The New Modernist Novel

The New Modernist Novel

Criticism and the Task of Reading

Elizabeth Pender

EDINBURGH
University Press

Edinburgh University Press is one of the leading university presses in the UK. We publish academic books and journals in our selected subject areas across the humanities and social sciences, combining cutting-edge scholarship with high editorial and production values to produce academic works of lasting importance. For more information visit our website: edinburghuniversitypress.com

© Elizabeth Pender 2024

Edinburgh University Press Ltd
13 Infirmary Street
Edinburgh EH1 1LT

Typeset in 10.5/13 Adobe Sabon by
IDSUK (DataConnection) Ltd, and
printed and bound in Great Britain

A CIP record for this book is available from the British Library

ISBN 978 1 4744 6148 1 (hardback)
ISBN 978 1 4744 6150 4 (webready PDF)
ISBN 978 1 4744 6151 1 (epub)

The right of Elizabeth Pender to be identified as the author of this work has been asserted in accordance with the Copyright, Designs and Patents Act 1988, and the Copyright and Related Rights Regulations 2003 (SI No. 2498).

Contents

Acknowledgements	vi
1. Reading a New Modernism	1
2. The Task of Reading and the Tasks of Criticism	30
3. Telling the Story of the Night Wood	77
4. *Adolphe 1920* and Modernism	108
5. *Insel* and Literary Value	138
Epilogue: Vocabularies	171
Notes	187
Index	228

Acknowledgements

Many people in literary criticism and beyond it contributed to the process of writing this book, and I am delighted to be able to make some acknowledgements here.

Thanks, first of all, to Drew Milne, who supervised the earliest version of this book as my PhD thesis. In that collaboration, the ideas here were first worked out. I am grateful for his support for the book, from its beginnings and over all the years of its composition. My examiners, Maud Ellmann and Stephen Heath, asked me attentive, exacting questions which improved the book. Ian Patterson gave valuable suggestions on John Rodker and generous advice on the book. Thanks too to others who read and commented on draft material in Cambridge: Beci Carver, Anne Fernihough, Ewan Jones, Jérôme Martin, Amy Morris, Rod Mengham, David Nowell-Smith, Sean Pryor and David Trotter, each of whom offered helpful criticisms and suggestions. The doctoral research was supported by the Cambridge Trusts and the University of Sydney Travelling Scholarship.

At the University of Cambridge and in the UK, many people formed the community in which the thesis was written. Graduate seminars in Cambridge and London gave me the chance to think with others over several years and were an immense source of vitality. I'm glad I had the chance to supervise the students I taught at several Cambridge colleges. I'm still grateful, years later, for the invitations to lunch and to other events. For these and other things it is impossible to separate the strands of my gratitude and acknowledgment across the people I knew in Cambridge and in the UK, whom I would like to acknowledge together here, among them especially Ruth Abbott, David Ashford, David Ayers, Oliver Brewis, Sarah Cain, Beci Carver, Daniela Caselli, Jamie Castell, Nick Chapin, Charlotte Charteris, Sara Crangle, George Danezis, Peter de Bolla, Cath Duric, Michael Englard, Ben Etherington, Anne Fernihough, Anna Fox, Andrew Francis, Geoff Gilbert, Peter Gizzi, Priyamvada Gopal, Aline Guillermet, Jeremy Hardingham, Antonia Harland-Lang, Stephen Heath,

Ewan Jones, Jenny Kaldor, Caroline Knighton, Sam Ladkin, Raphael Lyne, Jérôme Martin, Leo Mellor, Rod Mengham, Drew Milne, Robbie Moore, Amy Morris, Charles Moseley, Subha Mukherji, Jeremy Noel-Tod, Will Noonan, David Nowell-Smith, Redell Olsen, Jonathan Oppenheim, Ian Patterson, Neil Pattison, Michael Perfect, Sean Pryor, Amit Pundik, James Purdon, James Riley, Josh Robinson, Joseph Elkanah Rosenberg, Jaya Savige, Jan Schramm, Cathryn Setz, Kristen Treen, David Trotter, Bridget Vincent, David Whitley and Andrew Zurcher.

At the University of Sydney, where I was a Visiting Research Fellow, I received a warm welcome. I would like to acknowledge Melissa Hardie's generous and sustained support of this research and her welcome collaboration on Djuna Barnes, and the many opportunities she and Kate Lilley created for conversations around research. Over several years, Paul Giles gave generous and very helpful advice on publishing and on the content of this book. I am grateful for the intellectual company of Bruce Gardiner, who also gave sage advice on draft material. Bruce Gardiner, Melissa Hardie and Margaret Harris supervised earlier work that has been crucial to this book's project. At UNSW Sydney, where I was an Adjunct Associate Lecturer, I want to acknowledge the dedication of Julian Murphet, Helen Groth, Sean Pryor and others at the Centre for Modernism Studies in Australia to supporting research and community, from which I and others benefited greatly. Thanks too to John Attridge, Alexander Howard, Chris Oakey, Helen Rydstrand and Mark Steven, with whom I shared work and workspaces. I would also like to thank Ben Etherington and Sean Pryor, who have consistently welcomed this research, over the period of these affiliations and beyond, and who read and commented on sections of this book.

In Sydney, I appreciate the generous opportunities that were granted to me to take part in events and conversations that helped to shape the book. Many of those conversations took place on Bedegal land and on Gadigal land. Thanks especially to those I have mentioned above and to Mark Byron, Anthony Cordingley, Jennifer Crone, Anthony D'Agostino, Maud Ellmann, Toby Fitch, John Frow, Sarah Gleeson-White, Priyamvada Gopal, James Jiang, Sigi Jöttkandt, David Kelly, Daniel Kicuroski, Rónán McDonald, Peter Marks, Catriona Menzies-Pike, Alys Moody, Olivia Murphy, Lynda Ng, Joseph North, Lisa O'Connell, Nicola Parsons, John Plotz, Nick Riemer, Benjamin Riley, Brigid Rooney, Liam Semler, Paul Sheehan, Alecia Simmonds, Vanessa Smith, Matthew Sussman and Rebecca Walkowitz. Thanks to David Nowell-Smith and Aaron Nyerges for their thoughtful comments on draft material. Other people have shared friendship over the course of this book's composition, from the UK and in Sydney.

viii   *The New Modernist Novel: Criticism and the Task of Reading*

I worked closely across continents with Cathryn Setz, whose undimmable enthusiasm for Djuna Barnes has always been a boon to be around. I would like to thank Cathryn and the contributors to *Shattered Objects: Djuna Barnes's Modernism* for the chance to work with them on Djuna Barnes: Daniela Caselli, Bruce Gardiner, Alex Goody, Melissa Hardie, Tyrus Miller, Drew Milne, Peter Nicholls, Rachel Potter, Julie Taylor and Joanne Winning.

The archival material cited in the book was all consulted remotely, which meant considerable labour from several people, all of whom were incredibly helpful. Special thanks to Beth Alvarez, former Curator of Literary Manuscripts, and to Amber Kohl, curator of the Literature and Rare Books collections, at Special Collections and University Archives, University of Maryland, for their dedication and commitment to making the archives accessible. I would also like to thank Adrienne Sharpe of the Beinecke Rare Book and Manuscript Library, Yale University, for assistance with archival material relating to Mina Loy, and Katharine Beutner, Jill E. Anderson and Cristina Meisner of the Harry Ransom Humanities Research Center, University of Texas at Austin, for assistance with material relating to John Rodker. Thanks too to the Cambridge University Library Inter-Library Loans department, which sponsored the original transfer onto microfilm of several manuscript items held in the Mina Loy archive so that I could view them in Cambridge. I am grateful to Isabel Howe for additional assistance on Djuna Barnes. In Sydney, the University of Sydney library staff have always been wonderfully helpful.

At the Centre for English Teaching, University of Sydney, I want to acknowledge the conviviality of my colleagues and their support for this research, especially the support of Carol Wing-Lun, Carolyn Matthews, Tony Hickey and Mariela Mazzei.

This book is much better for the suggestions of my editor at Edinburgh University Press, Jackie Jones. The anonymous readers read the book extremely carefully and gave very helpful advice. Very many thanks to the staff I worked with: Susannah Butler, Fiona Conn, Ersev Ersoy, Elizabeth Fraser, Fiona Little and Elizabeth Parker.

I am very happy to be able to thank the many members of my family here, in this book.

The first three sections of Chapter 4 were first published as 'Mawkishness, or Literary Art: John Rodker's *Adolphe 1920* in Modernism', *Modernism/modernity* 21, no. 2 (2014): 467–85. Thanks to Nick Wolterman, who was then Managing Editor at *Modernism/modernity*, for helpful line edits on that material.

The work on Ezra Pound and F. R. Leavis in Chapter 2 uses excerpts of two of the five sections of my article 'Exemplarity and Quotation: Ezra Pound, Modernist Criticism, and the Limits of Close Reading', in 'Historical Poetics and the Problem of Exemplarity', ed. Ben Etherington and Sean Pryor, *Critical Quarterly* 61, no. 1 (2019): 67–81. The excerpts are slightly revised here. I am grateful to the editors of the special issue for their valuable assistance with the final form of that piece.

Quotations from Djuna Barnes's *Nightwood* are reprinted by kind permission of the Authors League Fund and St Bride's Church, as joint literary executors of the Estate of Djuna Barnes, and of Faber and Faber Ltd and New Directions Publishing Corp. Quotations from Djuna Barnes's correspondence held in the Djuna Barnes Papers, Special Collections and University Archives, University of Maryland Libraries, are reprinted by kind permission of the Authors League Fund and St Bride's Church, as joint literary executors of the Estate of Djuna Barnes.

Quotations from John Rodker's *Adolphe 1920* are reprinted by kind permission of Ernest Rodker and the Estate of John Rodker and of Carcanet Press, Manchester, UK. Punctuation and spacing in quotations follow John Rodker, *Poems and Adolphe 1920*, ed. Andrew Crozier (Manchester: Carcanet, 1996).

Quotations from Mina Loy's *Insel* are reprinted by kind permission of Roger L. Conover for the Estate of Mina Loy and of Melville House Publishing Ltd. Punctuation and spacing in quotations follow Mina Loy, *Insel*, ed. Elizabeth Arnold, introd. Sarah Hayden (Brooklyn, NY: Melville House, 2014).

Other quotations from fiction and poetry in this book follow original punctuation and spacing where indicated.

Chapter 1

Reading a New Modernism

The New Modernist Novel

The term 'modernism' has long had a productive dissonance with its content. Coined belatedly more than once to describe a movement or period or group of writers or group of texts and artworks, it has been the target of significant intellectual energy in the late twentieth and early twenty-first centuries regarding the tensions it maintains between the critical frame and the material under discussion.[1] In recent decades, the term has been the site of 'expansion', involving the recognition of writers whose geographical, temporal or cultural position placed them at a distance from earlier concepts of modernism. This expansion has involved new approaches: new kinds of critical work on modernist culture, history and politics, amounting to what has been termed a 'new modernist studies'.[2] These changes indicate a sustained discomfort with an earlier, mid-century version of modernism that was overly narrow.[3]

Among the oldest of the 'new' modernists are those who participated actively in settings of modern and avant-garde writing and sociality, and who avidly read – and were read by – their more well-known peers and contemporaries, but whose contributions were not well recognised, or not recognised at all, in the academic literary criticism of much of the twentieth century. Amid expansions into global or planetary modernisms or into a timeframe extending well into the late twentieth century and beyond, Djuna Barnes, John Rodker and Mina Loy may look decidedly establishment.[4] However, these writers and their novels *Nightwood*, *Adolphe 1920* and *Insel* have persistently troubled definitions and understandings of modernism, and they are rightly understood as recent additions. The recovery of these three novels in the late twentieth century poses a challenge: if an expanded modernism is now current, how can its literary works be read closely? An earlier version of modernism brought with it powerful strategies of close reading, strategies that were developed, challenged and consolidated over decades of criticism. The success of those strategies helped,

2 The New Modernist Novel: Criticism and the Task of Reading

in turn, to sustain that more selective version of modernism, even when that modernism was read in new ways. But Barnes's *Nightwood*, Rodker's *Adolphe 1920* and Loy's *Insel* read differently from fiction whose recognition as modernist was established earlier on. Reading these three newly recovered modernist novels closely suggests revisions and extensions to the vocabularies with which modernist fiction has been read.[5] More broadly, the expansions to canons in the new modernist studies invite new attention to close reading as a practice that may be changed by the text being read.

One of the many ways in which the selectivity of an earlier, established canon has been conceived is via periodical studies. This is a scene in which Barnes, Rodker and Loy were active. The scholarly return to the little magazines opened up an alternative, broader canon of writers, of whom some had later gained wider recognition while others had not. The limitations of a 'great minds' model of modernism have long been recognised, but reading modernism via its networks, and especially via the periodicals, has contributed to the dismantling of that model.[6] Within a modernism conceived as a collaborative enterprise, the active participation of Djuna Barnes, John Rodker, Mina Loy and many others in little magazines across the globe has more recently become significant.

Substantial work over the last few decades has sought ways to read authors who had been left out of earlier stories of modernism.[7] In the cases of Barnes and Loy, criticism informed by feminism and queer theory substantially restored these writers to view for teaching and criticism, and editorial labour over a number of decades saw their writings and art collected and republished.[8] Yet even if Barnes and Loy are now less marginal, nevertheless, fairly recently, at the end of the twentieth century, it was difficult to imagine how Djuna Barnes, Mina Loy or John Rodker could be made central to any textbook account of modernism. They had been absent from landmark accounts of modernism that informed teaching from the 1960s and 1970s, including Hugh Kenner's 1971 *The Pound Era*, and while the late 1970s and the 1980s saw significant new intellectual work on how to read Anglophone literary modernism, this work tended to rethink modernism through some of its most well-known proponents. Importantly, a core canon that had come together in the 1950s and early 1960s tended to be maintained, even if with some changes, into the 1980s, even through major challenges to how that modernism might be read.[9]

The recovery of formerly neglected modernist writers generated new reflections on modernism. This was in part because of tensions originating within the period. Neither Barnes nor Loy, for example, had ever quite suited an Eliot modernism or a Pound modernism, and they have challenged critics to read modernism again, and differently.[10] Tyrus Miller places Barnes, Loy, Samuel Beckett and Wyndham Lewis as 'late modernists'. My term 'task of reading' is Miller's too: 'it is high time to get on with the task of reading these works and discovering what we have missed'. In the last twenty years, Barnes and Loy have become more central, within a new modernism, and other new modernisms have emerged too.[11] Lawrence Rainey's 2005 *Modernism: An Anthology* showcased a reconfigured modernism: the anthology includes stories and plays by Barnes and poems and essays by Loy, and Rainey's introductory account of modernism's 'difficulty, its wild and irredeemable opacity, its resolute insistence on wonder so condensed that it turns into horror' has considerable power in suggesting approaches too to the longer works *Nightwood* and *Insel*, which are not included in the anthology, and even to *Adolphe 1920*.[12] The strong sense, brought home by several critics since the late 1990s, that modernism did always include Barnes, Rodker and Loy, along with many other writers, lends impetus now to an enquiry into how modernist studies came to be, in the first place, something to which they and others were also impertinent, 'improper'[13] or challenging.

To return to the question above, put differently: if modernism is now understood to include a range of writers, locations, and forms, how can new modernist fiction be read closely? How can this be done when the modes available for such reading have developed interdependently with a different canon of modernist literature – a canon that was narrower in scope and that largely did not include these writers? I address this question by asking what close reading might look like for these three novels, which were written in communities that included more established modernist writers, but which remained at a distance from literary modernism's twentieth-century critical afterlives. Responding to the new modernist studies, I aim to articulate some consequences of including these new modernist novels – of canonising *Nightwood* and beginning to read *Adolphe 1920* and *Insel* – for reading and literary value. Criticism of new modernist writing has already involved learning together to read that writing in new ways. But in its longer history as an academic practice, close reading has been trained more extensively on other modernist writing. Reading these novels closely suggests the potential that the new modernist studies offer to reconsider close reading not as a fixed set of strategies, but as a site of disciplinary change. By drawing attention to the contingency of close reading of fiction as a culturally and historically situated practice, and by challenging the perception of conservatism associated with close reading, the book aims to suggest ways in which habits of close reading have often been generated by specific texts and can continue to be so generated.

4 *The New Modernist Novel: Criticism and the Task of Reading*

The new modernist studies have been critiqued, for example, as identifying the artwork with its historical situation;[14] as failing to notice women;[15] as maintaining a 'primary (unmarked) modernism surrounded by (raced and gendered) satellite artists';[16] or as having the potential to overreach into dominance.[17] Rather than arguing directly for inclusion based on identity, this book considers the consequences for existing value structures of reading selected recovered modernist fiction. By moving the focus from the recovery of unjustly neglected authors to a study of strategies of reading, I suggest ways in which the discipline itself may be changing in response to the recognition of a broader expanse of modernist writing and conversations. The Epilogue steps carefully regarding the risk of overreach: the critique of the discipline offered here may be relevant for reading other newly recovered fiction, beyond the fiction considered in this book. But only close readers of that fiction can decide that. The book makes the addition of a set of reflections on close reading to a toolbox named 'new modernist studies', and makes the addition as one that critics can use as and when they find appropriate. In this, I hope to answer Douglas Mao's call for the new modernist studies to embrace 'the art of close reading, which sometimes looks in danger of being lost'.[18] But for fiction, close reading might look a little different when it has been trained not on a familiar modernism, but on a new modernism.

In this first section of this chapter, I go on to explain why *Nightwood*, *Adolphe 1920* and *Insel* might raise these questions now. In the following two sections, I first consider some connections between modernism and critical reading at mid-century, and then some connections between critical reading and productivity. In the final section of this chapter, I return to the question of close reading specifically, and I make an argument for recognising a firmer connection between modernism and close reading. In that final section I characterise, at least very loosely, some aspects of my own practice of close reading in relation to recent debates. Chapter 2 considers the changing meanings of reading for readers of modernism at key points in the twentieth century; Chapters 3 to 5 offer readings of *Nightwood*, *Adolphe 1920* and *Insel*, considering these novels' work with fiction and reading, their connections with modernist networks, and, in the cases of *Adolphe 1920* and *Insel*, the global consciousness of their modernism; the Epilogue considers what these readings may offer to readers of other new modernist writing.

§

In *Nightwood*'s fifth chapter, 'Watchman, What of the Night?', Nora seeks counsel from Dr Matthew O'Connor by asking him to tell her about 'the night'. 'Have you ever thought of the night?' he asks her, 'with a little irony':

> 'Have you', said the doctor, 'ever thought of the peculiar polarity of times and times; and of sleep? Sleep the slain white bull? Well, I, doctor Matthew-Mighty-grain-of-salt-Dante-O'Connor, will tell you how the day and the night are related by their division. The very constitution of twilight is a fabulous reconstruction of fear, fear bottom-out and wrong side up. Every day is thought upon and calculated, but the night is not premeditated. The Bible lies the one way, but the nightgown the other. 'Beware of that dark door!'[19]

With this, the doctor begins a long disquisition on the night that ends with his narrative of the night he met Nora's lover, Robin, when she was out with her new lover, Jenny. Matthew's disquisition mixes philosophy, anecdote and verbal performance, but its model is narration: sustaining teller and listener by the telling of the tale, in all its digressive wonder. Like Dante and like Dante's Virgil, the doctor provides for Nora a topography, here of the night: not 'calculated' and 'not premeditated', the night eludes analytical reasoning, and belongs instead in enchantment and storytelling.

Nightwood makes an enquiry into storytelling, and works with the capacities of narrative fiction in the early twentieth century in different ways from some of Barnes's more well-known contemporaries. Long sections of *Nightwood* consist of the doctor's disquisitions, which are spoken for Nora and, briefly, for Felix. These exchanges are marked as interpersonal, as here: 'Well, I, doctor Matthew-Mighty-grain-of-salt-Dante-O'Connor, will tell you [. . .].' Matthew is prompted throughout this section by Nora's questions: '"But, what am I to do?" she said.'[20] Nora will contribute her own narrative in a later exchange. The presence of these long exchanges in the novel is a recurring reminder that narration is an interpersonal act. And indeed, the complexities of the novel's own narrative voice go beyond what can be analysed formally. Formal models of point of view, or even Hugh Kenner's 'Uncle Charles Principle', developed for James Joyce's short stories, fall short of the complexities of tone and partisanship in *Nightwood*'s narrative voice, which exceed the studied precision of voice or interiority that has sometimes been observed in other modernist fiction.[21] It is the complex instabilities of tone in this narrative voice that begin my enquiry here. This includes problems posed by basic narrative structure: in the doctor's direct speech above, the narrator's own style is readily recognisable in the doctor's Wildean decadence and in his tendency to digression. Is it the doctor whose speech is recorded, or is his speech taken over by a

6   *The New Modernist Novel: Criticism and the Task of Reading*

narrator speaking for him? This question could be asked fairly innocuously of most fiction, where the spoken styles of characters may at times resemble the styles of their narrators. But in Barnes's *Nightwood*, questions about voice and tone arise so persistently, and so persistently escape formalising analytical frames, as to suggest aspects of a theory of narrative to this novel. Like *Nightwood*, *Adolphe 1920* and *Insel* try out the capacities of narrative fiction in the early twentieth century. Each of the three offers its own original departure from the modes of fiction developed by these authors' more well-known contemporaries.

The three novels were at a distance, however, from the modernism recognised by mid-century critics. *Nightwood* has been present at least at modernism's periphery since 1936, when it was published by Faber and Faber in the UK, and most editions from 1937 included T. S. Eliot's preface. But despite Eliot's praise, and despite a continuing public readership, *Nightwood* tended to disappear from criticism of modernist literature in the 1950s and 1960s until it was restored from the 1970s onwards.[22] Like Barnes, John Rodker and Mina Loy were both active in communities of avant-garde writers. Rodker was a poet and an accomplished critic, translator and publisher of modernist writing. *Adolphe 1920*, written in 1925–26, was serialised in Pound's little magazine *The Exile* in 1927–28, translated into French for *La revue européenne* in 1927 and then published in book form in English by the Aquila Press in 1929. However, the Aquila Press closed shortly after publication for financial reasons and the novel received very little publicity. It was first republished in 1996 in Andrew Crozier's edition of Rodker's work, *Poems and Adolphe 1920*.[23] Loy had already been recognised by her peers as a modernist poet for two decades by the late 1930s when *Insel* was written. But her poetry became hard to obtain, and after the Second World War Jonathan Williams edited her *Lunar Baedeker and Time-Tables* for publication in 1958, then in 1982 Roger L. Conover edited her poems as *The Last Lunar Baedeker*. *Insel* was read in draft form after Loy completed it following her move to New York in 1936, but it remained unpublished in the archive until Elizabeth Arnold edited it for Black Sparrow Press in 1991, and the novel was republished in 2014, edited by Sarah Hayden. Since their republication, both *Adolphe 1920* and *Insel* have been significant for broader enquiries into modernism.[24] *Nightwood* and *Adolphe 1920* offer an intriguing slice of a modernism that was known by contemporaries, but that was not well accessed by later critics. This means that these novels are well placed to provide a renewed understanding of how modernist fiction might be read. And so is *Insel*: not read by Loy's contemporaries, and not published until 1991, *Insel* is in some ways 'ephemeral'.[25]

But Loy's recognition as a poet, and *Insel*'s immersion in its Paris surrealist art world, connect *Insel* enough to the modernism of Loy's contemporaries for it to provide a renewed understanding of how that modernism might be read.

The three novels are clustered by their authors' inclusion in expatriate and European groups of writers and artists in interwar Paris: Barnes, Rodker and Loy each self-identified as modern, and each sought out and engaged with literary communities that are now recognised as modernist or avant-garde. Their writing in the 1910s and 1920s – fun, queer, modern, a bit deliquescent, and highly literary – is obviously deeply invested in these communities. Barnes's *Ladies Almanack* (1928), a satirical almanac featuring the Natalie Clifford Barney circle, might typify modernist queer fun, but Rodker's more serious ambition to publish modernist poetry was very much an engagement with community: at his Ovid Press he published T. S. Eliot, Ezra Pound, Wyndham Lewis, Oscar Wilde and himself, among other modernists. Barnes, Rodker and Loy read, were read and reviewed by, commented on and wrote for a moveable crowd of artists, writers and expatriates: a crowd that was key to, if in no way coterminous with, what came to be known as modernism. A parallel gesture to community is readable in the writing of Barnes, Rodker and Loy, where cultural references announce and reaffirm a modernist frame of reference, and where the figures of their contemporaries tend to reappear on the page. While their novels, as mentioned, are closer to a more established modernism than to a global modernism, each novel engages with a contemporary global literary and art context. The authors' choice of publication venues, too, indicates how they wanted their work to be perceived. They published in *Camera Work*, *The Trend*, *Others*, *The Egoist*, *Poetry*, *The Little Review*, *The Dial*, *Broom*, the *transatlantic review*, *Pagany*, *This Quarter*, *The Exile*, *transition* and elsewhere: as far as periodical publication is concerned, these authors were present and engaged across some of modernism's major published forums. Barnes's short stories and occasional poems appeared in step with episodes of *Ulysses*; Rodker, the only one of the three not based in Paris for much of the interwar period, published novels in French translation in *Les écrits nouveaux* as well as *La revue européenne*.[26]

In the case of Barnes, this self-identification as modern extended to her newspaper stories, interviews and articles, which frequently represented contemporary literary and art figures and bohemian characters, and which appeared in the mass media: in the Brooklyn *Daily Eagle*, the New York *Press*, the New York *Morning Telegraph Sunday Magazine*, *All-Story Weekly*, *Vanity Fair*, the *New Yorker* and many smaller newspapers.[27] Her well-known identity as a modern writer helped to sell

8   *The New Modernist Novel: Criticism and the Task of Reading*

her journalism.[28] For all three authors, their identification as modern involved affective connections to social networks connecting, between them, Paris, London, Berlin, Florence and New York: for Barnes and Loy this included their own friendship in Paris, and Rodker's early friendship groups included Isaac Rosenberg, Joseph Leftwich and others among the 'Whitechapel Boys' of London's East End.[29] Although Barnes was an American who lived for a time in Paris, Rodker British, and Loy British but resident in various European cities and later naturalised American, the three authors' work tends to underline the relevance of a continental frame for reading Anglo-American modernism.

Their self-identification as modern was accompanied by recognition granted their writing by other modernists. This is important, because it predates their relative absence in later accounts of modernism. As well as being published widely in modernist little magazines, Barnes, Rodker and Loy were anthologised by their contemporaries beyond periodical publication: poems by Loy and Rodker were published in Alfred Kreymborg's *Others Anthology* of 1917; a story by Barnes opened the 1925 *Contact Collection of Contemporary Writers*, which also included Loy's long poem *Anglo-Mongrels and the Rose*; both of Barnes's stories from Ford Madox Ford's *Transatlantic Review* were reprinted in his selection *Transatlantic Stories*.[30] Ezra Pound recognised Rodker and Loy in particular: he reported that he began the little magazine *The Exile* partly in order to print Rodker's *Adolphe 1920*, and Rodker and Loy both featured in key moments in Pound's thinking about literature, namely those of *belles lettres* and logopoeia.[31] *Nightwood* was published and prefaced by T. S. Eliot. In these acts of recognition, Kreymborg, Ford, Pound and Eliot endorsed the modernising ambition of the works they read, an ambition still readily visible for readers now in what might now be called these texts' 'difficulty'.[32] That endorsement was given too by other contemporary reviewers and critics, including each other.[33] Barnes, Rodker and Loy did not have the devoted support of a quorum of committed contemporaries, of the kind that Joyce and Eliot successfully cultivated.[34] But even so, all three authors were a well-recognised presence in the various cultures, coteries, networks and magazines that produced what would become known as modernism.

Despite their self-identification as modern and their recognition as modern by peers and contemporaries, all three writers' work later receded or disappeared from pedagogical and critical canons until their recovery in later decades of the twentieth century. This relative disappearance provides the second clustering of *Nightwood*, *Adolphe 1920* and *Insel*, beyond their first clustering as novels by writers who had energetically participated in modernism's networks since before the end of the First World War. *Nightwood* stands out, in this second clustering, as the work whose exit from canons was least complete, and whose re-entry came soonest and has been most comprehensive and most consequential. By comparison, the recoveries of *Adolphe 1920* and *Insel* have attracted less critical attention, yet their recoveries are consequential too for understanding anew what close reading can look like for modernist fiction.

How Modernism Was Read

While the reasons for renewed interest in each of the three writers have been made clear enough in the challenges to literary canons made since the late twentieth century, what the restoration of Barnes and Loy in the 1970s to 1990s and subsequently of Rodker in the late 1990s leave open to question are the reasons that earlier canons of modernist writing developed around authors other than these three. This is a complex question, comprising multiple processes of selection that were active from the 1920s to the 1960s and beyond.

The selectivity of a mid-century version of modernism provided a major impetus to the new modernist studies. Mid-century tendencies to overlook women modernists, writers of colour, LGBTQ+ writing and other work, including writing from across continents and timeframes, are now being recognised, following decades of work to redress these limitations. In the cases of Barnes, Rodker and Loy, factors of gender, sexuality, culture and ethnicity influenced others' decisions about the value of their writing. As a result of the substantial work of recovery that has been done so far, it is now possible to enquire how the mid-century's selections and exclusions were patterned into the tools of the discipline itself. That is, where the exclusions or inclusions made at mid-century may align with contemporary social prejudices, those selections and exclusions were also accomplished and sustained in different ways in the tools of the discipline. The selectivity was often not only at the surface of the discipline, in direct choices of authors, but embedded in its practices and strategies. I argue that at key points in the mid-century consolidation of literary criticism as a taught discipline, the value assigned to specific modernist literary works was interdependent with a particular set of strategies of reading that could be brought to those works as subjects for teaching and published criticism. That set of strategies in turn helped to sustain a narrowed canon that satisfied mid-century preferences for a certain kind of author and literary work.

10   *The New Modernist Novel: Criticism and the Task of Reading*

A related argument has been made in relation to modernist poetry and American New Critics. While the New Critics' essays ranged across centuries in their subject matter, the complexity of a version of modernist poetry was important in confirming and sustaining their methods of formal analysis.[35] However, the acceptance and legitimation of modernist fiction on the US academic syllabus crucially relied on critics whose work went beyond that of the New Critics. Despite significant criticism in the 1930s and 1940s on modernist fiction, much of the work that legitimised the study of modernist fiction in an institutional setting was done in the early 1950s and onwards by critics who were finding paths away from New Critical methods. In this sense, the development of a fuller, more stable modernist canon depended on further strategies of reading modernism, beyond New Criticism, that were developed in the postwar decades. That canon was then sustained enough, even through profound changes in reading, to be able to be challenged for its exclusions in the later decades of the twentieth century.

Writing on reputation, Aaron Jaffe corrects a flaw in the argument that modernism is a retrospective construction, forged in the academy, by showing how 'the historical "modernism" played an active part in its own reification'. For Jaffe, the choices made by academic critics depended significantly on the material effects of reputation, so that those writers who, like Eliot, Pound and Joyce, had already carefully shored up their reputations by their self-promotion were more easily and readily transposed into the academic study of modernist literature. Jaffe demonstrates the significant role that gender played in determining whose work would be read after the Second World War.[36] For both Jaffe and Rod Rosenquist, the creation of a widely accepted canon of representative modernist writing was a process that was actively undertaken and achieved within the interwar period, most actively by those who most benefited from it.[37] To this narrative of the selection, promotion and marketing of modernist writers in the interwar period itself, Catherine Turner's work adds the advertising work of publishers who promoted modernist works for commercial success in the interwar period, and Lise Jaillant identifies the popular readership of cheaply reproduced modernist fiction.[38]

I want to suggest, however, that reputation required something further: that is, strategies of reading that could support a fully fledged and widely teachable academic discipline. The term 'strategies of reading' covers sequences of steps in the construction of an argument about a specific text that could readily be taken up and used by other readers or critics, including students, to gain new insights into the text being read, or into other texts, or into the cultures that the text engaged with. For various reasons, Barnes and others lacked the reputation to remain current in the 1950s and 1960s, and, as well as that, strategies of reading that were being developed around other writers were less suited to criticism of their work, I argue, for complex reasons that to a degree were interdependent with, but went beyond, these authors' lack of access to the apparatus of promotion.

In 1985 Hugh Kenner observed that Ezra Pound's poetry had not been well suited to New Critical methods of reading:

> this was the key fact: nobody in 1949 knew *how* to talk about Pound's poetry. Cleanth Brooks, my mentor at Yale where I'd by then matriculated, was sympathetic both to the award and to my feelings, and not even he, the doyen of the New Criticism, knew how to talk about Pound. That was because the New Critical vocabulary – wit, tension, paradox – had been assembled around other poetry, notably Eliot's.[39]

The observation is from Kenner's retrospective preface to his book *The Poetry of Ezra Pound*. In the original 1951 book, he had written, 'It seems fair to say that most even of those who have looked at his pages have not *read* them.'[40] Kenner offered such a reading. The book was published by James Laughlin of New Directions and was the outcome of Kenner's and Laughlin's enthusiasm for Pound's poetry. Kenner's chosen grounds for the book, finding ways to read Pound that would open up the poetry to other readers, relied on the wager that the right strategies of reading were needed to bring modernism to its readers. Kenner's skill is evident in the book's success: in his own 1985 foreword, James Laughlin recalled that Kenner's book offered an 'explanation, the first significant one we were given, of what Pound was up to'.[41]

As Gregory Barnhisel records, Kenner's approach deftly sidestepped the issue of Pound's wartime activities, which aligned with Laughlin's approach to promoting Pound's poetry by arguing that the poetry 'must be judged strictly on aesthetic grounds'.[42] Pound had produced fascist propaganda in English before and during the Second World War, and these activities included making radio broadcasts in support of the Italian fascists.[43] In the preface, Kenner situates the book in the aftermath of the Bollingen prize that had controversially been awarded to Pound for *The Pisan Cantos* in 1948. Kenner's literary and formal readings of Pound's poetry and other writings avoided the need to consider their author's support for fascism. Criticism by Kenner and others helped to establish Pound's 'reputation' for university courses, along with the advent of trade paperbacks, so that the 1960s saw a flourishing of critical work on Pound, who then followed Eliot and others in being seen as a major modernist writer.[44]

12   The New Modernist Novel: Criticism and the Task of Reading

In the case of Pound, then, the way Pound's poetry might be read was still in question in 1951. This is suggestive of a broader pattern: even if many of the same works of modern writing had been read – and reread – by virtue of their status early on, they were not necessarily being read in the same way in the fifties, or the sixties, as they had been read in the twenties, or the thirties, or the forties. The way modernism was read was in flux, and the eventual construction of modernism around mid-century and after depended not only on whose writing was being read – and which work – but also on how that writing was being read. In other words, both the activity of texts in suggesting specific strategies of reading, and the activity of critics in developing specific strategies of reading those texts, helped to determine how modernism came to be read as it was read at different points in the twentieth century.[45] Further, some of the strategies of reading that were current in the 1910s, 1920s and 1930s were less amenable to academic requirements or were simply not picked up in any influential way.

In Chapters 3 to 5, I observe Pound dismissing Barnes, Wyndham Lewis satirising Rodker and Yvor Winters hesitating in praising Loy: these hesitations indicate differences in these writers' styles from the modernisms these critics promoted, as Jaffe and Rosenquist suggest. Yet specific doubts that Pound and Winters expressed about a perceived clumsiness in the work of Barnes and Loy, or that Richard Aldington expressed about a decadent sensibility in Rodker's work, took on a new aspect, I argue, in more general critical trends at mid-century that valued learnedness, coherence and a certain distance from decadence. At mid-century, the kinds of reading that could be done on specific modernist literature mattered for whether that literature was perceived as valuable. Even the support of T. S. Eliot was not enough to return Djuna Barnes's writing to prominence.

In Chapter 2, I ask what reading meant for selected critics of modernism. I look at how modernism was read at two key points: first around 1930 and then around 1960. This focus allows me to consider strategies of reading at a time when modernist criticism was being consolidated, and then at a time when an influential understanding of modernism was forming within academic institutions, especially in the US. Around 1930, I find modernist writing prompting a diverse new set of strategies of reading. Some of these strategies would be more suited to academic teaching and publishing than others. I focus on the essays on Joyce's *Work in Progress* collected in 1929, Edmund Wilson's 1931 *Axel's Castle* and the debate between Ezra Pound and F. R. Leavis over Pound's 1931 pamphlet *How to Read*. As literary criticism came to be produced more often in academic settings, the modernism that was read, and the

Reading a New Modernism 13

ways in which that modernism was read, changed under the pressures of a professional literary criticism. In the 1950s and early 1960s, Graham Hough, Harry Levin, Hugh Kenner and Wayne Booth were among many critics finding ways to respond to modernist literature in criticism. The entry of modernist fiction, in particular, into academic study provided one set of directions away from New Critical approaches to reading. While other selections of mid-century critics could readily be made, it is clear from reading these four critics that at this time, influential strategies of reading were developed for modernist fiction that then remained bound up in the selections of what writing might best be valued. These strategies of reading tended to seek coherences and to devalue decadent traits. They would soon be challenged, not least by more theoretically informed readings, but they served to support a narrowed canon of modernist literature that tended to remain relatively stable for some decades, even as approaches to reading changed.

Djuna Barnes's *Nightwood* is the key text of the three considered here, in that it was being read by both critics and a wider public at the time when an academic criticism of modernist fiction was coming together in academic settings, but *Nightwood* was not widely considered in that criticism. This specific act of deselection is the catalyst for the wider set of questions that I consider about how modernism was read at mid-century and how habits of reading that began in the academy with a mid-century canon may need revision for reading a new modernism. I originally arrived at this catalyst by finding for myself that my own habits of reading modernist fiction, which I had been learning at the time from reading *Ulysses* via the Hugh Kenner of the 1970s and 1980s among other modernists and critics, were not working for reading *Nightwood*. Many others before me have had similar experiences, and their experiences have generated an abundance of knowledge and thought about Barnes, reading and modernism as the result of observing *Nightwood*'s distinctiveness. To this abundance I wish to add the results of my own enquiry into how mid-century strategies of reading served to create literary value for a certain selection of modernist literature. Chapter 2 records some ways in which modernism and literary value were linked in criticism, and Chapter 3 offers a reading of *Nightwood* that considers how Barnes's novel brings to modernism an original set of ideas about the capacities of fiction, and how it resists reading in some of the ways that have been successful for reading other modernists. Barnes's readers, of course, have often been outside the academy, and the circulation of *Nightwood* across languages and in literature and film has long offered *Nightwood*'s global audiences alternatives to academic modes of interpretation.[46] Chapters 4 and 5

14   *The New Modernist Novel: Criticism and the Task of Reading*

consider *Adolphe 1920* and *Insel* as modernist novels that were, even more so than *Nightwood*, absent from much university teaching of modernism in the twentieth century.

Nightwood had featured as the representative modernist literary work in Joseph Frank's essay on 'spatial form' in 1945, which was revised and reprinted in 1963.[47] But it faded from academic criticism. *Nightwood* would have been a challenging book in the sexually conservative moral and political climate of the 1950s and early 1960s. Its lesbian, gay, queer and trans content is heartfelt and direct. *Nightwood*'s 1930s expatriate world ran counter to the social conservatism of the postwar academy in Britain and the US. Yet *Nightwood* is a challenging book for any moral universe, offering up suffering as it does for all its characters. That suffering may well have been too much for critics looking for moral guides for use in teaching. Joseph Frank's claims for *Nightwood* were unusual too in that they centred a woman writer, something that was unlikely to happen at mid-century, to the point that Bonnie Kime Scott's *The Gender of Modernism* (1990) contributed to a significant shift in critical understandings of modernism.

As Cathryn Setz and I outline in our piece on Barnes criticism, following Frank's essay, Melvin Friedman, Leslie Fiedler, Wayne Booth and Leon Edel all mentioned *Nightwood* or alluded to it, but declined to comment on it in detail, even though *Nightwood* seems key to their theories. Edel, for example, as Setz and I observe, draws on T. S. Eliot's preface and Joseph Frank's essay without mentioning *Nightwood* in his conclusion to *The Psychological Novel*. These critics' evasions suggest to us that while Barnes's novel may have been highly generative for their thinking about fiction, it still seemed to elude the critical frames that they were developing.[48] Perhaps tellingly, as Brian Glavey documents, Joseph Frank later revised his opinion of *Nightwood*'s importance in modernist fiction. Glavey's comment on this revision could well apply to some of Barnes's earlier critics too: 'Barnes's work thereby comes to be excluded from the theory of form for which it was the inspiration.'[49] In tandem with the social factors in *Nightwood*'s exclusion, there is evidently a strong interest among mid-century critics in how modernist fiction might be read formally, and it is possible now to consider how reading developed for modernist fiction in ways that made Barnes and others seem, to their critics, genuinely less valuable.

Reading these novels draws attention to the different kinds of difficulty developed by modernist writers and registered by readers. For Leonard Diepeveen, 'By the early 1960s, high modernism had rigidly established not just its canonical texts, but difficulty itself as the default aesthetic of high culture' via the activity of literary criticism.[50] Yet the academy's canons of modernist literature recognised some kinds of modernist difficulty more readily than others. The reading process, or strategy, or practice that seeks and values difficulty did not miss these novels because of simplicity: these novels further shore up the association that Diepeveen documents between difficulty and canon.[51] Yet they were missed – in the cases of Rodker and Loy partly for practical reasons – and their particular difficulties challenge strategies of reading that were developed for reading more established difficult texts. They remain challenging to read now, even with a century of criticism to draw on. On difficulty, J. H. Prynne writes, 'Difficulty, I suggest is the subjective counterpart to resistance: I experience difficulty when I encounter resistance.'[52] Experiencing the particular difficulties of these novels through close reading may leave a partial imprint of the resistance offered by each one to critical readers now.

Of course, canon-making of any kind is a fraught exercise. The mid-century critics who read *Nightwood* and demurred to write about it may have been troubled not only by its direct representation of queer lives and loves, or by the genuine questions it posed about what a novel was and how fiction might be read, but perhaps also by its representations of characters whose sexuality, religion or ethnicity is key to the representation. Indeed, *Nightwood* has long been a classic of lesbian, gay, queer and trans literature, even if it brings to that literature a rhetoric of deep heartbreak and tragedy.[53] The novel's radical potential is evident in such tensions.[54] Rather than being new models for modernism, *Nightwood*, *Adolphe 1920* and *Insel* offer cases for considering how close reading of modernist fiction might respond to the addition of new modernist fiction.

Productivity and Literary Criticism

The volume of published criticism on James Joyce versus the more modest, if still sizeable collection of articles and books on Djuna Barnes and other new modernists can be viewed in another way. Strategies of reading are complex, because they depend on both the work being read and the critic – each one of the two being both an agent and, at the same time, an instrument of specific social, political, institutional and other forces. If the strategies of reading that had been developed by around 1960 were interdependent with a set of selections, still the writing that was selected was a successful choice, in that it led successfully to criticism. What is it about Joyce's writing that still now leads successfully to criticism, in which it long differed from Barnes's, even if that difference has now lessened?

16   *The New Modernist Novel: Criticism and the Task of Reading*

An illustration of how *Ulysses* responds to critical labour is needed here. The 'Circe' episode of Joyce's *Ulysses*, which takes place in Dublin's 'Nighttown', is presented in the form of drama, as a staged hallucination. The episode has been an exemplary case of high modernism because of its work with other texts. It has provided critics with abundant comparisons of the episode's events and characters with their daytime alter-egos elsewhere in *Ulysses*, perhaps most famously the soap. Like the rest of *Ulysses*, it has tended to lead critics readily out from the text into myriad historically specific literary and cultural contexts, each one rewarding critical enquiry. Take, for instance, hypothetically, an account of theatre as used to represent dream, as hallucination, in the episode. Such an account might immediately find several literary contexts to be relevant. For example, the formal tensions that arise in reading 'Circe' as a play within a novel could well be illuminated by considering a range of challenges to theatre as performance, from Goethe's *Faust* and Flaubert's *La tentation de St Antoine* to Guillaume Apollinaire's surrealist drama and contemporary Dada performance.[55] In its resonances with these and other plays or theatre, Joyce's episode engages with texts that provoke consideration of limitations of theatre and performance, and following this engagement tends to be rewarding because it is fair to say that the representation of dream as hallucination in Joyce's episode is historically conditioned by these texts.

But such an account is sufficiently illuminating that it has scope to be structured instead as an account of a dialogue between literary forms about dream from Goethe's *Faust* to works written in the wake of Joyce, such as Samuel Beckett's early novels, enquiring into how the representation of dream has been historically shaped in interactions between plays and novels. The topical structure of such an enquiry about 'dream' would have the capacity to draw in a range of key works such as Henrik Ibsen's early 'unperformable' plays, August Strindberg's expressionist plays, including *A Dream Play* (1902) and German Expressionist theatre. Such an enquiry begs the question of Joyce's interest in cinema. In this case there is a small shift only between a question about the relation between a subject matter and form in 'Circe' and a more general discussion that can immediately put to use several well-known works across different literary forms and perhaps across media. That is, 'Circe' suggests a theory about the relationship between theatre and dream across a range of literary works and beyond; it can be read to orient other texts critically, and theoretical or critical claims readily extend beyond the purview of a study only of Joyce's book. In this example, the 'Circe' episode is a model of potential productivity for the critic, and typical of *Ulysses*. In existing criticism, that productivity has persisted across many different kinds of questions, among them questions about the episode's relationship to the complete *Ulysses*, genetic criticism and enquiries into popular culture, Irish history, early cinema and gender, for example.[56] Derek Attridge and Daniel Ferrer grant this quality of Joyce, writing in 1984 of the then very gradual critical 'realization that texts are unmasterable, and will return new answers as long as there are new questions, new questioners, or new contexts in which to ask questions', and they note that 'Joyce's texts display this characteristic more openly than most.' In their analysis, Joyce is a 'particular' case of such general textual qualities.[57]

A parallel example in the writing of Barnes, Rodker and Loy may be the circus as a special kind of cipher for the social worlds represented in their works. *Adolphe 1920* was originally titled *Circus*;[58] it opens in a fairground where the novel is set. *Nightwood*'s opening chapter features a room full of circus performers at a party. Loy's *Insel* is more distant, but shares in the café culture that both *Nightwood* and *Adolphe 1920* situate as connected to circus culture. Circus culture has a literary history in modern French poetry and in French and Anglo-American modernist writing and artwork, including in Loy's poem 'Crab-Angel' and Pablo Picasso's *La famille des saltimbanques* (1905), which intersect with a wider French literary trope of carnival in other kinds of popular entertainment, visible for example in Apollinaire's stories in *Le poète assassiné* (1916) but made current earlier on in a literary sense by Baudelaire and Laforgue. Joyce's 'Circe' episode also engages with this currency. But the way such literary or cultural contexts might shape a reading of the writing of Barnes, Rodker and Loy offers a less frenetic productivity than does Joyce's episode. The circus context is obviously important, but in these three writers the circus leads less immediately to problems of literary form as literary history or cultural history than it does in Joyce's episode, though it may still do so. Something else beyond intertextuality pulls readers through these texts. In a criticism that has long valued the congress of formal, literary historical, and cultural historical questions, the difference has registered. In recent decades, the increased recognition of ways in which literary texts work with culture defined more broadly has been crucial to the increase in published criticism on Barnes.

If, for the early episodes of *Ulysses*, 'the task of fiction was to discover the prose (and poetry) of inwardness', only to arrive in the later episodes at the 'inescapable multiplicity of styles',[59] then the achievement of the later episodes may be the fixing of the task of criticism. This task unfolds from the requirements on its readers of a novel that engulfs texts and histories as much as does *Faust II* or *La tentation de St Antoine* and, ostentatiously modern, does so in order to make of itself a monument.[60] The episodes of *Ulysses* present not just generic difficulty, but a gargantuan syllabus for future readers, who will, by necessity, be critical readers. The divergent tasks set by *Ulysses*'s later episodes are then performable not just on those episodes, but also on earlier episodes and on other modernist writing, and the tasks that they have set have not yet been exhausted. *Nightwood*'s different literary ambition queries the modes of storytelling available in fiction when it was written, spinning vertiginous impasses without offering ready theories. Where 'Circe' seems to condense a whole book in the density of its intratextual references, the connections within *Nightwood*, as I suggest in Chapter 3, operate more diffusely and less directly at the level of word choice than do those of *Ulysses*. Where *Ulysses* seems to invite inexhaustibly many intertextual references, in 1989 Victor Hugo's writing was identified as a precursor for *Nightwood*, referenced in the novel, yet Hugo has featured only fleetingly in subsequent criticism.[61] If both Barnes and Joyce produce a 'crisis of critical mastery', their disruption of authority and genealogy is pursued along different lines.[62] *Nightwood*'s work with characters and states of feeling delves deep into European prose, poetry and drama, and yet seems perpetually to refocus the critic on the representation of the people being written about. Such an ambition in no way precludes the kind of critical unfurling that *Ulysses* seems to require; but equally, it does not demand it.

The claim that works that seem to invite, require or reward critical labour of a specific, recognisable kind are likely to be valued is not a new claim. Northrop Frye cites it as the only quality of literary value he admits in the introduction to *Anatomy of Criticism*, observing experientially that 'the profound masterpiece draws us to a point at which we seem to see an enormous number of converging patterns of significance'.[63] Other critics have acknowledged that the hold that a literary work, once it has been granted canonical status, may have on subsequent processes of evaluation means that the work is likely to influence ideas about what is thought valuable.[64]

Discussing literary value, John Frow identifies a problem for the perceived legitimacy of 'value-based disciplines' in 'the fact that canonical texts have been taught in such a way as to sever them from the structures of social uptake in which their value has been constructed'.[65] In the case of modernist fiction, this suggests the need to revisit the historical construction of a teachable canon of modernist literature. But more than that, as approaches to criticism change, so too does the value of different literary texts. Further, different structures of social uptake make texts more or less readable in different ways. The recognition of new literary texts should, too, continually change the discipline's strategies of reading, including close reading of modernist fiction. In that sense, reading these three more established new modernists and registering the resistances they offer to familiar strategies of reading modernist fiction is likely to be valuable for learning to read new modernisms written in other circumstances, if only because it suggests how close reading can change when the text being read changes.

This is one of the deep values of literary study: when the subject of study changes, the science that can be brought to understanding or interpreting that subject changes too. In the cases of *Nightwood*, *Adolphe 1920* and *Insel*, strategies of reading that aligned with judgements of value in the years when academic modernist studies was first coming into being meet with intriguing deferrals. These novels complicate the more general valuing of coherence, of literary and cultural currency, and of a certain model of respectability that helped to establish the value of other modernist fiction at mid-century.

Nightwood, *Adolphe 1920* and *Insel* suggest a different set of attitudes to the boundedness of the novel form and to prose passages from those that tended to be valued at mid-century. In their privileging of passages as a locus of style, they tempt comparison with the *informe* expounded as an alternative Bataillean modernism in visual art by Rosalind Krauss and Yve-Alain Bois, but their commentary is more elusive.[66] The resistance to formalising reading in the novels by Barnes, Rodker and Loy sometimes takes the form of a pleasure in diffuseness, arch disintegration, inconsequence, even incoherence. This is in keeping with the kinds of pleasures valued by modernists in Laura Frost's analysis, in that the pleasure is deferred (consequence must first be sought in order to find inconsequence), but it differs from them in that the deferred pleasure is sometimes located, still, in the deferral: finding diffuseness in place of carefully constructed order.[67] Such resistances amount to a critique of the coherences that criticism has often found in the work of their more established contemporaries.

That critique can be understood to be implied by the novels at the time of their writing and also to be available for their readers now.[68] Matthew Sussman, commenting on Erich Auerbach, observes a 'difference between aesthetic standards derived from literary texts and those inherited through cultures of interpretation, which also have a history'.[69] This distinction is useful here. Although in practice the two sets of standards can, arguably, never be separated, nevertheless, the distinction opens up the possibility of deriving new modes of reading from newly recognised texts in ways that can challenge or enhance modes of reading that have been valued in criticism. In the specific case of more established modernist fiction, this perspective suggests that such established fiction need not

20   *The New Modernist Novel: Criticism and the Task of Reading*

necessarily be read as itself modelling coherence, but only as having supported a more focused interest at mid-century in coherence (along with other qualities) than the fiction of some of its authors' contemporaries.

There is an obvious relation between the short pieces that were published in modernist little magazines and processes of reading that value style in passages. Literary criticism in the academy has tended to prefer complete works of fiction, in part because they are easier to identify and set as reading for students. But modernism itself was not made up of complete, full-length works for much of its history, even in its fiction: *Ulysses* was published in instalments in *The Little Review*; so was Dorothy Richardson's *Pilgrimage*; *Finnegans Wake* did not exist until 1939, and before then, *Work in Progress* was readable in sections; and as poems, the *Cantos* appeared in successive instalments of an ever longer whole. Much of Gertrude Stein's work in *transition* and elsewhere is made up of short pieces that are fragmentary in their aesthetic yet not part of a larger work. Several anthologies in the 1920s included short pieces, sometimes both prose fiction and prose commentary as well as poetry and other forms, for example the prose fiction, poetry and criticism of the *Contact Collection of Contemporary Writers* and the essays, stories, poems, drama, music and artworks of Alain Locke's *New Negro* anthology, both volumes dating from 1925. While style may be a quality that is fully available only in a whole work – style may be a question of an author's individual 'vision' – still the styles of many modernist writers are readily recognisable from short pieces, or even from single phrases.[70]

One way in which published pieces were read and judged by contemporaries was for their style, which was only later to be incorporated into the completed work, if at all. Yet academic literary criticism has sometimes been uncomfortable with discussing style directly, so that for example *Ulysses* has still tended to be celebrated more for its intricate coherences than for its Dadaist and other informal tendencies, or Beckett's self-critical qualities valued above Wilde's eloquence. Despite the finished completeness of the novels by Barnes, Rodker and Loy, their novels still carry the flavour of the shorter pieces they wrote – and the flavour of the experimental milieu in which they were composed, where the flair of style livens the page, even if occasionally by flouting the formal structure of the whole. If *Ulysses* absolutely shares this investment in local style, it has not always been valued that way. Strategies of reading and valuing modernist writing at mid-century often sought formal brilliance, but earlier in the century, modernist writers and critics might be said to have prized the writing style first and the form second. The stylistic intelligence of Barnes's, Rodker's and Loy's resistances to strategies of reading that were later developed in formal academic criticism of modernist writing suggests that their novels were deeply, interestingly and intelligently engaged with the thinking about fictional prose being done in their own time, in the literary work of their contemporaries.

New attention to modernist cultures has brought with it a greater attention to Barnes. As a result, the discrepancy in volume of published work between Barnes and Joyce is diminishing as criticism changes in ways that mean Barnes has become, in an academic sense, far more read, and far more readable, than previously. On the measure of published criticism, *Nightwood* has now had greater productivity than most books ever published, greater even than many if not most books that have made it onto pedagogical or other canons. It is not only the ways Barnes's work can be read, but the whole literary field in which her work is now being read that has changed in this shift towards greater cultural awareness. This now includes reading the little magazines themselves as texts, as Cathryn Setz reads *transition*.[71] Still, kinds of close reading that have been productive for reading modernist fiction still now meet with interesting resistance in Barnes's writing. I locate the challenge that *Nightwood* and also *Adolphe 1920* and *Insel* make to an established modernism both in their styles and in the ways in which the styles of that established modernism have been read. In this I differ slightly from important work that has been done on different strands of modernism, such as Tyrus Miller's *Late Modernism*, where Miller writes about Djuna Barnes, Mina Loy and Samuel Beckett, along with Wyndham Lewis, as late modernists whose works show up the formal mastery of an earlier modernism by drawing on a 'marginalized "figural" tendency' within it – that is, a disruptive and transgressive tendency that was not foregrounded in the works of an earlier modernism.[72]

Close Reading and Literary Value

One value of these novels for their present-day critical readers, then, is their ability to prompt those readers to question some of their habitual and learned practices of reading. Before moving on to Chapter 2, I want to connect an expanded modernism with close reading in two ways: first, via the observation that literary critical close reading owes more to modernist literature itself than has been widely recognised, despite the selectivity of that debt; and second, by making the case for bringing close reading to a newly recovered modernism.

Close reading itself has proved difficult to define: fundamental to the discipline, yet apparently inadequate to a global literature, or at risk of forgetting the 'mediations of history'.[73] Examining the content of the

22   *The New Modernist Novel: Criticism and the Task of Reading*

terms reading, close reading, detail, form, formalist, history and historical, critique, criticism, and value is one way in which the discipline and its critics have sought to achieve self-definition.[74] This examination has brought reimaginations of reading with it. Rita Felski has registered a move away from reading as a 'hermeneutics of suspicion' whereby the critic diagnoses what the text cannot see about itself. She hopes for a future of greater attention to the embodied, affective processes that make up reading in individual, but heavily socially mediated engagements with texts. These involve both text and critic: 'interpretation', for Felski, might be seen as a 'coproduction between actors', where those actors include the non-human actor of the text along with the myriad other human and non-human actors that have brought about, for example, that text's presence on a reading list, or its reader's preconceptions about it.[75]

Responding to the perceived political conservatism or ahistoricism of close reading, Joseph North revisits the beginnings of close reading in the work of I. A. Richards and William Empson, both of whose left-liberal politics differed considerably from the politics that were associated with the success of close reading in academic institutions – the New Critics' southern agrarian conservatism and the Leavises' intellectual elitism. The point is significant for North because it allows for the possibility of close reading in a liberal future of the discipline. Yet the question valuably asked by North, 'where did "close reading" come from?', is complicated, beyond the work of Richards and Empson, by the significant connections between academic 'close reading' and modernist reading and writing.[76] The most concrete evaluation of such connections has been Donald Childs's observation that 'the story of the origins of New Criticism is fairly well known and fairly well agreed upon, yet it is not accurate: it leaves out Robert Graves'. Childs shows how Empson's 1930 *Seven Types of Ambiguity* and Richards's 1929 *Practical Criticism* are more indebted to Robert Graves's work and to Laura Riding and Robert Graves's 1927 *A Survey of Modernist Poetry* than has previously been recognised. For example, as Childs observes, for Richards, the meaning of 'a reading' changed under their book's influence from meaning, in the early 1920s, reading a poem out loud, to meaning, in *Practical Criticism*, a 'number of perusals made at one session' or a single 'slow reading' of the poem sustaining 'one single growing response' to it.[77] Riding and Graves read modernist poetry: their aim was to defend its perceived difficulty for readers by justifying that difficulty as necessary. In this sense, modernist poetry was the grounds for the critical method they developed. Their work on modernist poetry contributed to mid-century academic close reading via its influence, documented by Childs, on Empson and on Richards. In other words, both modernist literature and modernist criticism themselves were significant shaping forces in the various academic forms of literary criticism that developed in the mid-century. The history of literary criticism in the academy is closely bound up with modernist writing as a key link in that history.

Riding and Graves provide a specific instance of a method for reading modernist poetry influencing the development of close reading, but they are only one instance of a wider sympathy, even an interdependence, between modernist literature, with all its attendant formal and stylistic difficulty for readers, on the one hand, and on the other, ideas about reading in the 1910s, 1920s, 1930s and after. Modernist literature – as published in little magazines, and as written and read by those who identified with its milieu – tended to foreground reading as a problem. Its difficulty for readers was repeatedly recognised: in the debates of *The Little Review* in the 'Reader Critic' and 'Discussion' sections, which encouraged readers to respond to the magazine's contents,[78] and by its many contemporary critics and reviewers, among them Wyndham Lewis, Edwin Muir, Ezra Pound, May Sinclair, Edmund Wilson and Virginia Woolf. The published work of modernist writers is equally a record of a literature that was difficult and required attentive reading. As Max Saunders puts it, 'Close reading, as it gained prestige from the 1920s in Cambridge Practical Criticism and then the American New Criticism, was not only a product of the modernist period but a product of modernism.' Saunders makes the point that Riding's and Graves's work is 'only part of the story of close reading', and that modernist writing more widely was requiring close reading.[79] This interdependence between modernist literature and ideas about reading extended to the academy, where T. S. Eliot's criticism, for example, provided a precursor for the New Criticism as well as for Leavis, but where Eliot's poetry was also important.

The coming together of modernist literature and an enquiry into close reading is not accidental. Although modernist critics themselves were not always 'close readers' in the disciplinary sense that the term gained later decades, they nevertheless energetically asked how to go about reading the challenging works that they were discussing. The writing of little magazine contributors and their responses to each other's writing drew attention to reading and its attendant difficulties. Marjorie Levinson, in her survey of 'new formalism', suggests taking cognisance of 'a wider array of formalisms' beyond the well-known trajectory from New Criticism to poststructuralism: 'Russian formalism; Aristotelian and Chicago school formalism; the culturally philological formalism of Erich Auerbach and Leo Spitzer; the singular projects of William

24 *The New Modernist Novel: Criticism and the Task of Reading*

Empson, F. R. Leavis, I. A. Richards, Northrop Frye, Kenneth Burke, Wayne Booth.'[80] Her list could be extended to include the non-academic modernist formalisms of T. E. Hulme, T. S. Eliot, May Sinclair and Riding and Graves. So where 'close reading' has sometimes retained perceived associations with the conservative politics of the New Criticism, this has been in spite of the coexistence and cross-pollination of quite different kinds of close reading in the twentieth century.

The present book contributes to the project of working out what close reading can mean now, for an expanded modernism. It pursues the question not theoretically as North and Felski do, but by asking of specific new modernist novels, what does it mean to read *this* novel closely? When all is said and done, the best way to study the place of close reading in the discipline may be to see what it is like to read a specific text – and perhaps especially, to see what it is like to read a text that was not central at mid-century. In this 'coproduction', it matters that the critic is trained in a literary criticism that has not always seen these novels as important, and that the preferences and limitations of the critic get in the way and are the way the texts get read. Reading is never final, but reading these novels can tell us about their specific modes – about how they might be read now, and about how they were written to be read – and can do so not only beyond more general theoretical work, but also beyond the possibilities of direct historical enquiries into reception.[81]

This project of close reading might raise questions about historical context and about scale. I address these questions in turn. First, the association between close reading and American New Criticism is only a small part of a long history of close reading, which, as Mark Byron points out, extends back to coexist with the earliest written texts as an 'exacting attention to minute textual detail'.[82] Close reading need not be opposed to reading history and culture. Byron notes the significance of J. H. Prynne's long commentaries on single poems, among them *They That Haue Powre to Hurt: A Specimen of a Commentary on Shake-speares Sonnets, 94* (2001). In this commentary, 'etymology and intertextual references embedded in individual words are read within a discursive context of social, political, scientific, literary historical, and bibliographic information', and the possibilities of interpretation are considered: this close reading extends between the text and its many fields of meaning, engaging with other forms of social or cultural knowledge as readily as with literary knowledge.[83]

In an essay by Prynne on William Collins's poem 'Ode to Evening', a few lines from the poem prompt its reader to develop a detailed exposition of a concept, here of the 'hut', that is not fully available within the lines themselves or the poem.[84] Correspondingly, in the novels read in the following chapters, there are various details or scenes that could prompt a sustained enquiry into their meaning, so that the enquiry could become the subject of the chapter: for example, the band's performance in *Adolphe 1920*. Within the limits of the present book, close reading can never be close enough: indeed, even in the closest reading, meaning remains elusive. In the first section of Chapter 5, I attempt to date the action of *Insel*, which leads directly into *Insel*'s contemporary contexts. There I make a case for understanding historical and cultural context as an aspect of close reading, rather than as something separable from it. This is not context as general background knowledge but context as produced by the process of reading Loy's novel closely. Seen as a quality of the writing, style loses its independence from context of any kind (whether historical, literary or otherwise), since the material of context that enters the novels does so as part of their style, and questions asked about style may well lead to historical or other details.

The question of which context or which history remains.[85] In Chapters 3 to 5, the contexts that receive the most attention are the cultural networks immediately surrounding the composition and contemporary reception of the novels, such as nineteenth- and twentieth-century modern French literature; the representation of culturally marked identities in *Nightwood* and *Adolphe 1920*; the global consciousness of Paris surrealism and the novels' transnational interactions; and the interpersonal politics related to the novels' composition, publication and reception. Other contexts could easily come up from other close readings, but these are central to the readings here. Seen another way, of course, style itself is an index of context: the reading habits of these novels' imagined audiences are obliquely recorded in the writing style of the novels, and those imagined audiences are not so distant from the books' real contemporary audiences. This is reflected in the attention here to the literary and cultural company of those styles. The chapters' attention to context follows the book's overarching enquiry into the conditions of reading these novels – that is, the enquiry into how the novels resist or suggest strategies of reading that are themselves deeply culturally and historically nuanced.

Is this project scalable? The impetus to read beyond canons has famously led not to a call for close reading, but to a call for distant reading. In the essay 'Conjectures on World Literature', Franco Moretti asked how literary criticism can negotiate a global literature whose number of texts far exceeds the competence of any one reader. The answer, he argued, has to be not close reading, which can never manage the volume of works, but 'distant reading', which looks for a specific 'unit of analysis' across many texts, and even across national literary histories.

26   The New Modernist Novel: Criticism and the Task of Reading

Distant reading allows the critic to 'look beyond the canon' – reading further, by not reading closely.[86] In Moretti's account, the possibility of distant reading depends on the distant reader forgoing close reading of whole texts.

In the present project, close reading offers a different way to look beyond the canon. Here, the critic reads just beyond the canon – books that have more recently been added to a modernist critic's canon of fiction – and reads that writing attentively and closely. Doing so shows modes of reading being brought into play that are different from those that have been canonised and taught. This shifts the problem of literary value. 'You invest so much in individual texts *only* if you think that very few of them really matter';[87] or if you think that new texts, when read closely, can alert their readers to new things to look for, or even to new ways to look for new things. In other words, reading closely can provide a way of learning to know and value new texts. My assumption here is that literary texts involve difficulty for readers: they tend to resist reading, and close reading is a form of attention that can register literary texts, at least provisionally. Although reading is always provisional, the scale of attention to individual works in distant reading can tell very little about each work. The content of close reading cannot be predicted in advance, even when texts can be categorised by genre or some other feature. Reading beyond the canon might require close reading of new texts, then, rather than requiring that close reading give way to distant reading. And indeed, this was the substance of Gayatri Chakravorty Spivak's contemporary response to 'Conjectures', where, as she pointed out, Moretti's project already required the work of close readers from the Global South.[88] More recently, Ben Etherington makes the claim that 'particular experiences of literary works must always be the primary scene for conceptualizing literary totality'.[89]

In order to see close reading as having the potential to describe or interpret new texts from within literary criticism, it may be necessary to consider close reading's longer history. Angus Connell Brown asks what a 'more comparative history of close reading' might look like.[90] A small part of such a history might involve the selections from an Anglophone history of reading of modernist fiction that are sketched here. But such a history can be complemented by close readings that observe how specific newly recognised texts might be read, while at the same time registering those texts' resistances to familiar strategies of reading. Reading newly recognised texts closely has the potential to make an academic imprint of the text, but also to register the changes to close reading that the new text might bring about. As well as a reckoning with the history of close reading beyond the New Criticism, an expansion of canons will at some point require an associated expansion of strategies of reading, and at least at first, that expansion of strategies of reading may well need to be iterative rather than scalable.[91]

Considered in these ways, 'close reading' remains a non-specific term. In general that suits my purposes: in part the term sets up a space for trying out various kinds of reading of these novels. In the case of novels, even without any comparison to distant reading, close reading makes the problem of selection acute. If close reading involves close attention to the words on the page, which page is relevant? And which passage, or worse, which passages? This challenge recurs through the following chapters, where different approaches to selection are considered or worked through.[92] Another question is harder to address: what is the relationship between critical reading and close reading, where close reading is understood to involve enquiry into context? This more theoretical question leads to work done on reading in the last two decades.

The respect for texts that Rita Felski identifies as part of a shift away from a 'hermeneutics of suspicion' gives a broader perspective to the project of reading new modernist novels. In their introduction to the 2009 issue of *Representations* entitled 'How We Read Now', Stephen Best and Sharon Marcus state their interest in attentive 'modes of reading that attend to the surfaces of texts rather than plumb their depths', as against a depth model of symptomatic reading, in which the critic heroically restores the hidden depth of the text to readable meaning. Of the six types of surface reading they record, the three that speak most directly to the current project are reading surface as 'the intricate verbal structure of literary language'; the 'embrace of the surface as an affective and ethical stance', one that involves 'accepting texts, deferring to them instead of mastering them or using them as objects'; and 'attention to surface as practice of critical description', assuming that 'texts can reveal their own truths because texts mediate themselves', so that the critic's job is to 'indicate what the text says about itself'. In these notions of reading, agency is shared between critic and text, requiring 'a true openness to all the potentials made available by texts'.[93] This fields the possibility – at least in theory – of reading without a critical agenda determining in advance how the text might be understood or interpreted, a possibility that is needed for reading works that have not become canonical or have not long been canonical, but Marcus and Best's shared agency between text and critic avoids the critical naivety of an anti-theoretical reading. The gist of this respectful, attentive, observant, enquiring attitude to the texts is well suited to reading unfamiliar texts.

However, what the chapters here offer is not quite Best and Marcus's 'indicating what the text says about itself', because the task of reading as understood here is not finishable: the practice of critical description undertaken here is merely a contribution to understanding these novels, to be taken further by others. Like any reading, the readings here are necessarily partial: they assemble questions, insights and directions that can be mobilised in a future reading.[94] A reading that registers the novel being read, while it may have elements of description, and of critique, is also, in its provisionality, a performance of that novel: non-definitive but interactive, a practice as well as a task, public, and subject to criteria of art. Geoffrey Hartman's phrase 'the work of reading' draws attention to this parallel between the work of art and the work of reading.[95] For Rita Felski, too, reading is an 'act of composition', one in which both text and reader participate.[96] This kind of reading gestures to Felski's (and Bruno Latour's) 'critical ethos of attentiveness, respect, and generosity' towards the text being read. But the readings here make that gesture without discarding the critic's simultaneous knowing detachment, retaining that identification with critique, which shifts the performances here. As well, rather than traversing 'across multiple texts', the readings in Chapters 3 to 5 are a sustained process of reading one text seen as an actor, a process that cannot be completed but is only begun, three times.[97] By attending closely to how readers might be invited, now, to respond to these novels, I aim to register ways in which these texts can act on the strategies and vocabularies that are available for reading modernist literature critically, especially by expanding them.

This kind of reading is a task because it is not always quite the same as everyday reading, or lay reading. In 1966, Graham Hough called criticism 'a normal prolongation of intelligent reading', in which a student of literature then 'step[s] back to reflect' on that reading.[98] Perhaps the task is not the reading but the writing of that reading, as a commitment to others' future readings. John Guillory observes that literary study involves submitting reading to discipline. In Guillory's outline of differences between lay and professional reading – professional reading is a kind of work, is disciplinary, vigilant and communal – I note particularly that the discipline gives time and community to the development of professional reading, and I am taking advantage of those two conventions here.[99] Chapter 2 begins by enquiring into different ways in which modernist critics engaged with reading, and then considers some ways in which critical reading of modernist fiction came to be constituted in academic settings at mid-century. Chapters 3 to 5 articulate a series of questions about what constitutes attentive reading of three recovered novels, and in doing so, they undertake a 'sustained investigation' into each novel, addressing the conditions of reading them as modernist novels.[100] In the Epilogue I assess what reading *Nightwood, Adolphe*

1920 and *Insel* can bring to reading fiction by an established modernist, Samuel Beckett (the Beckett of *How It Is*), and another new modernist, Jean Rhys (the Rhys of the short stories).

If modernism was consequential for the development of literary criticism as a discipline in the early to mid-twentieth century, in the later twentieth century there was another set of changes that spurred literary criticism to do greater justice to the range of modernist writing across places and times, including in periodical publication. These changes led to the recoveries of texts as new modernist, including the novels by Barnes, Rodker and Loy, and one value of these novels is their capacity to critique earlier models of modernism and the modes of reading that have been learned from those models.

But that value depends on another, the value of these novels for their readers even without a knowledge of a wider modernism: while complex and challenging, they are worth reading in different ways for different readers. One way in which enjoyment of reading these novels can be thought of involves the pursuit of knowledge about them, or of knowledge held by them. This could be parsed, in Peter de Bolla's terms, as a 'kind of knowledge [. . .] within the artwork, something, as it were, known to it'. For de Bolla, this kind of knowledge might better be called a 'knowing' that is like a state of mind that he recognises as 'wonder'[101] – recalling Rainey's 'wonder' of modernism above. Another way to think about the knowledge pursued in the readings is perhaps not directly the search for understanding of community in the book's representation of a social world,[102] but a more abstract desire to know these novels' people by learning how those people are invited to read the novels: novels whose invited strategies of reading are drawn from their own social contemporaries and have travelled eventfully through other social worlds to the present. The task of reading is an unfinished process of continuing art-making between critics, texts and the expanding social and physical worlds they each travel.

Chapter 2

The Task of Reading and the Tasks of Criticism

Reading and Criticism circa 1930

The task of reading and the tasks of criticism have sometimes been at odds. One key aspect of modernist writing was that it required new kinds of attention from its readers. Repeatedly in modernist reviews and criticism, readers of the criticism were exhorted to read the literary texts being discussed, for example by Ezra Pound in special issues of *The Little Review*.[1] Over the course of the 1910s and 1920s, there developed a set of possibilities for demonstrating the process of reading modernist writing in published reviews and criticism. One of the most well-known examples is Laura Riding and Robert Graves's *A Survey of Modernist Poetry* (1927). But the question of what it meant to read this new writing attentively was being answered in substantially different ways by different reviewers and critics. In other words, modernist writing was generating a wealth of new questions about what reading meant, and in turn, new questions were being generated by critics about how the process of reading might be modelled or encouraged in reviews and criticism. At times, the aims of reading and the aims of criticism seemed to be directly in tension: for Edmund Wilson writing on James Joyce in *Axel's Castle* (1931), for example, the task of the reader and the tasks of the critic risked diverging.

New questions about what reading meant were being asked in an academic setting, too, where they were also prompted at least in part by modernist writing. I. A. Richards's role is well known here. His work with practical criticism – teaching students to read poems – connected with modernist criticism: Richards's 1929 *Practical Criticism* was indebted to Riding and Graves's *A Survey of Modernist Poetry*, and William Empson's 1930 *Seven Types of Ambiguity* directly acknowledged a debt to their book.[2] In the US, John Crowe Ransom outlined a *New Criticism* (1941), for which T. S. Eliot's criticism was key, along with that of Richards, Empson and Yvor Winters.

The diversity of answers to the question of what reading meant was reduced by the gradual convergence of literary criticism with an academic profession. As reading became understood by critics as professional reading, the aims of reading and criticism tended to become more similar.[3] Yet this academic criticism involved the selection of certain modernist texts and a certain set of strategies of reading those texts. A canon of modernist fiction became prominent in the 1950s to early 1960s that was selective, and that tended to meet the requirements not just of mid-century critics, but also of later and quite different readers.

The question of what reading meant for early critics of modernism is relevant here because the ways in which modernism tended to be read in the academy worked well for the development of an academic literary criticism, but worked less well for criticising or teaching novels by Djuna Barnes, John Rodker and Mina Loy. These writers' fiction appealed to their contemporaries, but it appealed less successfully to mid-century critics for whom reading and criticism were taking shape around other writers, and who were developing certain versions of close reading based on those writers. If we are to read Barnes, Rodker and Loy closely as new modernists – and it is of course not the only way to read them – then the question is, which modernism? Reading these authors against a mid-century version of modernism has the potential to return some virtues of an earlier modernism to current literary criticism. However, accessing this potential requires at least some understanding of ways in which reading was being thought about first by their contemporaries, and then by the mid-century academic critics who selected other writers than these.

Accordingly, this chapter first considers some ideas of reading around 1930. This was a time when a lively periodical culture of reviews and articles had led to the publication of several book-length works about modernist literature.[4] The chapter considers how reading took shape for critics of Joyce's *Work in Progress*; for Edmund Wilson in *Axel's Castle* (1931); and for Ezra Pound in *How to Read* (1931), as critiqued by F. R. Leavis in *How to Teach Reading* (1932). At this time, contemporary ideas about reading were changing directly under the pressure of modernist writing. Some of these ideas about reading would be more easily taken up in academic teaching and learning than others.

I then move to the 1950s and early 1960s, when the study of modernist fiction was taking shape in academic institutions. Douglas Mao identifies the late 1950s as the beginning of one of two 'flowerings' of modernist studies, the other being the new modernist studies beginning in the late 1990s.[5] I consider how four critics of modernism understood reading in the 1950s and early 1960s: Graham Hough, Harry Levin,

32   *The New Modernist Novel: Criticism and the Task of Reading*

Hugh Kenner and Wayne Booth. Another selection of critics would tell a different story. Asking how modernism was read at mid-century, especially how modernist fiction was read, means reading across critics, necessitating range, but it also means reading each critic reading, necessitating selection. What this particular selection makes obvious is the perceived value at mid-century of coherence, literary and cultural knowledge, and a certain social responsibility in modernist fiction. These four critics bring attention to the special productivity of modernist literature for criticism, particularly as that productivity is commented on by Hough and Booth. As they observe, at this time there developed an interdependence between modernist writing and literary criticism. This interdependence took shape at the time between a selected modernist canon and a set of ideas about reading and literary value that helped to sustain that canon. The nexus of a selection of writers and a set of strategies of reading that supported that selection was to have a profound hold on how modernism was subsequently read. If other critics developed different strategies of reading, still they were working within a similar set of literary and cultural values and on a shared modernist canon.

§

I begin with criticism of modernist literature from around 1930. It would require more than a chapter to study how meanings of reading varied among different critics at this time.[6] But only a few examples are needed to argue that the meaning of reading was changing significantly in this period, and that this change was at least in large part a response to modernist literature.

The essays on Joyce's *Work in Progress* that were collected in *Our Exagmination round His Factification for Incamination of Work in Progress* took on the challenge of providing critical commentary about a difficult, highly modern work. Not only that, but they commented on an incomplete work: *Work in Progress* had only been published in segments, largely in *transition*, and the completed *Finnegans Wake* would not be published for another ten years. The twelve positive essays turn the challenge of commentary to a contagious excitement about this new writing, ready to be shared with Joyce's other readers and potential readers.[7]

The main quality of *Work in Progress* that struck several of the critics was its use of language: Eugene Jolas confidently identifies Joyce with the figure of the 'new artist of the word' who 'has recognized the autonomy of language'. He looks through Joyce towards a 'complete internationalization of the spirit', for which the English language, which

The Task of Reading and the Tasks of Criticism   **33**

has been an 'amalgamation' from the start, is well suited.[8] Victor Llona correspondingly admires the international actors on Joyce's stage of words, but Jolas sees in *Work in Progress* no less than the possibility of a new language: 'language is being born anew before our eyes'.[9] John Rodker, like Jolas, finds Joyce 'revitalizing' words and language, but Rodker also asks a different question: how might we read this writing? He notices an extension of the reader–writer relationship: 'Here it is as though the words held in solution the elements, inarticulate in both reader and author, which we call dynamic'; this leads to a 'complete symbiosis of reader and writer'.[10] In this, Rodker directly addresses the difficulty of reading, a problem Samuel Beckett also addresses: 'Here is direct expression – pages and pages of it. And if you don't understand it, Ladies and Gentlemen, it is because you are too decadent to receive it. [. . .] Here form *is* content, content *is* form.'[11] Joyce is giving us a new language, say Jolas and Llona (and Rodker); reading it is difficult, say Rodker and Beckett.

The essays diverge between a kind of reading that happens privately, which the critic reports on, and a kind of reading that unfolds directly in the printed essay, in public. Some of this tension lies in the use of quotation. Two critics quote Joyce extensively: Stuart Gilbert, author of *James Joyce's 'Ulysses': A Study* (1930), and Robert Sage, an editor on *transition*. Gilbert, seeking the subject of *Work in Progress*, finds in it 'a synthesis of history and of language'.[12] This means, implicitly, that reading *Work in Progress* involves reading at the level of word and phrase. Accordingly, Gilbert quotes a long passage of three full pages which he then glosses phrase by phrase. His glosses identify the difficulty in reading with a difficulty in grasping the allusions in Joyce's words, and for Gilbert, that difficulty can be partly resolved, for other readers, by his recording for them his own processes of reading. Sage's quotations similarly aid readers to comprehend Joyce's text: he quotes several short passages from *Anna Livia Plurabelle* and explains how each quotation might lead to observations about words, rhythms, meanings or symbols, and ultimately about what Joyce is doing in his new book. Such observations are made in the course of an argument that 'his latest book *can* be followed in its large lines by any intelligent reader'. Sage hopes for a work that will never be overtaken by 'columns of footnotes', preferring that 'it will always have different meanings for different readers'. Perhaps for this reason – its 'inexhaustible promise of new revelations'[13] – for all that *Work in Progress* provokes critics' interest in language and in reading, the actual process of understanding the work remains opaque in many of the essays, with Gilbert's and Sage's essays an exception. Beckett's, Jolas's, Llona's and Rodker's neat

34   *The New Modernist Novel: Criticism and the Task of Reading*

arguments are stylish criticism, but in their essays, criticism is a wager on the text, with the working largely not shown, and only the finished results of private reading and thinking on offer. Jolas's explanations of a few misunderstood words are a minor exception, but for the most part in their essays, any quotation is largely illustrative, rather than forming part of the argument. Gilbert's and Sage's close attention to quotations is unusual: for most critics here, the initial process of reading is private, in that it is not yet a process that can be set out on the page in printed criticism.

What is shared, however, between these critics is a sense that the role of criticism is brought into question by Joyce's new work. This is put most forcefully by William Carlos Williams. In a tirade against what he calls 'British criticism', Williams rather viciously attacks Rebecca West for her essay on Joyce. Where for West, Joyce's 'sentimentality', what might perhaps be called his attention-seeking, including through obscenity, was 'entirely without taste', for Williams, Joyce's offence against taste is only an effect of the force with which he is breaking conventions, and it does not diminish his ability to make 'valid technical innovations' in literary form.[14] Williams, reading – 'Reading Joyce last night [. . .] I saw!' – realises that Joyce is 'restoring' words: as Joyce uses them, words are removed from their long-accumulated 'stultifying associations' and are 'freed to be understood again in an original, a fresh, delightful sense'. This argument pits reading against what Williams sees as an established version of criticism, which he casts as English or British. He attacks West as carrying the cultural weight of a criticism that is constrained to judge in advance. This criticism is rendered out of date by Joyce, Williams argues. For Williams, the appreciation of Joyce then falls to America's newer, 'undeveloped but wider criticism', a criticism that, he implies, will be free to read – to appreciate 'Joyce's true significance – his pure literary virtue'.[15] Jolas's essay also takes an unimpressed critic to task, schooling Sean O'Faolain on the long history of neologisms in and beyond English, and calling his critical philosophy 'dessicated'. The artist, for Jolas, 'makes no concessions to communication other than a tantalizing invitation to the reader to seek and continue to seek'. Here too, criticism that forgets to read with curiosity is lacking something important.[16]

For the *Exagmination*'s only woman contributor and its only claimed 'common reader', things are somewhat different: *Work in Progress* risks being not 'unintelligible' in an ultimately enlightening way, but merely disappointing. Reading seems to involve 'reading words for sound', which this reader records is a struggle.[17] Despite the differences among critics, it is clear from the anthology that Joyce's writing prompts these readers to think as critics about what it is they need to do when they

The Task of Reading and the Tasks of Criticism   35

read, and that there are many things that such reading, as prompted by *Work in Progress*, might become.

The complaint of the volume's 'common reader', who struggles to make sense of *Work in Progress*, lightly presages Edmund Wilson's serious respect for common readers in his 1931 *Axel's Castle: A Study in the Imaginative Literature of 1870–1930*. *Axel's Castle* identifies and theorises 'modern' writing, tracing its origins in symbolism, with reference to the work of W. B. Yeats, Paul Valéry, T. S. Eliot, Marcel Proust, James Joyce and Gertrude Stein, and an epilogue on Villiers de l'Isle Adam's *Axel* and Arthur Rimbaud. Wilson's book assumes a public readership of modern literature and sets about making modern literature understandable for that public. Where Laura Riding and Robert Graves chide their common or 'plain reader' to 'make certain important alterations in his critical attitude' so as to be able to read modernist poetry, Wilson is more likely to chide modernist writing for leaving its readers confused.[18] Nevertheless, Wilson's attention to the writers he discusses prompts several questions about reading.

Wilson's criticism of the 1920s and 1930s has a deep interest in people: writers and characters and their situations. Often, he will judge writer and oeuvre together. In *Axel's Castle*, on Proust, he states that

> The real elements, of course, of any work of fiction, are the elements of the author's personality [. . .]. His personages are personifications of the author's various impulses and emotions: and the relations between them in his stories are really the relations between these.[19]

Wilson's 'real' and 'really' are striking: in this study of Proust's novel as symbolist, the words mark a decisive departure from realism and even from the real of naturalism that, for Wilson, is symbolism's counterpart in the novels of Proust and Joyce. His statement effectively merges the author's work with his life, so that Proust's novel can be read by the critic, as Wilson reads him, with recourse to letters and anecdotes from friends alongside the oeuvre.[20] Within the following decade, this method will gain in depth and nuance, for example in Wilson's studies of Charles Dickens and Rudyard Kipling, which consider each writer within his contemporary moment.[21] But Wilson the moral arbiter is not at his best with Proust. He understands Proust's novel by understanding its author as a neurotic malingerer – rather than as an author who is able to write a character, Marcel, for whom as the novel ends, an hour of activity may mean twenty-three hours spent unable to speak or to sip milk. He carefully disapproves of Proust the writer's interest in homosexuality, and he goes so far as to claim authority on Proust's own sexuality.[22]

36   *The New Modernist Novel: Criticism and the Task of Reading*

Yet Wilson is a persuasive critic. Much of his thinking about Proust's novel is about a reader's processes, rather than a writer's processes. Wilson points out that the characters Swann and Charlus seem to have an unquestioned significance 'as we read'. But 'it is only when we think to examine Proust's novel from the point of view of ordinary fiction that we become aware of their irrelevance to the main narrative'. That is, we realise that they are nominally irrelevant because their fictional relation to the hero is only tangential, even though their stories fill much of the book. Examining the novel in this reflective way, beyond the initial process of reading, leads to critical insight: this novel 'stands alone as a true dream-novel among works of social observation'; it has the 'harmony, development and logic of the unconscious' (145). Reading is not explicitly isolated as a problem by Wilson, but the question of how Proust's novel can be read seems to require the division of reading into two kinds, 'as we read' and reflection, where reflection is required in order to perceive the 'architecture' of the novel – that is, the 'framework' that 'will bear the weight of all his longueurs and digressions'. Within this framework, Proust can be seen, for Wilson, to strive at a 'close unity and significant order' (121).

In the case of Joyce, Wilson is full of praise for Joyce's ability to create a social world and its people, and his chapter is highly positive. This positivity matches Wilson's regular references in passing to Joyce at around this time – in essays on other topics – as, for example, 'the greatest literary artist then alive'.[23] But Wilson regrets the demands *Ulysses* makes on its readers. This is a book whose 'key', the title that refers to the *Odyssey*, is 'indispensable if we are to appreciate the book's real depth and scope' (156). That is, merely reading the novel through will not lead to an understanding of its full significance: reading requires either existing criticism to illuminate the key, or something more than reading, perhaps reflection of the kind that generated insight about Proust's novel. However, Wilson observes, even reading with an understanding of the *Odyssey*'s relevance is not sufficient to see the complex schemata of organs, arts, sciences and other 'correspondences' that Joyce has used in his book. He looks back to T. S. Eliot's judgement: 'Joyce's handling of this immense material, his method of giving his book a shape, resembles nothing else in modern fiction' (169–70).[24] But for Wilson, unlike for Eliot, *Ulysses* 'suffers from an excess of design' (170), since it becomes clear that critical tools in the form of schemata are necessary for readers to try to understand Joyce's book.

The use of such tools is unsuccessful, Wilson argues, because the correspondences get in the way of reading. The difficulty is whether to follow the narrative of Bloom and Stephen or to follow the many

The Task of Reading and the Tasks of Criticism   **37**

other subjects and other orders of subjects that demand attention. In the 'Oxen of the Sun' episode, the difficulty becomes acute: 'If we pay attention to the parodies, we miss the story; and if we try to follow the story, we are unable to appreciate the parodies. The parodies have spoiled the story; and the necessity of telling the story through them has taken most of the life out of the parodies.' For Wilson, Joyce has 'as little respect as Proust for the capacities of the reader's attention' (173): it is the act of reading that brings out the limitations of Joyce's method, which seems to demand something readers cannot readily give. Wilson makes a similar point about *Work in Progress*: 'Joyce, with his characteristic disregard for the reader, apparently works over and over his pages, packing in allusions and puns' (188). Joyce, in Wilson's version of him, brings to an overt crisis the problems of reading modern writing that are already implicit in his contemporaries' fiction.

Yet within this is, for Wilson, an extraordinary rendering of each of *Ulysses*'s characters: the details of their environment documented in precise naturalistic abundance, and their mental worlds rendered through language in all the symbolist excess of those worlds. This is more important, for Wilson, than the problems he outlines: 'Joyce has undertaken in "Ulysses" [. . .] to find the unique vocabulary and rhythm which will represent the thoughts of each' of his people (164). The narrative voices that intervene on this combined rendering allow *Ulysses* to achieve a 'relativism like that of Proust: he is reproducing in literature the different aspects, the different proportions and textures, which things and people take on at different times and under different circumstances' (168). The admiration and praise that Wilson has for *Ulysses* come from the success of its rendering 'as exhaustively, as precisely, and as directly as it is possible in words to do, what our participation in life is like – or rather, what it seems to us like as from moment to moment we live' (175). The details of his enthusiasm about *Ulysses* echo critics of *Work in Progress* cited above, now Eugene Jolas – 'Joyce has found for this new vision a new language' (177) – and now John Rodker – 'Joyce is indeed really the great poet of a new phase of the human consciousness' (177–78).

The problems Wilson finds in reading *Ulysses* might be phrased as the extent to which the process of being temporarily absorbed in the book and its characters is necessarily interrupted by the process of reflecting on it at the level of a greater whole – a whole narrative, or a whole set of symbols, or parodies, or puzzles. Wilson's comments on correspondences in *Work in Progress* suggest a concept of reading that includes voluntarily surrendering to an illusion: 'And as soon as we are aware of Joyce himself systematically embroidering on his text, deliberately inventing puzzles, the illusion of the dream is lost' (188). Interrupting reading for criticism,

38   *The New Modernist Novel: Criticism and the Task of Reading*

allowing obfuscation of the story by the book's own technical apparatus, is for Wilson an excessive demand on readers, damaging to their experience. On Gertrude Stein, too, the quality Wilson most admires is to be found in her early novel *Three Lives*, which is less difficult at the level of sentences than her later work, and perhaps typically for Wilson, this quality is her work with character: 'one becomes aware of her masterly grasp of the organisms, contradictory and indissoluble, which human personalities are' (191).

By 1939, eight years after *Axel's Castle*, Wilson's vocabulary for expressing these difficulties has expanded via the figure of 'the reader': *Finnegans Wake* 'presents a more difficult problem to the reader as well as to the writer' than does *Ulysses*, so that 'it becomes on a first reading the reader's prime preoccupation to puzzle out who the dreamer is and what has been happening to him'. The obvious presence of Joyce in what should be Earwicker's thoughts leads to the 'reader's trouble'.[25] This prominence of an active 'reader' in 1939 is new. In the 1931 *Axel's Castle*, 'the reader' of Joyce is mentioned as quoted above (173, 188), but that reader is present only passively, as the reader forgotten by Joyce. Wilson does identify different groups of actual rather than hypothesised readers, as in the book's 'first readers' versus its later readers, but usually just uses 'we' ('the more we read *Ulysses*', 176). Any reader of Joyce in *Axel's Castle* is more like somebody trying to read a book for enjoyment and is not yet a figure defined by the act of reading – not yet someone who could be 'trouble[d]' or who could actively face problems in the work, as 'the reader' does, if still fleetingly, in the 1939 review of *Finnegans Wake*, a mere eight years later. For Wilson, distilling out 'the reader' as a variable to be monitored in critical reflection is helpful for refining his evaluation of Joyce across these two decades.[26]

Yet at the same time, *Axel's Castle* records qualities of modern writing that pull the focus towards reading. In the book, Wilson as reader offers critical reflection on reading, and he models it. Wilson's book plays out the extent to which coming to an understanding of these writers requires an extended process of absorption and reflection that extends beyond the timeframe of initial reading and requires readers to recreate these modern works in their own minds, even if doing so is an arduous, yet enjoyable task. Modern writing, the way Wilson portrays it in *Axel's Castle*, meant that reading had to become critical. By 1943, Wilson says as much directly in a comment on *Finnegans Wake*, when he asserts 'the peculiar kind of close attention to phrases, words and rhythms which the reader of *Finnegans Wake* must cultivate'. The association of an active verb, 'cultivate', with the 'reader' as subject here, almost four years after *Finnegans Wake*, is no longer new, and the idea that readers of Joyce's latest book must employ 'close attention' – to phrases, words and rhythms – is given as self-evident.[27]

This process of the reading evolving over many revisits in the course of two decades mirrors the kind of reading Rachel Sagner Buurma and Laura Heffernan identify as Wilson's kind. Referring to Wilson's 1942 course on Joyce, where Wilson explained in his opening lecture that he had reviewed *Ulysses* and *Finnegans Wake* on publication, but then had realised that the reviews were inadequate, they note that this kind of reading is most readily fostered not in reviews, which record a 'single act of analysis', but in classroom teaching, which often involves a repeated return to the same texts over decades, with different classes.[28] This kind of reading is critical, and also self-critical, as well as collaborative. In this process, parts of Wilson's critical style get trained over years by Joyce and other writers he reads, and by other readers' responses. Over these years, reading has become more complex.

Wilson's *Axel's Castle* connected to the contemporary literary worlds in which he worked and socialised, and its reflections on reading have a particular legitimacy for that reason. The book's subsequent passage into the academy was a circuitous one. For Wilson, 'smart commercial journalism' was one of the twentieth century's institutions that formed a social and economic base for the new American intellectuals, as Louis Menand puts it. The other was the university humanities department, with which his relationship was more fraught.[29] In this sense, it matters that Wilson cites T. S. Eliot declaring Joyce 'the greatest master of language in English since Milton'.[30] Wilson regretted that *Finnegans Wake* had been valued more inside the academy than outside it, and this claim for the value of Joyce by extension claims serious literature and serious reviewing for a still vital non-academic context. Wilson's hostility to the academy is clear in his charge that the academy tends to remove literary culture from 'historical action' in order to place it 'under glass': hence his own alarm at 'being bibliographed' while still alive.[31]

Yet as Paul Giles argues, while Wilson has been valued as a 'public intellectual' who resisted the specialising habits of the academy, 'it is arguable [. . .] that Wilson's position in American cultural history is more complicated and interesting than this, and that *Axel's Castle*, in particular, should properly be understood as one of the formative texts of American literary studies within the academy'.[32] This contribution to the academic study of modernism was completed after a delay, pending paperback and other editions of several of Wilson's books and essays in the 1950s, after which they were very widely read.[33] Despite Wilson's carefully maintained distance from academia, this places a stage in his academic reception chronologically alongside that of Lionel Trilling. But Wilson's criticism

40 *The New Modernist Novel: Criticism and the Task of Reading*

retained his closer identification with writers and artists who were his contemporaries. *Axel's Castle*, first reissued in 1959, registered questions about reading that were current to the early 1930s. Those questions about reading, as *Axel's Castle* shows, arose as a response to modern writing: this new writing required new, close attention to reading.

§

If modernist writing strongly prompted reflection on reading, answers as to what reading meant still diverged widely around 1930. One such set of reflections concerned reading as evaluation. This meaning of reading had already been active in criticism in *The Little Review*, where commenting on modern writing very often involved arriving at an evaluative judgement of that writing. Early on, in the first issue of volume 2 in 1915, Richard Aldington assumes that evaluation is a central aim of criticism and argues only over how it is to be arrived at. The problem, for Aldington, is not that 'the critic comes to judge a work of art', but that the critic does this 'not with an open mind but with a whole horde of prejudices, ignorances and eruditions which he terms "critical standards"'. Reading the writing carefully was already providing a solution to this problem, in Aldington's view.[34] Critics in *The Little Review* tend to assume that their readers will be just as capable of evaluation as they themselves are, so that the reading processes are often imagined to be shared by reader and critic and need not be dramatised on the page. Some fifteen years later, Ezra Pound and F. R. Leavis each saw evaluation as a key goal of readers. They each perceived the need to teach younger poets, or younger critics, how to read. But they disagreed over how literary writing might be evaluated.[35]

Pound first published 'How to Read, or Why' in the *New York Herald Tribune* in 1929. It was reprinted it as a pamphlet called *How to Read* in 1931.[36] Pound's occasion is dissatisfaction with the university teaching of literature that he had received. In response, he sets out a very roughly sketched history of literature that indicates what students should read in order to be able to make their own judgements about the value of any new work. *How to Read* emphasises that literature has a 'function in the state': writers are charged with maintaining 'the health of the very matter of thought itself' (*HR* 17). Pound's pamphlet therefore aims to help its readers to identify works 'where language is efficiently used' (*HR* 21). Some of its ideas were expanded into the 'text-book' *ABC of Reading* (1934), which has a stronger pedagogical bent. It aims more explicitly to equip students with the knowledge and ability to judge the value of a piece of writing themselves, and Pound emphasises the

The Task of Reading and the Tasks of Criticism   **41**

need to 'LOOK at' the texts rather than read criticism about them, his own included.[37] Both works address the general student of literature, but both intermittently assume that this student is an aspiring literary writer. Although these books are not directly concerned with reading modernist writing, they come from one of modernist literature's most active champions, and Pound insisted that *How to Read* concentrated more than two decades of his criticism.[38]

In *How to Read* and *ABC of Reading*, reading is framed by evaluation and judgement: from reading the best writers, the student can learn how to judge literary work and, in turn, how to write well. Pound's schema for classifying writers provides a method of evaluating writing. In both books, Pound's literary history is a history of inventions. The valuable poem is one that contains a 'discovery': that is, an 'invention, a definite contribution to the art of verbal expression' (*HR* 10) or a 'new process' (*ABC* 39–40). Such inventions are rare: conveniently for Pound's belaboured student of literature from antiquity to the present, inventions occur only in 'one or two men of genius' in each 'age' (*HR* 13), though other writers may master and use inventions, or dilute the work of the inventors, and so on (*HR* 21–24). In both books, these categories give rise to a reading list that represents 'the minimum that a man would have to read if he hoped to know what a given new book was worth' (*ABC* 41). Pound's schema reworks T. S. Eliot's notion of the 'new' in 'Tradition and the Individual Talent', though without naming Eliot explicitly (*ABC* 76, 91). In the preface to his *Active Anthology* (1933), however, Pound affirms Eliot's assessment that the 'existing works form a complete order which is changed by the introduction of the "really new" work'. In *How to Read* and *ABC of Reading*, his counterpart notion of the 'new' is a curriculum for students of literature, which will assist them to judge whether a given contemporary piece of writing is valuable. For Pound, the past is important for the training it offers to writers in the present – a training that finds knowing the 'results of processes' important for judging value.[39]

What do such judgements consist in? In *How to Read*, Pound declares that 'great literature is simply language charged with meaning to the utmost possible degree' (*HR* 21); he reiterates this twice in *ABC of Reading* (*ABC* 28, 36). Looking at 'what actually happens' in the writing will show the language charged by the music of its words (melopoeia), the visual images it casts (phanopoeia) or 'the dance of the intellect among words' (logopoeia; *HR* 25–26). As a prescription for reading and as a basis for judgement, this understanding of literature requires attentive, close work. Pound writes: 'The reader's first and simplest test of an author will be to look for words that do not function'

42   *The New Modernist Novel: Criticism and the Task of Reading*

(*ABC* 63). 'Dichten = condensare' (*ABC* 36, 92): to write poetry is to condense meaning into language. Consequently, close attention to the right works is an easier path than any attempt at comprehensiveness: 'a man can learn more about poetry by really knowing and examining a few of the best poems than by meandering about among a great many' (*ABC* 43). Pound thus proposes to list the best poems across multiple languages. Of course, the results of close examination are not fixed, and the best work will always support rereading. '"Literature is news that STAYS news"' (*ABC* 29), not just for centuries of readers, but also for the same reader. Implicitly, Pound hopes that different readers will make different judgements on the basis of their own reading, and he aims to cultivate those future judgements.

In *How to Read* and in the first half of *ABC of Reading*, reading lists of names and titles stand in for works and oeuvres, but the second half of *ABC of Reading* consists mainly of quotations or 'exhibits': passages excerpted from longer poems, and some short complete poems, presented for the student's examination and comment. The purpose of these quotations is primarily illustrative: they offer the student the chance to see what is valuable in a writer by looking closely at a short passage. Pound grapples with examples in both books, repeatedly observing a tension between his selections and his encouragement to read widely. On the one hand, the 'minimum that a man would have to read' traverses languages from Greek and Latin to Chinese to French, in a reading list that Pound asserts in *How to Read* 'would not overburden the three- or four-year student' (*HR* 51). On the other hand, the implication is that judgements of the value of a piece of writing can be arrived at quickly. Accordingly, in *ABC of Reading*, the student is presented with 'exhibits' consisting of passages: short poems and short passages excerpted from longer poems. As Pound reads, he cites 'half a page of Homer', 'a passage' of the *Odyssey* or 'another perfect strophe', as well as 'the author, poem or tale where a given quality exists in its purest form or its highest degree' (*ABC*, 43, 85, 53, 75).

But in this model of attention to how language is used, length, especially narrative length, poses a problem. Pound's selections from Arthur Golding's translation of Ovid's *Metamorphoses* seem to register most acutely the tension between passage and work.[40] Among the exhibits is a heavily excerpted selection from the story of Cadmus and Thebes (*ABC* 124–27). Apologising for the 'cuts in the story', Pound specifically exhorts the student to read all of Golding: 'I do not honestly think that anyone can know anything about the art of lucid narrative in English, or let us say about the history of the development of English narrative-writing (verse or prose) without seeing the whole of the

The Task of Reading and the Tasks of Criticism   **43**

volume' (*ABC* 126–27). Despite the beauty of Golding's *Metamorphoses*, Pound states that he is 'not here citing it for decorative purposes but for the narrative quality'. Pound's selections from book 3 are made with care: the three pages contain the salient events of the section he works with, and they cohere and develop as a narrative. They tell of Cadmus finding the plot of swampy land; the presence of the god Mars there in the form of a snake; Cadmus vanquishing Mars and encountering Athena; and, according to Athena's prophecy, armoured men growing out of the earth, some of whom will go on to help Cadmus found Thebes. Yet from his selection, it is hard to know how what Pound has left out might add to the story, or how these events fit into the longer narrative, or even which of them is the main story is at this point. Ovid moves quickly between stories – embedded, conjoined or otherwise linked. But it is hard for Pound to show how one story becomes another in his selection, and the selection struggles to demonstrate the 'narrative quality' that Pound claims for it.

The issue is not only that, as Pound regrets, he cannot reproduce a whole book of the *Metamorphoses*; it is also that the selection cannot adequately illustrate how different stories are woven together in the work. Pound demurred on his ability to analyse narrative form, commenting in *ABC of Reading* that 'I don't expect to write any novels and shall not tell anyone else how to do it until I have' (*ABC* 89). His comment is a response to Ford Madox Ford, who 'complained that no directions for major form were given in *How to Read*' (*ABC* 76).[41] If Pound's reading list on the novel aims at 'the underlying concept of FORM, the structure of the whole work, including its parts' (*ABC* 90), even so, the method of selection and comparative analysis in *ABC of Reading* founders on expounding form or structure. From *How to Read* and *ABC of Reading* comes the strong sense that the scales in operation are two: the level of lines and passages, and the level of literary history – a European history extended occasionally to Asia. The excerpts are reproduced in order to illustrate Pound's selected writers' styles for readers. But the level of form, narrative or otherwise, is harder to capture in excerpts, and reading, here, means first and foremost reading for style in excerpts.

Pound's model of reading can be compared with F. R. Leavis's response to *How to Read*, entitled *How to Teach Reading: A Primer for Ezra Pound* (1932). In it, Leavis criticises Pound for emphasising 'technique' at the expense of 'sensibility'.[42] For Leavis, 'technique can be studied and judged only in terms of the sensibility it expresses'; technique studied otherwise is an 'unprofitable abstraction' (12). In the training of students, a corresponding 'critical sensibility' should be

44   *The New Modernist Novel: Criticism and the Task of Reading*

'cultivat[ed]': that is, 'the power of responding fully, delicately and with discriminating accuracy to the subtle and precise use of words' (16). Yet such a sensibility is difficult enough to cultivate in one's own language, let alone in others. Beyond the difficulty for teaching, Leavis's concern is that Pound fails to understand the interdependence between language and literary tradition, where each is largely a product of the other. Instead, Leavis laments that for Pound, literature becomes 'a matter of mainly individual works [. . .] written by individual artists who invent – or borrow from other individual artists – devices, processes and modes of charging language with meaning', and the 'nature and conditions' of this 'meaning' remain unexplored (18). The critique here gets at Pound's use of authors in relative isolation, studied as exhibits of particular techniques in a translingual history of poetics. Reading and judgement, Leavis claims, require a different mode of thought. Literature must be read closely – 'everything worth saying in criticism of verse and prose can be related to judgements concerning particular arrangements of words on the page' (25) – but its reader must be ready to understand the writing within a 'cultural tradition' (19).

Leavis's distance from Pound is made especially clear on the question of reading literature in other languages: such reading should aim 'not at collecting a bag of tricks, but at realizing an order' (45). The bag of tricks is ultimately Pound the poet's, providing techniques gleaned from wide reading. Leavis finds in the *Cantos* a 'more or less elegantly pedantic dilettantism' (17), and this, for Leavis, corresponds to the idea in *How to Read* that technique is translatable across languages.[43] The realised order is, in turn, the critic's. Leavis glosses the 'order' as Eliot's from 'Tradition and the Individual Talent'. For Leavis, reading in other languages involves gaining familiarity with Eliot's 'mind of Europe' – that is, the order (or consciousness, or memory) 'within which English literature has its place' (19, 45).[44] Once a student has trained a sensibility in English literature as the primary interest ('the literature of one's own language', 42), the study can profitably be extended outwards. In this criticism of Pound, Leavis stakes out the ground of Eliot's essay in a way that pulls it away from Pound's interpretation. Where Pound seeks to aid the new poet to write what Eliot called the 'really new' work, Leavis reads Eliot's essay as leading the critic to position literary works within a larger tradition.[45] For both Pound and Leavis, the 'focus of interest is in the present' (39), but the meanings they give to Eliot's word 'tradition' differ considerably. Pound railed against Leavis by letter on his criticism of reading in other languages: 'GOD you ought to live and die in England.'[46]

Leavis's critique effectively distinguishes his own understanding of cultural tradition from the 'eclecticism' (18, 45) of Pound's literary history. Graham Hough would later call *ABC of Reading* 'a huge barbaric

The Task of Reading and the Tasks of Criticism   45

indigestible mass of gobbets'. Hough's word 'barbaric' perhaps refers obliquely (in 1960) to Pound's fascist sympathies, but his phrase also gets exactly at the kind of work that Pound was doing and that Leavis criticised.[47] In both books, Pound does indeed blend a diversified platter of national literatures into a meal edible for an expatriate, cosmopolitan twentieth-century writer. Both books aim to help the English-speaking student to become well versed in a broad literary tradition, ostensibly regardless of that student's cultural and geographical origin. Hough later commends 'Pound's commando raids on the whole history of poetry', observing in 1975 that 'the eclectic exploration of foreign literature at large in search of possibilities new to English' is a 'modern phenomenon'.[48] If the cultural diversity imagined by Pound only occasionally extends beyond Europe and North America, still, as Hough recognises, the catholicity built into Pound's gobbet-based programme for reading has wide resonance both with the expatriate status of individual modernists and, more significantly, with their movement's conception of style and newness as readable across a range of literary and cultural traditions. Hough's later comments on Pound show up the anti-modernism that is latent in Leavis's earlier response.

In calling for a different model for teaching literary critical reading, Leavis argues for what he later calls 'the development of more embracing critical thought out of local analysis' – that is, out of I. A. Richards's 'practical criticism'.[49] Quotation is imagined as serving a critic's analysis of a piece of writing, an analysis that will, it is understood, extend to 'an encompassing understanding of literature and culture', in Christopher Hilliard's words, concerning the whole oeuvre and, too, the whole 'age' – even if, in practice, Leavis's criticism often concerned itself primarily with specific passages.[50] Leavis did engage with Pound, however, and learned from him, as Ian MacKillop points out. Noting that the appendices to *Revaluation* (1936) are 'mostly quotation', and noting the 'astonishing amount of quotation' in the 1955 *D. H. Lawrence: Novelist*, MacKillop observes the similarity in Leavis's use of quotation to the 'procedure recommended' by Pound in *How to Read*.[51] Indeed, Leavis's introductory comments in *Revaluation* on the relationship of the poet to 'tradition' as being either an 'illustrative relation' or a 'significant development' carry strong echoes of Pound's categories of inventors and others in *How to Read*. Along with this enquiry into tradition, the drive to evaluative judgement that carries the book's critical analyses also bears close comparison with Pound's emphasis on judgement.[52] Yet for all their length, Leavis's quotations in *New Bearings in English Poetry* (1932) and *Revaluation* retain their status as evidence given in support for an argument being made about the text at hand, and in this way they still contrast with Pound's more general claims of value,

46   *The New Modernist Novel: Criticism and the Task of Reading*

where a passage quoted tends be more generally illustrative of a writer's style. Where Pound exhorts readers to read as a way to verify his claims of value, and more importantly to form their own claims, Leavis tends by contrast to use quoted passages as evidence in an argument being made at the time, on the page. In this, Leavis's use of quotation is more recognisable to criticism now.

Pound's goal of training young poets to think about literature differs from Leavis's of training young critics to think and write about it, and for Leavis, the printed page matters. Yet Pound's selective gobbets resonate directly with the version of modernism he helped to construct. What Leavis rightly calls the eclecticism of the reading lists in *How to Read* bears comparison with the range of allusions, citations and quotations in the literary work of the most familiar modernists – Joyce, Eliot, Pound himself – and of many other modernist writers. At the same time, in *ABC of Reading*, the brevity of the selections needed to judge the value of a piece of writing corresponds to an observable quality of good writing found by Pound the modernist reader in the work of modernist writers, among them Joyce, Eliot, Marianne Moore, Gustave Flaubert and others: that is, an exacting attention to style.[53] Pound's programme emerged interdependently with modernist literature: it affirmed and articulated many of modernism's criteria of literary value. But in the 1930s, Leavis's stated preference for unifying argument about a piece of writing's significance, supported by 'practical criticism' of selected quotations, was to lend itself to a more successful style of criticism that could be taught in academic institutions.

On fiction specifically, Leavis, like Ford Madox Ford, disputes Pound's assumption that one reads prose only in order to write verse: one might read prose for its own sake, Leavis argues. But to do so may be to find that the critical tools are lacking:

> With the novel it is so much harder to apply in a critical method the realization that everything that the novelist does is done with words, here, here and here, and that he is to be judged an artist (if he is one) for the same kind of reason as a poet is. Poetry works by concentration; for the most part, success or failure is obvious locally, in such passages as can be isolated for inspection. But prose depends ordinarily on cumulative effect, in such a way that a page of a novel that is as a whole significant may appear undistinguished or even bad (consider, for instance, Hardy: Virginia Woolf, on the other hand, like certain other moderns, stakes all on local success). (33)

Leavis's observation prefigures his later study of the novel in *The Great Tradition* (1948), one of whose strengths is to articulate the specific qualities of page after page of George Eliot, Joseph Conrad and Henry James

The Task of Reading and the Tasks of Criticism   **47**

within the cumulative effects of their novels. Leavis does so through the use of frequent, lengthy quoted passages, in a book that collates his earlier essays on fiction into a model for a discipline still developing models for writing about fiction. But just as interesting as this later work being prefigured in this quotation is the exception he makes here for 'certain' 'moderns', who stake all on 'local success'. The claim rings true for Virginia Woolf's poetic passages, even if most readers would want to make the added claim that her novels' cumulative effects are significant too. Beyond Woolf, the idea that some modern novels reward being read in part as poetry is highly suggestive for readers of modern fiction, even though a distinction between fiction and poetry tended to carry through academic criticism of the next few decades. Longer fiction is a challenge for Pound's method of teaching reading, but his sharp sense of the local success or failure of the writing being read coincides here with what Leavis finds in modernist fiction.

In the passage, F. R. Leavis is borrowing the term 'cumulative effect' from Q. D. Leavis: 'The novel's effect, then, is cumulative [. . .].'[54] Q. D. Leavis points out that 'A poem is so much more delicate and compact an organization than a novel that the whole depends on the quality of the part', whereas 'the novel does not stand or fall by its parts'. That is, 'in criticizing a poem one can safely bear out one's general impression by examining particular passages', since 'the poem succeeds or fails at every point'. By contrast, 'the novel is diffused, it cannot be read through at a sitting, and the whole is apt to be lost sight of in the immediacy of the parts'.[55] In consequence, she observes, the novel can, unlike poetry, be translated. In the case of Woolf, Q. D. Leavis observes that 'the technique and intention of *To the Lighthouse* are poetic', and that the writing requires the reader to 'allow the novel to act on him as "poetry"'.[56] For both F. R. and Q. D. Leavis, there is an element of newness to novels that are invested in the success of passages, yet where the writing still takes the form of the novel. Their terms 'local success' and 'poetic novel' indicate the new challenge that 'certain' modernist fiction presents to its readers.

Local success is at issue for other contemporary critics. I. A. Richards acknowledges the potential for tension between part and whole by setting whole poems in *Practical Criticism*, where he writes that 'no other critical moral, perhaps, deserves more insistence' than the need to judge details only with respect to the whole poem and the experience of reading it. Laura Riding and Robert Graves analyse poems line by line in *A Survey of Modernist Poetry*.[57] Local success is a defining criterion of modern fiction in Wyndham Lewis's 'taxi-cab driver test': the taxi-cab driver, awkwardly assumed not to know the book, is asked to evaluate a book on the basis of the writing on its first page.[58] But the tension specifically in

48   *The New Modernist Novel: Criticism and the Task of Reading*

modern fiction between local success and cumulative effects, articulated here by F. R. Leavis and Q. D. Leavis in the early 1930s, before academic criticism of modernist fiction had yet come into its own, was to remain a challenge for critics. Across the range of critical writing considered here – the critics in *Our Exagmination*, Edmund Wilson, Ezra Pound and F. R. Leavis, and those around them, including *Little Review* contributors, T. S. Eliot, Laura Riding and Robert Graves, Wyndham Lewis, Q. D. Leavis and many other readers – modern or modernist writing was prompting new attention to what was required from readers. For many of its readers, what was new about this writing was that it had to be read closely.

For Michael Levenson, it was in the early twenties that

> English modernism achieved its decisive formulation [. . .] not only because of legitimizing masterworks such as *Ulysses* or *The Waste Land* but because there developed a rhetorically effective doctrine to explain and justify that body of work. For this rhetoric and doctrine Eliot was in large measure responsible.[59]

In other words, Levenson established that Eliot showed how modernism could be read in a way that consolidated it and institutionalised it. Yet reading contemporary critics around Eliot suggests that despite this predetermined arrival, via Eliot, at a certain set of critical understandings of modernism, what it meant to read modern writing was by no means determined by the early 1930s, and major rifts in thinking about what reading involved were still underway between critics of larger and smaller influence. These questions about reading began to be answered with greater consensus in academic settings.

The Mid-Century Reception of Modernism

In 1972 Harry Levin commented on Edmund Wilson's 'Thoughts on Being Bibliographed' of 1944. Levin wrote that Wilson had 'expressed regret that younger men, possibly in recoil from the confusions and restrictions of the thirties, were turning from the present to the past and from Bohemia to Academe'. Levin continued, quoting Wilson,

> He was struck by 'the curious phenomenon—which would have been quite inconceivable in my college days—of young men teaching English or French in the most venerable schools and universities at the same time that they hold radical political opinions and contribute to "advanced" magazines'.

The Task of Reading and the Tasks of Criticism   49

In the 1944 piece, Wilson had taken Levin as an example: 'In the twenties, Mr. Harry Levin, who has written so brilliantly on Joyce, would undoubtedly have been editing the *Dial* and going to bat for *Ulysses* in its pages: today he teaches English at Harvard.'[60] Wilson's sense comes through that his own radical literary opinions do not match those of young academics now. Levin's later naming of a move into academia collects several changes, including a move away from the avant-garde and international little magazine scene, and among these changes is the reconceptualising of a literary movement into an institutional shape, ripe for new, institutionally friendly styles of criticism.

In 1944 Wilson had declared that '*Finnegans Wake* went straight from the hands of Joyce into the hands of the college professors, and is today not a literary issue but a subject of academic research.' This was partly because, he comments, making a living from reviewing and journalism had become more difficult, so 'literary men' were obliged to work for universities.[61] By contrast, of course, the sections of *Work in Progress* had gone straight into the hands of Joyce's earnest critics in the little magazine *transition*, a decade earlier in 1929. The scene of literary writing in journals registered a similar change. Where many modernist little magazines were run with no affiliation to academic institutions, often supported by benefactors, the magazines that were the venue for up-to-date criticism in the 1950s tended, by contrast, to be housed or sponsored by academic institutions.[62]

Of course, the process of change was complex. Stefan Collini, complicating the picture of the professionalisation of literary criticism, notes that in Britain between about 1930 and 1970, the preferred readership for ambitious literary critics was public, and that Chatto and Windus was the main publishing venue sought after by leading critics such as William Empson, F. R. Leavis, Raymond Williams and Richard Hoggart.[63] Hugh Kenner, too, in the 1950s and 1960s published with (for example) New Directions, Faber and Faber, Chatto and Windus and Grove, often with the same press as the author who was his subject. Yet in contrast to earlier decades, by the late 1950s and early 1960s in the UK and the US, everyday criticism was largely being written from universities, and despite a broader readership, modernism was now being written about in large part in that new context.

These significant shifts involved changes in how modernism was read. In the remaining sections of the present chapter, I first note that the 1950s was a time of change for academic criticism. One key change was the arrival of modernist fiction as a fully legitimate subject of academic study, which I suggest happened slightly later for modernist fiction than for modernist poetry. At this time, the most successful impetus for the study of modernist fiction tended to come from critics who were finding paths away from New Criticism. I then go on in the last two sections to consider the interdependence between some versions of mid-century criticism and a particular selection of modernist fiction. Despite their broad reading in modernism, the mid-century critics I read tended to return to a smallish group of writers in their criticism, and those writers tended to reward these critics' approaches with success. I consider how critical values attached to the perception of coherence and learnedness in literary works helped to support the selection of a narrowed modernist canon at mid-century.

How did this canon come about? The steps involved in the unravelling of mid-century canons are better recognised than the processes of their formation, in part because challenges to canons have involved explicit engagement with existing gaps: as for example in Houston A. Baker Jr's *Modernism and the Harlem Renaissance* (1987) and Bonnie Kime Scott's anthology *The Gender of Modernism* (1990).[64] If the unravelling of these selections was achieved by the conscious inclusions of women writers, writers of colour, LGBTQ+ writing, and other work, including more recently writers who engaged with modernism across the globe, that is because those inclusions correspond to earlier exclusions. As Merinda K. Simmons and James A. Crank put it, 'The critical praxis surrounding early modernist studies was anxiously crafting a canon that actively denied space to voices on the margins – women, people of color, and postcolonial writers and artists.'[65] The different choices being made regarding canonicity in each of the 1930s, 1940s and 1950s were ostensibly made on other grounds, but one determining feature was the use of work that looked culturally authoritative as a reference point for a movement that was in fact populous and diverse. To analyse how writers moved from active participation in the modernisms of the 1920s and 1930s to the periphery of an academic modernist literature, it is worth returning to the ideas about reading and value that accompanied that narrowing and that served to rationalise it. I consider some of these ideas below.

Writing of the American New Critics' efforts to decide canons, Alan Golding stresses the 'connection between evaluation and close reading in early New Critical methodology'. Close reading of a New Critical kind effectively became a tool for selecting canons, notably through classroom teaching of successive editions of Cleanth Brooks and Robert Penn Warren's *Understanding Poetry* (first edition 1938).[66] In the UK, the *Scrutiny* group had, too, prioritised the judgement of literary value in the selection of literature for study. For the Leavises, the moral value of literature mattered, and this had the effect of a hesitation on Joyce and Pound that persisted in British criticism in later years. Indeed, there was considerable hostility to modernism, for example among the Movement poets and other readers of the Oxford-based journal *Essays in Criticism*, who distrusted the surface complexity of many modernist writers.[67] Leavisism was less readily professionalised than the New Criticism, since, as Simon During argues, it constituted an 'independent critical engagement with the dominant culture', and for this reason, During argues, the New Criticism took root in the US, rather than Leavisism.[68] This may have given later US critics more freedom to write about the modernism that they then established, in which Pound and Joyce were central alongside others. But for these later critics, close reading and evaluation remained connected, even if in new ways.

The moral seriousness of the 1950s in the US also affected the selection of literature for teaching. Alan Filreis gives a detailed examination of the way the literary 1930s were repudiated in the 1950s under the pressure of anti-communism, despite questions over how far radical experiment in writing corresponded to radical left-wing politics.[69] Andreas Huyssen shows how the modernism established in criticism in the 1950s was a domesticated and politically expedient version of modernism, ripe for rejection by American postmodernists of the 1960s. As Paul Giles points out, commenting on Huyssen, the 'sanitizing and commodification of modernism during the 1950s', which involved an 'eagerness to canonize works of art and celebrate them for their qualities of formal innovation', have also distracted from political commitments associated with those works.[70] The choice of writers as subjects of study was never made solely on the grounds of literary qualities, and various social and political pressures were at play in the gradual selection of a body of modernist fiction for criticism. In Lionel Trilling's words, the novel was an 'agent of the moral imagination', a phrase which implicitly records the high stakes that were involved in selecting specific modernist novels to write and lecture about.[71]

The period from the 1930s to the 1960s also saw significant changes in the study and teaching of literature, and in the US in particular, these changes accompanied a greater emphasis on modernist literature. Indeed, the 1950s marked a moment of change, where, as Wallace Martin notes, the gradual fading of the work of Richards, Eliot, Leavis and the New Critics coincided with new thinking about literary criticism. Martin writes of the 1950s, 'that decade was one in which the reorganisation of knowledge established a groundwork for new modes of literary understanding'.[72] These new modes of understanding were to involve significant disagreement on several questions, not least on definitions of criticism and theory. But at the same time they accompanied a swiftly developing

52   The New Modernist Novel: Criticism and the Task of Reading

consensus in terms of the selection of literary works that could be taken to represent modernism, as well as how such modernist literature might be read. This growing consensus supported critical exchanges that helped to define the discipline, and concepts of value and rigour that still persist today were historically conditioned within a relatively small timeframe.

I comment below on these concepts with reference to four critics: Graham Hough, Harry Levin, Hugh Kenner and Wayne Booth. But first, some further detail identifies this moment of change in the 1950s as a significant one for academic criticism of modernist fiction, as distinct from modernist poetry. In the movement of modernist literature into academic teaching and research, modernist fiction emerged as a legitimate subject for criticism slightly later than modernist poetry. T. S. Eliot provides a convenient rough marker here: the entry of Eliot's poetry into the academy was aided by the importance of his critical essays for F. R. Leavis and for the American New Criticism. Leavis positioned Eliot's poetry as central in *New Bearings in English Poetry* in 1932, and he later cited his own book as the 'pioneering' reason why, by the time of F. O. Matthiessen's *The Achievement of T. S. Eliot* in 1935, Eliot's importance as a poet was already established,[73] though Matthiessen was also influenced by contact at Harvard with I. A. Richards in 1929 and with Eliot there in 1932.[74] In Cleanth Brooks's *Modern Poetry and the Tradition* (1939), not only Eliot, but also W. B. Yeats, W. H. Auden, Robert Frost and other 'modern' poets (though not Pound) were studied. In 1950, Leavis was able to tout Eliot as 'a public institution, part of the establishment'.[75]

Criticism of Anglophone modernist fiction gained momentum slightly later. Among the *Scrutiny* crowd, some serious criticism of modern fiction appeared in *Scrutiny* in the 1930s, and Q. D. Leavis gave important attention to modern fiction in 1932 in *Fiction and the Reading Public*, but F. R. Leavis's *The Great Tradition* appeared only in 1948. Harry Levin's *James Joyce: A Critical Introduction* was commissioned by James Laughlin after the ban on *Ulysses* was lifted in the 1930s and appeared in 1941. F. O. Matthiessen's *Henry James: The Major Phase* was published in 1944, and Leon Edel's five-volume biography of James began in 1953. Erich Auerbach's 1946 *Mimesis*, which came to Anglophone modernist literature (Virginia Woolf) by way of European literary history, was published in English translation in 1953. As Michael Levenson shows, in the US, it was in the 1940s that Jamesian criticism of the novel was reconciled with New Criticism by Cleanth Brooks and Robert Penn Warren, with *Understanding Fiction* (1943) standing 'at the confluence of the neo-Jamesian enquiry into point of view and the New Critical concern with poetic irony'.[76] Point of view provided an ongoing tool of

The Task of Reading and the Tasks of Criticism   53

analysis that was formal in nature and that was not intrinsically New Critical. Modernist fiction was thus being calibrated with prominent approaches to modernist writing by US critics in the 1940s, approaches that had already been worked through with modernist poetry. But despite work like Brooks and Warren's, the story of criticism of modernist fiction is not essentially a story of the New Criticism. This critical environment was one in which new modes of reading were developed for reading fiction, and in the postwar boom in US tertiary education in the 1950s, a number of studies of modernist fiction appeared, many of them moving away from the New Criticism.[77]

The acceptance of James Joyce as a legitimate subject for research and teaching in endowed US universities was one sign of modernist fiction's imminent arrival there. Joseph Brooker, telling this story, records that in 1946, Richard Ellmann warned Ellsworth Mason that Joyce was 'fine as a hobby but not dissertation material', and that Hugh Kenner in Toronto met with similar discouragement. Brooker gives a sense of the dedication that Kenner, Ellmann and others needed in order to be able to study modernist writers.[78] Brooker records Mason's reflection on *Ulysses* in the early 1940s: 'nobody really read it [. . .]. Nobody knew how to read it.'[79] In this reflection, which he made in 1987, Mason echoes Kenner, who in 1985 reflected similarly on Pound's reception: 'nobody in 1949 knew *how* to talk about Pound's poetry'.[80] As Brooker shows, it was continued work by Richard Ellmann and Hugh Kenner, beginning in the 1950s, that gradually made *Ulysses* and Joyce's writing respectable topics for academic literary study in US universities. This was so even if each brought respectability to the writing on markedly different grounds. Brooker records that in the biography *James Joyce* (1959), Ellmann sought 'an effect of unity', producing a 'fundamentally harmonious' view of Joyce's life and work. Ellmann's biography, shows Brooker, provided a vision of Joyce's essential humanism, showing Joyce as 'the democratic champion of everyday folk'.[81] Joyce's moral authority in these decades was important for the role his writing came to play in academic criticism of modernism. Yet, Brooker writes, 'While Ellmann and others, then, were securing Joyce's place in the novelistic canon, Kenner took the slightly different route of devising a new narrative of literary history around him', one that was European in focus, that excluded many of Leavis's 'great' novelists, and that was a precursor to more recent shifts in modernist studies.[82] The example of James Joyce suggests that the possible routes modernist fiction might take to seek legitimacy in the academy were still being worked out in the 1950s. This was at a time when the legitimacy of (at least some) modernist poetry had already been established – and when Ezra Pound's poetry was following suit by means of Kenner among others.

54   *The New Modernist Novel: Criticism and the Task of Reading*

The acceptance of modernist fiction coincided with changes in criticism that meant its strategies of reading could more readily accommodate fiction. In part, the relevance of biography, such as Edel's biography of James and Ellmann's of Joyce, studies of historical context and other extra-literary work at mid-century helped to result in 'the dominance of academic high modernism at mid-century', as Sean Latham and Gayle Rogers explain.[83] But new modes of close reading needed to be developed too. Although Kenner's 1951 book *The Poetry of Ezra Pound* concerns poetry rather than fiction, some groundwork for his criticism of modernist fiction in the 1950s and after can be traced in the antagonisms treasured there to F. R. Leavis and the New Critics. These antagonisms are a part of a larger reconsideration of criticism in that decade, which, among other changes, found new ways to read modernist fiction. Kenner responds to the skirmish between Ezra Pound and F. R. Leavis about Pound's *How to Read* (1931) that was considered earlier in this chapter and rejects Leavis's position on reading in favour of Pound's. Similarly, he jettisons the New Critical vocabularies of 'wit' and 'paradox' that he objected to in readings of T. S. Eliot.[84]

Continuing the disagreement between F. R. Leavis and Pound on how to read, Kenner redefines 'technique' in a way that neutralises Leavis's critiques of Pound as a mere technical innovator. Recommending 'line-by-line attention to the entire "How to Read"', Kenner glosses 'technical innovations' as 'incorporation into literature of new provinces of thought and feeling'. That Kenner understands this to unsettle Leavis's distinction between 'technique' and 'sensibility', in which Leavis attacks Pound for an excessive focus on technique and a failure of sensibility, is suggested by the motivation Kenner assigns to the technical innovator: 'The innovator handles language in novel ways because his expression is too deeply engaged with his sensibility, his sincerity is too urgent, for received moulds to suffice.'[85] Kenner claims the last word, matching his own use of 'sensibility' to Leavis's use of the term: 'The first requisite for judging any poetry is not analytic skill but a trained sensibility. Dr. Leavis, despite his stern disapproval of most of Pound's work, is nowhere more surprisingly Poundian than in his realization of this.'[86] To the cultural conservatism implicit in Leavis's requirement for 'sensibility', Kenner gives the implicit riposte: 'Pound is concerned with the progress of an art [. . .] international and interlingual in a way that our present hypertrophied neuro-muscular sensitivity to the morphologies of racial sensibility scarcely permits us to suspect.'[87] On translation specifically, the site of Leavis's major objection to Pound, Kenner writes of '"acquiring technique" by translation' as 'enriching the English tradition with a wealth of other modes of thinking and feeling'.[88] By reframing both 'sensibility' and 'tradition' in this way, Kenner undoes the force of Leavis's criticisms of Pound and explicitly values an internationalist bent in literature.

Kenner's study of Pound took part in a broader change for modernist poetry, since Pound was hard to fit into either a Leavisite practical criticism or a New Critical understanding of poetry. For the New Critics, the 'formless' quality of the *Cantos* meant that they missed unity in it, as they did in other work by Pound, and accordingly valued Pound's poetry less highly. This added to their sense that Pound's 'sociopolitical commitments' in his poetry diluted the quality of his art.[89] Kenner's book restored that sense of unity – the unity is there, if only the reader or critic knows how to look for it, Kenner argued[90] – but it did so in ways that differed from New Critical practices. Showing that Pound may require different kinds of reading from New Critical approaches, Kenner attacks the 'assumption that what can be taken apart equals what has been put together'. If a critical apparatus finds nothing in Pound, that may be, he observes, because of the limitations of the method.[91] Kenner's readings of Pound's work progressed via Pound's critical writing and his reading lists, alongside broader reference, such as to the possibility of an aerial view. The length and complexity of the *Cantos* meant it was hard to bring New Critical techniques of close reading to this ongoing long poem, and Kenner's more allusive techniques of close reading were, by contrast, more successful for Pound.[92] In turn, Kenner's version of close reading would later adapt well to Joyce and other modernist fiction writers.[93] His ripostes to F. R. Leavis and his differences from New Criticism helped to lay groundwork for a decade of his study of technical experiment in modernist literature, especially fiction. Following Kenner's books on Wyndham Lewis, Joyce, T. S. Eliot and Samuel Beckett, he makes a set of observations about modernist fiction in *Flaubert, Joyce and Beckett: The Stoic Comedians* (1962).

The move away from New Criticism was not only Kenner's project, but was shared by other critics, notably Harry Levin. In *The Gates of Horn* (1963), Levin makes the point that the New Criticism was not well suited to the study of the novel. He writes that a formalist criticism that has 'gone so far as to turn its back upon history' seems, in the form of the New Criticism, to 'have been put off by the very informality of the novel, its impertinent outercourse with the outer world'. Levin's point is important: the novel as a subject of study could not sustain the intensive formalism that poetry, by contrast, had been able to sustain in New Critical methods of study. Levin remembers the pressure in the 1930s in the other direction, towards a predominantly sociological criticism.[94] In the decades during which he wrote *The Gates of Horn*, the academic

56 *The New Modernist Novel: Criticism and the Task of Reading*

study of literature came to include the study of the Anglophone modernist novel, and as the subject of study changed, so did the kinds of criticism that could most usefully be brought to it.

Yet the strategies of reading that were developed tended to suit some writing more than other writing, whether fiction or not. The establishment of a teachable canon was important for showing how this new modernism – a 1950s new modernism – could be read and taught. Despite their wide reading, then, Kenner, Levin and others tended to work most intensively with a smallish group of writers whose literary work rewarded their criticism. These and other critics' published work attested to the depth of biographical, historical and critical labour that was required to understand the writers they worked on, including W. B. Yeats, T. S. Eliot, Ezra Pound, James Joyce, Henry James, Samuel Beckett, Gustave Flaubert, Marcel Proust and others. That labour gradually provided a basis for others to write about the same writers. The difficulty of these writers' work and that work's productivity for critical labour seem likely to have been significant factors in the relative neglect of other writers while critical groundwork on these writers was being done.

This selection took place alongside a much broader modernism that these critics read and cited. Poets, too, read widely, sometimes with different enthusiasms. Kenneth Rexroth was reading Mina Loy's poetry in the 1940s, and Loy's *Lunar Baedeker and Time-Tables* was published in 1958 by Jonathan Williams with introductions by William Carlos Williams, Kenneth Rexroth and Denise Levertov, despite little academic attention to Loy. In a 1982 review of Roger L. Conover's edition of Loy's poems, *The Last Lunar Baedeker*, Hugh Kenner briefly questioned why Mina Loy had been undeservedly forgotten as a modernist poet.[95] Alexander Howard observes that Charles Henri Ford's work with surrealism and his writing style were at odds with the critical values of Clement Greenberg and John Crowe Ransom, but Ford was recognised by Kenneth Koch and other emerging US poets, including Frank O'Hara, John Ashbery and Ted Berrigan.[96] As Stephen Heath records, while Mary Butts's work 'disappeared from attention', being 'barely mentioned, if at all, in literary histories', it was read by writers in the US, notably by poets, including Frank O'Hara, John Ashbery, Robert Duncan and Jack Spicer.[97] While the poetic reception of modernism differed at mid-century from its academic reception, the version of modernism that these and other poets were reading would become key to the new modernisms by the end of the century.

As well as this poetic reception, there was an active public readership of modernism, not just among poets. As Melissa Hardie discusses, Barnes's *Nightwood* was published for a general readership in the New Directions New Classics series, with Alvan Lustig's cover design from

1948, which presented 'the book as design object'.[98] By 1949, *Nightwood* was already a lesbian and cultural classic: when Harriet Sohmers introduced herself to a teenage Susan Sontag by suggesting she read *Nightwood*, Sontag had already read it.[99] Even within academic institutions, where instructors could set their own preferred texts, classroom teaching allowed for broad choice of literary work to be studied.[100] Any selectivity took place against a still very broad modernism that was being read inside and outside the academy.

Those writing about modernist fiction as professional literary critics, however, increasingly were academics, including the four critics whose reading practices I analyse in the next section. Analysing the reading practices of Graham Hough, Harry Levin, Hugh Kenner and Wayne Booth as they read modernist literature, especially modernist fiction, gives some provisional answers to the question of what reading, especially critical reading, meant for these critics. This selection of critics may risk ratifying the canonisation of a small group of white Anglo-American men. However, it is their and others' prominent position in a winners' history of twentieth-century criticism that makes them suitable subjects here.[101] They were influential, and that matters for my argument. I deal here not so much with their definitions as with what they do: I read them reading. That is to say – I read them writing about their reading. I argue that their modes of reading contributed to a set of criteria of literary value that effectively narrowed the conception of modernist literature, even through major theoretical challenges, prior to that conception's being challenged and its canons being widened later in the twentieth century and in the twenty-first. Three of the four were based in US universities: the mid-century reception of modernism outlined here is largely a US-based reception, and indeed, the concept of modernism that came together with enough force to produce – decades later – a new modernist studies came together first in the US.

Productivity and the Academy

Graham Hough's 1959 lectures on modernism were delivered in Washington DC, though Hough was based in Cambridge, UK, for most of his academic career. In the published lectures in 1960, Hough wrote, 'the years between 1910 and the second world war saw a revolution in the literature of the English language as momentous as the Romantic one of a century before'.[102] But at this point in time, for Hough, reading modern poetry remains a challenge, perhaps an insurmountable one. This is in spite of the achieved institutionalisation of a version of modernism

58   *The New Modernist Novel: Criticism and the Task of Reading*

via T. S. Eliot's criticism: 'A diluted version of Mr. Eliot's critical doctrine (and that includes, at one remove, a great deal of the doctrines of Hulme, Pound and Lewis) is by now the possession of undergraduates and schoolboys.' Hough continues, 'Yet the direct effect on literary practice has been strangely small.'[103] If Eliot's modernism is part of an institutionalised canon and syllabus, how it may be read remains a problem both within and outside the institution.

The account here of a community of readers who collectively found ways to read *The Waste Land* offers insight into the strangeness of this modernist poem for some of Hough's contemporaries. This community of readers found that where the general keys to the poem offered by the notes were fairly unhelpful, enquiry into specific lines in isolation was more productive, in that it offered a greater depth of understanding of those lines. Such enquiry increased the available volume of critical work on the poem, but it was insufficient to resolve the 'real' questions, chief among them that of 'what really makes the poem a totality, if it is one at all'. For Hough, reading *The Waste Land* involves not only understanding isolated lines, but finding the structure that holds the poem together. In the 1960 essay, Hough's deep puzzlement is clear: 'It is as though a painter were to employ a pointilliste technique in one part of a picture, and the glazes of the high renaissance in another.'[104] The concepts of 'totality' and 'structure' here are not New Critical unities, as each suggests a relation to the whole social world of which the literary work is a part – a relation that seems lacking to Hough in Eliot's poem.[105] The missing element for Hough here seems to match what he later terms 'consonance': 'the demand for coherence and proportion' where the diverse parts are brought together into 'harmony and unity'.[106]

Hough later tempered aspects of his critiques of Eliot, Pound and modernism. By the time of 'The Poet as Critic', written for publication in 1975, the observation that Eliot's poems 'have no rational structure at all' is no longer puzzling, and instead furnishes enquiry into the dissonance between the poems as 'brilliant collages' on the one hand, and Eliot's 'declaration of "classical" principles' in his criticism on the other.[107] But the concerns raised in the 1960 essay are reflected on repeatedly and generatively in his later work, and in expressing those concerns in 1960 Hough registers some of the challenge that this new writing presented to its readers. In the 1960 essay, the puzzlement occasioned by *The Waste Land* presents an issue for literary criticism specifically: 'it is very difficult altogether to dispel the notion that the objects, persons and ideas in a single poem should be in some intelligible relation to one another'. Fine passages, no matter how literary, are not enough to make great poetry without coherence, and reading is a process of finding coherence

The Task of Reading and the Tasks of Criticism   59

across the poem. The issue is that for a given disagreement about how the parts of the poem might fit together, Hough sees 'no means by which the matter could be decided'. This conclusion brings home the force of Hough's earlier protest: 'the methodological infractuosities of the piece have fulfilled one of the main economic functions of poetry in this century – they have given employment to a host of scholiasts'.[108] His account here of *The Waste Land* sees exegesis piling up endlessly without ever being able to offer clarity. In turn, modern poetry and the institutions that are devoted to it come to seem alarmingly insular. Read by students and professors, modern poetry and modern criticism are at the service of each other, and this is at the expense of a poetry which would speak to a public. Hough's essay astutely diagnoses a new relationship between modernist literature and literary criticism, and it does so by identifying a difficulty that inheres in reading.

Hough later identifies not modernist writing, but the academic setting of criticism as the source of the insularity he perceives. In 1970 he observes a loss of connection between criticism and culture, where criticism addresses a 'captive audience of students and teachers' rather than a 'diversified adult public', and as a remedy he calls for criticism to account for the 'relation of literature to the social order'.[109] In a later essay, he identifies the proliferation of multiple meanings as a new aspect of criticism, dating from Empson's *Seven Types of Ambiguity*.[110] Yet for my question of how modernism was read, the connection Hough makes a decade earlier between modernist poetry and its productivity for academic literary criticism registers a new challenge for academic readers in modernist writing, even if that challenge then gets absorbed into criticism.

The 1960 essay draws attention to another question: who was reading modernism? There is a set of complex changes recorded regarding the loss of a public sphere for literature. To some degree Hough inverts Q. D. Leavis's concern in *Fiction and the Reading Public* (1932): where she laments that good literature is not being read by a mass readership, who are instead reading second-rate work, he laments that what is on offer as 'good literature' is not readable by a mass readership. But he retains her divisions between the different capacities of readers, even if his sympathies lie with the 'common' reader, for whom *The Waste Land* may, to his regret in 1960, prove incomprehensible. The potential incoherence of modernist literature plays into both Q. D. Leavis's and later Hough's different ideas of the reading public, who, they record, are not reading modernism.[111] Hough would go on to write criticism that makes T. S. Eliot and others more readable. Echoes of concerns about a new, wider readership are differently evident in the more pedagogical tone of

60   *The New Modernist Novel: Criticism and the Task of Reading*

some of the other criticism of this decade, notably that of Harry Levin and Hugh Kenner. If the public are reading modernism but, these latter critics fear, don't know how, a pedagogical academic criticism takes on more importance, as it had for Edmund Wilson some thirty years earlier.

Harry Levin's essay 'What Was Modernism?' takes a different stance from Hough in the same year. Levin shares with Hough a sense that with the 'Moderns', a great movement had passed. He writes, 'we live at least in the afterglow of the Moderns'.[112] But he does not share Hough's conclusion that this relative poverty signifies any deficiency in the moderns that might have left an impasse for their successors. Rather, the essay carries the theme of taming the formerly shocking new, beginning with the example of Picasso, who has arrived so completely that his name will signify 'domestic respectability' to a consumer public.[113] In contrast to Hough, Levin sees such respectability exemplified in the career of T. S. Eliot, whom 'we have come to view as a living embodiment of tradition'; for Levin, Eliot's 'problematic endeavours startled and puzzled his early readers', but implicitly not 'us', who are no longer puzzled by the 'Modernists'. Levin observes the demands these diverse writers make on their readers, but he asserts their ethical seriousness.[114]

At the time when Levin's book *James Joyce: A Critical Introduction* was first published, in late 1941, it was among the first responses to modernist fiction from within the academy, and although Levin was an academic, the book had been commissioned by James Laughlin of New Directions. But when it was republished in revised form in 1960, it followed a good deal of subsequent work on Joyce and modernist fiction, by both faculty and students. In this sense, Levin's book helped to bring about the shift he later comments on, in which *Ulysses* became a classic as the study of twentieth-century literature was moving into the academy.[115] The 1941 edition helped to begin the process of making Joyce's writing a suitable, respectable topic for academic work.[116] Levin's 1942 preface articulates a version of what it meant to read Joyce critically: 'Now that [Joyce's] work is completed, we must try to understand its significance, and to place him – without extenuation or malice – against the broad perspectives of literary history.'[117] By making progress in understanding a valuable work, the critic can help to illuminate literary and cultural history as the wider object of study.

The steps of this approach – understanding through careful analysis of the work, and positioning within a literary and cultural tradition – can be found in Levin's discussion of the 'Circe' episode, which he identifies as 'the climax of *Ulysses*'. He cites John Middleton Murry's comparison of 'Circe' to Goethe's *Walpurgisnacht* and adds his own range of relevant literary references, moving for example within a sentence from

The Task of Reading and the Tasks of Criticism   61

the allegorical *dramatis personae* found in the medieval morality play to expressionist modern theatre. Such a mini-literary historical positioning constitutes a condensed history of drama into which *Ulysses* enters. But the work of analysis is also evident, here in Levin's careful analysis of apparent inconsistencies in 'Circe' (Bloom hears a phrase earlier read by Stephen; Stephen sees a face earlier remembered by Bloom), which lead back to consistency under the careful eye of the critic: for Levin, in this chapter, Stephen's and Bloom's 'streams of consciousness seem to converge'.[118] Such readings are evidently invited by 'Circe'. Yet Levin's reading makes *Ulysses* seem the kind of text any critic would value: one that not only engages with the history of dramatic literature, but rewards intricate, careful attention. For Levin, the thinking critical mind can, through patient work and careful reading, make sense of the text's complexities.

The approach is reiterated and clarified in his study of realism from Stendhal to Proust, *The Gates of Horn* (1963): 'We have not analyzed a novel until we have discovered its place in the mind of the novelist, in the movement of the age, and in the tradition of literature.'[119] Levin reads his selected novelists in the service of the idea that they are 'decisive points of reference, not only for one another, but for all subsequent practitioners of novelistic technique' and that they are 'united by their cumulative response to a continuous train of historic circumstance'. Accordingly, the chapters detail a literary and cultural history where these novels are decisive literary events. In this way, the various novels are no longer disparate, but connected. Indeed, the five novelists are called 'innovators' as opposed to 'imitators', presumably following Pound's terminology of inventors.[120] Here and elsewhere, in spite of the breadth of Levin's criticism, the sense is clear that in order to be valuable for Levin, a literary work must take part in a larger history and illuminate it. In the twentieth century, Proust and Joyce are especially worth writing about, since their writing lives are deeply embedded in literary and cultural history. Criticism of Proust and Joyce reads not just their novels but, through those novels, a connected cultural history.

Levin's critical project differs from the work of the younger critic Hugh Kenner. Yet the similarities between Levin's and Kenner's work suggest some of the concepts of criticism and literary value that helped to shape a canon of modernist literature in the mid-century. In the 1960 edition of *James Joyce*, Levin takes issue briefly with Kenner's approach. Levin suggests that now in 1960, the basic problem of understanding Joyce has generally been solved. As Joseph Brooker records, Levin cites Kenner's 1955 *Dublin's Joyce* as an example of a tendency for new interpretations 'to become capricious and doctrinaire through their very

62   *The New Modernist Novel: Criticism and the Task of Reading*

effort to discover novel readings'.[121] On the problem of the work that remains in reading Joyce, Levin sees the issues as already clear: 'In signalizing the dangers of subjective over-reading, I do not mean to suggest that we have wrested the last iota of meaning out of *Ulysses* or that significant researches are not continuing. Experts can still annotate it on technical matters', and these technical matters might include its use of music, Talmudic references or the process of composition. But the work of criticism involves this task of annotation, rather than 'novel readings'. On the whole, '*Ulysses* is no longer opaque', even though 'there are those who would restore its opacity'.[122]

Kenner, for Levin, is representative of a trend in criticism towards endless new interpretations. But for Levin, the critic or the critic's approach is the locus of the issue, rather than the (modernist) literary text itself. Kenner stands accused, if gently, by Levin of essentially creating critical work where there need not be any. In chapters on *A Portrait of the Artist as Young Man* and *Ulysses* in *Dublin's Joyce*, Kenner gives a new close attention to sentences and to correspondences, assessing meaning with a heightened awareness of the potential for irony provided by a completed work. In Kenner's book, Joyce's writing in these two books is indeed highly productive of newly meaningful correspondences, as if newly opaque. Beyond the correspondences within each book are the correspondences between Joyce's books and a whole literary, cultural and historical field, seemingly brought into relevance by Kenner's reading of Joyce. One figure for this is the exact parallel, a reflection of Joyce's text in another plane – another piece of writing or historical situation that it 'parallels exactly'. The mode of discovery for such correspondences is most often quoted passages. For Kenner's erudition, assembled through 'correspondence', 'analogy' and 'parallel', Joyce's texts seem to offer an 'inexhaustibly intelligible world', a phrase Kenner uses of Stephen's world in *Ulysses* and that contrasts with Levin's sense of Joyce criticism.[123]

Kenner's 1987 preface to the republished *Dublin's Joyce* brings out a different aspect of *Ulysses* from Levin's criticism. In the preface, Kenner comments on how each new generation of readers of *Ulysses* has read a markedly different book. In emphasising the generations' different understanding of the book, Kenner implies that there has been, at least in part, a cumulative aspect to Joyce criticism. That is, later critics have been able to learn about the meaning of Joyce's works from earlier critics, or from correcting earlier critics' errors: criticism has helped to clarify problems that Joyce's work raises and that can slowly be solved. For Kenner in this preface, the obvious example is Molly's relationship history, where he came to recognise his own error in assigning Molly so

The Task of Reading and the Tasks of Criticism   63

many encounters (following Edmund Wilson among others). He writes, 'each Joycean helps form the conscience the rest rely on'.[124] The idea of criticism as having a cumulative aspect differs from Levin's claim that Kenner's criticism is (merely) capricious. The difference here is more than a disagreement about the kind of text *Ulysses* is, since it is a disagreement about what it should mean to read a literary text critically. While for both Levin and Kenner, reading is a collectively performed process, and one that involves collective learning, their actual processes of giving close attention to the text differ. Patient and knowledgeable annotation come into conflict with a process that more radically seeks new correspondences, new coherence, new readings.

Yet the work of Pound, Wyndham Lewis, Joyce and Eliot remains explainable in Kenner's criticism in the 1950s. Like Graham Hough, Kenner in 1959 observes the challenge posed to readers by sudden shifts in tone of *The Waste Land*. But where Hough identifies a major change in poetic practice indexed by the juxtapositions in *The Waste Land*, Kenner undertakes to explain those juxtapositions. In *The Invisible Poet: T. S. Eliot* (1959), Kenner's account of the poem's 'many sudden transitions' links the shifts in tone to Eliot's earlier poetry, particularly *The Love Song of J. Alfred Prufrock*, which employs similar transitions, and to Eliot's critical writing. Kenner argues that Eliot's critical essays, especially 'Tradition and the Individual Talent' and 'Rhetoric and Poetic Drama', provided him with a way to raise what was 'at best an intuitive poetic method' to 'deliberateness', which in turn enabled him to use that method in *The Waste Land*. Having done so, Kenner observes, 'he wrote little more prose of concentrated urgency' after 1921.[125] This argument connects the critical writing and poetry up to 1922 into an internally coherent oeuvre. The implication is that formal questions about the work can be elucidated through scholarly and critical labour. Repeatedly, here and elsewhere, Kenner makes Eliot make sense, even in his most challenging poem, and even in its challenging last lines.[126] As with Kenner's criticism on Pound, Lewis and Joyce, such labour could seemingly be continued indefinitely, via any reader's process of adducing new relevant material from Eliot's writing or from others' writing and analysing its relevance. This is dramatised in the book's 'Supplementary Dialogue', for example. The implication is that other, similar labour could readily be similarly productive, for example when done by students. This implied productivity is predicated on the assumed value of the writing studied: this writing is worth scholarly and critical investigation, it is assumed, and so such investigation is likely to produce critically interesting results. In practice, such results underpin the value of the writing.

64 *The New Modernist Novel: Criticism and the Task of Reading*

In the case of *Ulysses*, one aspect of the productivity of Joyce's book for critical labour, for both Kenner and Levin, is an apparent coherence or consistency to the text. Both Levin and Kenner make reference to Stephen's quotation on beauty from Saint Thomas Aquinas in *A Portrait of the Artist as a Young Man* (1916) to give a method for reading *Ulysses*. Stephen quotes Aquinas saying that three things are required for beauty, 'integritas, consonantia, claritas', which he translates as 'wholeness, harmony and radiance'.[127] Stuart Gilbert, in his 1930 study of *Ulysses*, had made the quotation central to an understanding of the value of Joyce's work: '*Ulysses* achieves a coherent and integral interpretation of life, a static beauty according to the definition of Aquinas.'[128] For Levin, despite the diversity of his materials, 'Joyce learned how to reconcile the principles of unity and diversity', and even in *Finnegans Wake*, 'however unintelligible he may seem, he is never incoherent'.[129] But it is Kenner for whom *consonantia* is generative. For Kenner in *Dublin's Joyce*, it is fundamental that *Ulysses* is 'intelligible' at Joyce's level: this assertion constitutes a condition of his criticism on it.[130] This intelligibility operates in correspondences between situations, both within the book and between it and other books, cultural phenomena and histories. In *Flaubert, Joyce and Beckett* (1962), the seeming inconsistencies of *Ulysses* provide ample opportunities to be analysed back into consistency via new readings.

Kenner's reading of Joyce gains momentum in *Flaubert, Joyce and Beckett*, where he generalises its tendencies to the modern novel. He tackles *Ulysses* thus:

> On page 488 we read, 'Potato preservative against plague and pestilence, pray for us.' Now just sixty pages earlier, if we were alert, we may have noted the phrase, 'Poor mamma's panacea', murmured by Bloom as he feels his trouser pocket. And fully 372 pages before that, on the bottom line of page 56, we have Bloom feeling in his hip pocket for the latchkey and reflecting, 'Potato I have.' The serious reader's copy of *Ulysses* acquires cross-references at three points; and Bloom's potato, it is by now commonplace to remark, is but one trivial instance among hundreds of motifs treated very briefly at two or three widely separated points in the book, and not even intelligible until the recurrences have been collated.[131]

The observation seems little more than is required by *Ulysses* of diligent readers: to make sense of *this* novel, a reader might need to engage in more than usually assiduous cross-referencing. But Kenner immediately makes a claim for consistency beyond its relevance to Joyce's work. His point here is that this kind of collation is enabled for Joyce, as it was

The Task of Reading and the Tasks of Criticism   65

not possible for Homer, by the technological status of the printed book, whose numbered pages can be leafed through in any direction and annotated at the whim of the reader. Echoing Stuart Gilbert, Kenner writes of *Ulysses*,

> Nothing is more important, for this sort of enterprise, than consistency of cross-reference. [. . .] We may not check out many such references, but it is surprising how our sense of the book's integrity comes to depend on our faith that they will indeed check out.

This is the technology of the book:

> This sort of consistency was what Joyce came to understand by *consonantia*, the exact interrelation of parts; and apparently to value it, even to sense it, is a fairly late development of the Western imagination. Shakespeare notoriously doesn't bother to decide whether Lady Macbeth had any children or not.[132]

Within a couple of sentences, Joyce has here become an exemplary modern writer.

In the same book, the questions that emerge most prominently with Samuel Beckett are those of literary form and literary history: what does this writer do with the novel form, and how does that change the possibilities for the future of this form? These questions, too, are suggestive for reading modernist literature more widely. The power of Kenner's account is sufficient to suggest that one of the tasks of modern fiction is to address the conditions of its own existence, as literary historical and technological form: to be self-critical. Joyce, Beckett and Flaubert are evidently ideal subjects here, given their own works' ostentatiously self-critical stances on which Kenner draws. Aspects of Kenner's readings of Joyce and Beckett in particular have so strongly shaped subsequent literary critical imagination as to create a sense of the modernist novel, or of modernist *writing* in fiction, that goes beyond these immediate critical subjects. Reading Joyce in *Dublin's Joyce* and *Flaubert, Joyce and Beckett*, Kenner inaugurated a modernist fiction that would provide seemingly inexhaustible new material for readers and critics, including himself. Such a powerful set of strategies as he developed here unsurprisingly helped to shift canons in the direction of Joyce's work and other writing like it.

For both Levin and Kenner, the choice of Joyce's work as a major subject for their criticism is significant in terms of the formation of literary criticism on fiction at this time. For both critics, Joyce offered ample

66   *The New Modernist Novel: Criticism and the Task of Reading*

scope to develop a critical method that was successful, in the sense of, first, producing arguments about the work as literature and, second, doing so at a level of complexity and respectability that made those arguments compelling within institutional frames of criticism. On top of that, Kenner's style of criticism was something that students could do for themselves, using just the text in front of them – and could do not only with poetry, but with fiction. Margot Norris comments that 'the strategies of the early Kenner, produced in his Joyce criticism of the 1970s, have become for many of us a kind of critical unconscious'.[133] The Kenner of the 1970s notably includes the author of *Joyce's Voices* (1978). That book's astute work with voice must surely draw on the work of Kenner's Joycean colleagues who had, for the last decade, been more engaged with French literary theory.[134] It also develops Kenner's keen sense, evident in *Dublin's Joyce*, of the potential for irony opened up by Joyce's choices of words. The combination of its strategies of reading with Joyce's writing produced a testimony to the generative possibilities of literary criticism, mediated through Joyce.

The productivity of Joyce and other modern fiction writers, particularly Henry James, for academic criticism was examined by Wayne Booth in a spirited indictment of modern narrative fiction in *The Rhetoric of Fiction* in 1961.[135] Like Graham Hough on poetry in 1960, Booth is troubled by the proliferation of contradictory readings of modern fiction. For Booth, the source of the problem is the rhetorical disunity of this fiction, which means that the fiction fails to give its readers the necessary guidance. The way Booth analyses this problem can be read against Gerald Graff's account of literary criticism to suggest a different picture from Hough's 1960 sense of complicity between the unreadable modernist text and the proliferation of contradictory or incomplete readings, and to move, like Hough, towards the institutional setting of criticism as the source of the issue. Booth's account, too, as implicitly interpreted by Graff, finds a greater degree of selection and serendipity in the choice of Joyce than is allowed for by Levin's and Kenner's use of Joyce and others as key or representative modernist writers.

For Booth, coherence was not something valuable found in these esteemed works but something valuable which was distressingly lacking in modern fiction. Although Booth's examples of modern fiction are eclectic, Henry James features prominently and is followed in prominence by James Joyce. For Booth, there is a problem with *The Aspern Papers*: different passages present the narrator as a different 'kind of man', hampering any interpretive, even retrospective, realisation of the story for the reader. This disharmony means that 'good as it is, *The Aspern Papers* is not as good as James might have made it' if he had used a reliable narrator where suitable and limited the tasks of the existing, unreliable narrator. But the problem of disharmony is not limited to this tale. Neither can it be imputed to James alone: 'Yet if we exonerate James, must we not blame the critics? Or repudiate criticism itself as wholly capricious?' Booth identifies a problem that emerges in the criticism, and he finds that problem's ultimate source in modern fiction: 'it becomes more and more difficult to rely, in our criticism, on the old standards of proof; evidence from the book can never be decisive'.[136] This echoes Hough's lament, which Booth has quoted eight pages earlier in discussing *The Aspern Papers*, that nothing can be decided by recourse to the text of *The Waste Land*. For Booth there is a moral issue here, encapsulated in regular reference to *Lolita* in particular: does Vladimir Nabokov's novel present its narrator as compelling or horrifying, and is a reader's inability to decide this question a quality of the book or an indictment of it?

'Our lines of communication have been fouled': uncommented on in his book, Booth's metaphor suggests that reading is a war in which the author is a commander, one whose palpable presence is therefore required for the battle; or that reading is a path to a prelapsarian language, with the modern novel headed in the wrong direction.[137] Readers of modern fiction, on this metaphorical terrain, seem to hope in vain for the text to assert its authority, and they are left with the unsatisfying and morally dubious disunity of a rhetoric that in earlier literature had, according to Booth, proved unified. *Nightwood* is a key accused here, the first example named in relation to the questionable morality of the modern novel, but Booth says no more of Barnes's novel. Where for Hough the loss is the connection between literature and its public and between criticism and culture, for Booth the problem is cast as belonging to individual readers, who may be misled by modern novels. Steven Connor notes of Booth's *The Company We Keep* that 'Booth's ethic is based upon and finally referable to the individual person rather than the community',[138] and the same is true here: the danger is to readers reading alone, and the possibility of collectively calibrating our understanding of characters such as Humbert Humbert is regrettably remote.[139]

Booth's dissatisfaction with modern fiction suggests the peculiar productivity of fiction by James and Joyce. In a review of *The Rhetoric of Fiction*, David Lodge puts forward the history of Shakespeare criticism as an obvious counterexample to Booth's concern with proliferating and contradictory readings. For Lodge, 'It is surely every reader's experience that the great works are those which have the capacity to yield up an infinite number of meanings. No two readers read the same good book, and no reader reads the same good book twice.'[140] The second sentence in this claim remains persuasive now. But the first sentence is now up for discussion.[141] Its claim is complex. The complement structure with 'are'

68   *The New Modernist Novel: Criticism and the Task of Reading*

suggests that for Lodge, the statement could also be put as the converse: that is, that those works which have the capacity to yield up an infinite number of meanings are the great works. Put this way, the statement more clearly shows one effect of its original version, that of limiting the canon of important twentieth-century fiction to works which have this capacity to yield up many meanings. When Lodge reaches his statement by merely reversing the values of Booth's analysis, he implicitly endorses, and rearticulates, Booth's own assumption that the reading-producing works that Booth takes as examples represent the best that twentieth-century fiction has to offer. By these standards, works that produce or even have produced less in the way of critical response would be less valuable works. Lodge's statement locates a link between literary criticism and literary value that is of interest for the new modernist studies in the examples of Barnes, Rodker and Loy: not only because Barnes, Rodker, Loy and other new modernist writers have received less attention from critics, but also because for Barnes in particular, the ratio of attention has changed as the study of modernism has changed. Her work, granted greater value, has proved more productive; or the changes in modernist studies, for example greater attention to culture and history, have made it possible to write productively about the values of her work.

Lodge's analysis begs several questions. Among them is the question of the popularity of works: if each reader reads a different book, then the books that have had the greatest number of readers emerge here as a necessary comparison to those works that have produced the greatest number of published critical 'readings'. Within the scene of academic publication, Lodge's analysis invites a related set of questions, regarding what institutional pressures towards publication bore on these critics' choices and what economic advantages there were for universities in an increase in literary critical output. Neither question is given substantial attention by Booth. Gerald Graff analyses these pressures in retrospect, however, in an extended discussion of R. S. Crane's critical writing. Graff suggests that 'new uncertainties about what counts as valid proof have made questions of verification seem more debatable, and this has opened the way for new criteria in criticism that have coincided with increased production requirements'. The phrasing here suggests that the effects of such changes are still ongoing in 1987.[142] In this account, it is debates about how criticism should be done that have motivated expectations for swifter and more voluminous production of publications. Graff's sense that the institution has its own purposes that are different from, but bound up with, the practice of criticism suggests that modernist literature is not the sole source of the rapidly increasing volume of published criticism, nor is it the sole driver of disagreement within that criticism.

The Task of Reading and the Tasks of Criticism **69**

These changing requirements followed the expansion of literary study after the Second World War, which brought with it a greater scope for study of twentieth-century literature. Where Hough and Booth suggest that such changes are associated with modernist literature, Graff shows how the institutionalisation of New Critical approaches contributed to the rise of multiple readings, along with institutional pressures. As Graff puts it, a 'method that assumes axiomatically that all poetry is the "language of paradox" will find no great difficulty subsuming a more or less gratifying number of examples under it, especially when there are institutional rewards for doing so'.[143] In Graff's account, then, the volume of published criticism is also increasing for specific reasons which are in addition to those proposed by Hough in 1960 and Booth regarding the relationship between reader and modern text. This aligns with Hough's later analysis in 1970, which finds institutional criticism to be focused too exclusively on an audience of students and teachers, distancing it from a culture and a public with which it could engage.

One value of James and Joyce in such a context may be just their ability to help their critic to publish. Graff connects the productivity of criticism to perceived literary greatness:

> The point of criticism was no longer subtractive but additive, the idea being to produce more criticism, not less. This view dovetailed nicely with the growing view that literary meanings were in and of themselves aesthetically desirable, so that the more of them that could be attributed to a literary work, the more the work's value was presumably enhanced and the more the interests of literature and of humanism were therefore served.[144]

This shows the institutional convenience of David Lodge's implication that great literary works produce many different readings. Under this rubric, the value of writing by James and Joyce is enhanced at mid-century by its ability to support different readings. But also, the value of criticism of James and Joyce at this time is increased, since it generates new ideas about now valuable literature. Graff's account indicates the institutionally driven side not only of the growth of criticism in this period, but also of the selection of authors as subjects for that criticism.

Modernist Fiction and the Academy

The writers that Levin, Kenner and Booth selected up to and including the early 1960s were very often writers whose work did readily produce many successful new readings in their criticism. Harry Levin's

70 *The New Modernist Novel: Criticism and the Task of Reading*

impressively broad canvas of European and American writers in 'What Was Modernism?' and elsewhere was balanced by a smaller number of writers whose work offered repeated opportunities for close reading, and the canon of modernist literature that became current in the 1960s was well suited to new requirements of academic productivity. Even when general approaches to critical reading shifted, as they did noticeably in the case of Joyce in the late 1970s in Anglophone criticism, the proliferation of critical readings that Joyce and some other modernist writers tended to produce still remained suited to criticism in the academy for longer, since productivity was valuable even if critical approaches changed. In other words, postwar critics developed powerful techniques of reading that narrowed the canon not necessarily in the range of reference, but in the selection of authors for sustained critical attention. This narrower selection inevitably promoted strategies of reading that worked well on some authors, and so consolidated a canon that would serve for successive groups of later critics developing new approaches to reading.

As has been recognised, a factor in this situation, for modernist poetry, was the enabling relationship between, on the one hand, a formalist criticism which found its most prominent exemplar in the American New Criticism, and on the other, a body of modernist literature, especially modernist poetry, that responded well to formalist criticism.[145] Yet in the case of fiction, it was work that was neither New Critical nor merely formalist that most influentially brought modernist fiction into academic recognition. Rather, the 1950s saw critics move beyond the New Criticism in order to read modernist fiction. For Hough, Levin, Kenner, Booth and others, the modernist writing – both fiction and poetry – that they chose to discuss up to the early 1960s tended to reward the kinds of critical labour they or others did with success. In this sense, via many of its critics, modernist *fiction* complicates the acknowledged complicity between modernist *poetry* and formalist reading. That is, the work of Levin, Kenner, Booth and others suggests that the tendency of the texts they read to produce many questions or many different readings was a new, complementary form of complicity that held between mid-century academic criticism and a particular canon of 'modernist' fiction. This complicity operated beyond the now familiar complicity between modernist poetry and the New Criticism.

Seen in this way, fiction had a role to play in the academic institutionalisation of modernism, but its role was different from the earlier role played by modernist poetry. The choice of Joyce, Proust, Flaubert, Beckett and Henry James is important, since rather than being merely some among several possible selections, they model literary value for criticism.

The Task of Reading and the Tasks of Criticism   71

Joyce's writing as read by Levin and Kenner exemplifies texts that are highly literary: in Levin's sense, literary in that they engage deeply with a European literary and cultural tradition, and in Kenner's sense, literary in that they are what might now be termed self-critical. In its literariness, Joyce's writing exemplifies both a moral seriousness and an attendant critical productivity. These and selected other writers are readily shown to be valuable subjects for research and teaching. In turn, this selective mid-century group of literary works were influential for ideas of what might be expected from a properly 'modernist' novel, since these writers' novels were so often discussed at a key point when modernist fiction was beginning to written about and taught in the academy.

Other novels sometimes proved more troublesome. In *The Psychological Novel*, Leon Edel raises the possibility that some modernist fiction, here Dorothy Richardson's, might best be read as a series of 'intensities' or passages, encountered page by page, and without requiring consolidation. He concludes regarding the novels he discusses in the book, 'Since thought does not arrange itself in orderly sequence, the novel of subjectivity often gives an effect of disorder, and different readers, as we have seen, cope with this in different ways.'[146] At this point, Cathryn Setz and I note, Barnes's *Nightwood* is present only just below the surface of the writing, as Edel quotes from T. S. Eliot's preface to the novel and borrows terms from Joseph Frank's analysis of *Nightwood*.[147] For Edel, Richardson's writing brings out effects of 'disorder' that challenge contemporary strategies of reading and gesture implicitly towards *Nightwood*. Nevertheless, Edel retains the criterion of coherence: he borrows Frank's concept of a 'poetic synthesis' to describe the whole novel by Richardson, read as a series of moments of 'intensity' that are yet synthesised.[148]

The Wildean, surrealist and decadent heritages of passages that seemed not quite to cohere were far less substantially of interest for critics at this time. In 1949 Edmund Wilson had encouraged a 'revival' of Ronald Firbank, praising Firbank's carefully composed 'dense textures of indirection'.[149] Wilson added a hesitation in the revised 1951 version of the essay, where the aspect of Firbank that brings this author into closest kinship with Barnes, Rodker and Loy as read in the present book – Firbank's tendency to beautiful or sharp or witty passages that threaten not to cohere across the novel – is seen as a flaw by Wilson. Tellingly, the flaw is French in origin:

> the weakness of [Firbank's] narratives, like the weakness of [Anatole] France's, is a lack of continuous development. One chapter does not lead to another, but each makes a little vignette which, significant and finished though it is, does not always fall into place as part of a coherent scheme.[150]

72 *The New Modernist Novel: Criticism and the Task of Reading*

Vincent Sherry comments on Wilson's effort in the 1931 *Axel's Castle* to leave decadence out of the story of modern literature he writes. Sherry shows how influential this earlier suppression of decadence was for crucial explanations of modern writing after the Second World War, namely Frank Kermode's *The Romantic Image* (1957) and Hugh Kenner's *The Pound Era* (1971). Wilson's comment on Firbank suggests a similar impulse in the 1951 essay here. The modernism that was taking shape at this time was one that embraced symbolism in Wilson's terms, but not decadence.[151]

Peter Nicholls observes that 'The decadent style is, above all, excessive, always obsessed with local effect at the expense of overall sense.' He quotes the nineteenth-century critic Paul Bourget, who identifies a 'decadent style' as one where 'the unity of the book is broken down in favour of the independence of the page, where the page is broken down to allow the independence of the phrase, and [similarly] the phrase in favour of the word'.[152] For Bourget, by implication, decadence is identified with social anarchy. Bourget's 'theory of decadence' is interesting here because it identifies a preoccupation with style in passages as a decadent quality. Nicholls returns to the point in the context of observing that Ezra Pound took more from decadence than he let on, and that decadence plays a larger role in modernism than has been recognised.[153]

Even without decadence, passages as the locus of style were out. As Wilson notes in a 1947 review, Kafka's unfinished novels *The Trial* and *The Castle* consisted of 'mere loose collections of episodes', and Wilson compares Kafka detrimentally with 'great naturalists of human personality, great organizers of human experience', Joyce, Proust and Dante. As mentioned above, Proust's novel's potential to achieve 'close unity and significant order' was important to its value for Wilson in *Axel's Castle*. Wilson writes of Kafka, 'I do not see how one can possibly take him for either a great artist or a moral guide.'[154] The moral judgement weighs too, interconnected with the judgement on form. Wilson's responses in the 1940s to Firbank and Kafka, two figures who were at the edge of an Anglo-American modernism situated in Europe, diagnose the residual challenge that less systematic fiction posed to his thinking about modernist fiction, and a similar need for coherence persisted for other critics in a context where Wilson's work was widely read.

For Wilson and for Hough, Levin, Kenner and Booth, however, *consonantia* and its associated properties were important – consonance, coherence, consistency, the perception of formal harmony or proportion, formal harmony itself. In the case of Levin and Kenner, claims for the essential unity of the work were in part a response to the dismissal of Joyce and Pound by New Critics as disordered.[155] Stephen's translation

The Task of Reading and the Tasks of Criticism   73

of Aquinas – beauty as consisting in 'wholeness, harmony and radiance' – was significant, too, for Frank Kermode in *The Romantic Image* (1957), where it begins the volume as 'characteristic' of the moderns.[156] Kermode's use of Stephen's quotation underlines the depth of engagement in criticism of modernist literature at this time with the idea of beauty in the quotation from Aquinas that Stephen reflects on. Even if these properties seem not to be on offer in modernist literature, as for Hough and Booth, they are still important as criteria of literary value. For Kenner, the correspondences to be found within Joyce's texts accompany their correspondences with a wealth of other situations.

Yet the unity of the work was not the only way of interpreting consistency. In 1952 Raymond Williams glossed T. S. Eliot's 1945 observation of a 'deeper consistency' in verse drama, with respect to which the characters 'may behave inconsistently'. For Williams, Eliot's 'deeper consistency' can be taken to mean 'the reduction to essentials [. . .] of living experience', expressed through the various characters. This consistency is a 'radical reading of life', and the consistency is 'that of the pattern or structure of experience': implicitly both the experience that the play presents as art and the wider social experience it relates to. Williams later revised this introduction into an enquiry into the relation of conventions to 'structures of feeling' – that is, to the 'continuity of experience' beyond the specific work to other works and the period.[157] While Williams's context here, drama rather than fiction or poetry, differs from that of the critics discussed above, still his use of the term 'consistency' moves him towards the social significance of the form, rather than seeking wholeness only in the artwork itself. Of the four critics considered here, Hough's and Levin's criticism most shares with Williams's this directionality of consistency.

Where for Ezra Pound, style can be found in passages, and the value of the writing for literary history can be judged directly from excerpts, for Hough, Levin, Kenner and Booth, style and value are much more keyed to kinds of coherence sustained across a whole literary work or even oeuvre, a whole that is navigated in the process of judging the value of the writing. This process might begin with passages, as it does for Kenner in *Dublin's Joyce*, but for Kenner and others, the value of the writing is closely linked to its intelligibility as a completed whole. For Hough, Levin and Kenner, that wholeness includes the literary work's engagement with a whole social or cultural world; for Booth, coherence is needed by readers. Modernist literature did not necessarily come up as valuable in these judgements: for Hough and Booth around 1960, the failure of the high modernist writing they read to cohere in the process of reading led them to question its value.

74 *The New Modernist Novel: Criticism and the Task of Reading*

Yet the task of reading modernist literature into coherence, literariness and value provided an impetus for a relatively selective canon that could very successfully support literary study. Indeed, this newly formed consensus as to canon tended to be retained into the 1980s, even as consensus on what academic criticism could look like was being profoundly challenged by more theoretically informed readings. These more theoretically informed readings would critique the idea that texts can be analysed back into consistency. This critique found abundant material for new kinds of reading in modernist writing that had already been read as coherent. But in doing so, it helped to break the hold of that narrowed canon as authoritative, and so helped pave the way for reading more broadly.[158] The mid-century canon had always generated challenges: while a core canon remained central, other writers were continually being brought in, in a starting point to the new modernisms that stretches back at least to the 1960s, when, for example, Wallace Stevens was the subject of a book by Frank Kermode (*Wallace Stevens*, 1960). These challenges gained momentum from the 1970s onwards.

Had Hugh Kenner chosen in the 1950s or 1960s to write at any length on other writers, for example Gertrude Stein, Mina Loy, Djuna Barnes, Charles Henri Ford or Ronald Firbank, he might perhaps have contributed to bringing them or other writers closer to the centre of what would then be a different-looking canon, one with different or added reading strategies. LGBTQ+ writing and writing by women were less Kenner's territory than major modernist men in this decade, in spite of his interest in Marianne Moore, and his choice of writers at this time records more than just qualities of the writing. But the canon of modernist fiction that coalesced for Kenner around Joyce, Beckett, Flaubert, Pound and Eliot supported a sense that the most interesting writing was highly generative of new readings, that it was coherent at the level of the author's identifiable literary vision, that it was highly learned in a recognisably valuable canon, and that it had a self-critical intelligence that could be accessed and explained in the process of critical reading. Kenner's criticism of fiction by Joyce and Beckett modelled modernist fiction so well that it provided questions and tools that still remain relevant. Indeed, Kenner's process of focusing on passages and his wide-ranging familiarity with many different modernists across languages mean that his work was a significant precursor to the new modernist studies, with modernism conceived of as an international movement. Yet Kenner's skill in bringing out seemingly core qualities of each writer he wrote about also troubles the easy transfer of similar questions and tools to the study of other writers.

The recovery of a number of modernist writers from the 1970s onwards and especially in the 1990s brought a new and different modernism to critical consciousness. This was closer to the modernism that had been read, and that was continuing to be written, by a number of poets across continents. In time, the continuing poetic reception of modernist writing helped to make obvious the need for an academic modernist studies that would have the capacity to read works and writers whose poetics were valuable and relevant, but who had been sidelined in earlier critical frameworks, among them Rodker, Loy and Barnes.[159] In addition, a more urgent attention to modernist histories and cultures made relevant a much broader canon. Peter Brooker makes the point that Raymond Williams's work on modernism 'inspired and encouraged' much of the expansion that has now repositioned modernist studies.[160] Williams's attention to modernism, from *Drama from Ibsen to Eliot* in 1952 to *The Politics of Modernism* published in 1989, helped to bring about an expansion of its object of study to include a fuller social world.

What can be gained from this chapter's brief travel through a selection of critics? It is clear that the meaning of reading was changing in the 1920s under the pressure of modernist literature, and that reading itself was becoming a problem for readers of modernism. As modernist fiction moved into the academy, the tendency of modernist works to produce multiple readings was gradually absorbed into an institutional criticism in which the productivity of a work for criticism was associated with literary value. Yet this productivity still tended to depend on ideas of wholeness and mastery, and the decadent traits of works whose stylistic flair exceeded their formal structure tended to be associated less with literary value than those whose perceived traits of coherence, learnedness and mastery reliably led to coherent, learned and critically interesting readings.

If the work of Barnes and Loy now has a productivity that rivals that of more established modernist fiction writers at mid-century, that is in part because sustained critical work has shifted the discipline towards valuing a fuller understanding of modernism. Yet as writers whose work was read and praised by contemporaries, but was not central at mid-century, their writing potentially also engages tensions between ideas of modernist literature and of close reading that were operating at these two times. In *Nightwood, Adolphe 1920* and *Insel*, as the chapters that follow suggest, style and meaning are often found in passages, and patterns of coherence often meet with intriguing deflections when traced across the novels. In engaging such tensions, the novels suggest ways of reading and valuing modernist fiction that may (or may not) be useful for reading other new modernists. More generally, they suggest that modes of reading and value will necessarily shift according to the writing being read. In the remaining chapters, I consider the conditions of reading these novels. To do so, I draw on the last several decades of critical reading of modernist fiction, including readings by the critics discussed here and readings that then later brought to the discipline a new awareness of theory, politics, culture and history.

Chapter 3

Telling the Story of the Night Wood

Prose Style and a Passage

Ezra Pound laments what he sees as Barnes's lack of talent in *Nightwood*. His limerick, addressed to T. S. Eliot in January 1937, complains of *Nightwood*'s style:

Eminent Udder, S. C. D., etc.: — / — /

> *There onct wuzza lady named Djuna*
> *Who wrote rather like a baboon. Her*
> *Blubbery prose had no fingers or toes;*
> *And we wish Whale had found this out sooner.*

'Whale' is Frank Morley, Barnes's editor with T. S. Eliot at Faber and Faber, where *Nightwood* had just been published; Pound adds, '*This* exaggerates as far to the one side as you blokes to the other. I except *Ladies' Almanack*, which wuz lively.'[1] If the 'baboon' and the loss of 'fingers or toes' suggest a lack of intelligence or a lack of dexterity in the writing, it is the 'blubbery' that carries the criticism here, with its suggestions of soft, unstructured prose. Perhaps 'blubbery' prose is also overly feminine. Certainly the limerick feminises Barnes, then finds in that feminisation cause for contempt. The mock rhymes and odd line-breaks seem to lampoon a lack of formal poise, even a clumsiness in Barnes's writing. The force of Pound's limerick is exclusion: the in-jokes of the names recall a group of critics among whom Barnes does not number, so that her work is mocked as merely an object of criticism to be 'found out', and not as itself critical. But the wit or intelligence of Barnes's prose in *Nightwood* can be found in just the kind of style that Pound satirises in the limerick. The energies of Barnes's prose may well remain difficult to address critically, but such elusiveness may be much more interesting to read and write about than Pound suggests.

78   *The New Modernist Novel: Criticism and the Task of Reading*

Pound's limerick was written by a major contemporary reviewer and critic, one who was often perceptive about authors he read. In that sense it is worth looking past the dismissiveness and prejudice of the limerick to see what it records about how Barnes was read in her own time by others who identified as modern. In this chapter I explore what might be involved in the lack of poise or clumsiness that Pound imputes to Barnes. I argue that Barnes's writing in *Nightwood*, rather than being clumsy, seems unstable in ways that persistently draw attention to the critical decisions that need to be made in reading her novel. Unlike Pound, I find in this quality a basis for claiming the literary value of *Nightwood*, both as a novel and as modernist writing. A central issue here is one of tone. Barnes's prose in *Nightwood*, I argue, exploits the novel form's potential to weave complex relationships between the language of fiction and the characters whose stories the fiction narrates. *Nightwood* anatomises the ethics of this process. Often, its work with style is done most intensively in passages, which troubled some readers from the 1930s onwards who sought unity in her novel.

The following chapter offers, rather than a finished interpretation, a set of questions and paths in preparation for further reading. It builds on previous enquiries into resistances in Barnes's writing to the modernisms of Pound and Eliot as they were framed critically.[2] Where to begin? The process of selecting passages to discuss is a complex one. The opening of a novel has a special quality of reproducibility in printed criticism, since the reader reading the quoted passage is beginning with the beginning of the novel. The opening of any piece of fiction is usually one that the text itself prioritises as important for readers, and so such passages may be a privileged locus for reading 'what the text says about itself'.[3] So I begin here with *Nightwood*'s opening sentence.

The sentence undertakes to represent an event – a birth – which brings with it commentary, a character, a setting and a profusion of factual details. It might best be read as opening banter, as a quip ending in a punch line:

> Early in 1880, in spite of a well-founded suspicion as to the advisability of perpetuating that race which has the sanction of the Lord and the disapproval of the people, Hedvig Volkbein, a Viennese woman of great strength and military beauty, lying upon a canopied bed of a rich spectacular crimson, the valance stamped with the bifurcated wings of the House of Hapsburg, the feather coverlet an envelope of satin on which, in massive and tarnished gold threads, stood the Volkbein arms – gave birth, at the age of forty-five, to an only child, a son, seven days after her physician predicted that she would be taken.[4]

The summary content of this sentence is the birth of Felix, but the event is overwhelmed by an abundance of commentary, description and detail.

Telling the Story of the Night Wood   **79**

The sentence suggests that Felix will be the hero of the novel, in a game played with genre that suggests similar games played by Laurence Sterne in *Tristram Shandy* and Henry Fielding in *Tom Jones*. The birth of the epic hero is a trope already available for satire to François Rabelais in the births of Gargantua and Pantagruel. Barnes knew this literature.[5] But the instabilities of tone and direction here make the relevance of the canonical novel openings difficult to gauge, not least because the 'birth of the hero' seems tongue-in-cheek. The sentence's digressive energy makes it resistant to summary: there is a sense that the information in asides may be more important than the event narrated, and indeed, a dash is required to return to the birth and complete the sentence, even though no initial dash marked a first separation.[6] Readers who have read not just the opening sentence but the whole novel will know that Felix will not, in fact, be the hero of *Nightwood*, certainly not in any conventional sense. As a whole, the novel will digress from this opening, and the resistance that the sentence offers to summary is repeated at the level of the novel, where digressions provide much of the tale.

There is a dramatic quality to this opening. Read with or without further knowledge of the novel, the opening seems to be delivered by a narrator who is eager to make witty remarks for an audience, and who is already interrupting the telling of the tale to do so. This narrator seems to relish the role of introducing a cast of characters, layering ornate asides as if setting the scene of a play. Indeed, the content of the story and the commentary seem to converge only in the specialist knowledge of the punch line of the passage, 'seven days after her physician predicted that she would be taken'. This banter, whose point is not quite clear, introduces a strategy of wit, digression and performance that will be developed in the novel's exploration of the tropes of telling and reading.[7]

This opening line gives a sense of some of the complexities of tone in *Nightwood*. Before the sentence has a subject, the first aside intervenes with a comment on 'the advisability of perpetuating that race'. The euphemism 'that race' seems to refer to the Jewish heritage of Felix and his father Guido, and this is confirmed shortly afterwards in the chapter. In a novel that has long had a committed readership, this seems a perplexing, even troubling opening. In one sense, it is not immediately clear how to make sense of the comment: is this the narrator's opinion, or is it the character Hedvig's? If the 'suspicion' is Hedvig's, why does the narrator call it 'well-founded'? If the syntax suggests that the suspicion may be Hedvig's, further reading of the novel suggests otherwise, since according to the first chapter, Hedvig's husband Guido seems to have taken great care to hide his Jewish identity, apparently even from her. Yet the suspicion seems unlikely to be the narrator's too, since the narrator's sympathy for the plight of Guido drives much of the first chapter.

80   *The New Modernist Novel: Criticism and the Task of Reading*

The chapter's content seems mismatched to the tone of the opening sentence's comment, even if that chapter readily employs stereotype. Tone and voice are difficult to identify here. Perhaps the suspicion is the unhappy Guido's, affecting the narrative even at the distance of a paragraph, and even before he is introduced in the next paragraph – introduced as having died six months previously: comedy and tragedy have become inextricably intertwined, and reading the opening sentence seems to require reading at least the novel's first chapter in full, but the difficulty of reading the sentence persists even with further reading of the novel.

The wit here goes well beyond what can be analysed in Hugh Kenner's 'Uncle Charles Principle,' in which the narrative voice bends to the 'gravitational field of the nearest person', not least because in Barnes's opening paragraph, Guido is not present.[8] Guido's depth of despair may register in the narrator's choice of words, so that the narrator's opening line may display a strength of sympathy that breaks the bounds not only of formal narrative structure, but also of decent speech, to declare itself for Guido. But this wit has a troubling edge, since in this outburst of sympathy, the comment evidently echoes contemporary semitic discourse.[9] As Maren Tova Linett points out, the word 'sanction' is ambiguous here, too, meaning either 'chosenness by a Jewish god or criticism by a rejected Jesus', making the tone harder to identify.[10] Voice and tone are both difficult to gauge, and this narrative voice engages with its characters in ways that go beyond the reach of ready formal analysis and open up the more general question of the relationship of modernist styles to the representation of others as characters. The sentence falls at the border of style and tone in a novel that narrativises the 'shared humanity' of its characters, in Rachel Potter's phrase.[11] To return to Pound's limerick, reading *Nightwood*'s opening sentence suggests that, *contra* Pound, instability is not clumsiness: the sentence opens up a series of questions not just about style, but about the stakes of representation and voice in fiction in the early twentieth century.

Narration as Performance

This reading of the opening sentence furnishes specific questions about style that can be taken up in further reading of the novel. I first observe this style at more length, and then I return to the questions of representation raised above, this time in relation to the description of Robin and *Nightwood* as a *roman à clef*. Finally I consider modes of reading the novel as a whole and some ways in which *Nightwood* resists strategies of reading that have worked for other modernist novels.

Telling the Story of the Night Wood   81

The passages I have selected are ones that allow me to develop the questions about style raised above. They are frequently passages where characters are introduced, perhaps because at such points in the text, the juxtaposition of narrator's and characters' voices is thrown into relief. Different readers, and close readers of different passages, although they will find in *Nightwood* a different novel, will perhaps find one which still, or also, raises the questions considered here.

Later in the first chapter, 'Bow Down', Matthew is introduced with:

> The man was Dr Matthew O'Connor, an Irishman from the Barbary Coast (Pacific Street, San Francisco), whose interest in gynaecology had driven him half around the world. He was taking the part of host, the Count not yet having made his appearance, and he was telling of himself, for he considered himself the most amusing predicament. (13)

Surely the relative clause 'whose interest in gynaecology had driven him half around the world' is tongue-in-cheek. If the wry tone of that aside is in doubt, surely too, it is confirmed a moment later by 'for he considered himself the most amusing predicament'. But could this last phrase be a neutral statement of fact? In a novel that is so particular about the details of its characters' self-perception, the phrase could, at a stretch, read as unironic: as merely gently, non-judgementally informing readers about Dr Matthew O'Connor. But the irony would pop up again nearby, in the very idea of a narrator making this statement innocently and neutrally about a character. So it is hard to tell, then, whether 'an Irishman from the Barbary Coast (Pacific Street, San Francisco)' is barbed or not. Is this a narrator's affirmation of the character's multiple identities – multiple identities being a quality shared by the other characters and indeed by their expatriate author? Later in this first chapter, the doctor identifies as Irish in conversation with Felix, and in the second chapter he confirms an American identity in response to Felix's direct 'But you are American' (36). The key geographical identity recorded here might be the underground of San Francisco's Barbary Coast, which had been a port hotspot for drinking, sex work and drag performance in the early years of the twentieth century. There are historical parallels with expatriate American and other migrant identities, but such tensions need also to be read against the way in which *Nightwood*'s prose orients the conditions of reading them: that is, by navigating the awkward tones of the narrator's wit. Here, affectionate indulgence for the novel's characters doubles with a potential for sharp-edged mockery.

The doctor's first speech in 'Bow Down' is important because it transfers the narrative from the narrator to a character. Felix enters when the

82 The New Modernist Novel: Criticism and the Task of Reading

doctor is in the middle of speaking and begins to construe the doctor's discourse not as narrative, but as a collection of themes: '"We may all be nature's noblemen," he was saying, and the mention of a nobleman made Felix feel happier the instant he caught the word, though what followed left him in some doubt' (13). Felix, 'in doubt', is unable to predict what will come next. He is able to absorb only the theme, 'noblemen', but a causal narrative context is unavailable to him, and he is given only the doctor's definitions of legend and history. Here, the doctor fails to produce a narrative with a recognisable or inferable 'framework',[12] and the difficulty of the doctor's digressions for Felix resonates with the difficulties presented by the digressive tendencies of *Nightwood*'s opening sentence. Finding himself overtaken by his inability to control or understand the doctor's speech, Felix will later break into 'uncontrollable laughter', which he hopes is very much only laughter, and not 'anything else' (17). Felix here cuts a figure for first-time readers of *Nightwood*, for whom predicting the course of this novel might be an impossible task, enjoyable or vertiginous.

The momentum of the doctor's words seems to come not from its content, but from the relationship between himself and his audience. The Duchess's interruption 'was quite useless' at stopping him:

> Once the doctor had his audience – and he got his audience by the simple device of pronouncing at the top of his voice (at such moments as irritable and possessive as a maddened woman's) some of the more boggish and biting of the shorter early Saxon verbs – nothing could stop him. (14)

Matthew's audience is captive: he commands their attention to a performance, one whose contents he is free to take in any direction. This is an extreme of narration as exchange,[13] where the exchange for the doctor's narrative, if indeed it is narrative, is only the audience's attention to the doctor at the time of telling, but not necessarily their comprehension. That the audience is captive is particularly clear in the Dalkey Archive edition, where 191 lines of the doctor's stories are restored after being deleted during *Nightwood*'s editorial process.[14] The restored passage begins, '"Halt!" said the doctor', and is interrupted only by the line 'Frau Mann nodded, she wanted to say something, but she knew there was no hope.'[15] Yet in that long restored speech, the doctor offers his audience of outsiders, in return for their attention, something more communal than narrative, because of the confessional and queer content of his story, later lost to editors. In the passage quoted above, the narrator gently affirms Matthew O'Connor's gender in parentheses.

Matthew's performance is followed by Nikka's, as narrated by Matthew. This circus performer has elaborate tattoos covering his body, and the tattoos are described enthusiastically by Matthew. In the retelling, Nikka's past performance is used by Matthew for his own performance art of retelling, in the process both honouring the the Black performer's original performance and also rendering the performer merely an occasion for a new performance, with Matthew now the artist. The retelling is part of the circus theme of this chapter, in which the titles of the characters recall circus names from the Métropole circus in the early twentieth century – Baron Felix and '"baronne" de Holstein'[16] – and in which Frau Mann the trapeze artist links the Bohemian world of the novel with the circus. Yet the tone of Matthew's retelling of this performer's art is complex. Brian Glavey observes that Matthew emphasises his own verbal performance, yet that at least Matthew's 'queer ekphrasis preserves the object's anonymity'.[17] Nikka's own voice enters Matthew's description right at the end: 'I asked him why all this barbarity; he answered he loved beauty and would have it about him' (15). In response, Matthew details that beauty for listeners.

In the relationship between narrator and narrated, Matthew's enthusiasm for Nikka's performance situates narration as performance somewhere between recalling the original performance in homage and appropriating that performance via the wit of the teller. The vertigo that might be produced for Matthew's audience, or for a reader of the scene, is given its edge by the instability of the narrative tones already evident in this novel: just how far Matthew, and *Nightwood*, will veer towards comedy at the expense of the character whose tale is being told is impossible to predict. Even in rereading, the tones of this scene's racial representation shift in sharp-edged ways, making it radically difficult to know how to read the scene. As Merinda K. Simmons and James A. Crank write, 'racial play – that is, variations and improvisations on a theme of racial otherness – operated as a central and foundational part of modernism'.[18] Yet in one reading of this play here, the joke may be Nikka's at Matthew's expense, since his tattoos document much more than beauty, falling themselves between commentary on and pastiche of European literary and cultural history and that history's global reach and damage. The 'beautiful caravel in full sail' (15) suggests a more critical documentation accompanying 'beauty.' The allure, wit and scholarly puzzlement of the performer's combination of images are transferred intact in Matthew's retelling, so that the original performer's art remains present and available to readers of the novel. Yet for all its celebration, as homage, the tone of Matthew's retelling remains fraught. This scene dramatises some of the complexities of

84   *The New Modernist Novel: Criticism and the Task of Reading*

retelling as performance, and these are complexities that the novel will encounter again in other ways.

Barnes's work with tone and style are a reminder that modernism might be associated with a 'certain complexity of *tone*'.[19] But this work with tone differs in significant ways from the work of Barnes's contemporaries. At times, marks of performance in *Nightwood*'s narration can be made out. The complexities of Matthew's self-construction in this first chapter, 'Bow Down', draw attention to the way this novel's style sustains incomplete performances. Matthew's self-contradictions are sometimes openly claimed, as with his profession, but they are sometimes more obscurely woven into the threads of the narrative. For example, Laura Veltman notes that Matthew's use of the phrase *pecca fortiter*, a segment of a Lutheran epigram that is antithetical to Catholic doctrine, seems ill suited to the context in which he uses it in his commentary on Catholicism to Felix (18–19). The full epigram is *pecca fortiter sed crede fortius*, translated, according to Veltman, by the 1908 *Catholic Encyclopedia* as 'sin as you like provided you believe', and is considered heretical in Catholic theology. Veltman explains that that the phrase is 'misunderstood as an invitation to sin'. Her interpretation focuses on the Catholic Church's attitude to sexuality,[20] but Matthew's use of a Lutheran phrase to describe the Catholic priesthood might also be read as a non-sequitur or a moment of instability.

Nightwood suspends the seeming contradiction here between belonging to the character and belonging to a narrator: Matthew's possibly inaccurate use of Luther can be read as a performance by a narrator as much as by the character. Barnes commented to Wolfgang Hildesheimer, her German translator, on a phrase earlier in this same passage, as recorded by Daniela Caselli: 'The Doctors references are never to be taken as precise – – and as far as the rant on Luther, it was his own, taken down (in my own ignorance of exact history of Luther,) as I heard it for baudy <u>old</u> ram – the old is a gratuitous jesture on his part.'[21] 'His own' refers to Dan Mahoney, the real-life model for Matthew O'Connor, from whose conversation Barnes took copious notes.[22] Matthew's wit in the phrase that Veltman glosses contains the vestiges of another performance, Dan Mahoney's social persona, which provides initial material for both narrator and Matthew O'Connor.

Examining this phrase, then, yields not a tone of knowing literary or theological reference of a kind that may be familiar from T. S. Eliot, Ezra Pound or James Joyce, but a complex instance of the modes of performance and telling under scrutiny in *Nightwood*'s writing. The reference is most meaningful when traced back to another performance, Dan Mahoney's in cafés, rather than when it is traced back to its original doctrinal context. In this instance, an example of possible clumsiness is revealing, instead, about the intelligence of this novel: the ability of this prose style to give life to character, here regardless of the idiosyncratic juxtaposition of Catholic and Lutheran doctrine – or even through it, since the occasional inattention to the specifics of historical detail in favour of rhetorical force is characteristic for Matthew ('Remember your century, at least!' the ex-priest chides him in 'Go Down, Matthew', 147). Yet the narrator and Felix share this trait too.[23] In the flow of Matthew's rhetoric, the writing means less *through* its intertextual references than *in spite of* them, in this way disregarding high modernist conventions of prose fiction writing or of criticism that demand that what is mentioned in the writing be consequential for it.

This is not to deny the possibility of knowing or ironical literary reference in Barnes, however. Diane Warren points out that '*Nightwood*'s richness is further underscored as [Jane] Marcus observes that "We are not accustomed to thinking of Barnes as a learned woman", implying, correctly, that we should be.'[24] Barnes's writing documents the breadth and voracity of her reading, and it should be noted that she might well know more about the history of Luther than her character lets on – or than she lets on in her letter. But here, the awkward combination of different religious doctrines is a source of Matthew's and the narrator's wit, and it requires a different kind of attention from the more explicit learnedness of some of her contemporaries. Barnes offers a different model of the learned fictional text, one whose learnedness is not necessarily oriented towards scholarly examination. Unlike *The Waste Land*, *Ulysses* or the *Cantos*, *Nightwood* seems not to assign its readers an extensive reading list. The problem of 'grasping the tones and implications in play' has been analysed by Drew Milne as the 'sociality of wit'. *Nightwood*'s rendering of lived experience, Milne argues, goes beyond the reach of formal, academic analysis. Here, analysing literary allusions leads to an instance of the complexities and instabilities of voice and tone in this novel.[25]

For this narrator, characters matter. Yet tone may rupture, because the primary narrative contract holds between narrator and reader (or listener), and not between narrator and character: the narrator's performance for readers carries the novel's style.[26] Perhaps, the novel's first chapter suggests, the most apt mode of reading *Nightwood* is a critical wager: a reading as performance that runs the risk of failure in order to tell a story of the novel.

Narration as Storytelling

Nightwood's second chapter, 'La somnambule', introduces a new character in a way that parallels the introduction of Hedvig in 'Bow Down'.

86   *The New Modernist Novel: Criticism and the Task of Reading*

Yet there is a shift in tone from the first chapter to the description of Robin Vote lying on a bed in a faint. Where the opening lines in 'Bow Down' and the introduction of Matthew O'Connor might suggest the nuances of performance inherent in narration, the description of Robin seems a more serious attempt to represent a character in writing:

> The perfume that her body exhaled was of the quality of that earth-flesh, fungi, which smells of captured dampness and yet is so dry, overcast with the odour of oil of amber, which is an inner malady of the sea, making her seem as if she had invaded a sleep incautious and entire. Her flesh was the texture of plant life, and beneath it one sensed a frame, broad, porous and sleep-worn, as if sleep were a decay fishing her beneath the visible surface. About her head there was an effulgence as of phosphorus glowing about the circumference of a body of water – as if her life lay through her in ungainly luminous deteriorations – the troubling structure of the born somnambule, who lives in two worlds – meet of child and desperado. (31)

Robin is described through her physical qualities: perfume, texture, frame, effulgence. As with Hedvig, the writing immediately meets the difficulty of accounting for the character in description. But the figurative energies of the prose provide this character with a set of connotations, among which sleep is the most prominent, mentioned in each of the three sentences along with flesh or body. Where in the novel's opening sentence, asides and digressions proliferated, here the figuration carries the momentum of the prose style.[27] However, as in that sentence, this sentence's emphasis on the attempt at description can usefully be read as stemming from a describing consciousness.[28]

Is the describing consciousness merely reporting on a character who exists beyond the page, as the passionate efforts of this description suggest? Or is the character dependent on the description? As so often in Barnes, there is a strong sense of both a narrator's confidence in describing the character and the possibility that any description may not be enough. Mieke Bal notes that the description of Robin is initially given through Felix's focalisation but shifts to focalisation by the narrator of this passage. She asks, 'If this description is ekphrastic, does the ekphrasis produce the woman, or the woman the ekphrasis?'[29] Bal generalises the problem of the inaccessibility of Robin here to a 'paradox of description':

> Either the perceived other is easily objectified, which turns her or him into a dead thing and thus makes description epistemic murder; or the other is accepted, respected, indeed, welcomed, as irreducible, which turns her or him into an inaccessible subject, and makes description, then, impossible – and love kills *it*. The description of character is, therefore, the emblematic case of the paradox of description.

In this way, 'description is at the core of the novelistic genre', and Bal develops 'a view of narrative as generated by a descriptive motor rather than the other way around'.[30] The narrative energy generated by the descriptive motor is evident here in the passage's intense figurations, which make focalisation by Felix implausible. This sentence, then, shares with the novel's opening sentence an indication of the stakes of representation in narrative. Here, the irreducibility of the person described, Robin Vote, is much more strongly evident, since as subject she eludes even the extent of the rhetorical flamboyance deployed here, which can only describe her physically, and the tone of this passage is correspondingly more elusive. In the complex ambiguities of *Nightwood*'s narrative tone, the stakes of description as representation have a particular force, as Bal demonstrates.

The challenges presented by character description as representation can be observed not only in *Nightwood* but also in Barnes's short fiction of the 1910s and 1920s and the stage directions of her one-act plays. It is worth elaborating on why Barnes is so apt for Bal's example of a more general observation about narrative. Since Bal's focus is on description, I will give an example of another introductory description of a character, here from the short story 'The Robin's House'. The elaborate introduction of the character Nelly Grissard suggests the paradox that Bal summarises:

> Nelly Grissard was fat and lively to the point of excess. She never let a waxed floor pass under her without proving herself light of foot. Every ounce of Nelly Grissard was on the jump. Her fingers tapped, her feet fluttered, her bosom heaved; her entire diaphragm swelled with little creakings of whale-bone, lace and taffeta.
>
> She wore feathery things about the throat, had a liking for deep burgundy silks, and wore six petticoats for the 'joy of discovering that I'm not so fat as they say'. She stained her good square teeth with tobacco, and cut her hair in a bang.[31]

Nelly Grissard emerges from this description a being who remains a step ahead of even the expert rhetoric here. The first paragraph's enthusiasm might at first seem to capture her effectively enough to reduce her to the slightly sensational character it creates. But the second paragraph undercuts this effect by quoting from Nelly directly, suggesting the narrative's incapacity to represent Nelly without her own input.[32] Closer inspection suggests that 'feathery things' and 'good square teeth' might well be Nelly's terms too. If so, her idiom is still offset within the narrator's sentences, whose verbs deliver the relevant information, notably in the narrator's judgement, 'stained'. But it's hard to tell whose phrases

88   *The New Modernist Novel: Criticism and the Task of Reading*

these are, and 'feathery things' might also read as an awkward circumlocution with 'things', one that lacks, precisely, Nelly's own phrasing – indicating instead only her narrator's failing attempt to describe her before resorting shortly afterwards to quotation. As in some of the sentences quoted above from *Nightwood*, the complexities of voice are hard to discern in this passage, and tone remains unstable. The name 'Grissard', a possible pun on the French adjectives *grasse* and *grosse*, referring to fat, is a reminder of the edginess of this narrator's wit. The complexity here might be interpreted as a tension between reporting an independent character and creating her with description, similar to the tension Bal finds in *Nightwood*. Barnes's style hovers in the balance between, in Dora Zhang's terms, *'recording* reality' and *'inventing* it'.[33] In this description, there is the wit of a visible wager, that the description of Nelly will convince its readers.

The passage is helpful as an example too because it frames another issue with prose style involving the politics of narration. The portrait shows a sharp edge of homage in narrative fiction: for all this narrator's enthusiasm, would Nelly herself be flattered by the portrait? A reader might want to know whether this narrator will keep the character from stereotype and fatphobia. Even the narrator's minor judgements seem barbed: what is the tone of 'to the point of excess'? The complete story was not revised after the Second World War, and it did not undergo the revisions Barnes made to remove stereotyped language that her other stories published in the 1962 *Spillway* did. Other wording attributed to characters in this story reproduces contemporary stereotypes, not dissimilarly to *Nightwood*. But by 1929, Barnes had reprinted the story twice, and the passage quoted here helps indicate why Barnes's prose has been a key example for Bal.

In *Nightwood*, however, the challenge of character description is complicated by the biographical originals involved. Many of Barnes's fictional characters resemble people she knew, but *Nightwood*'s originals were close by: Robin Vote is a version of Barnes's lover Thelma Wood, Nora Flood corresponds to Barnes as Robin's lover, and Jenny Petherbridge is a version of Henriette Metcalf, who was Wood's lover after she left Barnes.[34] The challenge of description applies for example to Jenny Petherbridge, who is described scornfully by the narrator as giving off an 'odour to the mind [. . .] of a woman about to be *accouchée*' (59), which prefigures the doctor's 'with a smell about her of mouse-nests' (87). The narrator's scorn here maintains a tension with the actual narrative by implying fertility in Jenny, when she has married four husbands but has no children, and the personal investment in the narratorial judgement becomes evident. In this sense, in the passage Bal discusses, the question of whether the woman produces the ekphrasis or the ekphrasis the woman may not only be a formal question, since in one sense it is Thelma, not Robin, who produces this rhetorical density in Barnes's book, and whom the book represents or misrepresents in the character of Robin Vote.

Thelma indirectly produces other ekphrases in *Nightwood*. As Joanne Winning shows, Thelma Wood's silverpoint drawings closely correlate with some of the figurations in this introduction of Robin, most notably in the 'vision of an eland coming down an aisle of trees, chapleted with orange blossoms and bridal veil' (33). As Winning shows, this figure, along with the paragraph and text surrounding it, shares a vocabulary with Thelma's silverpoint of an eland (reproduced in Winning's article). Winning observes that 'we cannot understand [Barnes's] written line without reading it alongside Wood's bending of the silverpoint line'.[35] Thelma's presence in the prose style is likely to be complex, and Winning's work on the shared vocabulary of these artists suggests a significant context for that style.

Bal's interest is less in Barnes's modernism than in Barnes as novelist, but the prose style of *Nightwood*, and particularly the complexity of its tone, can be considered one of this novel's major contributions to modernism, and especially to modernist fiction. *Nightwood* persistently poses questions about the responsibility and ethics involved in the representation of another. In Nora's accounts of her dreams, such issues emerge with particular focus. This is perhaps because of similarities between dreaming; remembering and retelling dreams; and telling stories. Nora's accounts of her dreams suggest an elusive responsibility that inheres in acts of fictional creation and reception. This responsibility is reflected in the status of *Nightwood* as a published *roman à clef*.

Matthew's philosophy of the night has the sleeper take on a new identity inaccessible to the lover: 'The sleeper is the proprietor of an unknown land' (78). Earlier in *Nightwood*, Nora dreams that she is standing at the top of a house in her grandmother's room:

> standing, Nora looked down into the body of the house, as if from a scaffold, where now Robin had entered the dream, lying among a company below. Nora said to herself, 'The dream will not be dreamed again.' A disc of light, that seemed to come from some one or thing standing behind her and which was yet a shadow, shed a faintly luminous glow upon the upturned, still face of Robin who had the smile of an 'only survivor', a smile which fear had married to the bone. (56)

The elements of the dream are reflected in the narrative events of Robin's infidelity that are told immediately afterwards: Nora, looking into the garden for Robin, 'saw emerge from the darkness the light of Robin's eyes, the fear in them developing their luminosity until, by the intensity

90   *The New Modernist Novel: Criticism and the Task of Reading*

of their double regard, Robin's eyes and hers met' (57). This moment, where 'Nora saw the body of another woman swim up into the statue's obscurity' (57–58), ends the section and makes way for Jenny Petherbridge. The garden episode reworks the dream as 'reality'. In a later chapter, 'Go Down, Matthew', Nora, speaking to the doctor, figures Robin's predicament as a 'dream': 'she was in her own nightmare. I tried to come between and save her, but, I was like a shadow in her dream that could never reach her in time, as the cry of the sleeper has no echo, myself echo struggling to answer' (131). The waking lover cannot access the sleeping lover's dream. But in the earlier chapter, the echo becomes, for a reader, a re-enactment of the dream of one in the lives of both.

Although the dream might be analysed in terms of Freud's model of condensation and displacement, it departs from a Freudian model in that it has an effect on the one dreamed about.[36] It has now been '"well dreamt"' (55) and is now 'completed with the entry of Robin' (56); the phrasing of this change, 'Robin had entered the dream' (56), suggests volition on the part of Robin herself. The dream appears to Nora as 'something being done to Robin, Robin disfigured and eternalized by the hieroglyphics of sleep and pain' (57). Dreaming, then, touches those dreamed about; it is a hazard for them. Nora repeats this worry while recounting another dream of her grandmother to the doctor:

> This I have done to my father's mother, dreaming through my father, and have tormented them with my tears and with my dreams: for all of us die over again in somebody's sleep. And this, I have done to Robin: it is only through me that she will die over and over, and it is only through me, of all my family, that my grandfather dies, over and over. (134–35)[37]

Dreaming cannot take place in isolation from those it involves, but will be consequential for them. In what Nora says here, the potential harm of dreaming of others seems unlimited. In a novel intensely concerned with the situation of telling, this power that dream has perhaps finds its clearest analogue in the effect of the novel as retelling on Thelma as possible reader. Nora's desperation to understand the dream that she retells to Matthew parallels her confusion and questions to him about Robin. But it might also function as a disclaimer of some of the responsibility involved in retelling: '"What was that dream saying, for God's sake, what was that dream?"' (135). The teller of the story, like the dreamer of the dream, may choose to abdicate responsibility for the content of the tale.

Julie Taylor's comment about Barnes's fiction might serve equally to highlight an aspect in which it shares ground with dream. Taylor uses the term 'affect' to capture 'the ways in which Djuna Barnes refuses to organise feeling along narrative or moral lines and the ways in which, in her fiction, feeling functions not as a route to interpretation, but as a radical alternative'.[38] Dream, too, resists interpretation, even when it is subsequently interpreted by the events of the narrative. In Barnes's short story 'A Little Girl Tells a Story to a Lady' (1925), dedicated 'To T. W. [Thelma Wood]', there is a dreamlike strangeness to some of the lines: 'And somehow it did not seem funny that she spoke to me' or 'Then I got up and followed my lady, and we came to a big house and she let herself in with a key, and we were in her home.'[39] The dreamlike quality in these and other lines resonates with an artistic, rather than theoretical, representation of dream or reverie, since here, the simple, dreamlike events escape the narrator's interpretation, even when she desires interpretation. Peter Whitehead wrote of his 1978 or 1979 film scenario for the revised version of the story, 'Cassation' (1962), that: 'She seems to dream the episode with the woman . . . maybe it is her dream or vice versa but not true at all.'[40] Even the garden setting of the 'reality' referred to above, Robin with another woman in the shadow of the statue, which reworks Nora's dream as reality, has already been dreamed or written as the start of the short story 'The Robin's House'. Nora's garden's statue, a 'fountain figure' of a tall woman bending forward (50), recalls the story's fountain: 'in the back garden a fountain, having poured out its soul for many years, still poured, murmuring over the stomachs of the three cherubim supporting its massive basin'.[41] Rather than interpreting the earlier story, the later story seems merely to re-dream it.

The aspect of disclaimer to Nora's question to Matthew about her dream – 'what was that dream?' – can be read to apply obliquely to *Nightwood*'s effect on its readers. At the time when *Nightwood* was being edited by Emily Coleman, T. S. Eliot and Frank Morley, Thelma Wood was already based in America with Henriette Metcalf. Barnes writes to Emily Coleman of an instance where she was challenged with the effect the book might have on Thelma: at a party given by Natalie Barney, Barney induced an attack on Barnes in the form of the accusation that *Nightwood* had caused Thelma's illness and that Thelma was threatening suicide over it. Barnes's dizziness and tears following Barney's attack may also respond to an outcome Barnes might have anticipated or feared.[42] She later wrote to Emily Coleman that she 'knew (and got) Thelma's fury for *Nightwood*', which she had 'rather expected'. Thelma had thrown a cup of tea at her and knocked her down twice on 'that awful night I read it to her'.[43]

There is evidence in the drafts that Barnes made some attempt to soften the impact of *Nightwood* on Thelma as future reader. To

92   *The New Modernist Novel: Criticism and the Task of Reading*

Coleman, Barnes wrote of Thelma in September 1935 that she knew that 'as I [wrote] it I should have to read it so to her'.[44] This prospect seems to have limited her direct treatment of Robin: to Coleman's comment in 1932 that 'You should write of Thelma' (rather than of Dan Mahoney), Barnes responded that she 'had written about Thelma' and 'could not face Thelma's reading it'.[45] As well as leaving Robin focalised externally for almost all of *Nightwood*, and with very few spoken lines, Barnes showed a growing awareness of the potential effect of her depiction of Robin by making small changes to the way Robin's behaviour is recorded. At Coleman's instigation she left out the second clause in 'She stayed with Nora until the mid-winter, then she wanted to go', after first correcting it to 'then she became restless';[46] the record of the short time spans in 'It was not long after this that Nora and Robin separated; a little later Jenny and Robin sailed for America' (69) was softened in Barnes's hand to 'a little later' from 'and only a week later'. Barnes left out '[Robin] turned on her in a fury' from Robin's arrival with Jenny in America (150) and had Robin 'speaking in a low voice' rather than 'speaking harshly in a low voice' to the animals there (151).[47] Though the changes are small, they are all recorded late in the editing process, on the typescript carbon used as printer's copy or on the proofs to the first English edition (as collated by Cheryl J. Plumb). These minor late changes may reflect Barnes's continued unease with the effect that the novel might have on Thelma.

In her later reflection to Coleman, Barnes seems resigned to the other expressions of 'the hatred and disgust and malice of the world' she had received or might receive for writing *Nightwood*. She 'would not be at all surprised if Henriette stuck me in the back with a knife', but writes that she did not expect Dan's response: he had, like Thelma, hit her twice, knocking her down.[48] Dan's and Thelma's violent responses cannot be explained or justified.

Insofar as Thelma's response and Henriette's (unknown) response are anticipated by the novel's author, including in edits, that anticipation identifies a problem of the ethics of narration. Where Mieke Bal identifies the 'problem of description' as being at the core of narrative, *Nightwood*'s narration sustains the same questions beyond only description, into representation and storytelling: what is an ethical way to represent a character, or to tell the story of another? This is not only a formal problem, because the problem transfers from literary representation to the ethics of representation. Indeed, *Nightwood*'s author encountered the strong responses to the novel of those she fictionalised in it. *Nightwood*'s storytelling is bound up in the performative situation of a novel that was written for, or with the knowledge of, real readers.

This may be a situation that affects all fiction, since characters inevitably resemble real people, and readers inevitably recognise themselves in characters. In the complexities of its tone, *Nightwood* examines the ethics of storytelling.

Readings of *Nightwood* have been troubled by this partisan voice. Mia Spiro asks, for instance, 'Is it even possible to represent Jewish characters without characterizing them in identifiable ethnic or racial terms?' That is, without denying them 'diversity, specificity, subjectivity, and self-identity'?[49] Her question resonates with Bal's problem of description, of whether the other is 'easily objectified' and flattened by description or, by contrast, is 'irreducible' and inaccessible to all attempts at description. Spiro points out that Guido (senior) and Felix are represented in *Nightwood* as Jewish even though they do not identify themselves as Jewish. For Spiro, this involves the 'erasure of the historical reality of Jewish experience in the 1930s'.[50] As much as Barnes's characters tend to take on an aura of independence from their narrators, Barnes's writing about Thelma as Robin suggests the limits of such independence in any narrative. In the cases of Guido and Felix, the limits to these characters' independence also bear the imprint of semitic discourse in the 1930s. For Erin Carlston, *Nightwood*'s instances of semitic discourse are in tension with the way the novel 'calls into question fascism's utopic visions' by presenting characters who are caught in the general social predicament but who are neither its cause nor its cure. Calling *Nightwood* 'a dangerous book to read', Carlston observes its elusiveness to any critical interpretation.[51] Yet, as Rachel Potter shows, the act of storytelling matters, in that *Nightwood* finds a language with which to tell the stories of 'those on the outside of a humanism secured through national sovereignty', so restoring them to history.[52] These questions suggest the complexity of *Nightwood*'s anatomy of storytelling and, within it, of the language of representation.

Resistance to Formalist Analysis

By any standards, Barnes is a storyteller, from her early short stories and journalism onwards. Following Walter Benjamin's prominence in Anglophone literary criticism, the term carries some of his meaning. For Benjamin, writing of the Russian Nikolai Leskov, 'the storyteller is a man who has counsel for his readers', yet 'the psychological connection of the events is not forced on the reader. It is left up to him to interpret things the way he understands them.'[53] Leskov's stories differ starkly from Barnes's, perhaps most noticeably in the way Leskov's stories tend

94   *The New Modernist Novel: Criticism and the Task of Reading*

to leave readers to judge the motivations of their characters from their actions, where Barnes's narrators will jump in from the start to tell readers what kind of character we are dealing with.[54] But the balance of contrast in Benjamin's definition is maintained by Barnes's fiction. In *Nightwood*, often, interpretation and even understanding of events, or of conversations, are left to readers. Even the characters involved are often at a loss. Counsel, then, is not something *Nightwood* offers in any straightforward way. But on the other hand, counsel of a difficult kind may be *all* that it offers, and seeking or finding counsel may be one of the ends of interpretation, for both characters and readers. Benjamin also contrasts the oral nature of stories with the printed book, and in *Nightwood*, Matthew's long disquisitions recall the direct personal exchange involved in counsel, bringing out the spoken exchange as the medium of narration, among other forms of speech. In *Nightwood*'s narrator's voice, the tone of the speaker is significant, and in *Nightwood*, the undecidability of tone persistently calls attention to nuances of the telling of this story for readers. In that undecidability, and in other ways, *Nightwood*'s Barnes is not only a storyteller, but also a theorist of storytelling.

In Anglophone criticism of modernist fiction, for all its early attention to Henry James and its recent embrace of global fiction, analysis of storytelling has still in some ways been elusive. Joseph Frank's 1945 essay on 'spatial form' brought *Nightwood* into direct comparison with writers still now considered to be central to modernism: T. S. Eliot, Ezra Pound, Marcel Proust, James Joyce and Gustave Flaubert. The essay was later revised and republished, meaning that it was contemporary with two distinct moments in criticism of modernist fiction, 1945 and 1963, before it was republished again with Frank's foreword in 1991. Frank's treatment of *Nightwood* is highly sympathetic, and he positions *Nightwood* as the classic case of spatial form in modern literature. Yet his essay suggests by implication the difficulties of bringing an analysis of spatial form to this novel. I outline some of the difficulties below, in order to suggest some of what might be lost, even if much is to be gained, by reading *Nightwood* as modernist in Frank's formalist sense.

Frank develops Gotthold Ephraim Lessing's distinction between form in the visual arts as essentially spatial, because the artwork is seen in a moment of time, and form in the literary arts as essentially temporal, because it is based on narrative sequence, to argue that modern literature 'is moving in the direction of spatial form'. He quotes Pound's definition of the image and argues that in their major poems, Pound and Eliot attempted to force readers to 'perceive the elements of the poem juxtaposed in space rather than unrolling in time'.[55] Similarly to modern poetry, novels by Joyce and Proust require their readers to keep in mind and link together, or juxtapose, connected details from across the novel, independently of the progress of the narrative, in order to understand the whole work. Frank's essay is centrally concerned with *Nightwood*:

> The eight chapters of *Nightwood* are like searchlights, probing the darkness each from a different direction, yet ultimately focusing on and illuminating the same entanglement of the human spirit. [...] And these chapters are knit together, not by the progress of any action – either narrative action, or, as in a stream-of-consciousness novel, the flow of experience – but by the continual reference and cross reference of images and symbols that must be referred to each other spatially throughout the time-act of reading.[56]

Understood in this way, *Nightwood* fits well with *Ulysses* and *À la recherche du temps perdu*.

In the case of *Nightwood*, Frank's reading seems to require a process of cross-reference that can be worked through and at least partially completed. Yet at the same time, *Nightwood* seems to resist the kinds of knowledge that might be gained this way. Frank analyses *Nightwood*'s characters in some detail, and his commentary uses descriptions of the characters that are given in the narrative voice of the novel. For example, Felix's role is summed up with words Frank has recently quoted from the novel, 'give her permission to live' (105): 'Felix, then, makes the first effort to shape Robin, to give her permission to live by informing her with his own sense of moral values.' Jenny's chapter is 'appropriately entitled "the Squatter"'. Distilling the narrator's descriptions directly into criticism runs the risk of essentialising the characters: 'Characteristically, while Felix was drawn to Robin because he wished to use her, Nora is drawn to her through pity.'[57] The result is that the characters are read across the novel as unified beings, faithfully described by the narrative voice. Yet characters in *Nightwood* do not always correspond to their introductory descriptions, which can, I've argued, be read as performances on the part of a narrative voice. The early description of Nora, for instance, which Frank interprets soundly as one of 'faith in natural goodness',[58] is nonetheless sidelined by the doctor's later criticism of Nora's tenacious hold on Robin. The unifying trend of Frank's argument means too that he is obliged to set aside the obscurity of the final chapter ending: 'What this indicates, clearly, is that Robin has abandoned her efforts to rise to the human and is returning to the animal state; the somnambule is re-entering her age-old sleep.'[59] For other readers, part of the value of the ending has been that its meaning is anything but clear.

96 *The New Modernist Novel: Criticism and the Task of Reading*

This is not to deny the sharpness of Frank's analysis of the nature of the characters' 'entanglements' and the working through of the concepts of innocence and damnation, but to assert the disunity of *Nightwood*, a quality that seems precluded by Frank's reading. Frank's argument, which finds a method of reading spatially that will reveal a unity or pattern to the modernist texts he discusses, risks limiting the oddness of *Nightwood* in interpretation. Where Frank's faith in *Nightwood*'s narrative descriptions runs the risk of essentialising the characters, those descriptions might, I have argued, be read as performances by a narrator, rather than as a solid basis for factual development of the narrative. In other words, the novel makes an issue of the diffuseness of literary characters (and their narrators) in a way that tends to work against the specifics of Frank's analysis. *Nightwood*'s resistance to unifying reading brings out in Barnes's prose an engaging unpredictability that Frank's reading suggests but does not elaborate on. Read with this in mind, *Nightwood* becomes a different novel, one that hovers engagingly between virtuosity and instability, and that fits other potential contexts beyond the select grouping of high modernist literature that Frank identifies.[60]

Arguing that *Nightwood* is more than 'a collection of striking passages', Frank notes that 'thanks to a good many critics', it has become possible to 'approach *The Waste Land* as a work of art rather than as a battleground for opposing theories or a piece of literary esoterica', and he calls for *Nightwood* to be approached 'in the same way'. Identifying early on the problem of whether any of the other characters will be able to 'raise [Robin] to the level of the human', Frank writes, 'Once this fundamental problem is grasped, much of what we read in the rest of *Nightwood* becomes considerably clearer.'[61] The pedagogical aim is evident: Frank aims to set out the coordinates of this modernist novel in such a way as to facilitate further analysis of not just this valuable literary work, but modernist fiction and poetry more generally. But the analysis is limited by the way in which criticism on *Nightwood* may be even less accretive in a formal sense than criticism on *The Waste Land*. Frank's later comments on the essay's origins in his preoccupation with *Nightwood*, which he saw, at a later date, as not having been key, after all, to the way the novel form developed, hint at the different rewards of doing critical work on Eliot's poem.[62]

Yet *Nightwood* might well be closer to Frank's conceptual model than the specifics of his reading of it imply. In that sense, the essay might be considered an instance of what Paul de Man identifies in 1971 as a 'constitutive characteristic of literary language in general', which is that critics' 'findings about the structure of texts contradict the general conception that they use as their model'.[63] In other words, despite the difficulty of reading character in *Nightwood* in the way Frank does, Frank's concept of 'spatial form' and its ability to draw together poetry, visual art and novels remains highly suggestive for *Nightwood*.[64] *Nightwood* does lend itself to a reading that recalls 'images and symbols' from across the length of the novel, even if integration of those images and symbols is elusive. *Nightwood* does lend itself, too, to being read alongside not just modern fiction, but also modern poetry. The idea of 'spatial form' as something specific to modernism across forms differs significantly from, for example, F. R. Leavis's tradition of the novel along lines of form and genre, and suits *Nightwood*. Paul de Man, reviewing Frank's *The Widening Gyre* seven years earlier in 1964 alongside J. Hillis Miller's *The Disappearance of God*, observes that 'neither of these studies is historical or New Critical, and both – each in its own way – deal with the rejection of the concepts of form and of history that have been at the basis of much contemporary work'.[65] Frank's formal analysis can illuminate modernist fiction, not just modernist poetry. Yet *Nightwood* doesn't quite fit, and this is partly why the essay's argument for *Nightwood*'s 'spatial form' remains highly suggestive.

One thing that seems difficult to reconcile with Frank's reading is the resistance of *Nightwood*'s figures to integration. In *Ulysses*, repetitions of specific words have been seen by some critics as significant enough to sustain self-referential narrative and thematic threads across the novel: for example, the 'throwaway' motif, or Bloom's potato, or indeed much of what turns up again in 'Circe'. Yet *Nightwood* seems hardly to prompt the desire for an equivalent to a *Word Index to James Joyce's 'Ulysses'*.[66] If one were to be made, it might illuminate a different set of textual patterns. Word repetitions in *Nightwood* may or may not be significant: rather than recalling earlier uses of the word, a repeated word such as 'damned' may be more likely to refer to a figure that is active, changeable and resolutely opaque across the novel. As such, this word has prompted substantial critical exploration.[67]

Nightwood's dense figuration includes many tropes that recur at intervals through the novel. For example, the first of the passages below describes Felix's father Guido, and the second passage records Nora's meeting Robin:

> Childless at fifty-nine, Guido had prepared out of his own heart for his coming child a heart, fashioned on his own preoccupation, the remorseless homage to nobility, the genuflexion the hunted body makes from muscular contraction, going down before the impending and inaccessible, as before a great heat. (2–3)

> Then as one powerful lioness came to the turn of the bars, exactly opposite the girl, she turned her furious great head with its yellow eyes afire and went down, her paws thrust through the bars and, as she regarded the girl, as if a river were falling behind impassable heat, her eyes flowed in tears that never reached the surface. At that the girl rose straight up. (49)

98   *The New Modernist Novel: Criticism and the Task of Reading*

The figure of going down is one of the most frequent to recur in the novel.[68] It is evident in four of the eight chapter titles, 'Bow Down', 'The Squatter', 'Where the Tree Falls' and 'Go Down, Matthew'. Barnes claimed she named the chapter 'Go Down, Matthew' after the gospel song 'Go Down, Moses, Let My People Go'.[69] The Biblical reference is to the Israelites enslaved in Egypt, but the song had long been sung by African-American gospel singers. It was being sung by the Southern Syncopated Orchestra in London in 1919, for example.[70] The use of the song in Barnes's chapter title follows almost a whole book of figuration of going down, complexly woven across characters, so that the reference to 'Go Down, Moses' becomes a part of the density of the figuration of going down across *Nightwood*. The song may bring a politics of resistance to that imagery, but if the resistance is borrowed from gospel singers, it resonates in a general way with *Nightwood* and the specific context is not mentioned.

In the passages quoted, where Guido's 'hunted' body goes down, Robin's going down is enacted through the body of the lioness and contrasts with Robin's own movement, 'At that the girl rose straight up.' These passages, which are not associated with the same character over time, are an intriguing example for Frank's account of spatial form because it is not clear how the connection between them might be formulated. Through the novel, the figure of bodily downward movement tends to accompany Felix and Robin particularly, as in these passages, and at times the same figure also involves the relation of past and present. The bow given by Felix to his acquaintances is 'a reminiscent pardon for future apprehension' (7); he himself 'felt that the great past might mend a little if he bowed low enough, if he succumbed and gave homage' (8). Robin returns from the land of the sleeper: 'Such a woman is the infected carrier of the past: before her the structure of our head and jaws ache – we feel that we could eat her, she who is eaten death returning' (34). Among much that can be made of this description of Robin, the figure of 'eaten death returning' resonates with the sense of a past bound up with the present that dominates the characterisation of Felix, and the description implicitly involves the downward movement of death. Yet the figure extends to other characters too. Robin and Nora each go down in the last chapter. Felix's reflections on the doctor echo a downward movement:

> His manner was that of a servant of a defunct noble family, whose movements recall, though in a degraded form, those of a late master. Even the doctor's favourite gesture – plucking hairs out of his nostrils – seemed the 'vulgarization' of what was once a thoughtful plucking of the beard. (27)

Telling the Story of the Night Wood   99

The past here is seen in Felix's terms of the hereditary, and perhaps the echo is due to Felix's focalisation. But in these lines, the doctor is drawn in ways that resonate with the figure of going down and with figures of related past and present.

At these points and elsewhere, the diffuseness of the characters allows their fictional constitutions to be at risk, since they come close to being subordinated to the novel's development of figuration. Brian Glavey makes a similar observation of Robin's scene in the novel's final chapter: 'the significance of her final scene is not that she is absorbed into the animal kingdom but that she becomes part of the background of the novel's broader aesthetic pattern'.[71] At Guido's last scene in the novel, two chapters earlier, the figuration of the downward movement brings back into the novel's sphere of judgement a character whose presentation in this chapter has otherwise been far more sympathetic. Seeing a man who seems, Felix is sure, to be a member of the former Russian royal family, he 'could not keep his eyes away, and as they arose to go, his cheeks now drained of colour, [. . .] he turned and made a slight bow, his head in confusion making a complete half-swing, as an animal will turn its head away from a human, as if in mortal shame' (110–11). Exiting Nightwood, Felix carries the novel's shame and shares in its downward movement. The scene mortifies him, in the sense that it degrades his character by fixing that character in this behavioural trait and not another. This is the novel's chosen trait; these are, therefore, the fixtures of figures within which Guido must be represented. The final four lines of the chapter have Guido gently rubbing oil on his disabled son's cold hands, only partially redeemed from the novel's enactment through him of a downward movement of shame.

For Lara Trubowitz, this general formal trait – the diffuseness of characters within Nightwood's figurative style – can be analysed into greater specificity. For Trubowitz, the movement of images of 'going down' between characters is best read as an indication of the way the novel employs Jewishness at the expense of its Jewish characters:

> By the end of the text, everything that Barnes had initially described as qualities of the Jewish Guido and Felix is now fully associated with Robin, who reinforces the presence of Jewishness in Nightwood even after Felix and Guido, the novel's only actual Jews, have vanished.[72]

Trubowitz observes that this means that Jewish characters, through Robin, are 'fully central' to Nightwood. Her reading again suggests that the risks of the imagery that shifts between characters in this novel are not only formal risks, because identity is at stake. Nightwood, it seems,

100   *The New Modernist Novel: Criticism and the Task of Reading*

borrows their identity for the novel's own analyses. Trubowitz's analysis of this representation must sit alongside Scott Herring's observation of Barnes's newspaper work as a prelude to *Nightwood*: 'Within this epistemological uncertainty, ethnic and sexual freaks are lost the moment they are found.'[73] In *Nightwood*, for Herring, the more the doctor talks, the less the underworld he tells Nora of is intelligible as a real place. For Herring, it is the ability of *Nightwood*'s styles to keep the characters safely away from knowable identities that makes this novel valuable.[74] In each case, for Trubowitz and Herring, identity slips away from character.

This kind of diffuseness in character can be seen across many motifs and images, which are shared between characters. Matthew is called the 'Squatting Beast, coming out at night' (147), in an appellation that would seem to refer to Jenny as 'The Squatter', or to Robin as the 'beast turning human' (33), but the use of the phrase for Matthew strengthens the connection of figuration across the characters. As Peter Adkins notes, instabilities of meaning and difficulties of reading in *Nightwood* connect with its approach to representing animals.[75] The awkward connection of figures across *Nightwood* might be one of the sources of its intrigue, the sense that a pattern is constantly about to emerge, but that the pattern remains interpretable only in individual images, or at the general level of the novel as a whole. Carolyn Allen outlines a model of associative reading elicited by *Nightwood*:

> The language of *Nightwood* requires the reader to make associations among suggestions that are scattered throughout the novel. Thus the description of Robin as an 'infected carrier' of a past that extends backwards to the moment of the 'beast turning human' becomes meaningful as one of a number of references to the 'way back', to beasts both actual and mythical and to the pre-verbal realm from which she comes. These evolutionary references are related in turn to another set, again referring to prehistory but instead of beasts to 'the fossil of Robin, intaglio of her identity', 'the hieroglyphics of sleep and pain', figures of design, and references to tracing.
>
> Furthermore the sets themselves are not merely repeated patterns of images; they are groups of associations which have a collective meaning within each group and from set to set. Thus to understand Robin, the reader must respond to the language of evocation associatively rather than analytically.[76]

Nightwood, on this model, is a challenging and lively novel, where reading maintains or draws from many open threads of unsorted images or motifs, selecting between them. *Nightwood*'s density at the level of sentences and passages sustains a critically interesting tension with the boundedness of the novel form, where cross-reference is inevitable, and

Telling the Story of the Night Wood   **101**

inevitably produces meaning. Joseph Frank's spatial form identifies this tension, but with a different analysis from Allen's.

One way to extend Allen's model of *Nightwood* would be to ask, is *Nightwood*'s whole story best read not just by chapters, but by passages? In other words, is it passages, rather than characters, that are the key units of this novel? A relevant caution comes via Tyrus Miller, who suggests that each character offers desperate readers different 'allegorical clues about how to understand the book as a whole', before the novel 'undercuts the interpretive ground of the reader'. The same might be said of *Nightwood*'s passages: individual passages as much as characters might offer theoretical models for reading *Nightwood* as a whole, but they might be just as duplicitous.[77] Yet reading *Nightwood*'s passages without necessarily requiring from them a complete hermeneutics might be one kind of reading that this novel rewards. It is at least one kind of reading that the novel has rewarded in the past, not least in gaining publication at Faber and Faber in part on the strength of Emily Coleman's attempts at directing T. S. Eliot's attention to passages from *Nightwood* for his perusal, which persuaded him to read the book.[78] Edwin Muir likewise extolled to Eliot the 'extraordinary' nature of *Nightwood*'s passages.[79]

The brilliance of *Nightwood*'s passages was noted in early reviews, for example L. P. Hartley's: 'She has an amazing power of combining in a single phrase images that seem unrelated yet ignite at the contact – like incongruous objects in a *surréaliste* picture.'[80] Many of the early reviews praise the quality of *Nightwood*'s passages.[81] Indeed, the impetus for Joseph Frank's study of Barnes's novel is to dispel the idea that *Nightwood* is merely a 'collection of striking passages', as quoted above, though Frank sees the 'unit of meaning in *Nightwood*' as 'usually a phrase or sequence of phrases – at most a long paragraph.'[82] Hartley's claim for Barnes's 'power' as visible in passages is curiously echoed in Barnes's own reading of her friend the Baroness Elsa von Freytag-Loringhoven's letters, which she was planning to publish, along with poems and a biography.[83] She writes to Emily Coleman, 'really amazing lines in nearly every letter, but God, so many of them to go through'.[84] In this sense, the puzzlement and diffuseness of *Nightwood*'s imagery are linked to the way it elicits reading as a sequence of dense passages which yet tell a story. This novel's local density, wit and elusiveness tend less to give way to an underlying clarity of structure of the kind that Ezra Pound had found in Henry James: 'Here in a few paragraphs are the bare bones of the plan described in eighty of Henry James's pages.'[85] The local intensities of Barnes's styles might be read across the different forms she writes in: interviews, articles, short stories, plays, poetry, novels and *Ladies Almanack*. But in the novel form, the anatomy of storytelling is acute.[86]

102   *The New Modernist Novel: Criticism and the Task of Reading*

The problem of passages in relation to the novel form might usefully be referred back to Eliot's preface. The preface hovers about the question of value, seeking value in the experience of reading: 'A prose that is altogether alive demands something of the reader that the ordinary novel-reader is not prepared to give'; 'I cannot think of any character in the book who has not gone on living in my mind.' As has been noted by other readers, Eliot's preface records the uncertainty of a decision that is resolved by finding *Nightwood* valuable enough to preface, with some of the major insights of the preface depending on the recognition that what initially seems a flaw is in fact a strength: 'I am now convinced that the final chapter is essential, both dramatically and musically'; the doctor 'ceased to be like the brilliant actor in an otherwise unpersuasively performed play for whose re-entrance one impatiently waits'.[87] Critics have noted the preface's 'lingering ambivalence' about *Nightwood*.[88] The completed novel troubles Eliot's concept of literary value, but it also helps to reshape that concept, at least here in the preface. As far as the prose style is concerned, though, it seems clear that the value of Barnes's style is not in question for Eliot, unlike the value of her novel has been, for him, in the prelude to writing the preface. Praise for Barnes's prose style is the occasion of recognisably Eliotian hauteur, including in a comparison between Barnes and 'a competent newspaper writer or government official' that summarily dismisses the latter in spite of Barnes's two decades of newspaper work. Eliot simultaneously divorces *Nightwood* from its less admirable genre, the novel, and validates its prose style: 'it is so good a novel that only sensibilities trained on poetry can wholly appreciate it'. His comment identifies a gap in available modes of describing serious prose fiction, in that 'poetry' becomes a stand-in for a claim for literary value. So even if it is hard to work out what exactly is meant by Eliot's 'Miss Barnes's prose has the prose rhythm that is prose style', the complimentary tone of the comment is obvious, and 'style' is the word that carries it most strongly.[89] This praise for her prose style in *Nightwood* is supported by Eliot's writing advice to Barnes following *Nightwood*: 'Djuna, please write *prose*; I wish I could write prose as you can, why poetry? Prose please, from now on for three weeks at least, prose, or I'll give you a black eye (this from gentle Eliot) *no more poetry now!*'[90]

Eliot wrote to Coleman that it was the complete book that impressed him, and that the excerpts she had selected had given him a misleading impression.[91] Still, the 'whole pattern' that Eliot eventually finds in *Nightwood* is posited more tenuously: the book is 'not simply a collection of individual portraits; the characters are all knotted together [. . .]: it is the whole pattern that they form, rather than any individual

Telling the Story of the Night Wood **103**

constituent, that is the focus of interest'.[92] Eliot is a likely source here for Joseph Frank's reading of spatial form across the novel. Yet in this sentence of Eliot's, individual characters as the novel's focus are denied twice in favour of an elusive 'whole pattern'. At the same time, where the 'prose style' is an occasion for the critic's characteristic judgements of value, the 'whole pattern' is asserted more as a prelude to directly correcting future and already extant misreadings. Eliot's esteem is easily earned by *Nightwood*'s prose style, but Barnes's use of the novel's capacity for character representation poses a challenge to his sense of the genre.

The process of *Nightwood*'s composition could similarly suggest the importance of prose style to this novel over the details of its deployment of the novel form. As both Cheryl Plumb and Monika Lee observe, Barnes's correspondent Emily Coleman's letters show rearrangement of *Nightwood*'s chapters in 1935, with the chapters originally paginated separately and numbered consecutively only after the early drafts. Parts of chapters were also moved around, for example the Altamonte section, and the doctor's interlocutor was in two places changed to Nora, once from Felix and once from another character no longer included in the book.[93] Still, the resulting novel failed to satisfy Coleman. As Cheryl J. Plumb records, she wrote that to remedy the book, Barnes would need to reconceive it, placing the full emphasis on Nora and Robin so as to create unity.[94] To T. S. Eliot, Coleman had suggested that 'Bow Down' and 'Where the Tree Falls', both Felix's chapters, be removed from the book, in order to give it unity.[95] The difficulty of finding a structure to the novel through the process of reading also disturbed Eliot, who judged that Matthew's conversation 'distorts the shape of the book' and agreed to Coleman's deletions of sections of Matthew's lines.[96] This can be taken as evidence of the contemporary difficulty of reading a novel that, even on a completed reading, did not seem to match acceptable ideas of the novel form for both Eliot and Coleman, especially in terms of the kinds of coherence or unity they expected. Eliot and Coleman concur in finding that *Nightwood* seems to include the germ of two novels, though they identify these differently. Through her correspondence with both Barnes and Eliot, Coleman consistently identifies the writing in passages as the basis of her admiration for the book, over and above the arrangement of the novel, and her letters are often full of excerpts that she admires.

Similar questions about *Nightwood*'s structure occupied some of Barnes's critics in the 1960s and 1970s, with Charles Baxter and Alan Williamson identifying structural divisions operative in *Nightwood* and seeing the novel as a 'web of personal relationships' (Baxter) or

104   *The New Modernist Novel: Criticism and the Task of Reading*

a 'contrapuntal relationship between two distinct plots' (Williamson) divided between the doctor as centre and Robin as centre.[97] But the novel's frequent phrases in French, German, Italian, Latin and other languages suggest a partial identification of the Anglophone novel *Nightwood* with a modern French or German novel. In the guise of *fin-de-siècle* decadent fiction, on the model of Oscar Wilde's *The Picture of Dorian Gray*, or even on the model of French surrealist prose fiction, the work's tendency to produce admiration for style or passages over structure seems a valuable part of its style. *Nightwood* presents a nightworld situated geographically between the underworld milieus of Paris, Vienna and New York, and it resonates with some of the ways those underworlds had been represented in fiction in other languages and literatures. In this, Loy's *Insel* and Barnes's *Nightwood* are close, both meditating on a metropolitan underworld in a style suited to that space and valuing that style as a major medium of fiction.

A sense of harmony remained unstable, then, for these early readers of *Nightwood*, even on an informed reading, despite the polished feel of the novel. The novel they sought was not necessarily what they found, and coherence or unity was a special sticking-point. For Coleman, a reading that values the style of passages, as she does, meets a problem of where to begin with reading, since according to Coleman, Barnes begins in the wrong place, with Felix. In its high-wire performance of a knowing clumsiness, the challenges *Nightwood* posed to its critics, despite their enthusiasm, is one measure of its newness.

Ezra Pound's limerick about Barnes, with which this chapter began, recalls Eliot's treatment of *The Antiphon* in the draft blurb he wrote in 1956. In the draft, Eliot wrote, 'It might be said of Miss Barnes, who is incontestably one of the most original writers of our time, that never has so much genius been combined with so little talent.' This and other barbs in the draft blurb left Barnes 'furious'.[98] Phillip Herring notes that in response to Barnes's objection, Eliot 'squirmed and said he was only quoting', which Herring takes to refer to Isobel Patterson's review of *Ryder*, which used similar terms.[99] But Eliot may have been quoting a different source. In 1933, four years before Eliot had prefaced *Nightwood* in print, some of his verse was published in Ezra Pound's *Active Anthology* of that year. Pound's preface to the anthology quotes René Taupin quoting Condillac on genius and talent:

> Il y a deux espèces: le talent et le génie. Celui-là continue les idées d'un art ou d'une science connue, d'une manière propre à produire les effets qu'on en doit naturellement attendre. [. . .] Celui-ci ajoute au talent l'idée d'esprit, en quelque sort[e] créateur.[100]

In Condillac's original, the sentences leading up to Taupin's quote use the French word 'invention'. In English, the passage runs:

> We do not actually create ideas; what we do is to combine, by compounding and decompounding them, those that we have received from the senses. Invention consists in knowing how to form new combinations. There are two kinds: talent and genius.
>   Talent combines ideas of an art or science already known in the right manner to produce effects one would naturally expect. [. . .] Genius adds to talent the idea of the intellect as being somehow creative.[101]

The relation between genius and talent that Taupin cites in Condillac's work had a wider contemporary currency.[102] Given this quote from Taupin and in the context of Pound's lists of 'inventors', who, Pound deems, produce work that is genuinely new, Eliot's comment on Barnes might lose some of its harshness. Condillac's 'talent' sounds a little like Pound's category of 'masters', who popularise the new invention but are not inventors themselves. The category of 'genius' seems closer to Pound's rare instance, the 'inventor' who offers 'a definite contribution to the art of verbal expression'. These categories and associated reading lists are set out in *How to Read* (1931) and *ABC of Reading* (1934).[103] In Condillac's schema, it seems to be the inventor as genius, whose quality is 'original' and 'inimitable', whose work is valued artistically.[104]

In Eliot's cryptic tone, the senses of genius and talent are hard to pin down. But interpreted this way, his comment about genius and talent in the draft blurb may contain a compliment, even if it is insensitively and dismissively phrased. His 'genius' seems to pick up on the 'original writers' among whom Barnes numbers earlier in the sentence. In the context of Condillac's distinction, the sentence that immediately follows in Eliot's draft blurb, 'Her writing shatters the normal structure of the English (or of the American) language',[105] might now seem an impressive feat, adequate to 'genius'.[106] The idea perhaps picks up on the 'right to use words of his own fashioning' heralded by the 1929 'Proclamation' of the 'Revolution of the Word' in *transition*.[107] Eliot's blurb is for *The Antiphon*, but his assessment of Barnes's writing must also be shaped by *Nightwood*.

Indeed, two other sources close to Barnes during the revisions to *Nightwood* seem to share some of this vocabulary of genius. One is Edwin Muir, who described *Nightwood* as 'an undeniable work of genius' in a highly complimentary review,[108] and later used the word to describe *The Antiphon* in a letter to Eliot while Barnes was redrafting the play. Eliot's draft blurb to *The Antiphon* may reflect Muir's word.[109] The other source is *Nightwood*'s impassioned defender in extended

106 *The New Modernist Novel: Criticism and the Task of Reading*

correspondence to T. S. Eliot, Emily Coleman.[110] Eliot's distinction between 'genius' and 'talent' seems to echo Coleman's praise for Barnes's 'genius' alongside her outspoken reservations about Barnes's ability to organise her own writing. Coleman drafted to Eliot, 'It is strange, to me, that anyone of such great unconscious intelligence should be as wanting in a kind of intellect as the writer of this book seems to be.'[111] To Barnes, she wrote similarly, praising her intelligence yet characterising it as wanting in the same terms.[112] Coleman uses the word 'genius' to describe Barnes or her writing in both draft letters to Eliot, and she calls Barnes 'unconscious of the design' of *Nightwood* in the second letter.[113] Eliot later wrote to Barnes, of Coleman, that 'She certainly thought you the greatest genius living, which I won't deny either.'[114] Perhaps Eliot felt he was quoting Coleman.

Parts of Eliot's preface to *Nightwood*, including some of the lines quoted above, seem to respond to other vocabulary and judgements favoured by Coleman. She wrote to Eliot recommending that he think of *Nightwood* 'as a spiritual document, and not a novel'.[115] Eliot's assertion in the preface seems, in this light, to respond directly to such a claim: 'To say that *Nightwood* will appeal primarily to readers of poetry does not mean that it is not a novel, but that it is so good a novel that only sensibilities trained on poetry can wholly appreciate it.' He distinguishes Matthew as being more 'conscious' than those around him, echoing Coleman's vocabulary in describing Barnes's intelligence.[116] These echoes are merely suggestive, but it may be that Coleman's discussions with Eliot informed some of the questions and vocabulary of his preface to *Nightwood*. If so, it is worth considering that her sense of the book's value as accessible in excerpted sentences and passages may relate to Eliot's clear demarcation of the book's 'prose style' as the locus of its value. In other words, between Coleman and Eliot, *Nightwood* becomes a model for a modernism that can be read by passages or by style as a way to seek the whole work, even if that model troubles each critic in some ways. Eliot's unpublished draft blurb to *The Antiphon* may owe some of its ideas to Pound's introduction to his *Active Anthology*, and both it and the preface to *Nightwood* may owe some of their thinking about prose style to Emily Coleman.

Eliot clearly had serious misgivings about *The Antiphon*, and the draft blurb as a whole was unkind to a degree that Barnes had not anticipated. But the judgement of Barnes as genius is perhaps worth extracting from Barnes's disappointment to consider in its own right. Where in Coleman's letters, the word 'genius' signifies a congenital intelligence that is at odds with order, the more familiar meanings are 'an exceptionally intelligent or talented person' or 'innate intellectual or creative power of an exceptional or exalted type'.[117] Eliot's repeated use of the word (1945 in the letter to Barnes, 1956 in the draft blurb) offers a common thread between the two meanings. If, in line with Eliot's comment, Barnes is reconsidered as 'genius' rather than 'talent', as that suggested rare category of genuine creator, on Eliot's prompt if not according to him, then even within an established modernist framework, her work with narrative fiction might be more relevant to an established modernism than it has sometimes seemed.[118]

What Eliot still doesn't have available to him, in the late 1950s, is a more articulate vocabulary for describing the genius of Barnes's writing. The draft blurb is forced back only to comparison with 'Middleton, Ford and Tourneur' over 'any living writer', recalling the appeal to 'Elizabethan tragedy' in the preface to *Nightwood*.[119] But such a critical vocabulary for Barnes's work has been developing over several decades of Barnes criticism. The more complex critiques of modernism since the late twentieth century may be a required step for criticism to flourish on Barnes.[120] Barnes's writing, however, is not the only case of an author whose work may differ from Eliot's critical account of modernism, or from influential mid-century accounts of modernism accounts that he helped to shape – that differ by prizing style in passages, with all the complexities of tone that a devotion to style might bring out in the novel form. The following two chapters take up aspects of the relationship between critical reading and the text in John Rodker's *Adolphe 1920* and Mina Loy's *Insel*. These works have received comparatively little critical response, yet both were, like *Nightwood*, contributions to an active contemporary enquiry into the possibilities of narrative fiction.

Chapter 4

Adolphe 1920 and Modernism

'The finest French novel in the English language'

John Rodker's *Adolphe 1920* was recovered and republished in Andrew Crozier's 1996 selection of Rodker's work, *Poems and Adolphe 1920*. The novella was first published serially in 1927–28 by Ezra Pound in his little magazine *The Exile*, and Ludmila Savitzky translated it into French for serialisation in *La revue européenne* in 1927. *Adolphe 1920* was, in a sense, a French as well as an English novella. It was the third of Rodker's novels to be published in French translation, but only the first to be published in English. The two earlier published novels were *Montagnes russes* (1923, English title 'The Switchback') and *Dartmoor* (1926), both translated by Ludmila Savitzky.[1] *Adolphe 1920* was brought out in English by the Aquila Press in 1929, but as Ian Patterson notes, the press went bankrupt three days afterwards, which affected the distribution of the book.[2] Crozier's selection contains the first republication of *Adolphe 1920* since 1929. This makes *Adolphe 1920* an interesting case of a new modernist novel: one that was written from within modernist circles and published in modernist little magazines, but that was not generally recognised as part of the critical landscape of modernism before the 1990s.

In this chapter, I show how *Adolphe 1920* tends to elude description according to accounts of narrative voice sharpened on other modernist writing, in part because it prioritises the representation of mood and feeling over voice. The novella's prose style provoked strong responses from Wyndham Lewis and other contemporaries, and the chapter gives some context, both literary and cultural, to contemporary claims of distaste. While *Adolphe 1920* has a clear ambition to be read alongside Pound, Eliot and Joyce, its connections to modern French writing go beyond those of these authors. Rodker reportedly called Ford Madox Ford's 1915 *The Good Soldier* 'the finest French novel in the English language', but the compliment could be turned back to *Adolphe 1920*.[3] In the final section I consider this novella's version of the modern, and in particular its connections to nineteenth-century French decadence and to music-hall performance. This novella's decadent traits and its different version of the modern from Rodker's more well-known contemporaries suggest a different perspective on modernist fiction.

Before the recovery of his poetry and fiction, Rodker was known as a publisher and reviewer of modernism. In London in 1919 and 1920, his Ovid Press published quality editions of works by Ezra Pound, T. S. Eliot, Wyndham Lewis, Henri Gaudier-Brzeska, Edward Wadsworth and Roald Kristian, along with Rodker's *Hymns*, aiming 'to bring before the public work that was considered advanced'.[4] In 1920, Rodker printed Oscar Wilde's *To M. B. J.* without the Ovid Press imprint. Rodker's publications in 1919–20 show a sharp aesthetic and professional sense for what would later become known as British modernism.[5] In 1920 the Ovid Press encountered major financial difficulties and effectively closed, but Rodker continued to work as a printer and publisher,[6] and in 1922 he served as co-publisher, with the Egoist Press, of the second impression of *Ulysses*.[7] Rodker had also been a regular contributor of poetry, short pieces and reviews to literary magazines, among them *Poetry*, *The Egoist*, *The Little Review* and *Others*. His first volume of verse, *Poems*, was published in 1914.[8] In 1917 Pound wrote to Margaret Anderson, 'Rodker has convinced me at last, that he "has it in him"';[9] in 1919 Rodker took over Pound's position as London editor of *The Little Review*.[10] These involvements suggest a writer and reviewer with a strong enthusiasm for an emerging modernism and a publisher ready to take on considerable financial risks to make this new writing available.[11] Andrew Crozier details the debts of Rodker's later writing to his early work with theatre, music and the 'Choric School' of dance, and argues that 'if we are to read Rodker fully we need to renegotiate the canons of modernist decorum which condition our taste, and recognise that Rodker was able to make of modernism something more than we expect'.[12]

Rodker's reviews, publications and translations reflect a modern consciousness beyond an Anglophone modernism. He opened his Casanova Press in 1922,[13] and at the time of writing *Adolphe 1920*, he had evidently been occupied with this press, which published at least fourteen volumes and sets of volumes between 1922 and 1926. These included translations from Baudelaire, Balzac, Rémy de Gourmont and François Villon, and Rodker's own translation of *The Lay of Maldoror* by the comte de Lautréamont, of which five sections had been serialised in *Broom* in 1922.[14] The press also published a broader range of material: translations of Giacomo Casanova's *Memoirs* and translations of Arabic literature, including *The Book of the Thousand Nights and One Night* (printed privately); translations of classical texts by Juvenal and Theocritus; and other work. Returning Rodker to modernism brings

110   *The New Modernist Novel: Criticism and the Task of Reading*

Anglophone modernism closer to modern French writing. Rodker's literary interests indicate a modernism that even now, reads differently from the modernism of his contemporaries.

The Temporality of Reading

Citing Andrew Crozier's comment above, Drew Milne observes that:

> Rodker's importance as a publisher and translator in the London–Paris modernist nexus [. . .] has long been recognized by scholars of literary modernism. More difficult, however, is the process of learning to read Rodker's poetry and poetic novel *Adolphe 1920* as more than merely secondary examples of familiar modernist paradigms.

More generally, 'Within academic literary accommodations, the critical focus on the European and Anglo–American modernisms of Yeats, Joyce, Pound and Eliot has overshadowed the range of alternative modernist poetic practices developed in Britain', such as the work of Mina Loy.[15] In other words, learning to read *Adolphe 1920* may open up a new set of poetic practices to critical intelligence. It is possible that such work may also suggest renewed critical tools with which to approach both more familiar modernist writing and other new modernist writing.

Rodker writes about a new potential direction for literary writing in his pamphlet *The Future of Futurism*. In the pamphlet, Rodker uses the term 'Futurism' more widely than Italian Futurists did: 'To-day, if writing is called Futurist, it is generally because words or ideas are found in free association'; Rodker archly includes 'all those artistic activities called revolutionary by the academies, incomprehensible by the man in the street'. For Rodker, in one possible development of literature, 'descriptions' will be

> the slow motion film of writing. The deliberate dropping stars of the tiny parachute in the Naples aquarium will be taken in detail, caught at each momentary iridescent flash; or the detail of every least irregularity of some seemingly perfect surface analysed as far as human ingenuity will take it.[16]

This statement about writing in relation to detail and temporality is intriguing for considering *Adolphe 1920*'s exploration of a prose style.

Rodker's statement is also intriguing because of its dependence on a concept of film. In *Cinema and Modernism*, David Trotter notes that

Adolphe 1920 is 'a text preoccupied with cinema', focusing his discussion on the protagonist's encounter with a mutoscope in the first section. Trotter cites Pound's comment in the final issue of *The Exile* that the 'success' of films like Walter Ruttmann's *Berlin: City Symphony* 'should flatten out the opposition (to Joyce, to me, to Rodker's Adolphe) with steam-rolling ease and commodity, not of course that the authors intended it'.[17] My aim here is to open up an investigation of the prose style of *Adolphe 1920*, the source of the 'opposition' noted by Pound, and to address some aspects of this novella's contemporary reception. In doing so, I take up selected literary contexts of the problem of description in the prose style of *Adolphe 1920*.

Some account of the novella may be useful. *Adolphe 1920* follows its protagonist, Dick, through a single day, closely recording events, perceptions, and mental and emotional states. Dick awakes in a hotel and then wanders through the circus that is being set up outside it. He intends to meet his lover Angela, but he finds she has sent a telegram instead; he moves through the fairground, visiting stalls, and his ex-lover Monica finds him in the crowd. In the fairground, with Monica or alone, Dick ruminates on Monica and Angela, and the novella's meagre thread of story reaches a denouement of sorts in a visit to a bar where music-hall performers sing and dance. The action is most likely set in a town north-east of Bordeaux, a location suggested by the places that Dick expects the circus to visit and by the fact that Angela's telegram arrives from Bordeaux, this despite the fact that all the characters use English, the performers sing in English, and the printed funeral announcement is in English.

The novella opens with the following paragraph:

> What had slit up his sleep? His eyes opened but the mind closed again. Piercing sweet the dawn star pierced him, his bowels shivering round it. On swooning mist and the far billowing of a lugubrious howl he swayed, till falling nearer, high bursting bubbles pulled him from his sleep. Morning lies round him. Behind the inn a bugle, in a far land heard before. A tent. A child skips, a trumpet to its mouth; a Moor throws up a ball. His soul fled after her through the cold light; snow falls, whirling . . .[18]

Notable in this opening is an interest in narrative voice that does not seem to follow well recognised models. 'What had slit up his sleep?' seems to open the passage with free indirect style: it records the character's words and thought but keeps its distance with the past-perfect, narrative tense of 'had slit up' and the third-person pronoun 'his'. But from 'his eyes opened', or from 'the mind' rather than 'his mind', the sentences that follow are less clearly marked as free indirect style or otherwise.

112 *The New Modernist Novel: Criticism and the Task of Reading*

The pull of these sentences is the richness of the language rather than the illusion of closeness to or distance from a particular character. For example, the change to present tense in 'Morning lies round him' may indicate waking in a waking scene, and as such would render the earlier details inconsequential or merely dreamed, but the details of the present share an obscurity with those given in past tense. It is the illusion of the protagonist's feelings, rather than the illusion of sharing his consciousness, that seems to be at issue here. Comparison with the corrected typescript shows that before the final version of *Adolphe 1920*, Rodker suppressed some of the verbs identifying tense: that is, verbs limiting the subject's temporal relation to the sense perceptions.[19] In this opening paragraph, Rodker is working with possibilities of narrative voice that are available to him in 1925, but the work he does with them in this paragraph suggests a different technical focus, where he is less concerned with perspective or point of view than were some of his contemporaries. Notably, there is less concern here with perspective than there is in Joyce's *Ulysses*, which one might say is entranced with perspective. *Ulysses*'s use of perspective, in particular, does not equip us for Rodker's opening, where the poetics of the third sentence – 'Piercing sweet the dawn star pierced him, his bowels shivering round it' – are less concerned with voice than with the suggestive properties of language, or with the body's place in experience, or the temporality of the act of reading, or even the poetic resonance between Rodker's novella and his earlier work, here the poem 'Southern Syncopated Singers'.[20]

Andrew Crozier's comment on *Adolphe 1920* is also relevant here:

> The writing is Joycean in its formal concern for prose texture, and Joycean also in its device of the textual analogue. But whereas Joyce's textual analogy is an epic action, Rodker's is all psychology. *Adolphe 1920* can constitute an advance on Joyce [. . .] because Rodker's treatment of psychology does not give subjectivity textual privilege: the mode of narration has passed beyond interior monologue, and abolished the separation of interior and exterior domains.[21]

In other words, Rodker's prose might require tools different from those developed for subjectivity and related narrative modes.

In calling *Adolphe 1920* 'an advance on Joyce', Crozier echoes Pound, who in discussing William Carlos Williams's *The Great American Novel* identified *Adolphe 1920* as the only 'other offspring from *Ulysses* [. . .] I have seen possessing any value', and who asserted that Rodker's novella was 'indubitably a "development", a definite step in the general progress of writing'.[22] Certainly, the abundance of literary

Adolphe 1920 *and Modernism*   **113**

allusions in *Adolphe 1920* suggests that the novella be read alongside the work of Pound, Eliot and Joyce. Pound's comment is sufficiently general to assert a grouping and development without articulating specific common characteristics. But Crozier's point is that Rodker does something new and that his writing is worth reading as part of modernism. The comparison with Joyce, for both Crozier's and my arguments, opens up avenues for reading *Adolphe 1920* through its differences from *Ulysses*, and need not locate Rodker's art as derivative or corollary.

Crozier's statement of Rodker's 'advance on Joyce' locates the development as a treatment of 'psychology', where interior and exterior domains are no longer distinct. Edmond Jaloux used the word 'psychologie' in 1923 to introduce Rodker's fiction to a French readership, referring not to *Adolphe 1920* but to Rodker's earlier novel *Montagnes russes*, which was published only in French translation (English title 'The Switchback'), with a preface by Jaloux. Jaloux writes that as an English-language writer Rodker distinguishes himself by 'la profondeur de sa psychologie' (the depth of [his treatment of] psychology), among other things, and he praises the psychology of Rodker's novel as 'juste' (sound) and 'exacte' (precise). Commenting on Rodker's poem 'The Gas Flame', Jaloux observes that modern poetry is developing a new logic, 'une logique psychologique [. . .] au lieu d'une logique discursive' (a psychological logic in place of a discursive logic).[23] He places Rodker at the forefront of this movement, within both a Francophone literary heritage and an Anglophone one, and both backgrounds, for Jaloux, contribute to the innovation evident in Rodker's writing. For Jaloux, then, Rodker is working with other contemporaries, Joyce among them, and his representation of psychology is his distinguishing characteristic.

Rodker's primary 'textual analogue' in *Adolphe 1920* is a French novel, Benjamin Constant's novella *Adolphe*, published in 1816. However, although Constant's *Adolphe* is evidently concerned with the shaping of emotion, its relevance to Rodker's *Adolphe 1920* is complicated. Ian Patterson notes that Rodker, 'unsure' about the title's allusion to Constant's *Adolphe*, might have been persuaded by Pound to retain it, and he points out that the title is also an echo of *Paulina 1880* by Pierre Jean Jouve. Rodker knew of Jouve's novel in 1925, the year it was published, and in the 1930s he translated two works by Jouve.[24] *Paulina 1880*'s interest in its protagonist's mental and emotional development and disintegration offers substantial material for comparison with *Adolphe 1920*. But comparison with Constant's *Adolphe* is particularly revealing for Rodker's novella.

Although the two texts offer 'parallel' psychological investigations,[25] the inconsequential nature of decisions and actions in *Adolphe 1920* differentiates it sharply from *Adolphe*. The concept of inconsequence as

114   *The New Modernist Novel: Criticism and the Task of Reading*

a quality of the modern is discussed by David Trotter in relation to Ford Madox Ford's impressionism: 'For Ford, impressionism was a relation between consequence and inconsequence. [. . .] In Ford's impressionism, [. . .] it is paranoia which breaks chronology, which discerns the patterns of consequence buried deep beneath the ostentatiously inconsequential.'[26] In contrast to the carefully planned or 'ostentatious' inconsequence of the modernist text *Adolphe 1920*, Constant's preface to the second edition of *Adolphe* emphasises the weight of consequence that binds his characters in their impasse:

> Some people have asked me what Adolphe ought to have done in order to experience and to cause less suffering. His position and that of Ellénore were irremediable, and that is precisely what I intended. [. . .] What is necessary for happiness in life is not to begin such relationships: once you have started along that path, you have only the choice of evils.[27]

Constant's Adolphe, like Rodker's Dick, is irresolute, unable to break decisively away from Ellénore's love and dependence, but unlike Dick's his vacillation repeatedly precipitates increased responsibility in a worsening situation. His retrospective first-person account of the affair and the foreword and correspondence of the 'editor' lay out a frame in which the story can be told in the biographical detail of cause and effect. The story is framed in a way that anticipates a reader's moral judgement from above the characters – that is, from a position of greater moral understanding than is available to Adolphe or Ellénore.

By contrast, nothing is resolved at the end of *Adolphe 1920*, and no moral resolution is made available. None of the characters expresses any feeling of responsibility, and both Dick and Angela deny responsibility. Neither character provides a model of sincerity in love, although Monica's demands on Dick mirror Ellénore's dependence on Adolphe. Rather than telling the defining episodes of a life, Rodker's novella dramatises a single day and keeps open an irresolute state of affairs through the length of the novella. Its ending denies any finality, making its suggestion of a story merely a situation that is utterly repeatable and even likely to be repeated. The novella asserts its characters' relationships not as a phase common to the young, as they are in Constant,[28] but as intrinsically modern. Constant's novella, then, does offer a study of 'psychology', but comparison with Rodker's novella suggests the importance of inconsequence, repeatability, irresolution and their representation in prose in 1920. Dick is sketched as if he could be any other member of the crowd that fills the fairground in *Adolphe 1920*; the mood that Rodker's novella represents is located between the subjectivity of its individual protagonist and a more generic, collective 1920 set of postwar experiences.

Adolphe 1920 *and Modernism*   115

The representation of feeling is obviously important in *Adolphe 1920*'s movement away from various other poetic and narrative practices. Selecting a sample passage to analyse is fraught, since any selection meets the problem of variation across the novella. The passage is taken from the novella's seventh section:

> From time to time Monica would push up to him, murmuring you do love me, dont you, and he pushed roughly back, saying yes, or no, or do shut up. But both were happy that the air was no longer charged, and his gaiety was an armour through which her longings could not pierce. Now spongy and humid dark buoyed them up. Gaping unwinking fish nosed at them through square green portholes, glided to earth like birds, like birds swam up through yellow weeds or settled pecking into the fine sand like a flight of starlings; flat fish undulated rapidly across the tank like galloping horses, their eyes starting, their bellies rasing the earth, or flurried in the cascade of bubbles which spluttering into the tank rose again to run in clots of quicksilver on the waters surface.
>
> Some click of stone struck his middle ear; some other fish. Her cries came to him upon the water, she gaped bewildered in the hard ways his jealousy had circumscribed. Her watery world was wide. His heart leapt yearning after her. She swam from him through the cold sea, fluttering tight and small, her mind a blank but lured to a treacherous luminous point, or rose and sank to a vibration, not sensed by him. Undine . . . yet she had come to him. Transfuse me . . . give me a soul. How, why? Now he would not see the cheeks flush with blood again, the eyes soften, the breast rise, and his own soul was flying from him inside her, she unwitting; yet he must find her again where like a box, remotely hid she held his heart, a 'vanishing wife'. But it could not be himself had sent her off and there had been no compact. No compact, true, nothing was said, yet drifting to land, had he not pulled a twig, had it not cried out warning him, and when as though despite himself he plucked another, had she not come from the river. (156)

The passage is an instance of this text's ability to move between the perceived and mental worlds of its protagonist. These constitute a hermetic present, disconnected from the history of character and plot. There is no reference, for instance, to Monica's status as Dick's ex-lover: her existence in the passage is only in the terms of their momentary exchange, her advances that are answered indifferently by Dick. In the first sentence, Dick's shifting responses are held in suspension by the shape of the sentence, which indicates his indifference with the conjunction 'or', rendering each response inconsequential. Monica's gesture can be repeated indefinitely because none of Dick's answers has any finality. For the characters, the options are held in suspension and decision is postponed. The indefiniteness of their exchange, which remains inconclusive and open to repetition, camouflages the insistence of Monica's questioning and of

116   *The New Modernist Novel: Criticism and the Task of Reading*

Dick's refusal to give a consistent response. But at the level of the sentence, the reading progresses differently. The forward pull of the sentence means that each of Dick's responses is pushed aside and discarded by the one that follows, so that the sentence moves successively through the options rather than keeping them open as possibilities in the same way as the completed scene does. The shifts take place between the phrases in 'saying yes, or no, or do shut up', with each version replacing the previous one. At the level of the sentence, then, there is a forward movement through different states of mind, where the progression of the writing necessitates a constant movement onwards from momentary decisions, but the impression is one of sustained indecision and perpetual vacillation on Dick's part.

In the remainder of the passage, there are echoes of this unstable succession of moments. Dick and Monica's movement through the aquarium is given as a series of present moments; two successive groups of fish give way in the unruly figuration to other animals and to the 'clots of quicksilver on the waters surface'. Following the protagonist's mind, the writing remains at the border between external and mental apprehension, shifting between perception and interpretation. The paragraph break prefigures a leap from the aquarium to a world that is entirely mental. With the sentence 'Some click of stone struck his middle ear; some other fish', the focus shifts to Dick's thoughts of Angela. In this sentence, the pressure of plausibility is temporarily removed, but the aquarium environment provides a ready figural landscape in which to ground the mental images. In moving between the aquarium and Angela, the passage temporarily deprives a reader of the ability to anticipate its movement. This is already evident in the figurative excess of the description of the fish, which succeeded, above, in transforming them unexpectedly into birds and horses. Such temporary dislocations of a reader's grip on the text are a recognisable aspect of the dense prose of *Adolphe 1920*. In several figurative passages, a reader constructs what meaning is available on the basis of what has been read at the level of the sentence, and the process of reading in time is one of continually revising the context that would frame any emerging meaning. In this way the identification of significant contexts alters with the movement of a reader through Rodker's text, here shifting from the aquarium that Dick is watching to Angela, who occupies his thoughts. The novella's style offers not a syntactically wrought structure of suggestion on the model of Mallarmé's prose poems, but a focus on the temporality of the movement of reading through the fiction.

This temporality is evident too in the repetition of words, figures and motifs through the novella. In the passage quoted above, 'their eyes

Adolphe 1920 *and Modernism*   117

starting' repeats 'his starting eyes touch glass' of the mutoscope machine
(138); the fish are momentarily 'horses', which belong to the circus (133
and 134–35); the phrase 'her watery world was wide', of Angela, revisits
the 'wide empty street of Angela' in the novella's opening (133); 'some
click of stone' and the 'eyes' and 'breast' of Angela recall the mechanised
wax Snow White and the horror of mortal bodies (140). While such
reworkings invite a memory of the earlier figure, in each case they seem
not to require it. The word 'heart' occurs twice in the passage: 'His heart
leapt yearning after her [. . .] yet he must find her again where like a box,
remotely hid she held his heart.' This word has occurred in Dick's recol-
lection of the 'wagging heart' of mummified bodies in a crypt (136), and
it has been pivotal to another early moment, a confusion between technical and actual animation via the mutoscope machine: 'He put his eyes
on its eyes, his heart on its heart, listening deeply, anxiously; forgetting
the fair, his fellows reading other hearts round him' (137). In the passage
here, the 'box' that holds 'his heart' recalls the mutoscope machine, with
'a woman for a heart', but the figure is substantially restructured: Angela
herself becomes the 'box', which now contains 'his heart', which takes
the place of a mechanical animation. Elsewhere, inanimate hearts are a
direct reminder of death: in the tent showing preserved body parts is the
'airman's heart snapped from its two frail tubes in some vertiginous fall'
(141). These broken hearts are less a repository for accumulated meaning than an index of the shifts through which this text is passing: 'heart'
absorbs significance from successive contexts rather than accreting significance through the novella, as each new context revises the previous
one, temporarily replacing it. Progressing through this novella's dense
textual surface produces patterns of a long prose poem as well as patterns of narrative. A decadent treasuring of word over thing is partly
evident here, but the work that *Adolphe 1920* does with the narration
of mood and feeling renders the narrative form meaningful too, shifting
the essence of the style from dwelling on selected words to the temporality of reading this dense prose as narrative fiction.[29]

The trope of forgetting runs obsessively through Dick's reflections on
Angela, and it serves as the motif for their relationship: 'Merciful for-
getfulness, how much she had to be grateful to it. / But did he not forget
too? / They stood drinking, their bark drifting, eyes in eyes; and though
he knew the philtre good for three years only yet he drank to that eter-
nity' (151). Just such forgetting carries the inconsequence dramatised at
the level of the writing in Rodker's text. Individual moments of vacillation and forays into new scenes are often discarded by the movement
of the text, which yet collects them into a psychological account. The
result is a flatness that resists structuration by the conventions of voice

118   *The New Modernist Novel: Criticism and the Task of Reading*

or story, since every fictional moment here asks to be considered on its own immediate terms regardless of causal, perspectival or other references to the discourse.

In this way, the novella's images and scenes are presented without any scaffolding for judgement: the prose style excludes authorial or narrative comment. Such a style seems to offer no distanced position for a reader. The novella is invested in provoking an immersion in a 1920 mood, not in an evaluation of that mood. This interest in mood immersion resonates with the short, wordless mood dramas Rodker published in 1915–19, collected as *Theatre Muet*.[30] These short dramas portray situations of intense but nebulous emotional content, depicting the ebb and flow of emotional states without resolution. In his article 'The Theatre' in 1914, Rodker compares the effect of such plays to 'a smell of musk wafted through a theatre', affecting the audience more 'poignantly' and 'profoundly' than merely intellectual plays where, implicitly, judgement and engagement can potentially be withheld.[31] In *Adolphe 1920*, the suppression of either quotation marks or dashes as speech markers, as well as of apostrophes and some question marks, emphasises the drawing-back of authority. The novella's capacity, as a whole piece of writing, to collect its images without hierarchisation and in defiance of the principle of non-contradiction precludes judgement:[32] the events and thoughts that the writing claims to record are registered without narratorial comment. This lack of comment forces a reader to consider the vacillations and interpersonal exchanges as they stand, since the lack denies recourse to any pre-established, intellectual moral code.

'Mawkishness à la Lautréamont': Taste and the Reception of *Adolphe 1920*

This prose style suits its aesthete protagonist, who is forgetful of all but the present; but Dick is an aesthete protagonist with a literary history. That history is represented in part by Benjamin Constant's *Adolphe*, but in 1925–26 Rodker also had access to the *fin-de-siècle* type exemplified in the decadent Des Esseintes of Huysmans's *À rebours* (1884), 'the breviary of the decadence'.[33] Rodker commented enthusiastically in *The Little Review* that 'Des Esseintes has never been that exotic the 90's found him, for all men are his peers.'[34] There are resonances between Huysmans's Des Esseintes and the title characters of Wilde's *The Picture of Dorian Gray* (1891) and Baudelaire's *La Fanfarlo* (1847), the latter of which draws in turn on Constant's *Adolphe* and possibly on Balzac's

Sarrasine (1830). The structure of Baudelaire's story bears some resemblance to Constant's *Adolphe* in that its hero, Samuel Cramer, undertakes insincerely the seduction of Fanfarlo, and they fall in love. But the ending reverses *Adolphe*: Fanfarlo discovers Samuel's motivations, and she abandons him despite their love. The story's wit is of a sensational kind, with the plot frequently taking new directions resulting in a particularly playful ending. In this wit is an inconsequence that differentiates *La Fanfarlo* from Constant's *Adolphe* and looks towards the dramatisation of inconsequence in the prose of Rodker's *Adolphe 1920*.

A decadent heritage informs Dick's self-consciousness. At the same time, however, the aesthete protagonist is given a very different context in 1920s modernism. Dick's vacillation is incorporated into the prose style; the interrogation of contemporary states of mind also includes a record of the protagonist's momentary changes of mind, his bodily and emotional responses to his surroundings and the way his reflections and emotions are registered on the body. This departs from the decadence of Huysmans and others, but it seems to share with some decadent writing a sense of uncomfortable intimacy or awkward frankness. For example, a statement shortly after the passage quoted above has a confessional quality in its frankness about a harmful emotion: 'Sometimes he loved her, loving him; for that too he hated her' (156).

Other passages record the physical impact of sensations and emotions:

> He went into the street. The smell of garlic and vanilla was violent, made his mouth water, tempted him to a second meal. He wondered could he eat again, wanted to, yet tore himself away. But then he thought it would be good to have a weight in his stomach and at the next stove ate mussels with relish, with nausea too and an anxious rapidity. The weight inside him got comfortably heavier and he sat watching the street, which slow oily and with sudden eddies loitered under a storm of beating drums, blaring cymbals, rattling mechanical pianos, noises of all kinds from boxes of all shapes. (137)

These lines resonate with Rodker's motif of constipation in his later novel *Memoirs of Other Fronts*, where the motif assumes an intimacy of reader–text relationship not readily available in contemporary avant-garde writing in English. As discussed above, the events of Rodker's novella are not immediately offered for moral judgement by a reader, and in this way the novella assumes a reader's indulgence in any communication, regardless of propriety or decorum. This is a characteristic *Adolphe 1920* shares in part with *Ulysses*, where impropriety was a problem for early readers such as Rebecca West, as well as for the courts.[35] But in Rodker's case the interrogation takes place at the level of direct sensations and emotions, avoiding the narrative distance that tends to characterise even *Ulysses*'s more awkward moments.

Within the novella, the physicality evident in the above quotation is linked with the First World War, notably in the episode of the tent showing the preserved body parts of soldiers. One of the poems that was reworked for *Adolphe 1920* and included in the 1930 *Collected Poems* was 'War Museum – Royal College of Surgeons'. 'War Museum' displays a disgust with the destruction wreaked on the bodies of soldiers, one that is in use in the third section of *Adolphe 1920*. Among other uses of vocabulary and images from the poem, the line 'an airman's heart snapped from its two frail tubes in some vertiginous fall' (141) borrows from the poem's opening stanza. In the poem, 'This is the airman's heart. / He fell five hundred feet / and the impetus snapped the hurtling heart / from its two frail tubes.'[36] The satirical tone of this poem is not evidently taken up in the novel, but the poem is clearly reworked. Similarly visceral responses emerge at other points in the novella. Laura Marcus comments on Dick's 'nausea and fear' in response to the film he watches; she notes that the terms of this disgust also echo the images used to describe the facial close-up by Jean Epstein, who emphasises the close-up's 'proximity' and potential 'intimacy'.[37] *Adolphe 1920* returns repeatedly to the ideas of disgust, revulsion and rottenness, especially as associated with human skin, in the skin of the film's protagonist and of other characters and body parts elsewhere in the novella. Such disgust, or its double, the sense of potential intimacy, may also be passed on to a reader of the novella.

This is suggested by Wyndham Lewis's response to *Adolphe 1920*, which, as Ian Patterson notes, he records in his novel *The Apes of God*. In the chapter introducing the writer Ratner, who will be a central character in the book, Rodker's *Adolphe 1920* is satirised directly.[38] Ratner types the following:

> Why had Marjorie left him hanging on the railings ? A tide of nauseous scourings with sickening drops of livid foam poured over him, he made headway against it and he found the flood had subsided. He was free, but why had Marjorie not returned or sent a telegram to say not good enough or better luck next time, anything but *Marjorie* only, it was a sickening feeling. This was intolerable. It was the ravings of a lonely and forsaken chapman. *Marseilles*.
>
> How why and where ? Should he reach Marjorie if he was forced to return ? Had she really drowned herself ? For him ? The sickening thought that it might be for him almost prevented him from buying the ticket. The storm burst. He was overwhelmed with a tempest of tremendous jealousy, it turned his stomach and made up his mind that he must

leave her neighbourhood for ever, this was final. Next time. Why could he not away ? Why could he not hence ? Always frustration, always struggle ! Life ! Why could he not strike his tent and depart for good ? It was the best way. Was it not as easy to go as to stay ? Not quite. He had forgotten the magnetic brown, darker in the right eye, with an electric-blue spot on the left.[39]

This passage emphasises qualities of indecision and indirection. As Patterson makes clear, the target is evidently *Adolphe 1920*, but the satire takes in Rodker's earlier fiction and his poetry, as well as his wider life and interests.[40]

Lewis's parody of the syntax of Rodker's successive states of mind subtly shifts the sophisticated rendering of consciousness that Rodker's prose makes available, turning it instead towards a childishness that fits with his attacks in *Time and Western Man*. The parody apes signature aspects of Rodker's prose style, including the tensions in temporality of the kind explored above. An example is Lewis's sentence 'He was overwhelmed with a tempest of tremendous jealousy, it turned his stomach and made up his mind that he must leave her neighbourhood for ever, this was final.' This sentence presents its protagonist's thoughts as a succession of events, but it suppresses the conceptual links between the different events. Instead, each new clause begins with 'it' or 'this', apparently referring to an idea that is satisfactorily completed and can be built on. But Rodker's prose style rarely works this way. Rather, suppression of causal or other conceptual links in *Adolphe 1920* tends to allow for an indefinite and shifting state of mind, as seen above in the discussion of the passage from the novella's seventh section. In the prose style of *Adolphe 1920*, thoughts tend to extend through experienced mental impressions, which might succeed each other or might be contemporaneous. Lewis's parody, in contrast, makes both the logical and temporal progression of thought seem clear and uncomplicated, breaking off and beginning anew each time with 'it' and 'this' as stable references. It is not surprising that Lewis's parody takes this path. For the author of *Time and Western Man*, Rodker's representation of fluctuating psychological states and their related physical impressions relies on an unproductive concept of time in individual experience. Lewis's parody effectively renders Rodker's intelligent prose that of a childish character unsure of his own mind.

What makes the parody stick, however, is the savage attack on Rodker and his writing as 'sickening'. Although 'sickening' and 'sicken' appear in *Adolphe 1920* (see, for example, 136, 137), and although recurrent nausea and disgust do form a complex motif in the novella, the word 'sickening'

122   *The New Modernist Novel: Criticism and the Task of Reading*

is not heavily developed by repetition through the novella, at least not to the degree that many other words and motifs are ('heart', for example). Lewis reads *Adolphe 1920* against the grain to isolate this word as sharply as he does. Rodker's writing is 'sickening' because it records emotions and indecision; Lewis's sleight-of-hand rendering of the temporality of Rodker's prose style is the substance of his claim that this prose is disgusting. For Lewis, Rodker's prose does not offer the clarity of something that can be perceived visually. Ratner, Lewis's character, laments the shortcomings of his own writing, articulating Lewis's objection: 'This was a *personal* prose !'[41] The intimacy of a 'personal' prose is set up as distinctly unpalatable regardless of the successful literary work done in developing a style that could *be* so personal. But for Lewis, Ratner is himself distasteful, and the terms of this distaste draw on contemporary antisemitism. The portrait is a virulently antisemitic depiction of Ratner, accompanied by attacks on his overlapping interests as publisher and author, on his physical appearance and on his effeminate and impotent character. David Ayers observes that Lewis's antisemitism is central to the construction of his character Ratner as representing the opposite of Lewis's own positions.[42] Ian Patterson details this antisemitism and shows how Rodker readily recognised himself in the portrait of Ratner and wrote a rejoinder, the novel 'An Ape of Genius', which remained unpublished.[43]

If Lewis's disgust at *Adolphe 1920* was invited by the novella, it also carried an uncomfortable context in his personal response to Rodker. The portrait of Ratner in *The Apes of God* echoes Lewis's own response to Rodker on first meeting him some time before July 1915. In a letter to Pound, Lewis described Rodker as 'most poisonous' and informed Pound, '[Rodker] told me he had written a lot of filthy sexual verse, which, if he sends it, I shall hang in the W.C. He described it as Verlainesque.' Lewis then insults Rodker's appearance as 'dirty'.[44] Although Lewis was characteristically cantankerous, the bigotry expressed here is repeated in *The Apes of God* and is already linked, at this much earlier time, both to Lewis's response to Rodker himself and to Rodker's interest in nineteenth-century French poetry.

Very few reviews of *Adolphe 1920* appeared, but Lewis was not the only reader to respond in this way to Rodker's writing. Harold Munro and Richard Aldington also record distaste, both of them in response to Rodker's 1920 volume of poems, *Hymns*, the last book-length literary work of Rodker's to appear in English before *Adolphe 1920*. In a letter to Rodker, Munro expressed his 'disgust' at the 'style, form, and psychological content of the poems' in *Hymns*.[45] Aldington reviewed the volume for the little magazine *Poetry*, contrasting the contribution of imagist F. S. Flint with Rodker's contribution: 'Where one is all candour, simplicity, naturalness and health, the other is affectation, insincerity, falseness and disease. I can find little in Mr Rodker's hymns which is not the expression of a vain and morbid sensibility.'[46] This quality in Rodker's verse provokes a series of personal responses from Aldington: 'My compassion is quenched by repulsion from this mawkishness à la Leautréamont [*sic*] [. . .] I am frankly sorry for Mr. Rodker, who finds life such a devastating and unpleasant process.'[47]

Aldington's and Munro's responses carry echoes of Max Nordau's strong distaste for *fin-de-siècle* aesthetics. For example, Nordau writes of the Joris-Karl Huysmans of *Là-bas*, 'This furnishes M. Huysmans with the opportunity of burrowing and sniffing with swinish satisfaction into the most horrible filth.'[48] Aldington's comments suggest that the vestiges of decadence in Rodker's writing lie in the writing's demands on its reader's attention, for instance in Aldington's awkwardly combined 'compassion' and 'repulsion'. For him, a reader's attention is required to respond to the depiction of a psychological state in the character. Despite Aldington's own translations of sections of Lautréamont's *Chants de Maldoror* for *The Dial* in 1914, in citing Lautréamont as the pernicious influence, Aldington positions Rodker's poetry within a decadent *fin-de-siècle* aesthetics, implicitly justifying his distaste.[49] For Aldington, then, an assessment of 'bad taste' in Rodker's poems stands in for a judgement of low literary value.

Maxwell Bodenheim defended Rodker against Aldington's criticism in a letter to the editor of *Poetry*. Where Aldington had questioned the value of Rodker's writing, Bodenheim questions the value of Aldington's criticism:

> I do not dislike candor, simplicity, naturalness and health, but I cannot see why they should have an endless monopoly on English poetry. [. . .] Besides, this charge of 'unhealthiness' is an easy and hollow gesture used by critics who possess no better arguments.

Bodenheim claims that Aldington adopts the critical method of distorting Rodker's meanings and selecting 'the poet's least representative lines' in order to make his case.[50] His response flags up the lack of critical rigour in Aldington's use of taste to condemn Rodker's writing, and this also suggests the strength of Aldington's distaste, which is so strong as to be insubordinate to contemporary critical demands.

Others responded more positively to Rodker's work and to *Adolphe 1920*, notably by placing it within a respectable literary heritage. Ezra Pound's comments on the novella, including his possible input regarding its title, consistently aligned it with other tasteful books.[51] For Pound,

124   *The New Modernist Novel: Criticism and the Task of Reading*

in addition to being born of *Ulysses*, *Adolphe 1920* is positioned in the form 'whose ideogram has been composed by Longus, Prevost, Benjamin Constant' (though Pound leaves Rodker off this list of representatives of *belles lettres* in his 1931 *How to Read*).[52] The anonymous reviewer in *The Spectator* calls the style 'highly wrought and poetic' and mentions Constant's *Adolphe*, identifying *Adolphe 1920*'s 'great virtue [. . .] in its understanding of the main character's interior life, his subjectivity'.[53] Clere Parsons, writing favourably of *Adolphe 1920* in *The Criterion*, emphasises the novella's positioning among other literary tendencies or movements, notably surrealism. For Parsons as for Aldington, 'The major formative influence upon Mr. Rodker's style is surely Lautrémont [*sic*]'; Parsons finds, however, that 'this prose is romantic in the most admirable sense; to read it is a pleasurable experience, a prick to all sluggish minds'.[54] To reach this conclusion, Parsons identifies in *Adolphe 1920* a movement from the 'psychological problem' as it appears in Constant, and also in *Adolphe 1920*, towards a 'literary art': the literary art is visible in 'the surréaliste stream' of the protagonist's reflections, a stream made up of 'the noises, odours, shapes and colours of the varied spectacles, vulgar, exciting, nauseous or fantastic'.[55] Parsons's review puts forward a difference between Rodker's earlier novel *Montagnes russes* and *Adolphe 1920*: the latter work's interest in psychology is now more carefully developed into a 'literary art'. For Parsons, taste is an aspect of Rodker's manipulation of his material rather than the sole ground for literary evaluation.

The nod here towards 'the surréaliste stream' suggests a different critical positioning of Lautréamont, one that nudges *Adolphe 1920* from the influence of a decadence exemplified by him to a surrealism that boasts him as precursor. In *The Diabolical Principle*, Lewis weighs in on the problem of Lautréamont's influence, and objects to the contemporary enthusiasm for the poet held by the editors of *transition*. Lewis attributes the editors' enthusiasm to their 'new Romanticism', which he associates with the 'diabolism' of Baudelaire, Huysmans and Wilde.[56] Ian Patterson records that the translation of *The Lay of Maldoror* that Lewis quotes at length is Rodker's, as published in the October 1927 issue of *transition*;[57] Lewis discusses the surrealists' interest in Lautréamont, and as he mentions, Philippe Soupault's edition of Lautréamont's *Oeuvres* had appeared in 1927, with a substantial biographical preface. Richard Aldington, similarly, wrote to Rodker to thank him for the copy of his translation of Lautréamont: 'I don't put lautreamont [*sic*] anything so high as the Surréalistes do, but I am sure he deserved an English translation.'[58] The preferences that inform both Lewis's and Aldington's responses to Rodker are related to their self-positioning in wider debates about literary value. In

Adolphe 1920 and Modernism   125

1921, by deploring the potential influence of *Ulysses* on younger writers, Aldington had, in Eliot's words, 'wailed at the flood of Dadaism which his prescient eye saw bursting forth at the tap of the magician's rod'.[59] In the responses to Rodker, these readers' distaste is a reminder that Rodker's poems and *Adolphe 1920* were close to various strands of deliquescent nineteenth-century French literature, which worked against these readers' concepts of new writing. Rodker responded to Lewis's comments in *The Diabolical Principle* by reflecting on the wilfulness of Lewis's dismissal of Lautréamont as 'vicious' and by asserting parallels between Lewis's own writing and Lautréamont's.[60] Rodker thus turns the tables on Lewis's criticisms by suggesting that Lautréamont's work has more in common with the work of Rodker's Anglo-American contemporaries than they would like to claim.

Huysmans and Lautréamont might be said to share a literary interest in disturbing their readers' comfort; in Lautréamont's *The Lay of Maldoror*, the assault on the comfort of the reader makes way for a prose not grounded in naturalism and not bound by social models of propriety. *Adolphe 1920*, however, lacks such a strongly programmatic intention to shock its readers, and in Rodker's novella, it is perhaps rather the awkward intimacy with the protagonist that arrests a contemporary reader and allows for new work with representation. In this way, details in *Adolphe 1920* might be read as unpalatable, but they might also be read as enabling a new positioning of the reader. Rodker's interest in the relationship between author and reader is clear from his essay on *Work in Progress*, where he raises for Joyce's late work 'the possibility of a complete symbiosis of reader and writer; the only obstacle which now remains being the inadequacy of the reader's sphere of reference – not to the emotional content – but to the ideas, objects and events given'.[61] Such a complete symbiosis of reader and writer, rather than an interpersonal exchange, is perhaps what Rodker is aiming at in *Adolphe 1920* through the suppression of explicit or implicit moral judgement in the prose. Such a 'symbiosis' might disallow the possibility of impropriety. Rather, granting the required indulgence makes possible the psychological insights referred to by Crozier, Patterson and Jaloux, rendering the details no longer improper.

But Lewis's and Aldington's distaste also raises a more general problem of taste as a criterion of value in twentieth-century literary criticism. As quoted above, Andrew Crozier calls for a renegotiation of 'the canons of modernist decorum which condition our taste'. Implicit in Crozier's comment is the claim that 1996 critical taste in modernist literature is shaped and limited by familiar or canonical modernist works or by familiar readings of canonical modernist works.[62] In this sense, reading and

126   *The New Modernist Novel: Criticism and the Task of Reading*

valuing *Adolphe 1920* suggests that the perceived value of literary work can change for criticism, and close reading can register new ways of valuing literary work.

Crozier's term 'decorum' provides a focus for the vestiges of a decadent heritage that are readable in *Adolphe 1920*. In particular, if decorum is treated as an aspect of the relationship between author and reader, Rodker's transgressions of decorum link Anglo-American modernism with modern French writing. But Crozier's word 'decorum' also draws attention to potential problems of taste in other modernist writing. The unattractiveness of the aggression in 'the ideological and libidinal content' of Lewis's novels, for instance, might be considered stronger than the mild unpalatability of Rodker's work.[63] *Ulysses* was initially considered improper or unpalatable in a more moralistic sense, one related for some readers to its stylistic improprieties, and in a way that resulted in a somatic disgust.[64] In different guises, unpalatability is a recurrent issue in dealing with modernist literature.

In *Ugly Feelings*, Sianne Ngai analyses disgust as something that strengthens and polices the boundary between self and other in that it finds its object intolerable and demands the exclusion of that object. As she indicates, there is high potential for disgust to be mobilised in the service of racism, antisemitism, homophobia, misogyny. Ngai contrasts disgust with desire, noting that unlike desire, 'disgust has no keywords associated with it and has largely remained outside the range of any organised critical practice or school'.[65] In considering why this might be, she cites the ties between desire and consumer culture, and the close ties between desire and pluralist thinking (as opposed to disgust's movement towards exclusion). Her analysis is suggestive for analysing the responses of Rodker's contemporaries.

The questions raised by this analysis of contemporary responses to Rodker's writing concern what constituted differences between modernist writers, and how such differences were constructed in contemporary critical discourses. For contemporary readers of Rodker and *Adolphe 1920*, reading often involved positioning new writing within an existing literary framework, and it usually meant offering a value judgement, even if that value judgement was disguised as mere distaste. Such critical conventions helped to shape new writing and the ways in which new writing could be read; more generally, such conventions have inevitably contributed to present-day critical approaches to modernism. Reading Rodker 'fully' might mean addressing once again the blurring between British modernism and modern writing, in this case particularly modern French writing, including *fin-de-siècle* poetry and drama. It will require a further examination of the discourses that Rodker borrows from and inflects, and of those that are brought to bear by contemporary readers on his writing. But it will also mean looking more closely at habits of reading that were active at the time, habits that had been trained on other modernist texts and that were repeatedly being brought to new writing. Such habits of reading are evident only partly in reviews: they are also available in the terms of the new modes of reading suggested by texts that depart from existing models. These models of reading can be newly brought to modernism now, through reading the texts of a new modernism.

A Feeling for the Modern

This final section takes up the question of how *Adolphe 1920* positions itself within Anglo-American and European literary and performance cultures. It is already clear that in positioning itself as modernist, Rodker's novella reconsiders the bounds of Anglo-American modernism and extends them into European writing. In this novella, the prose style is a key locus for its self-conscious positioning, meaning that one way of investigating this positioning is via close reading. Unlike in the extended close reading above, here I begin not from selected passages, but rather from this question about how the novella positions itself within contemporary cultural contexts.

To begin with the title: *Adolphe* in the title was considered above in relation to Benjamin Constant's novella *Adolphe*. That leaves the year, *1920. Adolphe 1920* is not the only modernist text in Rodker's circle to use the year 1920 in its title as a cipher for a particular mood or mode of being. The second part of Ezra Pound's *Hugh Selwyn Mauberley*, which was published at Rodker's Ovid Press, is titled '1920 (Mauberley)', and *Adolphe 1920*'s record of its protagonist's interpersonal vacillations makes possible a glance, in Rodker's title, towards the difficulties of a Mauberley unable to reconcile decadent leanings with demands on poetry in 1920, and capable of 'Nothing, in brief, but maudlin confession'.[66] The possibility of this glance suggests, again, not merely that Rodker's novella is a French text that happens to be written in English, but that it involves an English-language engagement with the moods of both French- and English-language contemporary writing.

Yet the year 1920 remains conspicuous in part because, like *Ulysses*'s 1904, it precedes by some years the composition dates printed at the end of the text: *Ulysses* records 1914–21 and *Adolphe 1920* records 1925–26. This particular parallel with *Ulysses*, however, is a surface parallel. Unlike *Ulysses*, which is plausibly set in 1904, *Adolphe 1920* is not plausibly set

128 *The New Modernist Novel: Criticism and the Task of Reading*

in 1920. This discrepancy is most evident in the notice which is reproduced in the novella's final section. The notice is an invitation to the funeral of His Royal Highness Prince (Joseph) Tovalou Padonou Azanmado Houénou of Dahomey. Recipients are invited to the funeral ceremonies by his son, Prince Kojo Tovalou Houénou.[67] As Ian Patterson noticed, the reprinted newspaper advertisement is Rodker's altered translation of Nancy Cunard's original invitation to the funeral at Ouidah (in present-day Benin).[68] Rodker has suppressed the 1925 and 1926 dates that appear several times on the original invitation. A reference to the year '1925' has been visibly crossed out on the corresponding page of the typescript, and a reference to '1926' was suppressed at a later stage.[69]

Rodker's use of the invitation suggests that part of the work of writing *Adolphe 1920* was the collation of a wide selection of already written material. Unlike *Ulysses*, however, *Adolphe 1920* is unconcerned with a meticulous naturalism of events and story. This is also evident in the ambivalence of the setting, where English is the language of the newspaper, the songs in the bar and the snake trainer, despite an implied geographical location close to Bordeaux. The mismatch of 1925 for 1920 and other mismatches indicate a difference in the structure of titular analogue, day of setting and dates of composition that *Adolphe 1920* would otherwise share with *Ulysses*. The inconsistency marks Rodker's text as a prose foray, interested in the constitution of narrative events, but betraying an overriding concern with the construction of a plausible interior world through its form, rather than with grounding that mental world in a highly naturalist exterior. '1920' evokes a mood that might be found in other nearby years.

Indeed, as Evi Heinz records, the biographical original for *Adolphe 1920*'s Angela is likely to be Nancy Cunard.[70] It was in the summer of 1923, not 1920, that Rodker and Nancy Cunard took two trips together around the south of France, the second one to the Dordogne valley, where the circus in *Adolphe 1920* seems to be located.[71] The band's performance could plausibly have taken place in 1920, potentially in November, the last month when Lottie Gee of the Southern Syncopated Orchestra could still have been performing 'I Couldn't Hear Nobody Pray', and at a time when the colourful limelights used on stage were new. But the performance would have been in London, not near Bordeaux.[72]

For this novella's mood, the invitation matters, and it matters enough to break chronology. The reprinted invitation, in modified form, is the only visual departure in the novella from an otherwise uniform text, and in this way it suggests a deliberate inclusion. The acknowledgement indicated in this inclusion seems directed towards Kojo Tovalou Houénou, the son in whose name the invitation is made. Tovalou founded the Ligue

Universelle pour la Défense de la Race Noire in 1924 and edited its journal *Les continents*. He was an outspoken commentator in France on the French colonial administration in the former kingdom of Dahomey and for African independence from European colonisation.[73] Tovalou was part of Nancy Cunard's circle at the same time as Rodker, who would have met him at her dinner parties.[74] His recognition had increased in August 1923 following his requests to the French government for equality to be respected.[75] The inclusion of the invitation can be read as a deliberate marker of the politics that the novella claims for itself, a sign of an aspiring alignment with Tovalou's pan-Africanism. In this prose style, then, the representation follows a contemporary mood, feeling and sympathies, rather than a precise correspondence of dates and places.

This contemporary mood inhabits this novella's style, including in the music-hall performance in the novella's last chapter. I turn now to another set of questions about the novella's self-positioning. On the novella's second page, there is a riddle: 'and her tears congeal about you like amber'. Why are her tears like amber? This sonorous, morbid phrase has a haunting quality common to much of Rodker's prose. It may be that all the haunting is done by the phrase's evocativeness: of lost love, mourned even while already turning sour. Yet part of the haunting may be the sense that these words are not only Dick's or the narrator's or Rodker's. The passage is here:

> But I hate her. I have hated her from the moment our eyes first met. And never was a time that I left her but I said, I must never see her again, and something said Never? But how break? What letter write? Impossible! And if she comes for you? And her tears congeal about you like amber. And as if that were not enough, her tears speak to your tears, and they too flow in treacherous balm. (134)

The fact that this passage seems to be one source for Lewis's parody fails to dispel the appeal of its style. The reference here is perhaps to the tears of Phaethon's sisters. Phaethon, who persuaded his father Phoebus to let him drive the chariot of the sun, scorched the earth through his inexperience and was killed in anger by Jove. In Ovid's version, his sisters wept for him so long that they were turned into trees and their tears flowed as amber.[76] Rodker's 'congeal' recalls the sisters' metamorphosis, as does the mute 'speaking' through tears. Yet the solemnity of the sisters' love for their brother is dashed by Dick's annoyance at his ex-lover's tears, and Dick's own tears, 'treacherous', remove Rodker's image from one of solemn mourning. 'Congeal' reworks the Ovidian image for this text by overlaying it with a sense of entrapment. Its intensity is local, not needing

130   *The New Modernist Novel: Criticism and the Task of Reading*

seductive parallels of allusion that would cohere across the length of the novella. Here, the local allusion contributes most acutely to the poetic density of represented emotion in the current moment, and the three-beat line of the sentence etches the image and its reference through sound, maintaining a focus on the dense present of Rodker's novella.

By lending density to the text at this point, the reference cedes to a different, contemporary literary context: the highly allusive literary work of Pound, Joyce and Eliot, which Rodker published, and which is one of this text's most immediate literary and cultural contexts. The literary reference to Ovid's tale in fact opens more directly onto a culture of reading in which readers in the know will expect literary reference, including classical reference. Even Wyndham Lewis, ferociously flinging insults at his character Julius Ratner, a figure for Rodker, fails to find the mark in complaining that Ratner's 'ambition led him to burgle all the books of Western romance', since in this, Rodker is straightforwardly aligned with Joyce, Pound and Eliot among others. Ian Patterson discusses this passage in detail in his study identifying Rodker as Lewis's 'split-man'.[77] Lewis's insult suggests that one of the effects of this allusive style was to position Rodker in the community he had chosen via his publishing work, which Lewis and others had sought to divide him from. In *Adolphe 1920*, Rodker is indeed, among other things, a virtuoso compositeur of borrowed material, and the poetic density of *Adolphe 1920* is part of its attraction.

This borrowing extends to the modern French and European literary contexts of the novella. Some context from beyond the novella is relevant here. In *The Future of Futurism*, Rodker names the 'admired masters' of French literature as Baudelaire, Rimbaud, Lautréamont and Mallarmé.[78] He asserts the relevance of Russian writers and resolves his discussion of literature into an opposition:

> it seems to me we have on the one hand, Blake, Mallarmé, Roussel and the development of all those qualities we have called mental agility, the consciously prophetic, and so the consciously sublime, and then there is the sublimity of the bowels as in Tchekov and Dostoievsky.[79]

Edmond Jaloux anticipates Rodker's opposition in his preface to *Montagnes russes*: Jaloux names one strand of contemporary literature stemming from Maupassant and Chekhov and the other from Rimbaud and Lautréamont, and he places Rodker's work up to *Montagnes russes* at their meeting-point. For Jaloux, Rodker brings together the two literatures.[80] Jaloux's and Rodker's genealogies are suggestive for how *Adolphe 1920* works beyond an Anglo-American framework for modernist writing.

Adolphe 1920 *and Modernism*   **131**

Taking up Rodker's and Jaloux's immediate literary contexts in French and Russian literature could lead in many directions. For example, Rodker's *The Future of Futurism* devotes a chapter to the then enigmatic figure of Roussel, whose *Locus solus* Rodker tried to gain a commission to translate in 1924 and again in the early 1930s.[81] In a chapter entitled 'A New Storyteller', Rodker writes, 'Let us hope that with Roussel [. . .] the story is about to come into its own again and the marvellous, ousted by science and invention, become once more part of our lives.' Rodker figures Roussel's stories using the aquarium, a figure he also uses above to illustrate the 'slow motion film of writing': 'This story of the scientist in his lonely wood with his extraordinary inventions, takes us with every dramatic and curious detail through a host of incidents like the tanks of an aquarium one has watched for years.'[82] The aquarium is something of a feature of modern French writing. Aquariums had opened in London in 1853 and 1924, in Paris in 1867 and in Berlin in 1869 and 1913. Louis Aragon's 1926 *Paysan de Paris*, for example, compares the arcades of Paris to an aquarium: 'Toute la mer dans le passage de l'Opéra' (The whole sea in the *passage de l'Opéra*), and Mina Loy's *Insel* marks its affinities with surrealism by, among other things, frequent references to aquariums.[83]

Adolphe 1920's aquarium seems to carry echoes of an episode of Roussel's *Impressions of Africa*, where the metamorphoses of water-dwelling and other creatures are described. *Adolphe 1920*'s creatures appear between animate and inanimate:

> Threads of gut hung in water, glittering parachutes, falling arc lamps. Transparent the gut glowed, carrying dull stars in crinkled invisible streamers which slowly changed their length, the creature rising, falling, deliberate and all but water. It had a will, it shone with its own light. (157)

There is a resonance here with Roussel's creatures, which achieve their role in the spectacle being displayed by suddenly betraying themselves as alive, unexpectedly moving their bodies. Rodker's 'fin twirling busily like a propeller' of the seahorses in the tank, the 'equilateral triangles of fish' that are 'hung from invisible wires', an 'elliptical ball' and the jar containing a 'curled end of thick transparent tape', which 'flapped rainbow light along its oblong edges', resonate with Roussel's strange creatures (157). These include a 'cylindrical object, fitted with a propellor', a 'triangular piece of material, like a pennant' on a flagpole, a gelatinous cake of soap with lather and a sponge, set against a scene involving the play of electric light and colour.[84] The sequence of aquarium tanks in *Adolphe 1920*, in which each strange creature is seen in turn and its

132   *The New Modernist Novel: Criticism and the Task of Reading*

movement watched, recalls the sequence in Roussel's chapter, in which each object in turn is seen to move, demonstrating a transformation into a living, not mechanised, creature.

However, the same section in *Adolphe 1920* also holds a resonance with a specific passage from Laforgue's *Salomé*. Laforgue's passage is another aquarium, inspired by the Berlin aquarium:

> As far as the eye can see, meadows enameled with white sea anemones, fat ripe onions, bulbs with violet membranes, bits of tripe straying here and there and seeming to make a new life for itself, stumps with antennae winking at the neighbouring coral, a thousand aimless warts; a whole fetal, claustral, vibrating flora, trembling with the eternal dream of one day being able in whispers to congratulate itself on this state of things.[85]

The French original reads:

> Et, à perte de vue, des prairies, des prairies émaillées de blanches actinies, d'oignons gras à point, de bulbes à muqueuse violette, de bouts de tripes égarés là et, ma foi, s'y refaisant une existence, de moignons dont les antennes clignent au corail d'en face, de mille verrues sans but; toute un flore foetale et claustrale et vibratile agitant l'éternel rêve d'arriver à se chuchoter un jour de mutuelles félicitations sur cet état de choses . . .[86]

The rich profusion of over-ripe objects or images ties this passage to the aquarium description in *Adolphe 1920* and to the style of Rodker's novel more generally. The closeness is especially evident in Rodker's sentence:

> Yet next them a dense clot of anemones with deliberate swaying tentacles like a monstrous picture disquieted him, their brick reds, rotting whites and porous yellows transporting him to a lunar vegetation where his mind crawled and stumbled through a carnivorous forest. (157)

Laforgue's passage is quoted in the above translation by Peter Nicholls, who notes that it points to a tension in Pound's reading of Laforgue. Writing of the 'strand of decadent style' that 'runs through *The Cantos*', Nicholls observes that:

> These richly ornamental passages exploit linguistic density and sound-patterning to produce effects quite removed from Laforguian logopoeia as Pound had defined it in 1918. On the other hand, though, these highly stylized, Pre-Raphaelite tableaux, with their frozen gestures and inorganic landscapes, are reminiscent of some of Laforgue's prose writings, and notably of the celebrated prose passage about the Berlin Aquarium

which, significantly, Pound had cut from his 1918 translation of *Salomé* but to which the Laforguian 'deeps' at the very end of *The Cantos* undoubtedly refer.[87]

Nicholls observes an 'almost fetishistic delight in language for its own sake, in the rich "opacity" of words', which differs from Pound's logopeia and from his insistence on the relationship of word to thing.[88] As Nicholls writes, 'the decadent and the modern are, in fact, more closely interwoven than Pound would have us believe'.[89] Nicholls's commentary on Pound's reading of Laforgue is relevant to Rodker's positioning within Anglo-American modernism: although Rodker engages with the work of Joyce and others, this is combined in *Adolphe 1920* with a decadent deliquescence that draws more openly on Laforgue than do some of Rodker's contemporaries. Rodker's interest in Laforgue is flagged by his use of the title of a Laforgue poem in his *Little Review* prose poem 'Chanson on Petit Hypertrophique', and in 1917 he translated a Jules Laforgue play, but the Laforguian resonance of *Adolphe 1920* is evident from the comparison here.[90] Perhaps Pound's reading of Laforgue was mediated by *Adolphe 1920*. So where there are some similarities between *Adolphe 1920* and Roussel's *Impressions of Africa* in the representation of the animate and the inanimate, this brief investigation of a Laforguian connection is more revealing for the cultural issues of poetics surrounding Laforgue's English-language reception.

There is a tension in *Adolphe* 1920, then, between a poetic style more readily associated with Pound, Joyce, Eliot and others, and a more deliquescent tendency that fits Rodker with some aspects of Laforgue and Lautréamont among others and is characterised by vacillation and indulgence. Vincent Sherry identifies the resistance to decadence as degeneration that informs what he calls the suppression of decadence, in favour of symbolism, in Edmund Wilson's *Axel's Castle*, Frank Kermode's *The Romantic Image* and Hugh Kenner's *The Pound Era*.[91] The decadent strain of Rodker's writing, as against Pound's, in these passages that echo Laforgue suggests the critical power of the writing to re-narrativise the backgrounds of modernist literature. Here and elsewhere, Rodker lends more weight to the deliquescent than do his more outspoken modernist contemporaries.

This deliquescent style mediates the performance of the musicians and dancers in the novella's final section. In the limelights, a dancer takes the stage:

> Her skin was green-yellow, an unripe and downy peach, and her voice rose so sour, so sweet, he could not bear it. She was looking for a lamb, and her

134 The New Modernist Novel: Criticism and the Task of Reading

> voice, bubbling, moaning, complaining, shuddered and died tremulously murmuring, a child sobbing itself asleep. And again her voice rose mournful, swaying like the snake: I couldnt hear nobody pray, he gnashed his teeth, with my saviour by my side, his heart grew stronger, I couldnt hear nobody pray. He saw Babylon in a great sheet of fire, half the sky cut by lightning; terraces, frantic princes and their concubines in too heavy jewelled gowns, chariots galloping into the yawning earth. (165)

The passage arguably shares the 'rich ornament', 'linguistic density' and 'sound-patterning' that Nicholls identifies above in Laforgue. The voice 'so sour, so sweet, he could not bear it' belongs recognisably to *Adolphe 1920*'s emotionally highly wrought state of feeling and its links with decadence, as do the 'too heavy jewelled gowns' and other elements of the passage. Here, Rodker's character Dick is so deeply absorbed into the performance that he is provoked by it, in a decadent trope, to see the Biblical scene.

The energies of description and figuration here echo the energies of earlier passages in *Adolphe 1920*, especially that of the aquarium. Rodker's 1924 New York letter in the *Revue européenne* opens with a visit to the New York aquarium and connects it to the music-hall he then visits.[92] For Rodker, in the novella as in the essay, the aquarium is an indicator of modernity. In the novella, the transformations of the performers while they dance include their figuration as 'fish' (165), which specifically repeats the fish of the aquarium earlier in *Adolphe 1920*. The limelights accompanying the music echo the lights that were earlier reflected in the aquarium, and indeed, in a rare reference forward, the aquarium has already been described using this comparison in the last paragraph: 'As in the music-hall: the back cloth ripples shimmering purple and gold' (158). Angela then returns, and her return makes the segue between the novella's aquarium scene and its music-hall scene. For *Adolphe 1920*, the music-hall scene is key to the modern 1920 mood that the novella documents, and it is closely linked to its aquarium scene. The deliquescent style that the novella develops is brought to the music-hall performance as a key scene of the modern.

Indeed, the style in this section is not only brought from the novella to the performance, but incorporates remembered performances in the way the musicians and dancers are represented in it. The 1923 performance that Rodker records in the New York letter took place on 42nd Street, opposite the Ziegfield Follies,[93] which were then on show at the Liberty Theatre, placing the show he saw in the area that is now known as the New 42nd Street. There are many possible venues that could correspond to the one Rodker was in. For instance, in February 1924 George Gershwin and Paul Whiteman performed *Rhapsody in Blue* at the Aeolian Hall,[94] which had an entrance on 42nd Street. In 1922 Rodker had recalled another performance in the poem 'Southern Syncopated Singers', whose title refers to a band of Black musicians from the US led by Will Marion Cook, which included Sidney Bechet. The group formed to travel to London to perform from 1919, and it toured in the UK and Europe under various names, including Southern Syncopated Orchestra, though the orchestra is not recorded as performing in France except in Paris in 1921.[95] The Southern Syncopated Orchestra performed 'a wide variety of musical styles', not only jazz.[96] In several ways – notably the repertoire, which in 1919 and 1920 included 'I Couldn't Hear Nobody Pray', the lime green and other limelights that had recently been introduced and the audience's enthusiasm for the singers and the dancers – the performance recounted in *Adolphe 1920* shares elements of the Southern Syncopated Orchestra.[97] The match is not exact, and the 'dim, low room' (163) where the band performs is unlike the glamorous venues that the orchestra often performed in, such as the London Palladium. But it is likely that the account in *Adolphe 1920* draws on both of these originals and possibly other sources.

The novella records detailed sequences of specific movements and gestures, keeping the performers' own work present so that their art and performance are recorded in the prose. Yet their performance is interpreted too. The dense figuration of the novella's prose style casts the performers in the forms of other creatures as they dance, echoing the figurations in the aquarium. This deliquescent style commemorates the musicians and dancers, comparing their performance to the spectacle of the aquarium that, until this point, has generated the most stylistically dense passage in the novella, and the transformations celebrate their dancing. At the same time, the presence of the musicians and dancers within the novella also requires them to submit to that deliquescent style, whose figurations risk dehumanising the performers temporarily as they dance. Yet in the density of figuration prompted by the performance, the performance itself seems to be one of the sources for the set of styles that have been in play through the novella, even earlier on, in the aquarium scene and elsewhere. It may be that Rodker borrowed signature aspects of the highly dense, highly wrought modernist style of *Adolphe 1920* not only from modern French writing, but also directly from the bands he saw.[98]

Representation and style are specifically complex here. Catherine Tackley writes of the Southern Syncopated Orchestra in London that 'the feature of the performances that was often most appreciated by audiences was that the SSO represented an authentic cultural experience, unlike previous imitations'.[99] 'Imitations' refers to minstrel shows,

136   *The New Modernist Novel: Criticism and the Task of Reading*

but even so, a comparable authenticity becomes hard to pin down in fictional representation. Some of Rodker's briefly present rhetoric of 'drums', 'pulses', 'hearts' and 'frenzy' – 'A drum began to beat. It was their own pulses. It made the heart beat stronger' – echoes, for example, Zora Neale Hurston's provocative lean into the primitivist take on a jazz performance in 'How It Feels to Be Colored Me' (1928).[100] Rodker's rhetoric also echoes back through the novella: for example, the beat of the heart recalls the beating of Dick's heart as he looks into the mutoscope at the start of the fair. When the band performs, beating hearts briefly figure the performance as an alternative to the characters' persistent ennui. But this figuration holds only in passing, much like the novella's other frequent transitions from real to imagined scenes, and the ennui absorbs everyone present in the scene of the stacked glasses (171). In this rhetoric it is hard to tell how far the novella adds an appeal to a primitive 'remnant' when representing the band, and how far the novella locates that appeal to a 'remnant' as already present in the band's own performance for a mixed audience, whether or not it was actually there.[101]

Midway through the performance, the printed funeral invitation provides a social and political context for the band's performance. As discussed above, Rodker adapted the invitation printed in the novella from the invitation received by Nancy Cunard in 1925. Cunard later edited the *Negro Anthology*, published in 1934. Among stories, articles, poems, essays, photographs and other work, the anthology reprints a considerable amount of sheet music recording songs.[102] Rodker's prose style in 1926 can perhaps be seen as making an earlier attempt to record in prose if not the songs, then the gestures, moods and intensities of the varieties of musical styles in the performances Rodker saw that are remodelled into *Adolphe 1920*'s final section. The inclusion of the modified invitation is an indication that *Adolphe 1920* specifically identifies the band as a feature of the 'modern'. That identification is aligned to a larger contemporary pan-African movement via the invitation's connection to Kojo Tovalou Houénou. Both reproductions, that of the band's performance in the novella, and that of the authentic printed invitation, rely on Rodker's and *Adolphe 1920*'s capacity to record, borrow, or recreate other voices.[103] Rodker might have been disparaged by Wyndham Lewis as a burglar, but what he heard and employed went well beyond Lewis's printed, canonised 'books of Western romance' in its representation of the modern.

This novella's impression of the modern inheres substantially in its style. *Adolphe 1920* repositions modernism as international, bringing French modernism, including its deliquescence, into Anglo-American modernism, alongside the musical performance in the style of the Southern Syncopated Orchestra. Its style discomforted its contemporary critics and similarly, still now redraws modernism into a new set of connections. Criticism of modernism that suppresses decadence, including influential mid-century criticism, has risked missing the modernism of this novella; reading *Adolphe 1920* closely, for style, finds that feeling, in this novella, is a feeling for the modern.

Chapter 5

Insel and Literary Value

Insel's Paris

Unlike *Nightwood* and *Adolphe 1920*, Mina Loy's novel *Insel* remained unpublished in the interwar period, despite interest in 1938 from James Laughlin of New Directions. In 1961, after he considered it again, Laughlin 'questioned whether it was really a novel'.[1] *Insel* was first published in 1991, when Elizabeth Arnold edited it from the Mina Loy archive at the Beinecke Rare Book and Manuscript Library for Black Sparrow Press. Sarah Hayden's 2014 Melville House edition includes Arnold's afterword and adds further editorial material, including the text of a related story, 'Visitation of Insel'. This recent, asynchronous recovery follows the trajectory of Loy's marginalisation, exclusion and recovery more generally.[2] It makes *Insel*, like *Adolphe 1920*, an interesting case of a new modernist novel that was written from within modernist circles but that was not recognised critically until the 1990s, not least because it was unpublished.

Insel records the friendship between Insel, a German surrealist painter living in poverty in Paris in the mid-1930s, and Mrs Jones, a character who resembles Loy. From the first page, the novel's world is an art world, and from the first page, too, this novel works with a prose style that is distinctive, and that is perhaps recognisable as Loy's from her poetry. In this chapter, I first attempt to date the action of the novel, and in doing so I consider how context can be developed as an aspect of close reading, rather than as a counterpoint to close reading. I then follow some questions about coherence that echo questions that *Nightwood* and *Adolphe 1920* have raised, and finally I consider the commitments of *Insel*'s style, notably to European surrealisms. *Insel* is an intriguing work: it deflects some established kinds of reading that have been associated with the history of the novel and with modernist novels, and it lays claim to a relationship with surrealism that is hard to place. I find that valuing *Insel* requires reassessing some concepts of literary value that have long held in Anglophone criticism of modernist novels.

Loy spent time with a number of different avant-garde networks at different times, especially in Florence, New York and Paris. In Florence from 1906 to 1916, she was connected with the Italian Futurists and with Mabel Dodge's circle, including Gertrude Stein. In New York in 1916 to 1918 and after, she was connected with the Arensbergs' circle, which included Marcel Duchamp and William Carlos Williams. From 1923 to 1936 she lived in Paris, where she socialised with expatriate crowds among British, American and French writers, and was friends with Djuna Barnes.[3] In Paris, as an agent for her son-in-law Julien Levy's New York gallery from 1931, Loy successfully commissioned artwork by Giorgio de Chirico, Salvador Dalí, Max Ernst, Juan Gris, Alberto Giacometti, Arshile Gorky, René Magritte, Pavel Tchelitchew, Toulouse-Lautrec and others, before returning to New York in 1936.[4] These different social, literary and art contexts turn up in *Insel*.

Insel is set in the Paris art world of the mid-1930s. As Elizabeth Arnold noted, the character Insel resembles the German surrealist painter Richard Oelze, whom Loy knew in Paris between 1933 and 1936. Similarly, Mrs Jones resembles the Loy of this period, the Paris agent for Levy's gallery, where Oelze exhibited in 1936. Oelze left Paris for Ascona, Switzerland, on 1 October 1936. Arnold outlines how aspects of Oelze and Loy correspond to Insel and Mrs Jones.[5] Indeed, the readiness with which *Insel* lends itself to reading according to its biographical contexts is suggested by *Insel*'s relevance for Loy's biographer, Carolyn Burke: Burke draws directly on *Insel* as her source for biographical information about Loy's friendship with Oelze.[6] But despite the residual sense of memoir that hovers over this work, Insel does not correspond fully to Richard Oelze, nor do the novel's events always perfectly match the cultural history it sketches.

The composition and attempted publications of *Insel* can roughly be placed biographically. *Insel* is the most substantial of several autobiographical prose works by Loy. Sandeep Parmar finds that Loy wrote notes and initial drafts for the novel in Paris – writing down remembered or imagined conversations with Richard Oelze – and continued writing and compiled the typescript drafts after her move to New York in 1936. Loy wrote the short piece 'Visitation of Insel' in New York, most likely in 1938. She later excised it from the manuscript of *Insel*, and it is appended to the 2014 edition.[7] Attempts to publish *Insel* followed contact between Julien Levy and James Laughlin. In 1938 Laughlin wrote to Loy to suggest publishing a section of her manuscript in the New Directions anthology, and he and Loy also discussed possible publication of the novel in the 1950s and early 1960s. In the event, it was not published by New Directions, nor by Simon and Schuster, to whom Laughlin had recommended Loy send it.[8]

140　*The New Modernist Novel: Criticism and the Task of Reading*

In the early 1940s Julien Levy may have been referring to *Insel* when he asked Loy for 'the new draft of her novel, *Islands in the Air*'. Loy referred to her prose fiction generally as her 'novel', and *Islands in the Air* is one among the novels, but drafts of *Insel* bear the title 'Islands in the Air' as well as 'Insel', and so 'Islands in the Air' seems to have been used to refer to a larger fiction project that included *Insel*.[9] 'Insel', then, may be one of the 'Islands', even a German one: in 'Visitation of Insel', Insel is called an 'Island in the air'.[10]

But the novel's action is harder to place historically. One puzzle is provided by the possible timeframes of *Insel* – that is, the possible dates of novel's events from the first meeting of Mrs Jones and Insel to the last, and the subsequent narration of *Insel* by Mrs Jones. The general setting is clearly the mid-1930s: mentions by name of Salvador Dalí, Man Ray, Joseph Cornell and Raoul Dufy place the novel in the context of Paris thirties surrealism, of the kind supported and marketed by Julien Levy's New York art gallery. The novel seems also to include cameos by Max Ernst, André Breton and others, even if it is not always straightforward to match identities with the names in *Insel*.[11] The painter Insel's fear of being condemned as '*Kultur Bolshewik*' if he had returned to Germany also reflects the mid-1930s context of encroaching fascism.[12] His presence in Paris despite speaking very little French, socialising little with other surrealists and having no financial resources, obliquely registers the developing political situation in Germany. Within this general setting, *Insel* illuminates the situation Insel and others are in. These cultural settings have been admirably explored by Sarah Hayden. Hayden also argues that *Insel* is 'closer to a deliberately distorted fictionalization rather than a memoir' of the period.[13]

Some further information about the relevant timeframes can be gained from close reading – that is, here, of paying close attention to passages whose reference to historical timeframes is most obvious.[14] Insel's ready conspiracy theory, that the Frenchman Stavisky was involved in having tons of sugar poured into the concrete foundations of the Maginot line (42),[15] confirms the majority of the novel's events as occurring after February 1934, when Stavisky became well known. The fraudster Alexandre Stavisky's apparent suicide following legal pursuit was seen as a cover-up for government wrongdoing, and suspicions helped to prompt the 6 February 1934 crisis in Paris, an anti-government demonstration by far-right groups, in which fifteen people died and which subsequently forced the resignation of two prime ministers. The case was covered by the expatriate American journalist Janet Flanner, who in 1935 called Stavisky a 'swindler who twenty-two months ago posthumously twice broke up the government of France'.[16]

The disjunction between the narrator and her character Mrs Jones is dated in the novel's second last chapter, where, in a moment of mutual animosity, Insel suggests a Freudian reading of lampshade materials in Mrs Jones's flat:

> We had, in our 'timeless conversation', with Insel's concurrence in my 'wonderful ideas', superseded Freud. I must always have known he had never the slightest idea of what I was talking about—yet only now did this fact appear as negatory.
> The still life that intrigued him was a pattern of a 'detail' to be strewn about the surface of clear lamp shades. Through equidistant holes punched in a crystalline square, I had carefully urged in extension, a still celluloid coil of the color that Schiaparelli has since called *shocking* pink. Made to be worn round pigeon's ankles for identification, I had picked it up in the Bon Marché. (143)

In that word 'since', the 1936 creation of Elsa Schiaparelli's colour 'shocking pink' marks a divide between character and narrator with a reference to actual events of the Paris surrealist milieu: Mrs Jones the narrator has knowledge about Schiaparelli that is unavailable to the character. Schiaparelli's colour was created and marketed in 1936–37, and the association of Schiaparelli with the word 'shocking' was confirmed in April 1937 by the launch of her 'Shocking' perfume, its bottle designed in 1936 by the surrealist Leonor Fini, whose work Julien Levy exhibited in November to December 1936.[17] The passage does not date the narrator's comments exactly, but suggests, with its present perfect tense, that Schiaparelli's naming is still a recent event, perhaps for both narrator and author. Indeed, the passage suggests the resemblances of Mrs Jones to Loy, whose lampshades used materials from Paris markets.[18] It also reconfirms a late thirties Paris surrealist milieu: Schiaparelli worked with many Paris surrealist artists, not only Fini; her colours around this time included 'Maginot line blue'.[19] This suggests 1936–37 as a pivotal point where the character Mrs Jones becomes the narrator.

But there are limits to such calculations. The dates that the novel suggests for the beginning of the friendship or of the writing process are less clear. The novel's first chapter sees Insel's painting in the narrator's studio, awaiting a shipping consignment. Carolyn Burke records that Loy held Richard Oelze's *Expectation* (*Erwartung*) in her apartment, citing a letter to Fabienne in 1936 and the description in *Insel*.[20] Correspondingly, Renate Wiehager notes that Alfred Barr, then Director of the Museum of Modern Art, did not sight the work in Oelze's Paris atelier in the summer of 1936, and this may have been the time when it was at Loy's apartment.[21] This painting, completed in 1935–36, was first published in

142   *The New Modernist Novel: Criticism and the Task of Reading*

1936 in Levy's *Surrealism*, and first exhibited in 1938 at the 'Exposition internationale du surréalisme' in Paris.[22] It was Oelze's major work of the period and became a noted contribution to surrealism. The appearance of this artwork at the start of the novel would situate the entirety of the action in 1936, between the completion of *Erwartung* and the launch of the colour 'shocking pink'.

However, the canvas described in *Insel*'s first chapter is not *Erwartung*. This canvas is, or includes, 'a gigantic back of a commonplace woman looking at the sky' (4), not the waiting crowd of several people in Oelze's painting, though the closeness is obvious.[23] Oelze's *Erwartung*, which includes a woman in the foreground among its waiting crowd, might nevertheless be said to share with *Insel*'s painting the 'eerie' quality of the sky described by the narrator in a letter: 'whenever I'm in the room with it I catch myself staring at that sky waiting, oblivious of time, for whatever is about to appear in it. Most eerie!' (4). Loy's description in *Insel*, then, still reads as a response to *Erwartung* despite the differences in the detail of the painting described. In fact, it reads sufficiently powerfully so that Wiehager translates it as the opening of her book on *Erwartung*. The incomplete correspondence between the two paintings, however, suggests the difficulty of aligning fictional details with a real-world set of events and dates.

The observable closeness between Insel and Richard Oelze is then only a partial resemblance, where Insel resembles Oelze but is not Oelze. Here, the difficulties that arise from the attempt to date the novel historically extend back into its biographical parallels. In other words, as is suggested by the incomplete historical correspondences, the biographical correspondences are similarly close but mismatched. Alfred Barr records his visit to Oelze in 1936 in terms that do readily suggest *Insel*'s studio, while comparing Oelze to other hard-up artists in Paris. Barr writes that Oelze's studio, a single room, was shabbily furnished, but as orderly as Piet Mondrian's, which Barr had seen shortly beforehand. On a small stove in Oelze's studio, a few potatoes were cooking. Barr remembers that it was the middle of the depression years.[24] The resemblance between Oelze and Insel is traceable too in the language of Loy's novel, where Insel's idiom shares salient aspects with Oelze's. Oelze's response to a 1968 questionnaire begins, 'Es gibt nicht einen allgemeingültigen Weg, es wird immer eine Vielzahl von Wegen nebeneinander geben' (There is not one generally valid way, there will always be a great many ways alongside each other),[25] which recalls the 'thousand directions' of Insel's account of his work: 'A thousand directions are open to me, to take whichever I decide—I cannot decide' (150). In a 1948 letter to his former art teacher Johannes Itten, Oelze calls himself 'immer und überall allein' (always and everywhere alone) and again 'ganz besonders allein' (quite particularly alone), 'allein' being a word Insel favours, even when he is appearing in an English-language novel: '"*Allein—allein*," he chanted forsakenly. [. . .] "Always alone—alone in Berlin—alone in Paris—"' (37–38).[26] The letter gives evidence of a melancholy devotion recognisable in Insel's attachment to Mrs Jones. But the illusion of closeness in this shared idiom is made interesting by discrepancies. Insel's later painting *Die Irma* similarly includes definite, if small departures from its counterparts in Oelze's 1935–1936 works *Frieda* and *Frieda II*.[27] Similarly, although Oelze's 'Frieda' is named after the character in Kafka's *Das Schloß* (*The Castle*), which Oelze read on a friend's recommendation in Paris,[28] it is *Der Prozeß* (*The Trial*) that Insel recommends to Mrs Jones.

The possibility that 'Irma' is taken from Freud's textbook example of a specimen dream analysis early in *The Interpretation of Dreams* suggests that Insel, cast as Oelze, may be canny beyond the diegesis in his Freudian reading of Mrs Jones's lampshades, anticipating Loy's combining, in the guise of Mrs Jones the narrator, Freud and French surrealist origins in the renaming of Insel's painting from *Frieda* to *Irma*: by exchanging Kafka for Freud, Mrs Jones has subtly realigned Oelze's artistic affinities in the creation of Insel's.[29] Similarly, while Wiehager records that Insel's years in Paris, 1933–36, were 'for him' 'three extremely fruitful years',[30] Mrs Jones, by contrast, tells Mlle Alpha that 'He seemed so worth helping, I've only just begun to notice he *never* paints' (104). As Sarah Hayden argues, 'Loy's portrayal of Insel systematically undermines and obscures Oelze's artistic success', which by 1936 was considerable.[31] The details again show that Insel is not reducible to Oelze, nor is he a different character who borrows only some of Oelze's factual details. Insel borrows Oelze whole: Oelze is the catalyst for Insel's character, and Loy's novel builds its fictional world on a resemblance that includes a crucial sliver of difference.

The Joseph Cornell box, similarly, suggests Cornell without quite matching any of several reproduced artworks by Cornell. Mrs Jones gives Insel

> a small object by the American surrealist, Joseph Cornell, the delicious head of a girl in slumber afloat with a night light flame on the surface of water in a tumbler, of bits cut from early *Ladies' Journals* (technically in pupilage to Max Ernst) in loveliness, unique, in Surrealism— (144)

Loy and Cornell were friends in the early forties, but Burke records that Cornell sent Loy one of his boxes after 1931, which Loy kept until

144 *The New Modernist Novel: Criticism and the Task of Reading*

she gave it to Oelze. On this gift to Oelze Burke cites the description in *Insel* but gives no external reference.[32] The description given seems to place the work among Cornell's 1932–36 series of glass-paned boxes as available on DVD, but it does not perfectly match any of the reproduced samples of Cornell's work.[33] It is similar but not identical to an early 'Soap Bubble Set' of 1936, with its head of a sleeping girl, its lunar map from 'early *Ladies' Journals*' and the blue colouring.[34] By referring to 'Surrealism' in describing the box and calling its use of collage 'technically in pupilage to Max Ernst', Mrs Jones suggests the version of surrealism recorded in Levy's 1936 volume *Surrealism*, which included Cornell. Although Loy was fascinated by the aviaries in Cornell's 1949 exhibition in New York, and wrote about them in 1950,[35] the box described in *Insel* is not one of the aviaries. The Cornell box seems to mark not only a 1936 context, but also the absence of substantial revision to *Insel* after 1950, which could potentially have changed the resonance of this mention of Cornell. It is the charm of Cornell's interwar work that is preserved here in Loy's novel. This preservation is perhaps in part by virtue of, rather than despite, the gentle mismatch between the artwork described in *Insel* and any specific work available for inspection by Cornell. If the description faithfully records an original artwork that – perhaps after being given as a gift – was not available for later photographic reproduction, even so the narrative medium of *Insel* necessarily introduces a gap between its own description in language and any specific artwork.

Where, as argued in Chapter 4, *Adolphe 1920* disrupts a scrupulously factual reading that seeks harmony among the specific 1920 date of the novel's title and its events, the correspondence of Loy's narrative content in the reading to the events and people of contemporary Paris is more subtly askew. There is a quality of convincingness to *Insel*'s prose style, despite or because of the imperfection of its correlations to real people and settings. Close reading of the novel's time markers and other details can provide an extended imagined setting that corresponds to a mid-1930s Paris art-world scene, but such enquiry also highlights *Insel*'s ambivalence in response to investigations of its specific correspondences. Knowledge of context here is not preparatory background information for interpreting Loy's novel, but rather, such knowledge can be collected and collated by a reading that follows *Insel*'s suggested dates and points of reference. That is, context here is a product of close reading, not an antecedent to it. Details of context are generated by an attentive enquiry into style: in this mode of close reading, style opens out onto context. Some of *Insel*'s appeal is in the slight but stylistically persistent mismatch between Loy's novel and its

Insel *and Literary Value* **145**

historical correspondences, and its historical networks are generated by that suggestive shimmer.

One of the more puzzling details of context is the rarity of any mention of what is referred to in passing as 'a threatening war': 'he unfolded his ardent yearning to flee to New York from a threatening war' (44). The chapter that contains this reference sees Mrs Jones, in response to Insel's prayers for New York, envision herself as an 'undiminishable steak' (45), a potential source of passage to New York for Insel, but the chapter digresses to Insel's 'psychic exudence' (46). Despite what seems to be an intriguing reference to the Second World War, 'from the last war into the next' (50), and an acknowledgement of the 'menace of a war' in a siren (42), both wars are otherwise unmentioned, although Insel does intriguingly recount taking part in a war on a film set (13). Sarah Hayden notes the 'traces of military language' on the novel's last pages, where, for instance, Insel reacts to Mrs Jones's trite comments about artistic composition: 'I felt Insel crack as if he had been *shot* alert.' Instantly forgiving her, Insel has eyes that are 'missiles that have not gone off' (153–54). As Hayden argues, such rhetoric prefigures the violence Insel risks by remaining in Europe as a German national and 'degenerate' artist: 'these apparently throwaway military allusions incite the reader to reflect upon the circumstances to which his erstwhile protector is leaving him'.[36] In this reading, the relationship between the two characters is the locus for the novel's representation of the political situation that bears down on both of them and especially on Insel. Insel's possible fate is presaged only a few times in their conversations, and the conversations turn aside. The novel's or the characters' reticence to speak directly about the politics of Insel's situation becomes a marker of the edges of their friendship, which, as Hayden outlines, in the end does not assist Insel to reach America. In this way, it is hard to place the tone of the novel's portrayal of Insel, in part because the characters and situation both adhere so closely to, and yet fall away from, their historical parallels. Insel, not quite Oelze, also stands in for a more general figure of the displaced, impoverished artist of 1930s Europe.

'Momentum' and the Novel Form

Where can 'style' be found in a novel? How can it be excerpted for critical comment? In a 1996 review of Loy's poems and of Carolyn Burke's biography of Loy, Helen Vendler outlines some of Loy's 'characteristic poetic moves' but suggests that she was not 'innately a lyric poet'. Vendler concludes too that Loy 'was not by temperament a novelist':

146   *The New Modernist Novel: Criticism and the Task of Reading*

her criticism of *Insel* is that it 'reveals no sense of momentum'.[37] Yet Loy's writing in *Insel* has a sense of adventure. This might be evident from its intriguing first sentence: 'The first I heard of Insel was the story of a madman, a more or less surrealist painter, who, although he had nothing to eat, was hoping to sell a picture to buy a set of false teeth.' This prose style is not flat: rather, the writing is characterised by a local liveliness. In the same paragraph, Insel is described with, 'my impression faded off. For, to my workaday consciousness, he only looked like an embryonic mind locked in a dilapidated structure' (3). The impression he gives while present in this opening scene is that 'it was as if a dove had flown through the window and settled upon a chair' (4), and after his departure, that '[t]all, his torso concave, he was so emaciated that from his waist down he looked like a stork on one leg' (5). There is a 'momentum' in these comparisons, and it is a local momentum, suited to passing thoughts and impressions. The stork is a measure of the unexpected local adventures of the prose: reading might well be drawn to the local virtuosity of the prose, and from there to the questions of how that prose coheres into a novel and of how a novel invested in this prose style might be valued.

Insel abounds with figures. Events are often recounted in momentary segments that return only intermittently to a longer narrative. As in the scene where Insel asks, for three hours, '*An was denken Sie?* [. . .] of God knows what girl, in God knows what decade, and all the same of me' (75), the mesmerism of Insel's company is available to Mrs Jones in idle conversation between them. Indeed, the prose style of *Insel* draws energy throughout from the character Insel, who provides Mrs Jones with a seemingly endless stream of figures, halted only occasionally by her perception of the waning of his rays. His rays, the luminous *Strahlen* that so fascinate Mrs Jones, are the most sustained figure. But Insel leaps off the page, metaphorically, in chapter after chapter. He 'became so hilariously wealthy he juggled a fortune' (10); 'Whenever I let him in he would halt on the threshold drawing the whole of his luminous life up into his smile. It radiated round his face and formed a halo hovering above the rod of his rigid body. He looked like a lamppost alight' (31).

The figures condense an unusual prose energy. A dove substituted again for Insel is not primarily a symbolic but an actual dove, one whose figurative energy then becomes more palpable in the course of the sentence:

> Insel, unconvinced, let out a low growl which sounded like one more *lustig*—while that strange bloom, as if he were growing feathers, spread over his face. He turned into a sugar dove. It flew about the sitting room,

Insel *and Literary Value*　　**147**

dropping from under its wings a three-ring circus. In one ring echoed the cracks of a whip; in one ring rotated an insane steed of mist; and in the other ring Insel's spirit astride an elemental Pegasus—. (115)

At times the figuration satirises Gothic horror:

> As I ran up the one flight of stairs, I had to slow down. Surprisingly, on this warm day, an iciness was creeping up my ankles. I proceeded into a chill draught.
> 　'Insel!' I realized.
> There was nobody standing at my front door.
> Although well lit by a staircase window, it was hung with a square curtain of black mist. (106)

Such adventures stand at the threshold of metaphor, metonymy, anecdote, narrative and gossip. They are closer to metonymy than to metaphor, despite their evident challenge to realism.[38] At one point Insel momentarily becomes Arthur Cravan, whose features he has previously, flirtatiously, copied onto his own face from Mrs Jones's photograph of 'Colossus': '*Craven* to a degree that rendered his cowering august, of that meekness befitting a supplicant at the door of heaven, Insel was knowing an alibi so sublime—I again lost all knowledge of who he was' (135, my italics). This transformation of identity – and of medium, from Insel's 'television' of Colossus to Loy's writing – slips immediately into the vicinity of another artist, in that it prompts Mrs Jones to give the 'little box' by Joseph Cornell to 'the will-o'-the-wisp', Insel (144). Occasionally, Mrs Jones's impatience with Insel halts the careening figuration of the prose:

> I perceived the cafe clock. On that uncompromising dial all things converged to normal. I was a tout for a friend's art gallery, feeding a cagey genius in the hope of production. Insel's melodious ravings, an irritating whine— It was ten to eight. (55)

Loy's poetry obliquely offers suggestions for reading the liveliness of *Insel*'s prose. The condensation of ideas and vocabulary in some of Loy's poems from *Others* and *Lunar Baedeker* has been described in terms of a 'scintillating precision',[39] a detached 'exactness',[40] an 'arid clarity'.[41] For William Carlos Williams, 'When she puts a word down on paper it is clean.'[42] Ezra Pound's term 'logopoeia', famously used to describe Loy's and Marianne Moore's poetry in 1918, is explained as 'poetry that is akin to nothing but language, which is a dance of the intelligence among words and ideas and modification of ideas and

148   *The New Modernist Novel: Criticism and the Task of Reading*

characters'.[43] Pound's term is a response to the October 1917 *Others Anthology*, which included Loy's poems 'At the Door of the House', 'The Effectual Marriage' and 'Human Cylinders'.[44] Pound's later reiteration of the term in *How to Read* (1931) articulates that logopoeia

> employs words not only for their direct meaning, but takes count in a special way of habits of usage, of the context we *expect* to find with the word, its usual concomitants, of its known acceptances, and of ironical play.[45]

One of the early critical responses to Loy within the academy, Virginia Kouidis's, similarly focuses on Loy's words: 'The word – in isolation, in unlikely conjunctions, or intertwined in glittering patterns of sound – is the sinew of her technical experiments and the pulse of her metaphysics and aesthetics.'[46] Loy's 'clean' words tend to divest themselves of their pasts. For Peter Nicholls, 'Unlike allusions, the single and singular word constitutes a kind of Duchampian ready-made, freestanding, autonomous, and abstracted from context';[47] Rachel Potter writes of Loy's poetry that 'her Futurist writing dislodges words from their 'glass cases' [of tradition] and gives them to us anew'.[48]

In contrast to her poetry, Loy's prose is less condensed: its units are not words or lines but minor incidents, or figures. The sometimes jagged movement within and between these results from juxtapositions against expected usages similar to those that operate in the poetry, but with a different local momentum in the novel form. Loy's prose in *Insel* suggests a fruitful context for Peter Nicholls's and Rachel Potter's observations on Loy's poetry, in that figures in *Insel* have a tendency to 'dislodge' from the narrative and point in different directions. Another reader of Loy's poetry offers a further suggestion that can be brought to reading the prose: Sean Pryor writes of *Anglo-Mongrels and the Rose* that it 'makes music' of the unstressed syllables, those that generally do not carry the root meaning, 'those relatively senseless sounds' that Hegel has called 'insignificant by-play'. Pryor writes that this 'represents the poem's most radical rebellion against poetic tradition'.[49] There is something too in Loy's prose of the 'insignificant by-play' that Pryor finds sounding in Loy's poetry, in that the figurations sometimes bounce off not the central comparison of the figure, but its edges, as in the dove's three-ring circus. *Insel*, which might be called a poetic novel, brings together features of Loy's modernist poetry with possibilities of the novel form in English and French in the late 1930s.

The momentum into figuration, anecdote, or other kinds of wit allows the easy shifts between the 'everyday' and 'unreal' aspects of Mrs Jones's friendships with Insel, suppressing the gulf between literal and figural elements and sidelining the need for plausibility. Such patterns can be followed in the novel's sentences. The tendency to move into figuration, anecdote or wit presents an Insel who is intriguingly transformative: 'So now I descended the stairway—Insel leaned over it in his disgraceful grace, "When shall I see you again?" he implored, clutching his concave breast. An awesome lunar reflection lit up his face from within' (52). Here, the last sentence pauses to transform *Insel* into part-lunar reflection, and similarly, as here, the short paragraphs of *Insel* are often punctuated by a pithy comment from the narrator in their last line. Such closing comments frequently involve a sideways movement into a new figure or into a new aspect of plot. This at times provides the narrator with the wit of an arch rejoinder to the anecdotal content of the paragraph: 'His role was helplessness personified. So here he was without a roof. In spite of the ceiling a pitiless rain seemed to be falling upon him already' (21). As with Insel as sugar dove above, the 'momentum' of such figures is carried in part by the distance they travel in figuration. Their energy is less in any kind of symbolism or plot than in reimagining Insel in a new mode. Insel, neither sugar dove nor yet destitute, at the same time fills these and other roles, if only in passing.

The novel offers a putative guide for reading this set of prose mechanisms. Mrs Jones's memory of Insel's 'Parnassian guffaw' is described with:

> Brought to a halt under the full force of my mental hilarity, I felt constrained to *continue to share it*—with what?— with whom? To do so I turned sideways. Whenever this *idea* of Insel occurred I could not go straight ahead—I had to turn to it—as when I had tried to sum him up on the Boulevard. (128)

This bodily movement has occurred earlier: 'One seldom took leave of him; (walking along with him one would unexpectedly drift sideways into a cab)' (51–52). Mrs Jones turns aside to try to take stock of her idea of Insel, but the comment fixes a suggestive resonance between Mrs Jones's personal response to Insel and the tendency of her prose style to move sideways into figuration and anecdote in his presence. Her sideways turn is preceded on the same page by her own 'dematerialization', which is uncannily modelled on Insel's: 'Like the witch's cat when cut apart running in opposite directions, suddenly my left leg began to dance off on its own' (128). The sideways drift is a suggestive figure for the local momentum of this energetic prose style, where the act of returning to wholeness or reconjoining the figures is ever on the threshold of impossibility. It is a congruent physical movement that, in 'Visitation of Insel', marks the sudden re-emergence of Insel's unmistakeable yet ethereal presence: 'Drawn

150   *The New Modernist Novel: Criticism and the Task of Reading*

from my couch, I rose erect, walking, so far did my head turn sideways, rather like a crab.'[50]

This effect of dispersion, a tendency of ideas to shift away from their starting points, might be seen as a prose analogue to another effect that has been described in Loy's verse. Writing of a poem from Loy's 'Love Songs to Joannes', John Wilkinson observes that 'every line starts with an effort of resumption': the pauses are not at the ends of lines, but at the start of each line. Wilkinson observes that Loy's lines in this poem often begin with a conjunction, and indeed that 'the act of conjunction is thereby asserted as the central performative task of verse'.[51] Wilkinson's striking reading is inevitably suggestive for reading Loy's prose in *Insel*. By comparison, in *Insel*, an arch rejoinder that ends a description of Insel may run with local momentum, and its end may require an analogous effort of resumption in the next sentence's or next paragraph's return to the narrative. This novel repeatedly performs the integration of figures, observations, anecdote and gossip into a narrative, but sometimes those smaller moments seem to carry the liveliest wit.

Yvor Winters, even if writing somewhat condescendingly on Loy's poetry in 1926, still perhaps captures some of this paradox between anecdote and narrative, moment and progression, state and experience: 'She moves like one walking through granite instead of air, and when she achieves a moment of beauty, it strikes one cold.'[52] He at first calls this 'clumsiness', but then ascribes it to 'the inherently unyielding quality of her material'. In prose, *Insel*'s paragraphs register moments of beauty, or of clarity, that may seem only secondarily conjoined into narrative, and the writing in *Insel* is as engaged with the possibilities of its medium of fiction as Loy's poems are with poetry.

§

So far, the selection of quotations from *Insel* here has been prompted by the question of how style can be observed in this novel's local momentum. I turn now, instead, to selecting quotations from what might be considered nodal points of the novel: instances where the narrative seems to suggest a particular connection or disconnection to other parts of the novel, through plot or other links. These nodal points are interesting because in *Insel*, markers of plot that might be anticipated to be important sometimes remain intriguingly untethered to the narrative, despite the connection being strongly suggested. The plot itself elusively resembles now a biography, now a rendering of Kafka, an underworld tale, a romance or a flimsy set of reminiscences; it has persuasively been read as a *Künstler(in)roman*.[53] How these shifting levels interact depends in part on the answers to questions that are not straightforwardly answered by recourse to *Insel*: in particular, what the relationship is between the two artists, why their friendship comes to an end and how that friendship relates to the completion of the narrator's book and *Insel*. The last of these, the narrator's relationship to her character and the timeline of the eventual composition of her 'book', remains unstated. Mrs Jones, the older woman who befriends the younger artist Insel, will later be the narrator of the novel *Insel*; when she first becomes familiar with Insel, she is writing a book, but, oddly for a novel about two artists which is narrated by one of them, her 'book' is mentioned only twice, each time in passing and without explanation, near the beginning and the end of their friendship (20, 153). It has been suggested that the 'book' may be *Insel* itself,[54] but Loy sometimes referred to her autobiographical works generally as her 'novel' or her 'book'.[55] Sandeep Parmar identifies the 'book' as 'The Child and the Parent', which Loy was writing at the time she knew Oelze.[56] In the second chapter, the narrator already owes her insights about Insel to her having reached 'the final phase in [her] analysis of him' (12) and is able to elucidate her commentary from hindsight: 'Later, when Insel and I became uncannily intimate I understood [. . .]' (15). This suggests that *Insel* is not the 'book' referred to in the final chapter, and that the narrator and character Mrs Jones do not coincide within the novel. *Insel*'s silence on the 'book' that its writer character mentions returns us to the question of what modes of reading this novel elicits, since various genres for this novel are suggested but not confirmed.

One of the initial formats for the friendship between Mrs Jones and Insel is that of biographer and subject. Early on, Mrs Jones raises the possibility of Insel's writing his own biography, and Insel considers the proposal: '"Oh," said Insel disinhibiting, "very well. It's not the material that is wanting," he sighed wearily, "the *stacks* of manuscript notes I have accumulated!"' However, he declines, and instead an exchange is established: '"We will make a pact. Get me to America and you *have* the biography." / "Done," I decided. "I'll write at once. America shall clamor for you."' (14). This pact is not observed on either side. Mrs Jones encounters several difficulties in her plan to write Insel's biography: Insel is reportedly less than forthcoming with useful material, and she observes that he himself is unsuitable for a biography: 'He was so at variance with himself, he existed on either side of a paradox' (16). By the end of the following chapter, the proposed biography has collapsed onto fictional models: 'You atrocious fake—you have no life to write—you're *acting* Kafka!' (18).[57] At the end of the novel, Mrs Jones leaves for the US while Insel, leaving Paris but not for the US, says, '"*Ich komme nach Hause.*" / He was "coming home"' (154), suggesting

152   *The New Modernist Novel: Criticism and the Task of Reading*

a return to a German-speaking country; and *Insel* is not evidently a biography of Insel.

The exchange is interesting in part because the novel seems later to deny any significance to it. In a late chapter, Mrs Jones asks to see the notes Insel has referred to, remembering 'those stacks of manuscript he had assured me were at my disposal in the days of "biography"':

> After a long persuasion he brought out a blotter, the kind for *écoliers* sold in bazaars. [. . .] It contained a single sheet of paper which he handed me with great precaution. Very few lines were written upon it. They formed a square block in the center of the page covering little more than the area of a postage stamp. (124)

Insel reads aloud the entire three sentences with great seriousness. But the obvious discrepancy between his world-weary promise of '*stacks* of manuscript notes' and the sparse few sentences he finally produces receives no comment from the narrator, who instead emphasises the solemnity of the occasion. The discrepancy seems significant, not only because it runs so clearly counter to Insel's earlier claim to be a potential biographical subject, but also because it implies that his initial offer, 'get me to America and you *have* the biography', was a sham, aimed at gaining passage to political security in the US. The paradox of the narrative discrepancy here might be attributed to Insel's strange charm as a character, and indeed this is the reading the novel seems to encourage. In this way, *Insel* seems to disdain an approach to reading that is overly interested in reconstructing factual details of plot – to disdain the tallying up of paradoxical facts. While there are occasional exceptions – one such exception is the incident of Insel, in a state of 'unrest' in a cab, holding fast to Mrs Jones's hand, which the narrator refers to twice afterwards (78, 117, 128) – the exceptions stand out in contrast with the normally more piecemeal structure of the narrative. Rather than requiring the comparison of disparate pieces of information through the novel, as has been fruitful for many modernist novels, *Insel* instead remains immersed in the moments and anecdotes that comprise its account.

And yet it is not possible for even this poetic novel entirely to escape being read as a novel. The inexact match between these two interactions seems characteristic of *Insel*'s style, but at the same time, the narrator's silence on the discrepancy might persuasively be read to mask the economic complexities of their friendship. The narrator implies that Insel is merely aiming to get passage to safety in the US, and gently mocks his 'variance'. But Insel's predicament, as a surrealist artist of German nationality in Paris during the depression era of the mid-1930s, suggests

Insel *and Literary Value*   **153**

that desperation, rather than trickery, is a more likely subtext here.[58] Where Mrs Jones has easy access to political security and the US, Insel fails to acquire that access. This novelistic reading steps outside the narrator's commentary and so finds in her an untrustworthy narrator. Yet this reading, too, is only suggested and never quite confirmed by *Insel*. Is Mrs Jones an untrustworthy narrator of Insel's struggles?[59] Or is she merely fallible, faithfully recording his allure as a luminous being and distracted by it, while remaining more oblivious than her readers to her subject's political and economic distress? In answer, Loy's novel gives its readers, simply, more anecdotes about Insel.

In the references to Insel's 'manuscript notes' and Mrs Jones's book, Loy's novel disrupts a process of reading as integration: a reading that seeks progressively obtained mathematical coherence with other parts of the novel is gently deflected. To take an interest in the discrepancy of the manuscript notes is to read against the grain of the novel's prose style. Reading it as a novel will indeed draw attention to Insel's political insecurity and exile, as against the narrator's focus here on Insel's luminous strangeness. But even in this, *Insel* deflects a reading that draws strongly on the kind of information that may have been pivotal for earlier modernist novels or their readers, such as the artist's developing relationship to their book, as with James Joyce's *A Portrait of the Artist as a Young Man* or Marcel Proust's *À la recherche du temps perdu*; or the correspondence between events and their later remembered versions, as with Proust's novel, Ford Madox Ford's *The Good Soldier* or Joyce's *Ulysses*; or even the reconstruction of and careful reference to earlier details of plot within the novel, as with the works by Proust and Joyce mentioned here and the works of other major modernists, for example Henry James. These three areas of correspondences – artist and work, events and memory, plot and story – had already been central to major modernist novels that were read by Loy and her circle, and they were also brought out in key readings at mid-century such as Harry Levin's of Proust and Joyce. *Insel*, by contrast with these novels and against the tendencies of some of their later readers, disdains coherence at the level of plot in some of its centrally intriguing repetitions. The mismatch of plot elements exposes the grain of the contemporary novel form by simply not following it, and in that mismatch, the medium blurs.[60]

Neither does *Insel* straightforwardly offer the kind of formal structure of significant repetition that characterises some contemporary surrealist texts, for instance the sculptor Alberto Giacometti's short story 'Le rêve, le Sphinx, et la mort de T.', which shares a Paris café milieu with the characters of *Insel*, but which allows the 'jaune ivoire' (yellow ivory) and other repetitions to join uncannily the different times, places or panels of

154   *The New Modernist Novel: Criticism and the Task of Reading*

the story.[61] Diane Drouin observes that in *Insel*'s style, 'la phrase préserve une structure et une syntaxe cohérentes, [. . .] mais son sens résiste à l'interprétation' (the sentence preserves a coherent structure and syntax, but its meaning resists interpretation).[62] Drouin's observation suggests that *Insel* presents a style in the novel form that challenges habitual modes of reading modernist prose fiction. Indeed, this challenge amounts to an implicit critique of the contemporary novel form.

In a chapter entitled 'Perspective' in his *Memoir of an Art Gallery*, Julien Levy focuses on passages to characterise Loy's prose:

> Of course it was not only painters who were exploring the new prospects of space and time as modified by psychology, or the point of view. Some years ago James Joyce pointed out to me how time was frozen into a kind of stopped-motion heraldic insignia in some of Herman Melville's descriptive passages. His own *Ulysses* offers many examples of slow-motion, simultaneity, and speeded immobilities. Mina Loy, in the book she had been writing for more than fifteen or twenty years, based her entire approach on this sort of temporal disformation.[63]

Levy's comments suggest a consistency of style across Loy's prose writing in her 'book', so that his observations may be taken as relevant to *Insel*. For Levy, Loy's prose participates in a modernisation that aligns it with surrealist visual art as well as with English-language contemporary writing, including Joyce, and style in Loy's book is accessible in 'passages'. Style, for Levy, is the locus of her art in fiction – rather than, say, her art being in the architecture of her novel, its plot or the character of its protagonists. The passages that catch Joyce's eye and those that remain in Levy's mind are 'descriptive'.

Yet insofar as this is still a novel, character and tone matter. In the following exchange, Insel has been unable to afford shoes that fit properly. Here, the conversational clichés stand out against the prose style of Loy's novel: in comparison with the prose that surrounds them, they jar because of a too effective mimesis of the real of contemporary conversation, in a text whose prose is elsewhere so singular:

> 'Let's have a look at your feet,' I said as he came weightlessly towards me. He drew off his slippers, padding over the bare boards on the drained Gothic feet of a dying ivory Christ.
>
> 'What's this?' I teased, pointing to a lurid patch on his instep, 'a chancre?'
>
> 'No, it's only where my shoe rubs me. I bought new shoes when I sold that picture and they hurt me,' he explained, frowning helplessly.
>
> 'Why not try pouring water into them and wearing them till they "adapt"? It often works.'
>
> A strange bruise. It shone with the eerie azure of a neon light. (118–19)

Mrs Jones's homely advice to wet the leather so the shoes adapt is incongruous when set alongside Insel's eerie luminosity. Her line is closer to a cliché of conversation than to the habitual style of Mrs Jones. Its tone fits with Loy's practicality, for example in her lampshade designs and other practical plans. That voice of Loy is less apparent in Mrs Jones, however, and the line stands out in *Insel*, not as a nodal point of plot, but as a point of momentary disconnection in the novel's style.

In seeming awkwardly integrated into *Insel*'s style, the advice might have the effect of a conversation between real people who have not yet acquired the limitations and allure of their fictional versions. In other words, it might have the effect of retaining some of the character of a remembered moment with Richard Oelze before the moment and the character were made fictional. And in this way, by failing to integrate into prose style of the finished fiction, as a kind of glitch, the exchange hooks into an awkwardly inseparable narrative, that of the impoverished refugee from Germany from whom Mrs Jones is commissioning art. The lapse is brief: already by the next sentence, Insel's 'strange bruise', the physical result of poverty, is transfigured into a surrealist artwork: 'It shone with the eerie azure of a neon light.' He is once again the artist, his poverty now surreal. In this brief lapse, the impoverished artist seems incompletely assimilated to the character of Insel within the novel, since the prose momentarily presents his poverty directly, without the effects of luminosity and eeriness that Insel's struggles tend to carry for Mrs Jones.

This transformation runs through the sentences of the novel. Mrs Jones's tone, established from the opening page, furnishes the novel's sharp wit by recognising the deep desperation of Insel's situation and turning it to genius. Even in the first line, quoted above, his hunger is easily subordinated to his alluring strangeness with 'although': 'The first I heard of Insel was the story of a madman, a more or less surrealist painter, who, although he had nothing to eat, was hoping to sell a picture to buy a set of false teeth' (3). Yet on occasion, the ethics of that tone are gently subjected to question by the narrator. Mrs Jones's and Insel's major argument, which sees Insel living in her flat and which ends only at their last meeting, begins with her comments on Insel's visit to Mlle Alpha, where she has praised his 'knack of dying on doorsteps' and teased, 'Insel, I believe you put *lots* of money in the bank!' She has insinuated that he collects money from a number of women. Her narration acknowledges her character's failure to grasp the situation fully: 'I could feel a distinct change in his aural temperature, but I was laughing too much to pay attention' (140).The context of this exchange is their deciding together whether the shivering Insel can afford new boots out of Mrs Jones's loan to him. Later, Mrs Jones tells him she suspects that

156   *The New Modernist Novel: Criticism and the Task of Reading*

he has 'blown' the thousand francs she has given him for an overcoat. Although he humours her by praising Paris's nightlife, he objects: '"You told me," he burst out unhappily, writhing with reproach, "that I put lots of money in the bank"' (148). Here, Insel almost outdoes *Insel* in accurately remembering an earlier plot detail, an uncommon occurrence in the novel. His objection draws attention to the character Mrs Jones's light treatment of his suffering. Sarah Hayden meticulously documents the economic relationship that underpins this friendship, where Insel's livelihood is dependent on his benefactors' conviction that he is an artistic genius.[64] Yet the novel sympathetically witnesses his plight, and in response, *Insel* makes of Insel a luminous artist, the centre of a novel whose prose style seems generated by his antics. The narration skips away from his poverty, employing it instead as material for figuration and anecdotes. As David Trotter writes of Loy's 'Songs to Joannes', 'the noise is essential to the signal'.[65] The poverty of Insel comes through in the gaps and glitches in the anecdotes, only to be creatively transformed momentarily by the next anecdote. Insel's struggles provide material for Mrs Jones's sublimation of the impoverished artist into a magical being.

It is not only Insel who is made luminous in this prose style. In the café at the Dôme, Insel shares a table with two women he has been dating as sex workers. In the novel's record of the scene, the women are identified as Black. On Mrs Jones's return, Insel has argued with the women about a packet of cigarettes and has hit one of them. In response to Insel's actions, they insult him with '*maquereau*' (pimp) and '*salaud*' (skunk; 60). The scene is followed by Mrs Jones reprimanding Insel on his treatment of the two women. Admonishing him, Mrs Jones dwells on the sounds of their words: "It made such a gorgeous sound when they were shouting—almost *macrusallo*. Like crucified mackerel—' (71). Her attention to the strange sounds of the women's insults to Insel at once preserves the women's serious accusations against him and, equally, diverts attention from the meaning of the words to their sound. Arguing with Insel about his mistreatment of the two women, Mrs Jones comments, 'It was fun teasing him. Like tickling a dazed gnome with a spider's silk' (70). Her rejoinder, ending this short paragraph, shares the sense of adventure everywhere evident in this novel's style. Yet the adventure shows, as elsewhere, the prose style's tendency to move away from its subject, here the mistreatment of the two women by Insel. The poetic sideways movement is equally a movement away from judgement, comment and fuller analysis. This movement away from direct comment is complicated by the use of racialised vocabulary in the novel to describe the two women. They are identified, here and elsewhere in the novel, as 'negresses'. This episode leads to the question: beyond Loy's own poetry and fiction, what are the commitments or attachments of this style?

For Susan Rosenbaum, this incident is an instance of the surrealist 'double image' that was popularised by Salvador Dalí, and that can be seen for example in Man Ray's portraits. The double image is where an image that represents one object simultaneously represents another completely different object.[66] Rosenbaum notes the double image in use in the group Insel makes with the two women, where the image represents both a fight over cigarettes and the 'double starfish' image made by the women (59). Similarly, she finds in the word '*macrusallo*' a 'double auditory image' providing both the original words and the audio counterpart of their combination, 'crucified mackerel'. As Rosenbaum notes, Man Ray's photographic 'double images' juxtapose sexual and racial difference without comment, in ways that are calculated to scandalise bourgeois sensitivity. Using this technique in the 'auditory double image', argues Rosenbaum, allows Loy to 'comment[] wittily on Insel as a parasite'. Rosenbaum's analysis of the 'double image' is suggestive for Loy's style: the movement between two images in the 'double image' bears a resemblance to what I have analysed as the sideways movement into figuration, or the local momentum of Loy's prose in *Insel*. For Rosenbaum, this use of the double image links Loy's style with a key surrealist trope. Rosenbaum, too, notes the absence of explicit judgement accompanying such images, for example in Man Ray's politically provocative photographs.[67]

In the course of Insel and Mrs Jones's conversation about them, the women undergo their own transformation, when they are present not in person, but in Insel's memory. Insel, goaded to regret his disrespect to them by Mrs Jones, swears to 'renounce' the women, whose imagined presence he accordingly throws aside, and whose mental image 'melted and dripped like black tears into limbo', into the metro station, there to be 'borne away on a hearse of the living throbbing along an iron rail which must be a solidified sweep of the Styx' (69). Here, the local momentum of the prose style allows the two sex workers to create their own performance art, even when they are not present. There is plenty to comment on in this image, which suggests a level of consciousness within the novel of the political stakes of Insel's mistreatment of the women. One quality that can be taken up here is that, in the melting and dripping bodies, and in the image of a 'hearse of the living', the women's performance art has a distinct surrealist edge.

Style's Company

What are this style's attachments to surrealism? Can the surrealist commitments of *Insel*'s style add to these women's performance art in the

158   *The New Modernist Novel: Criticism and the Task of Reading*

narrator's voice? What are the politics, surrealist or otherwise, of this piece of performance art? If *Insel* is in some ways unlike more recognised modernist novels, how far is it more like a surrealist novel? If a context for the artist Insel is provided by a cosmopolitan mix of European surrealists in Paris in the 1930s, that mix may offer a corresponding context for Loy's novel's style – not just in surrealist art but in the figure of the artist more generally. The process of reading Loy's style closely leads here to questions about the novel's relationships to contemporary surrealism.

Mrs Jones's responses to Insel's art offer a reasonably direct commentary on his version of surrealism. Mrs Jones is cautious in her commentary, but a muted critique emerges of the painting *Die Irma*. The narrator's description of *Die Irma* identifies the hands as 'as if nailed to her hips like crossed swords'. This description carries a suggestion of violence that remains vague, and that is given no specific points of resonance in the remainder of the discussion. The painting is quite close to Oelze's 1935–1936 works *Frieda* and *Frieda II*, which show a figure with a swollen lip and crossed hands that, like those in Insel's painting, are oddly paired. Although *Frieda II* shows deep red colouring on the clothing near the neck of the figure, comparing the two suggests that the violence here is introduced in the description of *Die Irma*, since it is not obvious from Oelze's painting.[68] When Insel shows the painting to Mrs Jones, the narrator comments, 'the magnetic bond uniting her painted body to his emaciated stature – as if she were of an ectoplasm proceeding from him – was so apparent one felt as if one were surprising an insane liaison at almost too intimate a moment'. The oddly intimate relationship between the painter and his painting provokes an objection from Mrs Jones: '"But Insel," I asked, "her upper lip is about to burst with some unavowable disease. You have formed her of pus. Her body has already melted."' Insel's control over his subject's body is a problem, a cause for remonstration and for Mrs Jones's dislike of the work. Insel interprets the relationship differently: '"Exactly," he answered with mysterious satisfaction' (110–11). Insel is undisturbed by what Mrs Jones sees as the mutilation of *Die Irma*'s body, taking her comment not as criticism but as description of an artistic intent.

Mrs Jones's objections remain unstated. But there are several suggestions through the novel that her criticism may relate to gender. Notably, these suggestions include her objections to Insel's treatment of women elsewhere in the novel, particularly after the episode at the Dôme cafe.[69] In their exchange over *Die Irma*, Insel's distress at Mrs Jones's dislike of the painting suggests that he is unaware of this dimension of her dislike: '"She ought not to be," he cried out, "if you don't like her, I am going to destroy her"' (111). His overwrought response displaces the criticism of his painting onto the grounds of personal approval or disapproval from Mrs Jones and avoids further confrontation of its gender politics.[70]

Mrs Jones's briefer comments on Insel's other work do not share her negative opinion of *Die Irma*. But the painting remains a focal point for their interaction as artists. The nature of her response to it suggests a wider commentary on art and artists that is mediated by the figure of Insel the surrealist artist. This broader reflection, which goes beyond surrealism, is made possible by Insel's interchangeability with other artists besides Oelze. In the figure of Insel, Loy's novel offers comment on artists loosely in Loy's milieu. For example, Julien Levy's later *Memoir of an Art Gallery* portrays the painter Arshile Gorky as a melancholy and troubled, but gentle and generous, gifted artist in way that resonates with Loy's Insel.[71] Since Levy knew Loy's unpublished novel, the novel may have lent imaginative shape to Levy's later description, but the resonance between Levy's Gorky and Loy's Insel also suggests that Insel draws on other artist figures, living or mediated in literary form. In the transfer of the 'Powell film' from experience to fiction, for instance, Insel has replaced not Oelze but, more probably, Constantin Brancusi.[72] The cafés visited by Mrs Jones and Insel – the Café Select, the Dôme and the Lutetia – were artists' cafés in Paris, peopled at various times between the wars by Djuna Barnes at the Dôme,[73] Samuel Beckett and friends at the Select[74] and James Joyce and Robert McAlmon at the Lutetia.[75] Ernest Hemingway gives an account in *A Moveable Feast* of meeting the painter Jules Pascin at the Dôme with two models, which recalls the painter Insel's interaction with two sex workers in the Dôme.[76] The sculptor Alberto Giacometti writes a short story based in late-night cafés of Paris, similar to those frequented by Insel;[77] even Samuel Beckett, translator of Paul Éluard, André Breton and René Crevel for the surrealist issue of *This Quarter* and subsequently for Levy's volume *Surrealism*, might be recognisable in Insel.[78] Rather than specific character traits, what seems relevant here is a concept of the avant-garde artist that was shared, and lived, in the thirties. The fact that Beckett was stabbed by an underworld figure in 1938 eerily matches the world of *Insel*.[79] *Insel's* portrait of a surrealist seems a point of departure for a more general meditation on avant-garde art and artists, in the terms of a prose style that is ideally matched to its subject, Insel.

One of Insel's namesakes may be the German-language little magazine *Die Insel*, which ran from 1899 to 1902 and was edited by Otto Julius Bierbaum, Alfred Walter Henmel and Rudolf Alexander Schröder. Loy may have encountered the magazine when she was studying art in Munich as a teenager in 1900.[80] This magazine's first issues, with their ornate decorations, Fraktur script and intricate *fin-de-siècle* drawings, suggest the decadent devotion to art that Insel exhibits. Authors published in German

160   *The New Modernist Novel: Criticism and the Task of Reading*

original and in German translation included Aubrey Beardsley, Albrecht Dürer, André Gide, Hugo von Hofmannsthal, Maurice Maeterlinck, Heinrich Mann, Friedrich Nietzsche, Rainer Maria Rilke, August Strindberg, Paul Verlaine, Frank Wedekind and others.[81] From 1900 the magazine appeared in modern script. In the inaugural issue, the editors comment on their choice of name in ways that quite closely echo Insel. *Die Insel*, they say, is not meant to denote exclusivity or seem excessively bourgeois, but rather suggests a refusal to join the cries of triumph for modern art, and a recognition of how hard it is to achieve development in the life of the artist against the difficulties that fall in the way of such development. In order to recover art that can later serve as a document and a justification for their magazine, they know that 'man mit sorgfältigen Händen, mit liebevollen Augen und mit viel Anstrengung suchen muß, um die wenigen Keime, die wenigen schönen Reste zusammen zu tragen und sich mit ihnen gleichsam einen Garten, eine Oase auszuschmücken' (one must seek, with careful hands, with loving eyes and with great effort, to bring together the few seeds, the few beautiful remnants and with them to decorate for oneself a kind of garden, an oasis) and that 'man die spärlichen Strahlen einer karg gewordenen Sonne sammeln und ausnüßen muß, um irgendwo versteckt und einsam Lebensspuren zu erhalten, die vielleicht später zu fruchtbarer Entwicklung reifen mögen' (one must gather and make use of the thin rays of a faded sun in order to preserve, somewhere hidden and lonely, traces of life, traces that may perhaps later ripen to a fruitful development).[82] Their vocabulary very closely resembles Insel's: Mrs Jones comments that 'This very word, *Entwicklung*, was so much Insel's word; its sound seemed to me onomatopoeic of his intellectual graph' (123); their word *Strahlen*, which in *Insel* designates Insel's rays, is perhaps the closest word to him in the novel. More generally, the editors' devotion to art, including their sense of the rarity of good art, resonates with the absoluteness of Insel's dedication to his art. The magazine's commitment to nurturing modern art and writing, along with its actual historical role in doing so, thirty-odd years before *Insel* was written, implicitly lend gravity to the portrait of this German surrealist devoted to his art and centre him in a European modern art movement.

However, various modern art movements are present in *Insel*. The novel itself carries vestiges of Loy's engagement with the Italian Futurists: Mrs Jones's 'metal beetles', for instance, cast a satirical glance at F. T. Marinetti:

> Darting about amazingly in the autumn vapor innumerable metal beetles of various species with which modern man, still unable to create soft-machines and so limited to the construction of heavy plagiarisms that sometimes crush him, had sprinkled the *carrefour* facing us, where gasoline impregnating the dust had begotten a vitiated yet exhilarating up-to-date breath of life. (37)

Marinetti's 'Manifesto of Futurism' hymns 'a new beauty; the beauty of speed. A racing car whose hood is adorned with great pipes, like serpents of explosive breath – a roaring car that seems to ride on grapeshot – is more beautiful than the *Victory of Samothrace*.'[83] But the slightly satirical tone is also a reminder of Loy's break with Futurist outlooks. Here, the beetles are already vestiges, 'heavy plagiarisms', and the satirical glance could equally be directed at Salvador Dalí's 'soft-machines' of an avant-garde belonging to a generation later, after the purchase of *The Persistence of Memory* by Julien Levy in 1931,[84] or even to Loy's own conceptions of soft-machines: Mrs Jones refers to Insel as a 'soft-machine' (7).[85] So there are a number of modern art movements that leave traces in the novel.

Nancy Cunard's likely presence in *Insel*, then, is not surprising. Mlle Alpha resembles Cunard: her eyes, 'volcanic' (29) and 'like coals, continent, of their fire' (103), recall the lights of Nancy Cunard's eyes that begin Loy's poem 'Nancy Cunard'.[86] While the connection is not confirmed, Mlle Alpha's day-bed decorated with African sculptures also suggests a match with Cunard, who was known as a collector of objects of African art and who edited the *Negro Anthology*, which came out in 1934, shortly before the period covered by Mrs Jones's and Insel's time in Paris.[87] The anthology included photographs of African artworks from different regions, and among many other entries, it included essays by surrealists, notably the Surrealist Group's anti-colonial 'Murderous Humanitarianism'.[88]

These different reflections complicate what it might mean when Mrs Jones says to Insel, 'you are organically surreal' (108), with the suggestion that Insel is 'too surrealistic for the surrealists' (104). Rather than aligning with Breton's Paris surrealism, Insel is closer to the strand of surrealism that Loy and Levy helped to establish in New York, where Richard Oelze's major work *Erwartung* was first published in Levy's 1936 *Surrealism* and where Alfred Barr's 1936 'Fantastic Art, Dada, Surrealism' exhibition was held at the Museum of Modern Art.[89] Insel collects resonances from different avant-garde groups, but focuses them on a portrait of a late thirties destitute artist, a German surrealist in Paris, and on the literary and cultural milieus associated with this figure.

This tension between Insel as a character in a novel who carries a special aura and Insel as a locus of commentary is a novelistic tension, an aspect of the problem of representation in the novel form. This brings us back to the question of what kind of novel *Insel* might be. Insel the artist suggests a broader figure of the displaced artist in the 1930s, but *Insel* the novel can helpfully be read against surrealist novels. Louis Aragon's *Paysan de Paris* (1926) and André Breton's *Nadja* (1928) situate 'surrealism' as involving a repudiation of the 'novel' in favour of newly experimental modes of prose fiction, as does Philippe Soupault's *Les dernières nuits de*

162   *The New Modernist Novel: Criticism and the Task of Reading*

Paris (1928), which was translated by William Carlos Williams in 1929 as *Last Nights of Paris*. Like Insel, Breton's Nadja and Soupault's Georgette have a special aura for their narrators. As characters, like Insel, they are also generic markers of the surreal coexisting with the real of Paris.

The context of these novels offers some answers to a puzzle posed by Loy's novel. The strangeness of Insel's rays or *Strahlen* and of other effects of his luminous being are difficult to place generically in an Anglophone context, because they resist reading in the terms of any of various contemporary Anglophone concepts of the novelistic real.[90] What remains opaque to reading the following passage is what the two characters actually see. Insel has requested peppermint tea:

> 'The peppermint won't grow out of the floor,' I advised.
> 'It will,' said Insel. 'You're to stay here.'
> And I found myself staring together with him.
> It was no peppermint growing out of the planes of polished oak. Only the creeping organic development of a microscopic undergrowth such as carpeted chaos in his work, almost as closely cramped as the creamy convolutions of a brain. Foliage of mildew it spread—and spread. (80–81)

Such shifts in reality, where Insel gives off sparks, or where his suit, when cleaned, turns white as he has predicted and finally black again when 'Insel must have forgotten about it' (92), offer, first, a descriptive sense of Insel's impression on the character Mrs Jones. In this sense, what the characters see might look like one of Insel's paintings, with their 'almost invisible herbiage' (122), or even one of Richard Oelze's, for example *Phantastische Komposition* of 1935.[91] But the implausibility of such moments renders them also, second, a generically oriented gesture: they are part of Insel's luminous, astral qualities, but they also pull away from the language Loy writes in towards contemporary French and German surrealist fiction and art. In this way, the conditions of plausibility and implausibility in *Insel* offer grounds for testing this novel's style against contemporary art and writing. Indeed, since many of the novel's sideways movements into figuration of Insel involve transitions that are implausible on a literal level, they are connected with moments of the eruption of the marvellous into the everyday of fiction.

In fiction, it is possible to find an affinity in Insel's rays with the stories and novels of Kafka, who was recognised as a surrealist by Breton in the 1930s, or the fictions of another reader of Kafka, Bruno Schulz, who translated Kafka's *Der Prozeß* (*The Trial*) into Polish in 1936. In his short fiction, Schulz develops a strangeness eloquently distilled from implausibility that has affinities with Loy's writing in *Insel*.[92] But it is French surrealist work with chance that seems to offer the most far-reaching comparison. In Insel's rays there is an affinity with the 'marvellous' as explored by French surrealists, including in fiction. Aragon's *Paysan de Paris* locates the 'marvellous' in the Paris nightworld, where *Insel*, *Last Nights of Paris* and *Nadja* take place; the latter three all involve the appeal of a person who figures the surreal possibilities of the city. Georgette's mystique in *Last Nights of Paris* prefigures Insel's, and like him, she sometimes detaches from her mystery, which is hers only at night:

> I felt that she was not the same since I had learned that she could be Georgette of the day and Georgette of the night, that two women, as different from each other as darkness and light, dwelt in that pale and supple body, that shadow dressed in black. She seemed to attract mystery as water attracts the light. About her danced I know not what cold and inviting flame. Georgette possessed the charm of the invisible.
>
> Since our first meeting in the place Saint-Germain-des-Prés, she had taken part in every event possessing an element of strangeness at which I had been present. She was at once the witness and the cause of this incomprehensible succession of mysteries.[93]

Like Insel, Georgette is accompanied by strange and mysterious events; she seems to share his incandescence (she is 'phosphorescent');[94] like Insel too, Georgette is – for the narrator – unsettlingly capable of losing her mystique and reverting to plain humanity. Unlike Insel's charm, Georgette's mystery appears to the narrator as inseparable from that of Paris: she is the city.[95] What read in *Insel* as moments of mild, witty implausibility in English involving his luminosity might then more interestingly be understood as moments of the French and German surreal permeating Loy's novel. In *Last Nights of Paris*, the density of generic markers of surrealism emphasises the surrealist context even to the point of satire: the extended meditation on chance; the preoccupation of the narrator and all the characters with the night and its mysteries; the easy familiarity with a Paris underworld and with sex work. It is hard to tell whether the gender essentialism on show in the novel, in the persistent identification of Georgette with sensuality and sex, is satire or not. If *Last Nights of Paris* is not itself satire, then it is gently satirised in *Insel*, whose wit at the expense of Insel's relationships with women hints at the comedy of surrealism's relationships with women.

William Carlos Williams's translation of Philippe Soupault's *Les dernières nuits de Paris* makes available the French surrealist text as an American modernist novel, with the result that the translation sets in play a dialogue of forms between modernist novel and surrealist text. In an afterword to the translation, Soupault draws attention to the work's being the product of 'poets', himself and Williams, and disclaims

164   *The New Modernist Novel: Criticism and the Task of Reading*

the generic marker '*roman*', instead calling his book 'my "testimony"', incorrectly subtitled "novel"'.[96] Williams, however, refers to the book as a 'novel' and then a 'Dadaist novel' in his 1958 poem *Paterson*.[97] Williams's use of the English term 'novel' to describe his own prose works of the period condenses an antagonistic engagement with the history of the term in these works that gives a precedent to this description. There may be an allusion to the title of Williams's translation, *Last Nights of Paris*, towards the end of *Insel*, where Mrs Jones observes Insel's new 'lubricity' with women: '"the last nights in Paris"'—he raved ecstatically. '*Es ist so schön das Leben, wenn man so leben kann*—It is so beautiful living, when one *can* so live"' (145–46). Like Williams's translation, Loy's *Insel* brings surrealist connections into the novel form in English.

In the context of *Last Nights of Paris* and *Nadja*, *Insel*'s tension between a character whose personality so captivates the narrator, and a character understood as a generically representative artist figure seems an especially acute tension. Insel, Nadja and Georgette are represented as themselves, but they are also figures for understanding a key but elusive set of ideas within surrealism as an evolving set of literary and art concepts. In a walk with Breton in Paris, Nadja's turning aside seems as generative for Breton's novel as Insel's is for Loy's novel: 'Nous tournons par la rue de Seine, Nadja resistant à aller plus loin en ligne droite. Elle est à nouveau très distraite.' ('We reach the corner of the Rue du Seine, where we turn, Nadja no longer wishing to continue straight ahead. She is still quite distressed.')[98] The haphazard journeys Nadja and Breton have traced through Paris and its cafés have been the physical correlation of the Nadja whose unexpected turns of thought, feeling and phrase have so captivated Breton. *Nadja*, too, finds the traces of the surreal in implausibility, here theorised via chance:

> Le regard de Nadja fait maintenant le tour des maisons. 'Vois-tu, là-bas, cette fenêtre? Elle est noire, comme toutes les autres. Regarde bien. Dans une minute elle va s'éclairer. Elle sera rouge.' La minute passe. La fênetre s'éclaire. Il y a, en effet, des rideaux rouges. (Je regrette, mais je n'y puis rien, que ceci passe peut-être les limites de la crédibilité.)[99]

> Nadja's eyes now sweep over the surrounding houses. 'Do you see that window up there? It's black, like all the rest. Look hard. In a minute it will light up. It will be red.' The minute passes. The window lights up. There are, as a matter of fact, red curtains. (I am sorry, but I am unable to do anything about the fact that this may exceed the limits of credibility.)[100]

Notwithstanding the explanatory note on the following page for 'the partisans of easy solutions' ('les amateurs des solutions faciles'), *Nadja* revels in the way this and other chance events supervene on reality in the presence of Nadja. Breton's novel's philosophising bent distinguishes *Nadja* from Loy's more sardonic takes on Insel's moments of implausibility, but the generic voltage of surrealism achieved via the meticulous description of idle habits of the narrator's protégé(e) belongs to both novels, as well as to *Last Nights of Paris*.

Insel's flickering transfiguration in *Insel* from desperate political refugee into radiant being retains some of the strain of the transfiguration, but this is a strain that is perhaps more readily readable in *Nadja* and *Last Nights of Paris*. In the cases of all three characters, Insel, Nadja and Georgette, the representation that binds the character as surrealist draws awkwardly on that character's material circumstances, which in all three cases are wretched. Yet the charm of Soupault's text is not any rigorous social analysis of Georgette's situation or her brother's, but an admiring observation of them as genuinely mysterious within the wretched, ordinary situations they find themselves. Nadja asks Breton to write a book about her, which he does, but at the same time her situation at the end of *Nadja* might be summed up with: 'Mais Nadja était pauvre, ce qui au temps où nous vivons suffit à passer condamnation sur elle [. . .]. Elle était seule aussi' ('But Nadja was poor, which in our time is enough to condemn her [. . .]. She was also alone'). She is 'alone' to the narrator Breton even though Nadja has said to Breton's wife, 'Je n'ai que vous pour amis' ('I have no friends but you'), referring to Breton and his wife. At the time of finishing his book, he has not yet 'osé m'enquérir de ce qu'il était advenu de Nadja' ('dared investigate what has become of Nadja') after hearing that she has been committed to the Vaucluse sanatorium, but he rails against state care for mental ill health.[101] This hospitalisation was the situation of the real person who inspired the character Nadja.[102] Both Breton and Mrs Jones try to give money but without effect; both voluntarily farewell their subject into dire circumstances before writing about them – yet they write about them as not just ordinary beings, but as sublimely surreal.

Still, there are differences between these novels. Mrs Jones insists that Insel is 'organically surreal', much as their authors insist of Georgette and Nadja. But Insel differs from Georgette and even from the artist Nadja in that he is a recognised artist in his own right, in theory independently of Mrs Jones's written portrait of him, and perhaps even of her patronage. Bearing in mind Nadja's own voice in *Nadja*, for example in its illustrations, Insel's art of surrealist performance, unlike both Georgette's and Nadja's, is not ultimately reducible to Mrs Jones's performance or dependent on it, as theirs may be to their authors' book. In this sense, once again, Insel is not only 'organically surreal', as they are,

166   *The New Modernist Novel: Criticism and the Task of Reading*

but is also a more generic figure for a displaced starving artist, surrealist or otherwise.

Of course, in Insel's role as this broader figure, there is also a feminist dimension, also not missed by Loy. In Alys Moody's analysis, 'Loy insists throughout *Insel* that the brilliance of the starving artist relies for its shine on the network of women who feed him.' Moody wittily observes that Mrs Jones 'closes the novel by usurping Insel's own position as starving artist', and her new position is confirmed in 'Visitation of Insel' where she is materially dependent on her daughter.[103] These various permutations go beyond the binary gendered roles envisaged in *Last Nights of Paris* and *Nadja*. Questions about the ethics of Mrs Jones's friendship with Insel flicker through these different critical positions available in the novel. Insel, lent extra life by Georgette and Nadja and but not constrained by them, remains both a luminously surreal character and a figure for struggling modern artists more generally.

Loy's modernism is café-based, rather than salon-based, and in this it is inclusive of outsider figures such as Oelze, whose counterpart Insel struggles to be accepted by the Paris surrealists, and such as the two women in the Dôme, whose act is transformed into surrealist performance with Insel, first in the café and then again later, in the course of Insel's and Mrs Jones's conversation about them. Susan Rosenbaum, in a wide-ranging and persuasive argument, finds a critique of 'surrealists' beliefs about sex and race' in Mrs Jones's criticisms of Insel for his treatment of the two women.[104] Mrs Jones's objection to Insel's disrespect towards the two women and to his mistreatment of them is clear, and in that critique the episode suggests and frames a broader critique of the racial politics of the Paris surrealists' aesthetics. As Rosenbaum convincingly argues, the episode comments on, rather than merely reproducing, stereotypes that surrealists reproduced. In addition, the women are memorialised in the novel, which gives them their own performance art, even when they are absent. They are figured as artists, even if the presence of their art in the novel is dependent on Insel's presence. Yet the sparseness of commentary in this novel's prose style means it is challenging to gauge the extent of the critique, since the novel skips away from commentary and analysis at these points. *Insel*'s critique of surrealism's politics of race remains less developed than its critique of surrealism's gender politics.

This may be partly, however, because Loy's novel is actively partaking in a surrealist mode. In the mention of the sculpted day-bed in Mlle Alpha's flat (103), *Insel* bears comparison specifically with the primitivism of *Nadja* in its reproduction of two artworks from Pasifika cultures: a mask from New Britain in Papua New Guinea, and a sculpture from

Rapa Nui (Easter Island). Breton's novel reproduces photographs of the two artworks, but the only identification given them is Nadja's naming of the artworks in her own idiom, as respectively 'Tiens, Chimène!' ('Goodness, Chimène!'), which refers to the French opera of that name, and 'Je t'aime, je t'aime!' ('I love you, I love you').[105] Will Atkin identifies the sculpture from Rapa Nui as a wooden Moai Kavakava statuette, which Breton had bought in France from a sailor as a teenager.[106] *Insel*'s mention of Mlle Alpha's sculpted day-bed aligns to the pan-Africanism of the 1936 *Negro Anthology* rather than to *Nadja*'s reproduction of the artworks from Papua New Guinea and Rapa Nui.[107] However, Nadja's discussions of artworks also include a mask from Guinea, which is now in Breton's home, and a 'small statue of a seated Cacique', presumably from the Caribbean.[108] As Claire Howard notes, 'Beginning in the 1920s, the Surrealists collected and displayed Oceanic and Indigenous North American objects as a counterbalance to Cubism's formal appropriation of African art and as an attempt to decolonize aesthetics.'[109] As a gesture that reaches beyond European art, the sculpted day-bed carries elements of both surrealist collections and Nancy Cunard's collections.

In *Nadja*'s naming of the two artworks, they become the artworks they are in the novel through Nadja's presence, with her responses providing the captions to the illustrations. Unlike the art objects reproduced in Nancy Cunard's *Negro Anthology* and the reproductions in Alain Locke's 1925 collection *The New Negro*, *Nadja*'s art objects do not carry authentic names. There is a suggestion in the way the objects are presented in *Nadja* of the idea of 'deux images différentes', a version of the double image, which was elaborated later by Breton in his essay 'Crisis of the Object'. Breton's essay was originally written to accompany the 'Surrealist Exhibition of Objects' of 1936. Breton expounds the 'suite ininterrompue de latences' ('endless latent possibilities'), beyond daily usage, that arise for the viewer of the object when its 'pouvoir évocateur' ('evocative power') is perceived. For Breton, quoting Gaston Bachelard, there is more to find in the hidden reality than in what is directly manifested. Christina Rudosky comments on Breton's idea here of *détournement*, a turning away of the object towards a new identity created by how it is perceived in the space it is in.[110]

This analysis of *détournement* links a key characteristic of *Insel*'s prose style, its tendency to turn sideways into figuration, with Breton's account of surrealist objects in the 1930s. There is an echo here of Nadja's surreal tendency to turn, or no longer to wish to continue straight ahead. Later, Loy glosses the surrealist use of objects as 'superimposed viewpoints as partial creation', which echoes these ideas.[111] Discussing Breton's and Gérard Legrand's *L'art magique* of 1957, Will Atkin argues

168   *The New Modernist Novel: Criticism and the Task of Reading*

that 'the surrealists credited Pacific culture with demonstrating complex mechanisms of symbolic slippage that afforded a means of reinscribing western culture from within'.[112] Maia Nuku affirms the agency given to Oceanic art in this positioning by surrealists, and explains of Oceanic art that in its unknowability, 'it is the art itself, released from the constraints of meaning, that creates a space for expansion, for action, for the radical enchantment that so enthralled its Surrealist admirers'.[113] The wider context of the reproductions in *Nadja*, then, is the global aesthetic connections that Breton's surrealism aimed at.

These aesthetic aspirations were accompanied by a distinct political stance. The 1934 piece by the Surrealist Group in *Negro Anthology* rails against 'the imperialist war' and its effects on Europe, Africa, Oceania and Asia and advocates 'changing the imperialist war, in its chronic and colonial form, into a civil war'.[114] Breton's 1934 'What Is Surrealism?' argues for these two distinct purposes for surrealism, the examination of the relation of the conscious to the unconscious mind and the question of what social action to undertake.[115] In *Insel*, in relation to Mlle Alpha's day-bed, tone remains hard to place. Yet in mentioning Mlle Alpha's collection, Loy's novel hints at the global consciousness of the Paris surrealist art world.

What Insel shares most directly with Nadja and Georgette is that his mere presence is eventually generative of the novel that is written about him. Loy's novel is the most suggestive of the three about how the represented subject can change the writing's style: despite the strong resonances of this novel's prose style with Loy's style recognisable across her fiction and poetry, there remains a sense in *Insel* that the novel's style at the level of its sentences is generated by Insel's effects on Mrs Jones. His tendency to make her turn aside is there in the local momentum of the prose. *Insel*'s poetic prose style records a set of effects of chance at the level of style, available in short passages as the narrative moves sideways into the figuration of Insel as artist. As far as *Insel* celebrates Insel, other artists are occasionally drawn in to the transformations of the prose style, where they can work their own illusions, most notably the two women in the Dôme.

In this way, Insel the character generates a style in fiction for a novel that is both a surrealist novel in English and a modernist novel. In this sense, while the momentum of *Insel* has much in common with the study of chance in *Nadja*, or the more playful enquiry into chance and coincidence in *Last Nights of Paris*, Loy's novel's style seems more challenging to align with the achieved and tonally complex plot structures of some major modernist novels. It might, however, be considered closer to aspects of Gertrude Stein's writing. The resonances of Loy's novel extend beyond an Anglophone modernist framing and interact directly with strands of European modern writing, including decadence and surrealism. Both Peter Nicholls and Michael Levenson make similar points about Loy's poetry.[116] These correspondences are important, because they allow *Insel* to be read, and to be valued or judged, on specific terms other than concepts of the novel based on influential readings of, for example, Joyce, Proust and Henry James. More generally, reading *Nightwood* in Chapter 3 of the present book has suggested that the diffuseness of that novel's style in the representation of character set Barnes's novel at odds with a concept of unity that was valued at mid-century by Joseph Frank. Here, in *Insel*, it is rather the tendency of the style to pull away from an integrated novel plot that differentiates it from novels that can more readily be read as interestingly coherent. One value of this style, then, is its capacity to challenge habitual links between legitimacy, coherence and literary value in an Anglophone critical context.

For its readers, *Insel*'s lively prose style functions in part as a Baedeker for its milieu of artists' cafés and art worlds. *Insel* brings into English a mode that in French has a history of surrealist, early twentieth-century and late nineteenth-century novels that take sex work and the demi-monde as their setting, and this is a mode that may be disorienting for readers who lack this context.[117] Like *Nightwood* and *Adolphe 1920*, *Insel* sustains a local richness in passages whose integration in the novel is intriguingly unstable. As with *Nightwood* and *Adolphe 1920*, *Insel*'s elusiveness to certain kinds of formal analysis carries an implicit critique of the literary values of coherence and authority. In this implicit critique, there is some overlap with the qualities Beci Carver finds in 'granular modernists' Henry Green, Evelyn Waugh and William Gerhardie: a tendency to 'discoherence' and 'futility'.[118]

French surrealist writing was not prominent in major strands of the Anglophone institutional study of modernist fiction at mid-century. Even if Hugh Kenner's modernism is international in its affiliations, including in its engagement with nineteenth-century French writing, Louis Aragon and André Breton scarcely feature in Kenner's criticism in the 1950s and early 1960s. In part, this is because they had not featured prominently for Ezra Pound, who wrote many of his major reviews before the first manifesto of surrealism in 1924. Harry Levin, similarly, in writing a cultural history of the novel, is steered away from the broader cultural shocks of Dada and Paris surrealism and towards Marcel Proust, despite his wide interest in contemporary French fiction.[119] By 1967, Frank Kermode would be writing of Jean-Paul Sartre's novels and the French *nouveau roman* in his *The Sense of an Ending* and beginning to engage with French literary and narratological theory.[120] But in the 1950s and early 1960s,

170　*The New Modernist Novel: Criticism and the Task of Reading*

with some exceptions such as the work of Marcel Proust, Anglophone literary criticism was at more of a distance from post-1920 strands of modern French writing, especially from those strands that inform *Insel*. When Laughlin read *Insel* again in 1961, although New Directions had published Rimbaud, Baudelaire, Jean Genet and Jean-Paul Sartre as well as William Carlos Williams, and although Grove had published Breton's *Nadja* in translation the previous year, nevertheless the academic criticism of the time seems not to have provided a ready context for *Insel*'s disintegrations of novelistic form or for its affiliations with surrealism. Aragon's *Paysan de Paris*, too, would not be first translated until 1970 by Frederick Brown, aptly entitled *Nightwalker*, perhaps after Djuna Barnes.

Like *Nightwood* and *Adolphe 1920*, *Insel* remains interesting in part because it eludes systematic strategies of reading – and it is not only those strategies that seek formal consistency that this novel eludes. In its local momentum, *Insel* works against the novel form as progressive integration of details and events and offers an intensity of focus on the moments that make up the novel as the focus of fiction. In this way, it develops a style that resists strategies of reading that were developed for the modernist novels that were most valued at mid-century, and that brings surrealist modes into poetic prose in English. But like Man Ray's 1920 sculpture *L'énigme d'Isidore Ducasse*, *Insel* is an artwork that resists classification, a witty suspension between the strangeness of an experimental prose style and the homage to an artist.[121]

Epilogue: Vocabularies

Modernist literature helped to bring about some of the twentieth century's major changes in critical reading. I have argued here that one of the things that made modernist writing new was that it needed to be read closely. Different readers and critics found different ways of reading this writing closely, and of writing about it, through the twentieth century. Of course, some of the twentieth century's major changes in critical reading came after the period studied here: in the later twentieth century, the fundamental terms of reading and criticism were rethought in readings that were newly theoretically, historically and culturally informed. Going back to the mid-century in order to understand reading, even close reading, may seem to miss some of the major literary critical work of the twentieth century. But one of the things that has interested me here has been the past activity of selection that has effectively made a new modernism 'new' since the late twentieth century.

The recent expansions to pedagogical and critical canons of modernism have challenged the selections that were consolidated at mid-century and that tended to remain relatively stable over the next decade or two. These expansions have involved returns to modernism's histories, cultures and geographies to make space for a much broader set of conversations: a new modernist studies. Among the many things that are different about this new modernism, one is that the fiction of the new modernists I read here interestingly resists some of the strategies of reading that were being developed for reading and valuing other modernist fiction at mid-century, when certain kinds of coherence and learnedness were being valued and when *fin-de-siècle* decadence was less valued. Of course, the shortcomings of mid-century modes of reading for more established modernist fiction were a major impetus for the fundamental challenges to established modes of reading and criticism that followed those decades. But even now, because a new modernism has involved a broader set of texts, the twentieth and twenty-first centuries' existing tools of critical reading may need to be adapted for reading a new modernism. When the texts being read change, it is likely that the critical tools will need to change too.

172   *The New Modernist Novel: Criticism and the Task of Reading*

In other words, a meaningful expansion of modernist studies to include new modernist writing will require corresponding expansions in modes of reading. Barnes and Loy faded from accounts of modernism in part because of their gender, but the gendered bias of mid-twentieth-century criticism may be just as readily traceable in that criticism's antipathies to decadent traits as in the personal gender, or degree of gender conformity, of the women and others who were marginalised at mid-century. Expanding current versions of modernism to include more French decadence or surrealism, or more Irish wit, might well help critics to be better readers of Barnes, Rodker or Loy, or other modernists. But the resistances their novels present to familiar strategies of reading are strong enough to pose a more difficult problem: the problem of the complex relationship between the discipline's history of reading and valuing literary texts on the one hand, and its potential subjects of study on the other. *Nightwood, Adolphe 1920* and *Insel* are well placed to indicate some ways in which habitual modes of reading fiction closely may need to change for reading newly recognised voices.

This makes *Nightwood, Adolphe 1920* and *Insel* relevant to an expanded modernism. For Eric Hayot and Rebecca Walkowitz, modernism is already global.[1] Indeed, each of these novels engages with strands of transnational interaction: European literature and history, or contemporary art forms, including contemporary African-American music and performance in the case of *Adolphe 1920*, and French and German surrealisms in the case of *Insel*. The further question that is raised by reading these novels as new modernist novels is: how relevant can the readings here be to reading other new modernist writing? To assert that they are necessarily relevant might be to follow a diffusionist model of modernism, where an established modernism is perceived as central, given that these writers are among the more established new modernists. But modernism's global circulations, as well as the conversations that may take place between scholars studying 'similar aesthetic objects' in different global contexts, may yet render the readings relevant: only readers of other new modernist fiction can decide that relevance.[2] In this epilogue, I collect some of the vocabulary that I have used for reading these novels, and I bring that vocabulary to fiction by Samuel Beckett and Jean Rhys: one established modernist and one new modernist, each of whom shared a milieu with Barnes, Rodker and Loy.

One driver of expansion to new modernist texts and new approaches to them has been the renewed attention given to little magazines and their networks. As indicated in Chapter 1, renewed interest in the little magazines was prompted by their status as historical artefacts of what was actually being published and read by modernist writers and artists

Epilogue: Vocabularies   173

and their circles. But the shift is also instructive, because it offers a way of understanding a shift in concepts of modernist forms over several decades of criticism. For example, *Finnegans Wake* has provided a model of modernism or of the literary object in very different ways. On the one hand, the *Wake* has been a vast machine for generating new readings, welcoming new readers and new interpretations. Jean-Michel Rabaté refers to this *Wake*, quoting Jacques Derrida: 'you can say nothing that is not programmed on this 1000th-generation computer – *Ulysses, Finnegans Wake* [. . .]'. In concert with Mallarmé's *Livre*, for Rabaté via Derrida, this is modernism as game: the wager of the reading played against or with the text, an ultimately critical wager, one that can be played inexhaustibly and differently each time. Rabaté's question is how theoretical and political readings of Joyce can be reconciled – as they can be, he argues, by seeing readings of Joyce's texts as necessarily provisional.[3] On the other hand, Joyce's last work began as a series of instalments published in the little magazine *transition*, where each instalment of *Work in Progress* could potentially be extended in different ways in the next issue. One aspect of the new modernist studies to which Rabaté has contributed has been the recognition of the work of writers who were published in little magazines and their networks – and here, by contrast, it was possible to write a sampler or a new style that would be published across a few pages, but that could in theory be extended indefinitely. This more eclectic, less monumental mode of publication leans a little more towards modernism as work being done provisionally in style, and a little less towards modernism as a complex, unfinishable formal game to be played out on a complete text, as exemplified by Joyce's texts. In such games, reading is potentially inexhaustible; in the more recent move towards the study of little magazines, the style at hand, sketched in a few pages, is potentially inexhaustible.

There are some echoes of these aspects of style in *Nightwood, Adolphe 1920* and *Insel*. In these novels, critical reading often meets an associative logic or richness in local passages that is subject to alluring kinds of disintegration and puzzlement in reading across a larger whole, yet this allure was valued less at mid-century by critics who assembled a modernism that is now more established. Reading these novels here has involved, in part, a now familiar vocabulary learned from twentieth- and twenty-first-century criticism and theory: narrator, narration, voice, representation and misrepresentation, reading, form, difficulty and, especially, passages. But the readings here have needed to add other terms to that vocabulary, terms that I have deployed or borrowed: instability, diffuseness, temporality of reading, inconsequence, local momentum, borrowing, and close reading understood to involve

174 *The New Modernist Novel: Criticism and the Task of Reading*

reading into history and other contexts. Other vocabulary has been reclaimed or redeployed by others since its earlier use in criticism of modernist fiction, or has been introduced later to Anglophone criticism, and carries some of those newer connotations here: prose style, tone, mood, feeling, storytelling, wit, performance, digression and disgust; decadence and surrealism have been reasonably stable in meaning. What has not worked as straightforwardly is some of the older critical vocabulary, where attempts to join that vocabulary with the texts have met with resistance in interesting ways: point of view, literary reference, correspondences, spatial form, unity, coherence, consistency, and close reading understood as valuing form or style as separate from context.

There is a difference in the way these novels' literary references respond to reading: where more ostentatiously self-critical texts such as *The Waste Land*, *Ulysses* or the *Cantos* might seem to assign their readers an extensive reading list, in the novels by Barnes, Rodker and Loy, it might seem hard to identify any necessary reading beyond the text itself (*Nightwood*), or such reading, merely suggested rather than assigned by the text, may be found to lead less to another text than to the styles of other modernists (*Adolphe 1920*), or the meaning of intratextual and intertextual references may remain unstable (*Insel*, *Nightwood*). These novels obviously participate in a modernism of quotation and allusion, but they offer alternative modes to the encyclopaedic critical ambition of some of modernism's most well-known works. A key locus of their work with fiction and with modern writing is in style and in an aesthetics of passages, drawing on decadent models of style. In this work, these novels offer alternative investigations into the capacities of narrative fiction.

Barnes, Rodker and Loy, who were writing and publishing at the same time as high modernists, are also late modernists because *Nightwood*, *Adolphe 1920* and *Insel* appeared later than more well-known modernist work: these novels are belated in the sense of consciously being written after high modernism; their styles may respond to those of their high modernist peers; and the time period in which they were written was different – either the late 1920s (*Adolphe 1920*) or the late 1930s (*Nightwood* and *Insel*).[4] Yet Barnes, Rodker and Loy were beginning to develop those styles before 1920, in writing they published in the same magazines as high modernists. There is a chronological slip, then, between the context of the modernist little magazines and the novels I read here: the novels come later, especially *Nightwood* and *Insel*. I have argued that the context of the little magazines remains relevant for reading all three novels. The styles they developed are, for each writer, recognisable across fiction, short drama, poetry and other forms – even if the styles are very different, as in the case of Barnes's novel *Ryder* (1928). The styles they develop in their novels can be read as critiquing their contemporaries' styles, both at the time and for later readers, and the implication of that critique that is most carefully worked through here is that the novels resist strategies of reading that were developed in academic settings at mid-century for reading the fiction of their more well-known contemporaries.

The critical potential of these novels then is to challenge some of the modes of reading that were established by readers of their contemporaries' fiction, and a corollary of that challenge now is that reading these novels offers revisions and extensions to vocabularies with which modernist fiction has often been read. A first implication of this critical power is that these novels' specific challenges to established strategies of reading modernist fiction can then be brought back to more established modernist fiction, in order to read that work in new ways. Many modes of reading run through all texts, and reading more established modernist fiction alongside newly recovered fiction by contemporaries may illuminate other ways in which more familiar writing might be read. In this sense, there is no clear division between the novels read here and a more established modernism, but the readings here emphasise different traits from those that have tended to be noticed over decades by critics in more familiar modernist writing. That familiar writing can be read again, and differently.

A second implication extends beyond established modernists to other new modernist fiction. It is possible that reading these three novels may be directly useful for reading other writers, and that the vocabulary teased out as above may help with reading other new modernist fiction, including writing whose value has not been recognised. But equally, other new modernist fiction is likely to invite quite different modes of reading. One purpose of outlining challenges that *Nightwood*, *Adolphe 1920* and *Insel* make to the vocabularies with which modernist fiction has tended to be read is to reassert the contingency of disciplinary modes of close reading and the contingency of ideas of literary value that accompany them, and so to suggest the possibility of reading new modernist writing that goes beyond the critical vocabularies that are currently available for it. In this sense, rather than being a conservative force, close reading can be a site of progressive change in the discipline, because it can so readily learn from new authors and new texts. The close reading that might be brought to new modernist writing may change, then, depending on what critics have been reading, and depending on that new writing itself. Obviously, this does not set up *Nightwood*, *Adolphe 1920* or *Insel* as model new modernist novels. Rather than models of any kind, they are case studies: finding new modes of reading encouraged by these novels

176   *The New Modernist Novel: Criticism and the Task of Reading*

can contribute to a toolbox for reading an expanded modernism and for valuing that newly read work more fully.

Samuel Beckett's *How It Is* provides an example, below, for how more established modernist fiction might be read in new ways. Beckett translated his French '*roman*' *Comment c'est* (1961) as *How It Is* (1964). I suggest that a vocabulary developed on reading Barnes, Rodker and Loy is relevant for reading the prose of Samuel Beckett. This relevance includes the resistances outlined above to certain terms in the cases of *Nightwood*, *Adolphe 1920* and *Insel*. Beckett was himself a reader and critic of European and Anglo-American literature of the late nineteenth and early twentieth centuries. He shares the affinities of Barnes, Rodker and Loy with modern European writing, and shares expertise with Rodker as a translator of French literature and criticism into English. For modernist fiction that was recovered later for criticism, as new modernist writing, Jean Rhys's short stories provide an example. Rhys's first book, *Stories of the Left Bank*, was published by Jonathan Cape in 1927 with an introduction by Ford Madox Ford. In this, she shares with Barnes, Rodker, Loy and Beckett a role in the production of modernism in the interwar years that was not at first registered in major critical accounts of modernism. Sue Thomas draws attention to the scope of Rhys's references to British, Irish and French decadence, especially Oscar Wilde, in *Voyage in the Dark* (1934).[5] Indeed, Rhys is said by Ford to have been reading almost exclusively 'French writers of a recent, but not the most recent, date' before publishing *Stories of the Left Bank*,[6] and the title of the story 'La grosse Fifi' echoes Guy de Maupassant's 1882 'Mademoiselle Fifi'. Nine of those early stories were then republished in 1968 with the later collection *Tigers Are Better-Looking*. As Peter Kalliney observes, Rhys 'became more recognizable as a postcolonial writer just as her identity as a modernist became available once again'. New attention to postcolonial writing had the additional effect of increasing the recognition of particular modernist writers.[7] Reading two of Rhys's short stories suggests some observations regarding the significance and complexity of style in her short stories.

§

Samuel Beckett's sequence of short, unpunctuated paragraphs, the novel *How It Is*, makes fun of coherence. This wit is already present in the opening paragraph:

> how it was I quote before Pim with Pim after Pim how it is three parts
> I say it as I hear it[8]

Epilogue: Vocabularies   **177**

The comedy is Beckettian: in the three parts of the novel, the narrator moves towards Pim through the mud, tortures him to produce speech and, once Pim has left, reflects alone on the operation of the space he is in. Trying in part 3 to conceptualise the landscape of mud where these three parts take place, he remains stumped.[9] Questions mount as to whether the progression of torturer/tortured pairs is circular or linear, the latter involving the possibility of an end to suffering and therefore the possibility of 'grace' (124); how the sacks of provisions are distributed; and whether there is in fact anyone else in the landscape besides him. The problem of how things operate in the mud is expounded at length in the terms of mathematics and justice, but the problem remains unresolved, with repeatedly 'something wrong there' (115). The generative mechanism of the prose is for some time an extended comedy on the impossibility of a knowable coherence or unity within this story, or any piece of fiction. Correspondences preoccupy the narrator, but the greater problem of coherence is only closed off, but not resolved, with the conclusion that the 'whole story from beginning to end yes' has been 'completely false yes' (144). As is the case for *Nightwood*, seeking coherence in *How It Is* meets the difficulty of integrating correspondences productively into coherence, but in *How It Is*, the critique is generative of the fiction. *How It Is* is a step ahead of coherence as a literary value for its contemporary critics of modernism, having taken the idea of coherence and made comedy at its expense.

Learned literary reference is mocked just as keenly as narrative coherence, and the references are encyclopaedic but arch. Single words airily conjure whole literary movements, for example 'tohu-bohu' (42), which looks back to Beckett's translation of Arthur Rimbaud's 'Le bateau ivre', where Beckett preserves Rimbaud's word,[10] or 'yellow book' (83), which echoes the *fin-de-siècle* journal *The Yellow Book*. The mud of *How It Is* is recognisable in Dante's *Inferno* without quite matching it: canto 7 of *Inferno* sees the shades of the Slothful lodged underneath the mud of the Styx, so that they 'gurgle in their throats / but cannot sing in words that truly sound', and Virgil must interpret their words for the pilgrim from the bubbles that come up through the mud; above them, the Wrathful hit and tear at each other in perpetuity.[11] Never quite finding coherence to the telling of the landscape, *How It Is* never quite settles into a Dantean *Inferno*, not even Limbo, or into *Purgatorio* as its preferred literary company, with an end to suffering remaining elusive no matter how many 'P's are inscribed and erased in Pim's skin (71) – while the novel's ruminations in part 3 on the question of 'how it is' in this landscape recall Dante's mathematics in *Paradiso*. As Daniela Caselli argues, 'there is in Beckett no stable Dante': rather, 'Beckett's

178   *The New Modernist Novel: Criticism and the Task of Reading*

texts invent their own precursors.'[12] In the case of *How It Is*, it is clear that the landscape is a Beckettian one, not a Dantean one, and the relationship to canto 7 is as dependent on the whims of the narrator as anything else in *How It Is*. Dante's *Inferno* is one among many possible paths of reference both suggested and thwarted by this text. This novel's range of reference rewards critical work and scholarship to an extent that differentiates it from *Nightwood*, *Adolphe 1920* or *Insel*, yet it persistently resists stable identification with any reference. These new modernist novels provide a context for *How It Is* where intertextual references give a flavour of the writing style without necessarily opening out onto meaningful literary correspondences.

But there is also a flavour of violence to this text. The level of violence in the narrator's interaction with Pim is egregious: it seems to require explanation or justification, yet none is forthcoming within the novel. Not quite matching canto 7, the violence in *How It Is* goes far beyond transposing the fisticuffs of the Wrathful. This violence provides the narrative with a major event, a beginning (and so provides a passage with which to continue my reading here):

> first lesson theme song I dig my nails into his armpit right hand right pit he cries I withdraw them thump with fist on skull his face sinks in the mud his cries cease end of first lesson (62)

This develops further:

> with the nail then of the right index I carve and when it breaks or falls until it grows again with another on Pim's back intact at the outset from left to right and top to bottom as in our civilisation I carve my Roman capitals (70)

What can be made of this violence? *How It Is* was divided by the Second World War from the earlier novels by Barnes, Rodker and Loy. Beckett worked with the French Resistance in the Second World War and later worked in a field hospital at St-Lô.[13] While writing *Comment c'est*, as Emilie Morin, Adam Piette and Dominic Walker outline, Beckett closely followed news of the war in Algeria, which included personal accounts of torture written by members of the Algerian Front de Libération Nationale. Piette reads *Comment c'est/How It Is* 'as a response to and satire of the ambiguous French position' on human rights in the late 1950s, under which torture was used in Algeria.[14] He argues that like Henri Alleg's *La question* (1958), which was published by Beckett's publishers Jérôme Lindon and John Calder, *Comment c'est* 'bear[s]

Epilogue: Vocabularies   **179**

witness to the abuse of torture' by France in Algeria. He shows how closely Beckett's novel coincides with personal accounts of torture, even being written in small pieces as if smuggled out, and he finds in *Comment c'est* a call for 'recognition, agitation, and legislation'.[15] Anthony Cordingley argues that the public objections in France to the use of torture in Algeria 'renewed in Beckett a reflection upon his own sense of complicity with Anglo-Irish Ascendancy and the history of Ireland's colonisation', and that the novel registers this set of historical events.[16] Dominic Walker, responding to Piette, details the close relevance to *How It Is* of the torture of Algerian *pris les armes à la main* (PAM), who were not protected as prisoners of war. Pim, who is tortured to produce speech, is also called Pam, and the working title of the novel was 'Pim'. Yet as Walker details, the names 'Pim' and 'Pam' also lead to Beckett's ex-lover Pamela Mitchell, with whom Beckett broke off in 1956. In each case the historical particularity of the parallel deflects formalist reading.[17] Both parallels are relevant, but neither is solely explicative for Beckett's text. These multidirectional possible particulars can take from their contexts as well as give to them: as Walker observes, the victims of torture and the rejected lover are made to stand in for each other.[18]

What can reading *How It Is* against Barnes, Rodker and Loy bring to this set of problems? In *How It Is*, it is difficult to account for any qualities of the space divorced from their relation to the narration. The narrator's words dictate the landscape, and as he vacillates, so it changes. From the opening paragraph, that narration is identified as interpersonal with 'I say it as I hear it.' The main narrated interaction of *How It Is* – the narrator torturing Pim to produce sounds, song and speech – is similarly interpersonal. It is suggested – but also contradicted – that the words recorded in the book are those spoken under another episode of torture where the narrator is tortured. Reading *How It Is* alongside *Nightwood* and *Insel* suggests that another piece in the puzzle of this violence can be gained by looking at the narrative situation in terms of the contemporary history of narrative fiction. That history suggests that for a strand of prose fiction in English and French around the mid-twentieth century, the act of narration of another's story is a potentially an ethically fraught act. The complex ethics of narration provide not any equivalent to the physical violence in *How It Is* or any answer to it, but merely a potential resonance in the form of the novel at this time in the way narration is being thought through. This is especially so because of narration's equally generative potential, which *How It Is* also puts into play.

A strand of modernist novels that includes *Nightwood* and *Insel* registers the risk of harm that inheres in the intimacy of narrating another's

180 *The New Modernist Novel: Criticism and the Task of Reading*

story – whether those risks are incurred by telling the story of another, or by the desire to produce in another the telling of one's own story. These risks are lightened in Beckett's prose by comedy:

> my part who but for me he would never Pim we're talking of Pim never be but for me anything but a dumb limp lump flat for ever in the mud but I'll quicken him you wait and see how I can efface myself behind my creature when the fit takes me now my nails (52)

The narrator boasts that what makes Pim himself is that he speaks as directed by the narrator. Part of the joke here is that this is the risk anyone runs who is transformed into a writer's fictional character. Alongside such risks, in their use of narrative fiction, these writers register the creative potential of narration, its potential to bring another into being. Each of *Nightwood* and *Insel* tells the story of a loved one, and so does *How It Is*. Two pages later, Beckett's comedy carries the disjunction:

> in the dark the mud my head against his my side glued to his my right arm round his shoulders his cries have ceased we lie thus a good moment they are good moments
>
> [. . .]
>
> a little tune suddenly he sings a little tune suddenly like all that was not then is I listen for a moment they are good moments it can only be he but I may be mistaken (54–55)

Reading *How It Is* alongside *Nightwood* and *Insel* brings out this reading focused on narration as the engine of the fiction in *How It Is*, since each of the earlier novels presents a set of problems around the limitations of telling another's story, or of seeking to involve another in the telling of one's own. Barnes's anatomy of the ethics of storytelling is especially revealing for *How It Is* because of its examination of the degree of dependence of the narrated character on the narrator and the author. When Nora is distressed by her dreams, saying 'this, I have done to Robin' and, in her distress, disclaiming her responsibility by asking 'What was that dream?',[19] it is because her dream Robin resembles, but also threatens to erase, the real character Robin. When Barnes as author anticipates anger – but she could never have anticipated their unjustified violence – from Thelma Wood and Henriette Metcalf, who, she knew, would recognise themselves in Robin Vote and Jenny Petherbridge, she is responding to a problem in the ethics of narration where the author must speak for the character, writing over their biographical original. Mieke Bal calls description in fiction 'epistemic murder',[20] but it is awkward that in Bal's example, the description of Robin is given within a story about Robin as a character whose biographical original, her author knows, will recognise herself in the character. Beckett's narrator aspires, he says, to 'efface myself behind my creature', but Beckett's complex tone suggests that this narrator is in fact, rather, effacing his creature behind his own narration, which in turn is ceded in *How It Is* to yet another. This problem of the ethics of representation belongs of course to narrative in general, which involves telling the story of another, or of oneself, but in such a way that the narrated other, or self, acquires reality in seemingly greater proportions than its original: it becomes larger than life. 'I say it as I hear it' involves, to borrow Dora Zhang's terms, both inventing another's reality and merely recording it, in a problematic close to the description of character in Barnes's short stories.[21] But Beckett's use of this capacity of narrative fiction is not only a critique of a general structural quality of narrative. This particular ethical problem of how to tell the story of another was one that was acutely at issue in a community of writers that he took part in and whose work he read.[22]

Beckett's study of narrative fiction in *How It Is* analyses the interpersonal quality of narration, and this means the form itself of the *roman*, or of the novel, supplies a part of the capacity for *How It Is* to carry the complex interpersonal ethics that is a part of fictional narration in the early twentieth century. The strands of violence in modernist aesthetics can be followed back more generally to the aesthetic of a late nineteenth-century decadence.[23] In addition, there is a specific association here with the narrative form of the contemporary novel and the contemporary *roman*. The ethics of telling the story of another were analysed by Barnes in *Nightwood* and by her contemporaries: by Mina Loy in *Insel*, Ford Madox Ford in *The Good Soldier*, Oscar Wilde in *The Picture of Dorian Gray*, Pierre Jean Jouve in *Paulina 1880*, André Breton in *Nadja* and others. Their analyses made the *roman*, or the novel and prose fiction in English, into something that in the late 1950s Beckett could use for the complex analyses of *How It Is*. Reading *How It Is* against *Nightwood* is a reminder that Beckett took part in a community of writers who were asking what it means to represent another person, or another self, in narrative fiction, and who were alert to a particular set of stylistic and ethical challenges of doing so. Adding this layer to *How It Is* adds a cultural history to this use of narrative form by Beckett. Beckett chooses, rather than invents, these capacities of the form in his first novel since *L'innommable*, also his last, and the resulting novel works with the avenues of reflection that were being opened up by the novel form and the possibilities of style.[24] Reading *How It Is* via *Nightwood* draws attention to a strand of fiction that makes the form of the novel and of the *roman* something that can carry the intimate interpersonal complexity of *How It Is*.

182 *The New Modernist Novel: Criticism and the Task of Reading*

In the ways outlined above, *Nightwood, Adolphe 1920* and *Insel* draw out both informal tendencies in *How It Is* – in the mockery of coherence at the level of narrative and at the level of reference – and anti-formal tendencies, in its work with the ethics of narration. As with *Nightwood, Adolphe 1920* and *Insel*, the work with fiction and reference in *How It Is* is work with prose style. In *How It Is*, coherence lasts only as long as the passage being read or narrated. In other words, the resistances outlined above to specific critical vocabulary are shared by *How It Is*. This novel's investment in passages and in style resonates, too, with the investment in prose style and passages in *Nightwood, Adolphe 1920* and *Insel*. In this resonance of style between the new modernist authors read here and *How It Is*, there can be identified, too, a site of strong resonance in terms of attention to style in passages between the novels by Barnes, Rodker, and Loy and *Ulysses*, a novel that for much of this book has by contrast been a source of strategies of reading that have not served as well to elucidate writing by less established modernists, or the decadent tendencies of that writing – but *Ulysses* lends itself to being read in many ways.

In the following short comments I test some of the vocabulary I have outlined above against two of Jean Rhys's short stories, one from each of two collections: *Stories of the Left Bank* (1927), which was published two years before Barnes's *A Night among the Horses* and contained one story Ford had already published, and *Tigers are Better-Looking*, the 1968 collection that also included a selection from *Stories of the Left Bank*. The 1927 collection contains several quite short pieces, of which 'Hunger' is the shortest one to be reprinted in the 1968 selection. It narrates five days without food, dramatised by the narrator's voice and that voice's shifts in tone. 'On the second day', the narrator informs readers, 'you have a bad headache. You feel pugnacious. You argue all day with an invisible and sceptical listener.' This disbelieving listener's voice is not heard, only the narrator's imagined responses to it: 'I tell you it is *not* my fault . . .'[25] But the narrator absorbs the listener's sceptical tone, declaring in the account of the fifth day, 'Women are always ridiculous when they struggle.' A moment later, the story denounces the women who 'stamp' on the clinging fingers of those who struggle. These contrapuntal observations presage the return of the sceptical listener, so that the line 'Well, you are doomed' may be that imagined listener's, the character's to herself, or the narrator's comment, and the tone of the wit is hard to judge. As soon as the moment threatens to turn morbid, the story situates itself as literary: 'If I were Russian [. . .] had I been French [. . .].' By the time of 'I love her most before she has become too vicious', the attacks from all sides have piled up in the story's shifting tones, and

Epilogue: Vocabularies   **183**

it is clear that no voice is safe: a meal is the only way out, and yet the present simple tense in this line suggests that any exit is only temporary. An arch final sentence ends the story without completing it: 'I have never gone without food for longer than five days, so I cannot amuse you any longer.'[26] This comment defends the character's dignity against the disbelief of all the voices by dismissing her suffering as merely an exercise in style. In this, Rhys's story shares with writing by Barnes, Rodker and Loy an investment in prose style in sentences and passages. Its immersion of its reader in the moods of the present moment of hunger recalls similar immersion in moods as a quality of much of Rodker's prose, including Rodker's prose poems, and indeed in prose poems by Stéphane Mallarmé or Ernest Dowson.

'Till September Petronella' was first published in the *London Magazine* in 1960. This story shares with 'Hunger' some of the earlier story's work with voice. In the later story, voice attaches more predictably to character, but the story's characters are created almost entirely by what they say. In this way, voice becomes not so much an aspect of character, as each character is only an aspect of style: Rhys's people's words are there on the page almost before the people themselves are. This style is invested in tone, not accretion: as in 'Hunger', the mood shifts line by line, as protagonist and reader are immersed in the story's present moment. Yet despite that immersion, the passing moments of the earlier story have been replaced by a carefully managed coherence across a sequence of events separated in time. Throughout 'Till September Petronella', correspondences stressed within the story confirm its events and sharpen its social critique. Petronella's companion Marston tells her she looks as if she has 'lost a shilling and found sixpence', and she reflects that this is 'the way they always talk', repeating the phrase herself. The story confirms her sense: the man who gives her a lift, a farmer, greets her with the same comment.[27] Both Marston and Melville, the man she meets in the taxi, vary another phrase, the story's title, 'Till September, Petronella' (32, 38). She begins to sing the same song in the taxi with Melville as she has sung on request for the farmer in his car; she compares their small generosities, implicitly comparing their broader failure to be generous. Each man coerces her in small ways, as with the farmer's instruction: '"Good-bye." / "No, say fare you well." / "Fare you well."' (32). These repetitions enhance the dull repetitiousness of Petronella's reliance on three different men in one day, none of whom succeeds in supporting her in any meaningful way, but they also give a sense of a narrative style that is carefully invested in plausibility. The repetitions suggest that the story's material is overlaid with an acknowledgment of the effort to write in a way that will be believable, combining a mastery

184 *The New Modernist Novel: Criticism and the Task of Reading*

of storytelling with a carefully ironic failure to believe that the story could ever be believed by a reader. In this, the more careful correspondences of this and other later stories revise some of the earlier stories' delight in passing moments and situations, where the dare to readers to believe the narrators is enough. This is not the gentle, radiant if elusive coherence sought by Rhys's contemporaries, the mid-century critics in Chapter 2 of the present book. The correspondences here critique the function of correspondences and coherence in creating literary value, and they critique their own mismatch with the unruly material of fiction. This is correspondence and coherence in a new, different sense.

The most cutting of the moments in the later stories are those that involve complex social interactions. Petronella's hosts are 'respectable' young men, British artists. The man she prefers, Julian, is dating another model, Frankie. Frankie, well aware of the rival presented in Petronella, carefully displays her literary wit, figuring for example Samson and Delilah: 'He said he'd lose his strength if I cut my hair' (15). In contrast, Petronella's conversation is repeatedly unsuccessful, sometimes for reasons that are not obvious from the words she says. When she assays to Marston, 'So that I long for death?' Marston's startled objection suggests that unlike Frankie, Petronella is not considered the right kind of person to play with register – whether or not her apologetic explanation, that she had been joking, is true. Marston has just given away why: he has questioned whether her name is real, and on being told the name is her grandmother's, has insulted her with 'Oh, you've got a grandmother, have you?' (17–18). Petronella Gray knows the stakes of this mockery: she thinks, 'If you knew how bloody my home was you wouldn't be surprised that I wanted to change my name and forget all about it' (17). Rhys's stage surname between 1909 and 1911 was Gray, and Marston's mockery hovers over Rhys's own biography.[28] Later, Julian sums up her relationship with her hosts: '"Can't you see she's fifth-rate?"' (24). His insult is loosely linked with Petronella's place of origin too, since his words lightly echo Anna's repetition in *Voyage in the Dark* that she is the 'fifth generation on my mother's side' to be born in the West Indies.[29] Like Marston's, his comments seem mismatched as a response to Petronella's direct banter to him, which while bold – she has called him a 'ruddy respectable citizen' – has seemed only to echo the similar edginess of her companions' jokes. In these failed exchanges, the insults arrive regardless of what her tone might be: Julian's comment gives the impression of responding merely to Petronella's presence, rather than to what she says.

Julian's insult echoes through the story's correspondences in the betrayals of Petronella by the other men: Marston who insults her for being an immigrant but feels entitled to her; the farmer who won't give her a lift without asking for sex; and the stranger, Melville, who pays her for sex and then hesitates on his offer to write to her. The earlier story 'Hunger' provides one key to this repeated situation: Petronella is at the mercy of this treatment because she lacks the money for independence. As she explains to Melville, her 'desperate expression' is simply hunger (35). But the later story provides another key, in the way the taunts from her friends and companions centre on her status as an immigrant rather than her poverty. The 'Poudre Nildé basanée' (28), or bronzed powder, that she applies to her face is a complex figure for this status.[30] Rhys's story figures the immigrant as central to the world she writes about, despite the consistent attempts by others to deny her protagonist's importance.[31] In the earlier stories, immersion in a sequence of moments suggests the lack of control that the protagonist has over her narrative, and the later story adds to this immersion a deep coherence, of a kind that suggests that, if the Rhys protagonist is not in control of the unfolding of events, others are. Their social consensus is repeatedly that she doesn't belong, and the judgements of others shape her plot through the story. This is dramatised at the level of style in the way Petronella's sometimes unknowable tone makes her voice – and her character – seem replaceable by other voices, or other tones of voice, while her hosts' responses remain unchanged. As in the 1939 novel *Good Morning Midnight*, this later story's style supports both a profound inconsequence at the level of events and a profound consequence at the level of narrative: whatever she does, things will go badly for her.

And yet the immersion in moments and the loss of coherence have the last word: the story is set on 28 July 1914, the date Austria-Hungary declared war on Serbia, meaning that the men who mistreat Petronella are likely to be sent to fight in the First World War. Even for them, too – even though they have paralleled each other in disrespecting her – things will go badly, whatever they do. Even this assiduous coherence unfolds within another moment, before things change.

How It Is and Rhys's short stories each read in their own way, but reading them after the readings here of *Nightwood*, *Adolphe 1920* and *Insel* brings out shared questions about the capacities of fiction to represent its people. In the case of Rhys's stories, the decadent immersion in mood in 'Hunger' gives way in the later story 'Till September Petronella' to a complex interaction between style and coherence that foregrounds the narrative possibilities of a decadent investment in style in passages, especially when those passages represent the voices of characters.

Of course, fiction has long been a site of formal experiment, and there are many novels written before the early twentieth century whose formal awkwardness has left them at odds with literary criticism. Transnational exchange has long brought new and different kinds of writing with it. The resistances traced here to historically conditioned kinds of formal analysis apply more broadly to any literary text, which is necessarily an object resistant to critical reading – an inscrutable subject. The modes of reading tried out here offer some familiarity with these novels; but equally, they may detract from other modes of reading that could allow these texts to speak more directly for themselves. Yet the resistances to critical reading that are part of the history of literature and of fiction are, too, intrinsic to the interest of these novels. Reading new modernist novels closely in written literary criticism offers one mode of engagement that can preserve an imprint of the text and an imprint of the discipline as each one changes, notably as the discipline changes to value a broader range of modernist writers and texts.

Notes

Chapter 1: The New Modernist Novel

1. See, for example, Laura Riding and Robert Graves, *A Survey of Modernist Poetry* (1927), repr. in Riding and Graves, *'A Survey of Modernist Poetry' and 'A Pamphlet against Anthologies'*, ed. Charles Mundye and Patrick McGuinness (Manchester: Carcanet, 2002), and Harry Levin, 'What Was Modernism?', *Massachusetts Review* 1, no. 4 (1960): 609–30, repr. in Levin, *Refractions: Essays in Comparative Literature* (New York: Oxford University Press, 1966), 271–95. For discussion, see Sean Latham and Gayle Rogers, *Modernism: Evolution of an Idea*, New Modernisms (London: Bloomsbury, 2015); Rachel Potter, '*CQ* and the Invention of Modernism', *Critical Quarterly* 61, no. 2 (2019): 32–37; Lawrence Rainey's introduction to *Modernism: An Anthology* (Oxford: Blackwell, 2005), xix–xxix; John Harwood, *Eliot to Derrida: The Poverty of Interpretation* (New York: St Martin's Press, 1995), chap. 1; and Houston A. Baker Jr, *Modernism and the Harlem Renaissance* (Chicago: University of Chicago Press, 1987).
2. Douglas Mao and Rebecca Walkowitz, 'The Changing Profession: The New Modernist Studies', *PMLA* 123, no. 3 (2008): 737–48.
3. For a history of the new modernist studies, see Michael North, 'History's Prehistory: Modernist Studies before the New', in *The New Modernist Studies*, ed. Douglas Mao (Cambridge: Cambridge University Press, 2021), 25–40. On discomfort, see Mark Wollaeger, 'Scholarship's Turn: Origins and Effects of the New Modernist Studies', in Mao, *New Modernist Studies*, 41–63.
4. For a sketch of such expansion, see Susan Stanford Friedman, 'Periodizing Modernism: Postcolonial Modernities and the Space/Time Borders of Modernist Studies', *Modernism/modernity* 13, no. 3 (2006): 425–43.
5. The need for such revision is suggested by Eric Hayot and Rebecca Walkowitz in their introduction to *A New Vocabulary for Global Modernism* (New York: Columbia University Press, 2016), 1–10 (1), where they write: 'Our contributors ask what happens to the foundational concepts of modernism and to the methods we bring to modernist studies when we approach the field globally.'

6. See George Hutchinson, *The Harlem Renaissance in Black and White* (Cambridge, MA: Harvard University Press, 1995); Suzanne W. Churchill and Adam McKible, eds., *Little Magazines and Modernism: New Approaches* (Burlington, VT: Ashgate, 2007), 1–18; Peter Brooker and Andrew Thacker, eds., *The Oxford Critical and Cultural History of Modernist Magazines*, 3 vols. (Oxford: Oxford University Press, 2009–13); and Robert Scholes and Clifford Wulfman, *Modernism in the Magazines: An Introduction* (New Haven, CT: Yale University Press, 2010).
7. See, for example, Maud Ellmann, *Elizabeth Bowen: The Shadow across the Page* (Edinburgh: Edinburgh University Press, 2003).
8. See, for example, Bonnie Kime Scott, *Refiguring Modernism: The Women of 1928* (Bloomington: Indiana University Press, 1995); Mary Lynn Broe, ed., *Silence and Power: A Reevaluation of Djuna Barnes* (Carbondale: Southern Illinois University Press, 1991); and Maeera Schreiber and Keith Tuma, eds., *Mina Loy: Woman and Poet* (Orono, ME: National Poetry Foundation Press, 1998). Douglas Messerli edited a number of Barnes's books for Sun & Moon Press and Green Integer, and Roger L. Conover edited two volumes of Loy's poetry and essays for republication.
9. This point is made in Latham and Rogers, *Modernism*, chap. 2, esp. 97. See, for example, Bernard Benstock, introduction to *James Joyce: The Augmented Ninth: Proceedings of the Ninth International James Joyce Symposium*, ed. Benstock (Syracuse, NY: Syracuse University Press, 1988), 3–24.
10. See Peter Nicholls, *Modernisms: A Literary Guide*, 2nd ed. (Basingstoke: Palgrave Macmillan, 2009), 193–218; Daniela Caselli, *Improper Modernism: Djuna Barnes's Bewildering Corpus* (Burlington, VT: Ashgate, 2009); Julie Taylor, *Djuna Barnes and Affective Modernism* (Edinburgh: Edinburgh University Press, 2012); and Rachel Potter, *Modernism and Democracy* (Oxford: Oxford University Press, 2006).
11. Tyrus Miller, *Late Modernism: Politics and the Arts between the World Wars* (Berkeley: University of California Press, 1999), 6. See also Rachel Potter, *Literary Modernism* (Edinburgh: Edinburgh University Press, 2012), and on other modernisms, for example, Beci Carver, *Granular Modernism* (Oxford: Oxford University Press, 2014); Alys Moody and Stephen J. Ross, eds., *Global Modernists on Modernism: An Anthology* (London: Bloomsbury Academic, 2019); and Aaron Nyerges, *American Modernism and the Cartographic Imagination* (forthcoming).
12. Rainey, introduction to *Modernism: An Anthology*, xxvi. Stephen Heath makes a similar observation about Mary Butts's *Armed with Madness* (1928): 'Wonder and horror come together.' Heath, 'Chances of the Sacred Game', preface to Mary Butts, *Armed with Madness* (London: Penguin, 2001), vii–xxiv (xxiv).
13. Caselli, *Improper Modernism*.
14. Charles Altieri, 'How the New Modernist Studies Fails the Old Modernism', *Textual Practice* 76, no. 4 (2012): 763–82, and Peter Howarth, 'Autonomous and Heteronomous in Modernist Form: From *Romantic Image* to the New Modernist Studies', *Critical Quarterly* 54, no. 1 (2012): 71–80.

Notes   189

15. Urmila Seshagiri, 'Mind the Gap: Modernism and Feminist Practice', *Modernism/modernity Print Plus* (17 August 2017), https://doi.org/10.26597/mod.0022. For discussion and a bibliography, see Sara Crangle, 'Feminism's Archives: Mina Loy, Anna Mendelssohn, and Taxonomy', in Mao, *New Modernist Studies*, 246–77. On the new modernist studies and non-modernist women writers, see Kristin Bluemel and Phyllis Lassner, 'Feminist inter/modernist studies', *Feminist Modernist Studies* 1, nos. 1–2 (2018): 22–35.

16. Patricia Chu, *Race, Nationalism and the State in British and American Modernism* (Cambridge: Cambridge University Press, 2006), 14. See also Laura Winkiel, 'Gendered Transnationalism in the "New Modernist Studies"', *Literature Compass* 10, no. 1 (2013): 38–44 (39).

17. Paul K. Saint-Amour, 'Weak Theory, Weak Modernism', *Modernism/modernity* 25, no. 3 (2018): 437–59: 'Even as scholars of modernism seek, with good reason, to make the field more inclusive, we need to be vigilant lest inclusivity become a byword for instrumentalizing the work or presence of others' (453).

18. Mao, introduction to *New Modernist Studies*, 16.

19. Djuna Barnes, *Nightwood* (1936; London: Faber and Faber, 2015), 72.

20. Barnes, *Nightwood*, 76.

21. Hugh Kenner, *Joyce's Voices* (London: Faber and Faber, 1978), 16.

22. For public readerships, see Laura K. Wallace, '"My History, Finally Invented": *Nightwood* and its Publics', *QED: A Journal in GLBTQ Worldmaking* 3, no. 3 (2016): 71–94.

23. For details, see Andrew Crozier, introduction to *Poems and Adolphe 1920*, by John Rodker, ed. Andrew Crozier (Manchester: Carcanet, 1996), vii–xxiii, and Ian Patterson, 'The Translation of Soviet Literature: John Rodker and PresLit', in *Russia in Britain, 1880–1940: From Melodrama to Modernism*, ed. Rebecca Beasley and Philip Ross Bullock (Oxford: Oxford University Press, 2013), 188–207 (191).

24. See, for example, on Rodker, David Trotter, *Cinema and Modernism* (Oxford: Blackwell, 2007), 151–53, and Laura Marcus, *The Tenth Muse: Writing about Cinema in the Modernist Period* (Oxford: Oxford University Press, 2007), 87–90; and on Loy, Miller, *Late Modernism*, 207–21.

25. Sean Pryor writes of Hope Mirrlees's *Paris*: 'The value and significance of *Paris* may lie, instead, in its having been so rare, peculiar, and ephemeral.' Pryor, 'Who Bought *Paris*?', *ELH* 88, no. 4 (2021): 1055–82 (1074).

26. John Rodker, '*Montagnes russes*, roman', trans. Ludmila Savitzky, *Les écrits nouveaux*, nos. 3–9 (1922). See Ian Patterson, 'Writing on Other Fronts: Translation and John Rodker', *Translation and Literature* 12, no. 1 (2003): 88–113 (94).

27. On the modernism of Barnes's journalism, see Alex Goody, 'Djuna Barnes on the Page', in *Shattered Objects: Djuna Barnes's Modernism*, ed. Elizabeth Pender and Cathryn Setz (University Park: Pennsylvania State University Press, 2019), 26–45.

28. On this identity, see Caselli, *Improper Modernism*, chap. 1, and Goody, 'Djuna Barnes on the Page'.

29. Evi Heinz, 'John Rodker', ed. Anna Mukamal and Dominic Williams, Modernist Archives Publishing Project, accessed 18 December 2022, https://www.modernistarchives.com/person/john-rodker. See also Elizabeth Dunn, 'Joyce and Modernism in the John Rodker Archive', *Joyce Studies Annual* 4 (1993), 191–201 (191–92).

30. Alfred Kreymborg, ed., *Others: An Anthology of the New Verse* (New York: Alfred A. Knopf, 1917), 64–72 and 92–95; *Contact Collection of Contemporary Writers* (Paris: Three Mountains Press, 1925), 1–10 and 137–94; Ford Madox Ford, ed., *Transatlantic Stories* (London: Duckworth, 1926), 38–60.

31. Ezra Pound to William Carlos Williams, 27 October 1934, in *Pound/Williams: Selected Letters of Ezra Pound and William Carlos Williams*, ed. Hugh Witemeyer (New York: New Directions, 1996), 150, and Ezra Pound, 'The Exile', *The Exile*, no. 1 (Spring 1927): 88–92 (89). On *belles lettres* and logopoiea, see Ezra Pound, *How to Read* (London: Harmsworth, 1931), 24 and 25–26.

32. On the experience of difficulty as a key characteristic of modernism, see Leonard Diepeveen, *The Difficulties of Modernism* (New York: Routledge, 2003).

33. For Loy and Rodker's exchange of reviews, see Mina Loy, 'John Rodker's Frog', *The Little Review* 7, no. 3 (1920), 56–57; John Rodker, 'To Mina Loy', *The Little Review* 7, no. 4 (1921): 44–45, with a greeting by Loy to Rodker 'as one European to another'; John Rodker, 'List of Books', *The Little Review* 5, no. 7 (1918), 31–33. In Paris in the 1930s, Loy read *Ladies Almanack*, in which she appeared as Patience Scalpel, and read drafts of *Nightwood*. See Carolyn Burke, *Becoming Modern: The Life of Mina Loy* (New York: Farrar, Straus and Giroux), 368.

34. On this success, see Aaron Jaffe, *Modernism and the Culture of Celebrity* (Cambridge: Cambridge University Press, 2005).

35. On this point, see Latham and Rogers, *Modernism*, esp. 49.

36. Jaffe, *Modernism and the Culture of Celebrity*, 12, 88.

37. See Rod Rosenquist, *Modernism, the Market, and the Institution of the New* (Cambridge: Cambridge University Press, 2009), chap. 1.

38. Catherine Turner, *Marketing Modernism between the World Wars* (Amherst: University of Massachusetts Press, 2003); Lise Jaillant, *Cheap Modernism: Expanding Markets, Publishers' Series and the Avant Garde* (Edinburgh: Edinburgh University Press, 2017). See also Pryor, 'Who Bought *Paris*?'

39. Hugh Kenner, 'Retrospect: 1985', in *The Poetry of Ezra Pound*, with a new preface by Kenner, foreword by James Laughlin (Lincoln: University of Nebraska Press, 1985), 1–9 (6). Jaffe discusses *The Poetry of Ezra Pound* in *Modernism and the Culture of Celebrity*, 71, 164.

40. Kenner, *The Poetry of Ezra Pound*, 13, 15.

41. James Laughlin, 'Some Irreverent Literary History', foreword to Kenner, *The Poetry of Ezra Pound*, ix–xiii (xiii).

42. Gregory Barnhisel, *James Laughlin, New Directions, and the Remaking of Ezra Pound* (Amherst: University of Massachusetts Press, 2005), 93.

Notes   191

43. For Pound's engagement with and support of fascism, see Matthew Feldman, *Ezra Pound's Fascist Propaganda, 1935–1945* (Basingstoke: Palgrave Macmillan, 2013). For a reflection on reading Pound, see Peter Nicholls, '"You in the dinghy astern there": Learning from Ezra Pound', in *Ezra Pound and Education*, ed. Steven G. Yao and Michael Coyle (Orono, ME: National Poetry Foundation, 2012), 137–61.

44. Barnhisel, *James Laughlin, New Directions*, chaps. 4 and 5.

45. In this phrasing, I am indebted to David Trotter's pursuit of a related question: how works of modernist literature 'came to be written as they were written'. See Trotter, *Cinema and Modernism*, 3.

46. On the circulation of *Nightwood* in film, see Melissa Hardie, 'Djuna Barnes: The Flower of Her Secret', in Pender and Setz, *Shattered Objects*, 178–92.

47. Joseph Frank, 'Spatial Form in Modern Literature', in *The Widening Gyre: Crisis and Mastery in Modern Literature* (Bloomington: Indiana University Press, 1963), 3–62, repr. in Frank, *The Idea of Spatial Form* (New Brunswick, NJ: Rutgers University Press, 1991), 5–66.

48. Pender and Setz, introduction to *Shattered Objects*, 5–6.

49. Brian Glavey, *The Wallflower Avant-Garde: Modernism, Sexuality, and Queer Ekphrasis* (Oxford: Oxford University Press, 2015), 53.

50. Diepeveen, *Difficulties of Modernism*, 223–24.

51. Diepeveen, *Difficulties of Modernism*, chap. 5.

52. J. H. Prynne, 'Resistance and Difficulty', *Prospect 5* (1961): 26–30 (28).

53. See, for example, Mia Spiro, *Anti-Nazi Modernism: The Challenges of Resistance in 1930s Fiction* (Evanston, IL: Northwestern University Press, 2013), and Ery Shin, 'The Apocalypse for Barnes', *Texas Studies in Literature and Language* 57, no. 2 (2015): 182–209.

54. Glyn Salton-Cox uses the phrase 'radical potential' in a similar sense in the context of 1930s political radicalism in *Queer Communism and the Ministry of Love: Sexual Revolution in British Writing of the 1930s* (Edinburgh: Edinburgh University Press, 2018), 43.

55. See, for example, Harry Levin, *The Gates of Horn: A Study of Five French Realists* (New York: Oxford University Press, 1963; repr., 1966), 241.

56. For example, Cheryl Herr, *Joyce's Anatomy of Culture* (Urbana and Chicago: University of Illinois Press, 1986).

57. Derek Attridge and Daniel Ferrer, 'Introduction: Highly Continental Evenements', in *Post-structuralist Joyce: Essays from the French*, ed. Attridge and Ferrer (Cambridge: Cambridge University Press, 1984), 1–13 (8, 10).

58. Corrected typescript draft of *Adolphe 1920*, John Rodker Papers, Harry Ransom Centre, University of Texas at Austin. I am grateful to Ian Patterson for drawing my attention to this.

59. Michael Levenson, *Modernism* (New Haven, CT: Yale University Press, 2011), 238.

60. The word is Levenson's, in *Modernism*, 271; see also 'monument' as used by John Guillory, *Professing Criticism: Essays on the Organization of Literary Study* (Chicago: University of Chicago Press, 2022), chap. 4.

192　*The New Modernist Novel: Criticism and the Task of Reading*

61. Jane Marcus, 'Laughing at Leviticus: *Nightwood* as Woman's Circus Epic', *Cultural Critique* 13 (1989): 143–90 (151); repr. in Broe, *Silence and Power*, 221–50.

62. Caselli, *Improper Modernism*, 10; Attridge and Ferrer, 'Introduction: Highly Continental Evenements', 10.

63. Northrop Frye, *Anatomy of Criticism: Four Essays* (Princeton, NJ: Princeton University Press, 1957), 17.

64. Barbara Herrnstein Smith, 'Contingencies of Value', *Critical Inquiry* 10, no. 1 (1983): 1–35.

65. John Frow, 'The Practice of Value', in *The Practice of Value: Essays on Literature in Cultural Studies* (Crawley: University of Western Australia Publishing, 2013), 87–107 (105).

66. Rosalind Krauss and Yve-Alain Bois, *Formless: A User's Guide* (New York: Zone, 1997).

67. Laura Frost, *The Problem with Pleasure: Modernism and Its Discontents* (New York: Columbia University Press, 2013).

68. For historicism and presentism as relevant here, see Pryor, 'Who Bought *Paris?*', 1057.

69. Matthew Sussman, 'Aesthetic Historicism Now', *Modern Language Quarterly* 84, no. 3 (2023): 347–60 (351).

70. Marcel Proust, *À la recherche du temps perdu*, vol. 7, *Le temps retrouvé*, pt. 2 (Paris: Gallimard, 1927), 43; Proust, *In Search of Lost Time*, vol. 6, *Finding Time Again*, trans. Ian Patterson (London: Penguin, 2002), 204. On 'style' as 'the realization of artistic vision' in Flaubert's *Madame Bovary*, see Stephen Heath, *Flaubert: Madame Bovary*, Landmarks of World Literature (Cambridge: Cambridge University Press, 1992), 2.

71. Andrew Thacker, 'Spatial Histories of Magazines and Modernisms', in *Historical Modernisms: Time, History, and Modernist Aesthetics*, ed. Jean-Michel Rabaté and Angeliki Spiropoulou (London: Bloomsbury, 2021), 55–72 (55–56); Cathryn Setz, *Primordial Modernism: Animals, Ideas, transition (1927–1938)* (Edinburgh: Edinburgh University Press, 2019).

72. Miller, *Late Modernism*, 16.

73. Franco Moretti, 'Conjectures on World Literature', in *Distant Reading* (London: Verso, 2013), 43–62; Yopie Prins, 'What Is Historical Poetics?', *Modern Language Quarterly* 77, no. 1 (2016): 13–40 (22).

74. See, for example, Barbara Herrnstein Smith, 'What Was Close Reading? A Century of Method in Literary Studies', *Minnesota Review* 87 (2016): 57–75; Terry Eagleton, *How to Read Literature* (New Haven, CT: Yale University Press, 2013); Susan Wolfson, 'Reading for Form', *Modern Language Quarterly* 61, no. 1 (2000): 1–16; Caroline Levine, 'Structures All the Way Down: Literary Methods and the Detail', in 'The Detail, Revisited', special issue, *Modern Language Quarterly* 84, no. 2 (2023): 129–46, and the other essays in that issue; Marjorie Levinson, 'What Is New Formalism?', *PMLA* 122, no. 2 (2007): 558–69; Rónán McDonald, ed., *The Values of Literary Studies* (Cambridge: Cambridge University Press, 2015), including Derek Attridge's chapter 'Literary Experience and the Value of Criticism', 249–62.

Notes   193

75. Rita Felski, *The Limits of Critique* (Chicago: University of Chicago Press, 2015), 174.

76. Joseph North, *Literary Criticism: A Concise Political History* (Cambridge, MA: Harvard University Press, 2017), chap. 1 (26).

77. Donald J. Childs, *The Birth of New Criticism: Conflict and Conciliation in the Early Work of William Empson, I. A. Richards, Laura Riding, and Robert Graves* (Montreal: McGill-Queen's University Press, 2013), 332–34.

78. For comment on *The Little Review*'s 'Reader Critic' section, see Alan Golding, '*The Little Review* (1914–29)', in *The Oxford Critical and Cultural History of Modernist Magazines*, vol. 2, *North America, 1894–1960*, ed. Peter Brooker and Andrew Thacker (Oxford: Oxford University Press, 2012), 61–84.

79. Max Saunders, 'Modernist Close Reading', in *Modernism and Close Reading*, ed. David James (Oxford: Oxford University Press, 2020), 19–44 (19, 32).

80. Levinson, 'What is New Formalism?', 563.

81. Here I differ from Diepeveen's enquiries into the documents of reception in *The Difficulties of Modernism* by looking instead at how the novels anticipate habits of reading in their readers.

82. Mark Byron, 'Close Reading', in *Oxford Encyclopedia of Literary Theory*, ed. John Frow with Mark Byron, Pelagia Goulimari, Sean Pryor and Julie Rak (Oxford: Oxford University Press, 2022), https://doi.org/10.1093/acrefore/9780190201098.013.1014, section 'Theory and Close Reading'.

83. Byron, 'Close Reading', section 'How Close Is Too Close?'

84. J. H. Prynne, 'Huts', *Textual Practice* 22, no. 4 (December 2008): 613–33.

85. Christopher Bush, 'Context', in Hayot and Walkowitz, *A New Vocabulary for Global Modernism*, 75–95 (87).

86. Moretti, 'Conjectures', 48.

87. Moretti, 'Conjectures', 48.

88. Gayatri Chakravorty Spivak, *Death of a Discipline* (New York: Columbia University Press, 2003), 107–109n1 and passim.

89. Ben Etherington, 'World Literature as a Speculative Literary Totality: Veselovsky, Auerbach, Said, and the Critical-Humanist Tradition', *Modern Language Quarterly* 82, no. 2 (2021): 225–51 (232).

90. Angus Connell Brown, 'The World of Close Reading', *Modernism/modernity Print Plus*, 3 October 2018, accessed 6 October 2022, https://modernismmodernity.org/forums/posts/world-close-reading.

91. On 'scalability', see Aarthi Vadda, 'Scalability', *Modernism/modernity Print Plus*, 2 January 2018, https://doi.org/10.26597/mod.0035. For a different opinion and a glimpse in 2000 of the possibilities offered by digital humanities, see Matthew Wilkens, 'Canons, Close Reading, and the Evolution of Method', in *Debates in the Digital Humanities*, ed. Matthew K. Gold (Minneapolis: University of Minnesota Press, 2000), 249–58. For more recent reflection on possibilities similar to Wilkens's, see Katherine Bode, 'The Equivalence of "Close" and "Distant" Reading; or, Toward a New Object for Data-Rich Literary History', *Modern Language Quarterly* 78, no. 1 (2017): 77–106.

92. On the problem of the exemplary passage, see Paul Fleming, 'Tragedy, for Example: Distant Reading and Exemplary Reading (Moretti)', *New Literary*

194   *The New Modernist Novel: Criticism and the Task of Reading*

History 48, no. 3 (2017): 437–55. On the interdependence of distant and close reading, see Andrew Piper, 'Novel Devotions: Conversional Reading, Computational Modeling, and the Modern Novel', *New Literary History* 46, no. 1 (2015): 63–98, and Andrew Goldstone, 'The *Doxa* of Reading', *PMLA* 132, no. 3 (2017): 636–42.

93. Stephen Best and Sharon Marcus, 'Surface Reading: An Introduction', in 'How We Read Now', special issue, *Representations* 108, no. 1 (2009): 1–21 (1–2, 10–11, 16).

94. For a model of notes for a future reading, see Stephen Heath, 'Ambivalences: notes pour la lecture de Joyce', *Tel quel* 50 (1972): 22–43.

95. Geoffrey H. Hartman, *Criticism in the Wilderness: The Study of Literature Today* (New Haven, CT: Yale University Press, 1980), 162.

96. Felski, *The Limits of Critique*, 182.

97. Rita Felski, 'Latour and Literary Studies', *PMLA* 130, no. 3 (2015): 737–42 (741).

98. Graham Hough, *An Essay on Criticism* (London: Duckworth, 1966), §3.

99. Guillory, *Professing Criticism*, 338 and 347–48.

100. 'Sustained investigation' is Drew Milne's term in 'Modernist Poetry in the British Isles', in *The Cambridge Companion to Modernist Poetry*, ed. Alex Davis and Lee M. Jenkins (Cambridge: Cambridge University Press, 2007), 147–62 (160).

101. Peter de Bolla, *Art Matters* (Cambridge, MA: Harvard University Press, 2001), 134–35.

102. See Raymond Williams's conclusion to *The English Novel from Dickens to Lawrence* (London: Chatto and Windus, 1970).

Chapter 2: The Task of Reading and the Tasks of Criticism

1. Ezra Pound, 'A Study in French Poets', *The Little Review* 4, no. 10 (1918): 3–61; Pound on Henry James, *The Little Review* 5, no. 4, Henry James issue (1918): 5–41.

2. See Donald J. Childs, *The Birth of New Criticism: Conflict and Conciliation in the Early Work of William Empson, I. A. Richards, Laura Riding, and Robert Graves* (Montreal: McGill-Queen's University Press, 2013).

3. For a history of these changes, see John Guillory, *Professing Criticism: Essays on the Organization of Literary Study* (Chicago: University of Chicago Press, 2022), chaps. 1, 2 and 12.

4. For example, Virginia Woolf, *The Common Reader: First Series* (1925); Laura Riding and Robert Graves, *A Survey of Modernist Poetry* (1927); Wyndham Lewis, *Time and Western Man* (1927); T. S. Eliot, *Selected Essays 1917–1932* (1932); Virginia Woolf, *The Common Reader: Second Series* (1932); Ezra Pound, *Make It New* (1934); and three studies of the novel for which modernist novels pose some of the most urgent questions about the form: E. M. Forster, *Aspects of the Novel* (1927), Edwin Muir, *The Structure of the Novel* (1928) and Ford Madox Ford, *The English Novel: From the Earliest Days to the Death of Joseph Conrad* (1930).

Notes 195

5. Douglas Mao, introduction to *The New Modernist Studies*, ed. Mao (Cambridge: Cambridge University Press, 2021), 1–21 (1).

6. For an overview, see Terry Eagleton, *Critical Revolutionaries: Five Critics Who Changed the Way We Read* (New Haven, CT: Yale University Press, 2022). See also Helen Thaventhiran, *Radical Empiricists: Five Modernist Close Readers* (Oxford: Oxford University Press, 2015).

7. Joyce did have a hand in the book but perhaps slightly less so than has long been assumed, most likely not having written 'A Litter', despite Sylvia Beach's hint in the introduction. See Fritz Senn, 'The Pleasure of Meeting Mr Dixon', in *Joyce's Disciples Disciplined: A Re-exagmination of the 'Exagmination' of 'Work in Progress'*, ed. Tim Conley (Dublin: University College Dublin Press, 2010), 143–46, and Sylvia Beach, introduction to *Our Exagmination round His Factification for Incamination of Work in Progress* (1929), repr. with the introduction (London: Faber and Faber, 1961), vii–viii.

8. Eugene Jolas, 'The Revolution of Language and James Joyce', in *Our Exagmination*, 77–92 (79, 82).

9. Victor Llona, 'I Dont Know What to Call It But Its Mighty Unlike Prose [*sic*]', in *Our Exagmination*, 93–102; Jolas, 'The Revolution of Language and James Joyce', 89.

10. John Rodker, 'Joyce and His Dynamic', in *Our Exagmination*, 139–46 (143, 144, 142).

11. Samuel Beckett, 'Dante... Bruno. Vico.. Joyce', in *Our Exagmination*, 1–22 (13–14).

12. Stuart Gilbert, 'Prolegomena to *Work in Progress*', in *Our Exagmination*, 47–75 (54).

13. Robert Sage, 'Before *Ulysses* – and After', in *Our Exagmination*, 147–70 (169).

14. William Carlos Williams, 'A Point for American Criticism', in *Our Exagmination*, 171–85 (177, 178); Rebecca West, 'The Strange Case of James Joyce', *Bookman: A Review of Books and Life* (US) 68, no. 1 (1928): 9–23 (9).

15. Williams, 'A Point for American Criticism', 184–85.

16. Jolas, 'The Revolution of Language and James Joyce', 81, 89.

17. G. V. L. Slingsby, 'Writes a Common Reader', in *Our Exagmination*, 189–91. For the gender of this contributor, see Finn Fordham, '*Finnegans Wake* in a Dentist's Waiting Room', in Conley, *Joyce's Disciples Disciplined*, 128–42 (129).

18. Laura Riding and Robert Graves, 'Modernist Poetry and the Plain Reader's Rights' (1927), in Riding and Graves, *'A Survey of Modernist Poetry' and 'A Pamphlet against Anthologies'*, ed. Charles Mundye and Patrick McGuiness (Manchester: Carcanet, 2002), 5–16 (5).

19. Edmund Wilson, *Axel's Castle: A Study in the Imaginative Literature of 1870–1930* (1931; Glasgow: Collins, 1961), 143–44. Further citations of this edition are given in the text.

20. For discussion of this aspect of Wilson's criticism, see Morris Dickstein, 'The Critic and Society, 1900–1950', in *The Cambridge History of Literary Criticism*, vol. 7, *Modernism and the New Criticism*, ed. A. Walton Litz, Louis Menand and Lawrence Rainey (Cambridge: Cambridge University Press, 2000), 322–76 (esp. 334).

196   *The New Modernist Novel: Criticism and the Task of Reading*

21. Edmund Wilson, 'Dickens: The Two Scrooges' and 'The Kipling That Nobody Read', in *The Wound and the Bow: Seven Studies in Literature* (New York: Oxford University Press, 1947), 1–104 and 105–18. The essays in *The Wound and the Bow* were first published in that book's first edition in 1941, with the Dickens material being based on essays published in the *New Republic* and the *Atlantic Monthly* in 1940. For this method, see also Wilson, 'The Ambiguity of Henry James', 1938 version with 1948 revisions, in *The Triple Thinkers: Twelve Essays on Literary Subjects* (New York: Oxford University Press, 1948), 88–132.
22. However, for Wilson as challenging Wyndham Lewis's attack on the excessive subjectivity of Joyce, Proust, Stein and others, see Jeffrey Meyers, *Edmund Wilson: A Biography* (Boston: Houghton Mifflin, 1995), 142.
23. Edmund Wilson, 'Mr. More and the Mithraic Bull', in *The Triple Thinkers*, 3–14 (11). The essay was written in 1937 and the reflection on Joyce in 1929. See also the regular references to Joyce in the essays collected in *The Triple Thinkers*.
24. See T. S. Eliot, '*Ulysses*, Order and Myth' (1923), in *Selected Prose of T. S. Eliot*, ed. Frank Kermode (London: Faber and Faber, 1975), 175–78 (177): 'It is simply a way of controlling, of ordering, of giving a shape and a significance to the immense panorama of futility and anarchy which is contemporary history.'
25. Edmund Wilson, 'H. C. Earwicker and Family', *New Republic*, 28 June 1939, 203–6; Wilson, 'The Dream of H. C. Earwicker', *New Republic*, 12 July 1939, 270–74, both rev. as 'The Dream of H. C. Earwicker', in *The Wound and the Bow*, 243–71 (243–44 and 257; see also 266).
26. In 1925, the interest and challenges of Joyce's writing are more consistently assigned to the use of 'language' than to the actions required of a reader. See Wilson, 'James Joyce as Poet', *New Republic*, 4 November 1925, 279–81 (280).
27. Edmund Wilson, 'The Antrobuses and the Earwickers', *Nation*, 30 January 1943, 167–68, rev. in Wilson, *Classics and Commercials: A Literary Chronicle of the Forties* (New York: Farrar, Strauss and Company, 1950), 81–86 (83).
28. Rachel Sagner Buurma and Laura Heffernan, *The Teaching Archive: A New History for Literary Study* (Chicago: University of Chicago Press, 2020), 152.
29. Louis Menand, 'Edmund Wilson in His Times', in *Edmund Wilson: Centennial Reflections*, ed. Lewis M. Dabney (Princeton, NJ: Princeton University Press, 1997), 253–65 (256).
30. Edmund Wilson, 'A Guide to *Finnegans Wake*', *New Yorker*, 5 August 1944, 54–60, rev. in Wilson, *Classics and Commercials*, 182–89 (183). See also Wilson, 'The Dream of H. C. Earwicker', in *The Wound and the Bow*, 255.
31. Edmund Wilson, 'Thoughts on Being Bibliographed', *Princeton University Library Chronicle* 5, no. 2 (1944): 51–61 (54–55), rev. in Wilson, *Classics and Commercials*, 105–20. On the way US academic criticism of the 1930s and 1940s marginalised Wilson's approach in *Axel's Castle*, to

Wilson's chagrin, see Paul Giles, '*Axel's Castle*', *Essays in Criticism* 61, no. 3 (2011): 275–300, esp. 294–96.

32. Giles, '*Axel's Castle*', 276.
33. Menand, 'Edmund Wilson in His Times', 263–64.
34. Richard Aldington, 'A Young American Poet', *The Little Review* 2, no. 1 (1915): 22–24 (24).
35. The discussion of Pound and Leavis here reproduces parts of my article, 'Exemplarity and Quotation: Ezra Pound, Modernist Criticism, and the Limits of Close Reading', in 'Historical Poetics and the Problem of Exemplarity', ed. Ben Etherington and Sean Pryor, special issue, *Critical Quarterly* 61, no. 1 (2019): 67–81. For discussion of their debate specifically in relation to the use of quotation, including in *The Little Review*, see the article.
36. Ezra Pound, 'How to Read, or Why', Books, *New York Herald Tribune*, 13 January 1929, 1, 6; 20 January 1929, 5–6; 27 January 1929, 5–6; *How to Read* (London: Harmsworth, 1931), repr. as 'How to Read', in *Literary Essays of Ezra Pound*, ed. T. S. Eliot (London: Faber and Faber, 1963), 15–40. Citations of the 1931 edition, abbreviated *HR*, are given in the text.
37. Ezra Pound, *ABC of Reading* (1934; New York: New Directions, 1987), 23. Further citations of this edition, abbreviated *ABC*, are given in the text. For discussion of the contradictions in Pound's approach to pedagogy, see Michael Kindellan and Joshua Kotin, 'The *Cantos* and Pedagogy' and Steven G. Yao and Michael Coyle, 'Glass Slippers vs. Winged Shoes', *Modernist Cultures* 12, no. 3 (2017): 345–63 and 384–87; and related responses. On Pound as teacher, *How to Read* and *ABC of Reading*, see Robert Scholes's preface, 'Back to Basics', in *Super Schoolmaster: Ezra Pound as Teacher, Then and Now*, by Robert Scholes and David Ben-Merre (New York: SUNY Press, 2021), xi–xvi.
38. See Pound to Ford, 5 September 1932, in *Pound/Ford: The Story of a Literary Friendship*, ed. Brita Lindberg-Seyersted (New York: New Directions, 1982), 111; and *HR*, 20, 29.
39. T. S. Eliot, 'Tradition and the Individual Talent' (1919), in *Selected Prose of T. S. Eliot*, ed. Frank Kermode (London: Faber and Faber, 1975), 37–44; Ezra Pound, preface to *Active Anthology*, ed. Pound (London: Faber and Faber, 1933), 9, 24.
40. I discuss Pound's selection from Golding in more detail in my 'Exemplarity and Quotation'. Pound's selection as discussed here corresponds to *Ovid's Metamorphoses*, trans. Arthur Golding (1567), ed. John Frederick Nims (New York: Macmillan, 1965), 3, lines 1–12, 33–43, 46–50, 71–72, 108–17, and 120–25.
41. Ford Madox Ford, 'Pound and *How to Read*', *New Review*, April 1932, repr. in Lindberg-Seyersted, *Pound/Ford*, 101–7. For Ford identified, see Pound, *Active Anthology*, 25–26.
42. F. R. Leavis, *How to Teach Reading: A Primer for Ezra Pound* (Cambridge: Minority Press, 1932), reprinted in slightly revised form as 'How to Teach Reading' in *Education and the University*, 2nd ed. (London: Chatto and Windus, 1943), 105–40. Further citations to the 1932 edition are given in the text.

198   *The New Modernist Novel: Criticism and the Task of Reading*

43. See also F. R. Leavis, *New Bearings in English Poetry: A Study of the Contemporary Situation* (1932), with 'Retrospect 1950' (London: Chatto and Windus, 1961), 155–57, and F. R. Leavis, 'The Case of Mr Pound: *Active Anthology*', *Scrutiny* 2, no. 3 (1933): 299–301.
44. See Eliot, 'Tradition and the Individual Talent', 37–44 (39).
45. Eliot, 'Tradition and the Individual Talent', 38.
46. Ian MacKillop, *F. R. Leavis: A Life in Criticism* (London: Allen Lane, 1995), 210–11. For discussion of Leavis's critique of Pound in relation to Eliot, see also Donald Davie, 'Second Thoughts: III F. R. Leavis's "How to Teach Reading"', *Essays in Criticism* 7, no. 3 (1957), 231–41. Davie points out that Leavis's and Pound's differing positions on technique have corresponded to the positions of British and American criticism since the early 1930s (232).
47. Graham Hough, *Reflections on a Literary Revolution* (Washington DC: Catholic University of America Press, 1960), 107–8.
48. Graham Hough, 'Dante and Eliot' (1975), in *Selected Essays* (Cambridge: Cambridge University Press, 1978), 200–216 (209).
49. F. R. Leavis, 'How to Teach Reading' (1943), 121.
50. On *How to Teach Reading* and Leavis's criticism, see Christopher Hilliard, *English as a Vocation: The 'Scrutiny' Movement* (Oxford: Oxford University Press, 2012), chap. 1 (38); on Leavis and Richards, 34–39.
51. MacKillop, *F. R. Leavis*, 16.
52. F. R. Leavis, *Revaluation: Tradition and Development in English Poetry* (New York: George W. Stewart, 1947), 2–3.
53. For example, see Pound on *Dubliners*: 'Mr Joyce writes a clear hard prose.' '*Dubliners* and Mr James Joyce', *Egoist* 1, no. 14 (1914): 267, repr. in *Literary Essays of Ezra Pound*, 399–402.
54. Q. D. Leavis, *Fiction and the Reading Public* (1932; London: Penguin, 1979), 173.
55. Q. D. Leavis, *Fiction and the Reading Public*, 172.
56. Q. D. Leavis, *Fiction and the Reading Public*, 180, 61.
57. I. A. Richards, *Practical Criticism: A Study of Literary Judgment* (1929; London: Kegan Paul, Trench, Trubner, 1930), 295; Riding and Graves, *A Survey of Modernist Poetry*.
58. Wyndham Lewis, *Men without Art* (1934), ed. Seamus Cooney (Santa Rosa, CA: Black Sparrow Press, 1987), 237–45.
59. Michael Levenson, *A Genealogy of Modernism: English Literary Doctrine, 1908–1922* (Cambridge: Cambridge University Press, 1984), 218–19.
60. Harry Levin, 'A Personal Retrospect', in *Grounds for Comparison* (Cambridge, MA: Harvard University Press, 1972), 1–16 (3). See Wilson, 'Thoughts on Being Bibliographed', 53 and 58.
61. Wilson, 'Thoughts on Being Bibliographed', 58.
62. On the finances of modernism's little magazines, see Lawrence Rainey, *Institutions of Modernism: Literary Elites and Public Culture* (New Haven, CT: Yale University Press, 1998). On academic magazines, see the section 'The Critical 1940s', in *The Oxford Critical and Cultural History of Modernist Magazines*, vol. 2, *North America, 1894–1960*, ed. Peter Brooker

and Andrew Thacker (Oxford: Oxford University Press, 2012), 923–58, esp. John N. Duvall, 'New Criticism's Major Journals: *The Southern Review* (1935–42); *The Kenyon Review* (1939–70); and *The Sewanee Review* (1892–)', 928–44. See also Eliseo Vivas, 'Criticism and the Little Mags', *Western Review* 16, no. 1 (Autumn 1951), 9–19, cited in Gerald Graff, *Professing Literature: An Institutional History* (Chicago: University of Chicago Press, 1987, repr. 2007), 187.

63. Stefan Collini, '"The Chatto List": Publishing Literary Criticism in Mid-twentieth Century Britain', *Review of English Studies* 63, no. 261 (2012): 634–63 (637).

64. See also Shari Benstock, *Women of the Left Bank: Paris, 1900–1940* (London: Virago, 1987); Joseph Allen Boone, *Libidinal Currents: Sexuality and the Shaping of Modernism* (Chicago: University of Chicago Press, 1998); George Hutchinson, *The Harlem Renaissance in Black and White* (Cambridge, MA: Harvard University Press, 1995); and Rita Felski, *The Gender of Modernity* (Cambridge, MA: Harvard University Press, 1995).

65. Merinda K. Simmons and James A. Crank, *Race and New Modernisms* (London: Bloomsbury Academic, 2019), 34–35.

66. Alan Golding, *From Outlaw to Classic: Canons in American Poetry* (Madison: University of Wisconsin Press, 1995), 112.

67. Blake Morrison records that Donald Davie, taking his lead from F. R. Leavis, rejected the politics of Yeats, Lawrence, Pound and Lewis as 'dangerous' and aligned the surface complexity of their work with a politically unsound challenge to the social order. Although Morrison does not articulate it, there is too an element of homophobia and anti-queer sentiment in the Movement writers' enmities to 'phoneyness', to 'London haut-bourgeois', and to specific writers taken to represent class privilege, among them, for Davie, W. H. Auden, Stephen Spender, John Lehmann and Cyril Connolly. Later, in 1959, Davie regretted that the prejudices of readers of *Scrutiny* and *Essays in Criticism* had weighed heavily on Movement writers: they had conceded too much, he observed, to 'the insularity which has ready its well-documented and conclusive sneer at Colette and Marianne Moore, Cocteau and Gide and Hart Crane'. As Keith Tuma and Nate Dorward observe, 'The Movement did not invent anti-Modernism; rather, it manipulated an existing discourse in which "Englishness" had long figured as the opposite term to "Modernism"' – as can be seen in the earlier exchange between Leavis and Pound. Blake Morrison, *The Movement: English Poetry and Fiction of the 1950s* (Oxford: Oxford University Press, 1980), 212–13, 52–53, 58; Donald Davie, 'Remembering the Movement' (1959), in *The Poet in the Imaginary Museum: Essays of Two Decades*, ed. Barry Alpert (Manchester: Carcanet, 1977), 72–75 (72–73); Keith Tuma and Nate Dorward, 'Modernism and Anti-Modernism in British Poetry', in *The Cambridge History of Twentieth-Century English Literature*, ed. Laura Marcus and Peter Nicholls (Cambridge: Cambridge University Press, 2008), 510–27 (514).

68. Simon During, 'When Literary Criticism Mattered', in *The Values of Literary Studies*, ed. Rónán McDonald (Cambridge: Cambridge University Press, 2015), 120–36 (135).

200 *The New Modernist Novel: Criticism and the Task of Reading*

69. Alan Filreis, *Counter-revolution of the Word: The Conservative Attack on Modern Poetry, 1945–1960* (Chapel Hill: University of North Carolina Press, 2008), esp. chap. 2.

70. Andreas Huyssen, *After the Great Divide: Modernism, Mass Culture, Postmodernism* (Bloomington: Indiana University Press, 1986), 190; Paul Giles, *The Global Remapping of American Literature* (Princeton, NJ: Princeton University Press, 2011), 139.

71. Lionel Trilling, 'Manners, Morals, and the Novel', in *The Liberal Imagination: Essays on Literature and Society* (London: Penguin, 1950), 208–23 (223).

72. Wallace Martin, 'Criticism and the Academy', in Litz, Menand and Rainey, *Modernism and the New Criticism*, 267–321 (321).

73. F. R. Leavis, 'Retrospect 1950', in *New Bearings in English Poetry*, 215–38 (217–20).

74. Kermit Vanderbilt, *American Literature and the Academy: The Roots, Growth, and Maturity of a Profession* (Philadelphia: University of Pennsylvania Press, 1986), 476.

75. F. R. Leavis, 'Retrospect 1950', 220. However, for Eliot's continuing relative absence from anthologies, see Golding, *From Outlaw to Classic*, 111.

76. Michael Levenson, 'Criticism of Fiction', in Litz, Menand and Rainey, *Modernism and the New Criticism*, 468–98 (485).

77. Chris Baldick, *Criticism and Literary Theory 1890 to the Present* (London: Longman, 1996), 119.

78. Joseph Brooker, *Joyce's Critics: Transitions in Reading and Culture* (Madison: University of Wisconsin Press, 2004), 92–93. See also Ellsworth Mason, 'Ellmann's Road to Xanadu', in *Essays for Richard Ellmann: Omnium Gatherum*, ed. Susan Dick, Declan Kiberd, Dougald McMillan and Joseph Ronsley (Kingston: McGill-Queen's University Press, 1989), 4–12 (10). For a detailed analysis of Joyce's growing legitimacy in universities at this time, see Brooker, *Joyce's Critics*, chaps. 2 and 3.

79. Brooker, *Joyce's Critics*, 92; Mason, 'Ellmann's Road to Xanadu', 5.

80. Hugh Kenner, 'Retrospect: 1985', preface to *The Poetry of Ezra Pound* (Lincoln: University of Nebraska Press, 1985), 1–9 (6), as discussed in Chap. 1 of the present book.

81. Brooker, *Joyce's Critics*, 109, 111.

82. Brooker, *Joyce's Critics*, 135.

83. Sean Latham and Gayle Rogers, *Modernism: Evolution of an Idea*, New Modernisms (London: Bloomsbury, 2015), 68.

84. See Kenner, 'Retrospect: 1985', 6.

85. Kenner, *The Poetry of Ezra Pound*, 30.

86. Kenner, *The Poetry of Ezra Pound*, 65.

87. Kenner, *The Poetry of Ezra Pound*, 30.

88. Kenner, *The Poetry of Ezra Pound*, 134.

89. Barnhisel, *James Laughlin, New Directions*, 108–9.

90. On this point, see William Harmon, 'Beat, Beat, Whirr, Pound', *Sewanee Review* 94, no. 4 (1986): 630–39.

91. Kenner, *The Poetry of Ezra Pound*, 64–65.

Notes   201

92. The word 'allusive' is used in this context in Michael North, 'History's Prehistory: Modernist Studies before the New', in *The New Modernist Studies*, ed. Douglas Mao (Cambridge: Cambridge University Press, 2021), 25–40 (31).

93. For an account of Kenner's relationship to New Criticism in his work on Joyce, see Joseph Brooker, 'Slow Revelations: James Joyce and the Rhetorics of Reading', in *Modernism and Close Reading*, ed. David James (Oxford: Oxford University Press, 2020), 86–112.

94. Harry Levin, *The Gates of Horn: A Study of Five French Realists* (New York: Oxford University Press, 1963; repr., 1966), 16, vii.

95. Hugh Kenner, 'To Be the Brancusi of Poetry', *New York Times*, 16 May 1982, 7, 30.

96. Alexander Howard, *Charles Henri Ford: Between Modernism and Postmodernism* (London: Bloomsbury Academic, 2017), 121–33.

97. Stephen Heath, 'Chances of the Sacred Game', preface to *Armed with Madness*, by Mary Butts (London: Penguin, 2001), vii–xxiv (x).

98. For commentary on *Nightwood*'s cover in this series, see Melissa Hardie, '*Nightwood* in the Cybernetic Fold: The Book as Networked Object', part of John Frow, Melissa Hardie and Kelly Rich, 'The Novel and Media: Three Essays', *Journal of Language, Literature and Culture* 66, no. 1 (2019): 1–15 (6).

99. Laura K. Wallace, '"My History, Finally Invented": *Nightwood* and its Publics', *QED: A Journal in GLBTQ Worldmaking* 3, no. 3 (2016): 71–94 (72).

100. For an example, see the authors of poems taught in a single course by Cleanth Brooks, as discussed in Buurma and Heffernan, *The Teaching Archive*, 137.

101. I borrow the term 'winners' history' from Christopher Prendergast's response to Franco Moretti's *Graphs, Maps, Trees*, 'Evolution and Literary History', *New Left Review* 34 (2005): 40–62 (62).

102. Graham Hough, *Reflections on a Literary Revolution*, 2. Originally delivered as lectures for the Catholic University of America in 1959. See Hough, *Image and Experience: Studies in a Literary Revolution* (London: Duckworth, 1960), chap. 1.

103. Hough, *Reflections*, 7.

104. Hough, *Reflections*, 29–30, 32.

105. For 'totality', see Graham Hough, *An Essay on Criticism* (London: Duckworth, 1966), §36; and Hough, 'Criticism as a Humanist Discipline' (1970), in *Selected Essays*, 1–22 (22).

106. Hough, *An Essay on Criticism*, §16.

107. Hough, 'The Poet as Critic', in *The Literary Criticism of T. S. Eliot: New Essays*, ed. David Newton-De Molina (London: Bloomsbury Academic, 2013), 42–63 (52–53). For a detailed analysis of a contrast between Eliot's aims and his methods in *Four Quartets*, see Hough, 'Vision and Doctrine in *Four Quartets*' (1973), in *Selected Essays*, 173–99.

108. Hough, *Reflections*, 32.

202 *The New Modernist Novel: Criticism and the Task of Reading*

109. Hough, 'Criticism as a Humanist Discipline', 10–13, 20.
110. Hough, 'An Eighth Type of Ambiguity' (1974), in *Selected Essays*, 23–45.
111. However, on readerships of modernism, see also Huyssen, *After the Great Divide*, 193.
112. Harry Levin, 'What Was Modernism?' *Massachusetts Review* 1, no. 4 (1960): 609–30 (618). The essay was reprinted, with a new preamble, in Levin, *Refractions: Essays in Comparative Literature* (New York: Oxford University Press, 1966), 271–95.
113. Levin, 'What Was Modernism?', 609. For the details of Picasso's initial move into respectable, successful circles, see Bernard Smith, *Modernism's History: A Study in Twentieth-Century Art and Ideas* (Sydney: UNSW Press, 1998).
114. Levin, 'What Was Modernism?', 611.
115. See Harry Levin, preface to *James Joyce: A Critical Introduction*, rev. ed. (London: Faber and Faber, 1960), 14.
116. For discussion of this impact, see Brooker, *Joyce's Critics*, 93.
117. Levin, preface to *James Joyce*, 9.
118. Levin, *James Joyce*, 97–98.
119. Levin, *Gates of Horn*, 81–82.
120. Levin, *Gates of Horn*, 446–47, 81.
121. Brooker, *Joyce's Critics*, 97–98; Levin, *James Joyce*, 193.
122. Levin, *James Joyce*, 193–94.
123. Kenner, *Dublin's Joyce* (London: Chatto and Windus, 1955), 147, 199.
124. See Kenner's 1987 preface to *Dublin's Joyce* (New York: Columbia University Press, 1987), xiii.
125. Hugh Kenner, *The Invisible Poet: T. S. Eliot* (1959; London: Methuen, 1965), 126, 99.
126. Kenner, *Invisible Poet*, 147–48, 153. For a contrasting reading of Eliot, see Maud Ellmann, *The Poetics of Impersonality: T. S. Eliot and Ezra Pound* (Cambridge, MA: Harvard University Press, 1988).
127. James Joyce, *A Portrait of the Artist as a Young Man*, ed. Hans Walter Gabler (New York: Routledge, 1993), 239; Harry Levin, *The Essential James Joyce* (London: Jonathan Cape, 1948), 18.
128. Stuart Gilbert, *James Joyce's 'Ulysses': A Study* (1930; Harmondsworth: Penguin, 1963), 20.
129. Levin, *The Essential James Joyce*, 18; Levin, *James Joyce*, 151.
130. Kenner, *Dublin's Joyce* (1955), 198.
131. Hugh Kenner, *Flaubert, Joyce and Beckett: The Stoic Comedians* (Boston: Beacon Press, 1962), 32.
132. Kenner, *Flaubert, Joyce and Beckett*, 60. See L. C. Knights, 'How Many Children Had Lady Macbeth?', cited in F. R. Leavis, 'How to Teach Reading' (1943), 125.
133. Margot Norris, 'The Voice and the Void: Hugh Kenner's Joyce', *Modernism/modernity* 12, no. 3 (2005): 483–86 (484).
134. For discussion, see Brooker, *Joyce's Critics*, 127–28.
135. Wayne Booth, *The Rhetoric of Fiction* (Chicago: University of Chicago Press, 1961).

Notes 203

136. Booth, *Rhetoric*, 363–4, 366, 369.
137. Booth, *Rhetoric*, 372.
138. Steven Connor, *Theory and Cultural Value* (London: Blackwell, 1992), 19.
139. Graham Hough seems to comment on Booth's question about *Lolita* in 1966: 'As to the effects of literature on character and conduct – the lasting effects, that is to say, of the temporary imaginative identifications made during reading – the truth is that we know very little about them.' *An Essay on Criticism*, §86.
140. David Lodge, review of *The Rhetoric of Fiction*, by Wayne Booth, *Modern Language Review* 57, no. 4 (1962): 580–81 (581).
141. On this point, see Northrop Frye's quality of literary value: 'an enormous number of converging patterns of significance' (also quoted in Chap. 1 above). Northrop Frye, *Anatomy of Criticism: Four Essays* (Princeton, NJ: Princeton University Press, 1957), 17.
142. Graff, *Professing Literature*, 238.
143. Graff, *Professing Literature*, 238. Graff is quoting the opening of chap. 1 of Cleanth Brooks's *The Well Wrought Urn: Studies in the Structure of Poetry* (1947), following Crane. See R. S. Crane, 'Criticism as Inquiry; or, The Perils of the "High Priori Road"', in *The Idea of the Humanities and Other Essays Critical and Historical*, vol. 2 (Chicago: University of Chicago Press, 1967), 25–44 (32). Crane's essay is based on a 1957 lecture.
144. Graff, *Professing Literature*, 238.
145. Brooker, *Joyce's Critics*, 95.
146. Leon Edel, *The Psychological Novel 1900–1950* (1955; rev. ed. London: Rupert Hart-Davis, 1961), 72, 137.
147. Elizabeth Pender and Cathryn Setz, introduction to *Shattered Objects: Djuna Barnes's Modernism*, ed. Elizabeth Pender and Cathryn Setz (University Park: Pennsylvania State University Press, 2019), 5–6.
148. Edel, *Psychological Novel*, 137.
149. Edmund Wilson, 'A Revival of Ronald Firbank', *New Yorker*, 10 December 1949, 141–50 (143).
150. Edmund Wilson, 'A Revival of Ronald Firbank', in *Classics and Commercials*, 486–502 (495).
151. Vincent Sherry, 'Modernism under Review: Edmund Wilson's *Axel's Castle; A Study in the Imaginative Literature of 1890–1930*', *Modernist Cultures* 7, no. 2 (2012): 145–59.
152. Peter Nicholls, *Modernisms: A Literary Guide*, 2nd ed. (Basingstoke: Palgrave Macmillan, 2009), 58–59, quoting Paul Bourget, *Essai de psychologie contemporaine* (1883–85; Paris: Plon, 1924), 1:20; Nicholls's translation.
153. Peter Nicholls, '"Deeps in him": Ezra Pound and the Persistent Attraction of Laforgue', *Revue française d'études américaines* 84 (2000): 9–19.
154. Edmund Wilson, 'A Dissenting Opinion on Kafka', *New Yorker*, 26 July 1947, 58–64, rev. in Wilson, *Classics and Commercials*, 383–92 (385, 392).
155. See, for example, John Crowe Ransom, 'Bright Disorder', review of *James Joyce: A Critical Introduction*, by Harry Levin, *Kenyon Review* 4, no. 3 (1942): 430–32 (432).

156. Frank Kermode, *The Romantic Image* (London: Routledge and Kegan Paul, 1957), 1.

157. Raymond Williams, *Drama from Ibsen to Eliot* (London: Chatto and Windus, 1952), 19–20; Raymond Williams, *Drama from Ibsen to Brecht* (1968; Harmondsworth: Penguin, 1973), 8–9.

158. In terms of the challenge in relation to Joyce specifically, classic examples here are Colin MacCabe, *James Joyce and the Revolution of the Word* (London: Macmillan, 1978), and Derek Attridge and Daniel Ferrer, eds., *Post-structuralist Joyce: Essays from the French* (Cambridge: Cambridge University Press, 1984). For comment see Guillory, *Professing Criticism*, 77.

159. For example, Andrew Crozier, a founder and editor of the *English Intelligencer* (1966–68), later restored John Rodker to critical view in his edition of *Poems and Adolphe 1920* in 1996. In the 1990s and early 2000s, new modes of reading modernism were being generated for example in *Parataxis*, edited by Drew Milne in Cambridge, which brings new writing together with reviews and criticism of a range of modernist and neo-modernist poetics and styles, and in *Jacket* and *Jacket2*, in which poems, reviews and commentary showcase a poetics that includes Barnes and Loy. On 'neo-modernism', see Drew Milne, 'Neo-modernism and Avant-Garde Orientations', in *A Concise Companion to Postwar British and Irish Poetry*, ed. Nigel Alderman and C. D. Blanton (London: Blackwell, 2009), 155–75.

160. Peter Brooker, 'Modernism under Review: Raymond Williams's *The Politics of Modernism*', *Modernist Cultures* 6, no. 2 (2011): 201–14 (206–7).

Chapter 3: Telling the Story of the Night Wood

1. Ezra Pound to T. S. Eliot, January 1937, in *The Letters of Ezra Pound, 1907–1941*, ed. D. D. Paige (London: Faber and Faber, 1951), 377. For 'whale', see J. J. Wilhelm, *Ezra Pound: The Tragic Years, 1925–1972* (University Park: Pennsylvania State University Press, 1994), 88; for Pound's naming of his friends after characters from *Uncle Remus*, see Humphrey Carpenter, *A Serious Character: The Life of Ezra Pound* (Boston: Houghton Mifflin, 1988), 414.

2. Daniela Caselli, *Improper Modernism: Djuna Barnes's Bewildering Corpus* (Burlington, VT: Ashgate, 2009); Julie Taylor, *Djuna Barnes and Affective Modernism* (Edinburgh: Edinburgh University Press, 2012); Drew Milne, 'The Critique of Modernist Wit: Djuna Barnes's *Nightwood*', in *Shattered Objects: Djuna Barnes's Modernism*, ed. Elizabeth Pender and Cathryn Setz (University Park: Pennsylvania State University Press, 2019), 114–29; Peter Nicholls, afterword to Pender and Setz, *Shattered Objects*, 207–14.

3. Stephen Best and Sharon Marcus, 'Surface Reading: An Introduction', in 'How We Read Now', special issue, *Representations* 108, no. 1 (2009): 1–21 (11).

4. Djuna Barnes, *Nightwood* (1936; London: Faber and Faber, 2015), 1. Further citations of this edition are given in the text.

Notes   205

5. Barnes refers to *Ulysses* as a 'great Rabelaisian flower' in her interview with Joyce: Djuna Barnes, 'James Joyce', *Vanity Fair*, no. 18 (April 1922), 65, 104, repr. in Barnes, *I Could Never Be Lonely without a Husband: Interviews*, ed. Alyce Barry, foreword by Douglas Messerli (London: Virago, 1987), 288–96 (295). The University of Maryland Libraries Shelf List (catalogued) for Djuna Barnes contains the Urquhart translation of *Gargantua and Pantagruel*, published by Chatto and Windus, 1921. Janet Flanner writes of Barnes, 'only she would have so thoroughly and deliberately steeped herself in the eighteenth century' in *London Was Yesterday, 1934–1939*, ed. Irving Drutman (London: Michael Joseph, 1975), 67, first published in the *New Yorker* as 'Letter from London, February 10, 1937'. For Edwin Muir reviewing *Nightwood*, though, it was the seventeenth century: 'New Novels', *The Listener*, no. 16 (28 October 1936), 832.

6. The Faber and Faber first edition follows this typography, but the New Directions edition carries an added initial dash. Djuna Barnes, *Nightwood* (London: Faber and Faber, 1936; New York: New Directions, 2006). On the relative importance of 'two textual states, one as it were the tonic, the other parenthetical to the tonic', see John Lennard, *But I Digress: The Exploitation of Parentheses in English Printed Verse* (Oxford: Clarendon Press, 1991), 242.

7. For mention of *Nightwood*'s 'lyric obscurity' in relation to the 'poetics of the canting song' of the late eighteenth and early nineteenth centuries, see Daniel Tiffany, 'Infidel Culture: The Brands of Cupid', *Area Sneaks* 1 (2008): 163–82 (163).

8. Hugh Kenner, *Joyce's Voices* (London: Faber and Faber, 1978), 16.

9. For the term 'semitic discourse', see Bryan Cheyette, *Constructions of 'the Jew' in English Literature and Society: Racial Representations, 1875–1945* (Cambridge: Cambridge University Press, 1993).

10. Maren Tova Linett, *Modernism, Feminism and Jewishness* (Cambridge: Cambridge University Press, 2007), 116. For commentary on this passage, see also Mia Spiro, *Anti-Nazi Modernism: The Challenges of Resistance in 1930s Fiction* (Evanston, IL: Northwestern University Press, 2013), 161 and 164; Mairéad Hanrahan, 'Djuna Barnes's *Nightwood*: The Cruci-Fiction of the Jew', *Paragraph* 24, no. 1 (2001): 32–49 (33–34); and Jean Radford, 'Race and Ethnicity in White Women's Modernist Literature', in *The Cambridge Companion to Modernist Women Writers*, ed. Maren Tova Linett (Cambridge: Cambridge University Press, 2010), 110–28 (118–19).

11. Rachel Potter, '*Nightwood*'s Humans', in Pender and Setz, *Shattered Objects: Djuna Barnes's Modernism*, 61–74 (65). On *Nightwood*'s representation of its Jewish characters, see, for example, Spiro, *Anti-Nazi Modernism*; Lara Trubowitz, *Civil Antisemitism, Modernism, and British Culture, 1902–1939* (Basingstoke: Palgrave Macmillan, 2012); Linett, *Modernism, Feminism and Jewishness*; and Alex Goody, *Modernist Articulations: A Cultural Study of Djuna Barnes, Mina Loy and Gertrude Stein* (Houndmills: Palgrave Macmillan, 2007), chap. 6. For the observation that fascism's stereotypes can readily be

206   *The New Modernist Novel: Criticism and the Task of Reading*

found reproduced in modernist writing, including Barnes's, see Erin Carlston, *Thinking Fascism: Sapphic Modernism and Fascist Modernity* (Stanford, CA: Stanford University Press, 1998), esp. 76.

12. Roland Barthes, 'Introduction to the Structural Analysis of Narratives' (1966), in *Image Music Text*, trans. Stephen Heath (London: Fontana, 1977), 79–124 (129).

13. For a concept of narration as exchange, see Roland Barthes, *S/Z*, trans. Richard Miller (New York: Hill and Wang, 1974), 88–89. See also Ross Chambers, *Story and Situation: Narrative Seduction and the Power of Fiction*, foreword by Wlad Godzich, Theory and History of Literature (Minneapolis: University of Minnesota Press, 1984).

14. Cheryl J. Plumb, in Djuna Barnes, *Nightwood: The Original Version*, ed. and annotated Cheryl J. Plumb (Normal, IL: Dalkey Archive Press, 1995), 189–90.

15. Barnes, *Nightwood: The Original Version*, 26–28.

16. Cirque Métropole, Paris, 1906. Dominique Jando, *Histoire mondiale du cirque* (Paris: Éditions Universitaires, Jean-Pierre Delarge, 1977), 103.

17. Brian Glavey, *The Wallflower Avant-Garde: Modernism, Sexuality, and Queer Ekphrasis* (Oxford: Oxford University Press, 2016), 59.

18. Merinda K. Simmons and James A. Crank, *Race and New Modernisms* (London: Bloomsbury Academic, 2019), 34.

19. Peter Nicholls, *Modernisms: A Literary Guide*, 2nd ed. (Basingstoke: Palgrave Macmillan, 2009), 1.

20. Laura J. Veltman, '"The Bible Lies the One Way, but the Night-Gown the Other": Dr Matthew O'Connor, Confession, and Gender in Djuna Barnes's *Nightwood*', *Modern Fiction Studies* 49, no. 2 (Summer 2003): 204–27 (211–12).

21. Caselli, *Improper Modernism*, 176n98. Caselli reproduces Barnes's original spelling and punctuation. See Barnes to Wolfgang Hildesheimer, 11 March 1959, Djuna Barnes Papers, Special Collections and University Archives, University of Maryland Libraries. Subsequent citations from this collection are recorded as 'Djuna Barnes Papers'.

22. Phillip Herring, *Djuna: The Life and Work of Djuna Barnes* (New York: Viking, 1995), 210.

23. On Felix, see for example Plumb, *Nightwood: The Original Version*, 218, note to p. 33.

24. Diane Warren, *Djuna Barnes' Consuming Fictions* (Burlington, VT: Ashgate, 2008), 16. See also Jane Marcus, 'Laughing at Leviticus: *Nightwood* as Woman's Circus Epic', in *Silence and Power*, ed. Mary Lynn Broe (Carbondale: Southern Illinois University Press, 1991), 221–50 (232).

25. Drew Milne, 'The Critique of Modernist Wit: Djuna Barnes's *Nightwood*', in Pender and Setz, *Shattered Objects*, 114–29 (118).

26. For the term 'narrative contract', see Chambers, *Story and Situation*, chap. 1.

27. For a discussion of metaphor in this passage, see Alan Singer, *A Metaphorics of Fiction: Discontinuity and Discourse in the Modern Novel* (Gainesville: University Presses of Florida, 1983), 57.

Notes   207

28. For a critique of the link between a style and a fictional being responsible for that style in the context of readings of episodes of *Ulysses*, see Derek Attridge, *Peculiar Language: Literature as Difference from the Renaissance to James Joyce* (London: Methuen, 1988), 174.
29. Mieke Bal, 'Over-writing as Un-writing: Descriptions, World-Making, and Novelistic Time', in *The Novel*, ed. Franco Moretti (Princeton, NJ: Princeton University Press, 2006), 571–610 (575–76).
30. Bal, 'Over-writing as Un-writing', 593 and 571–72.
31. Djuna Barnes, 'The Robin's House', in *A Night among the Horses* (New York: Horace Liveright, 1929), 117–30 (117). First published in *The Little Review* 7, no. 3 (1920) and revised and reprinted in *A Book* (1923).
32. Alyce Barry also observes the uncertainty between whether Barnes 'extracts' or 'creates' her subjects' words. Barnes, *I Could Never Be Lonely without a Husband*, 10.
33. Dora Zhang, *Strange Likeness: Description and the Modernist Novel* (Chicago: University of Chicago Press, 2020), 27.
34. See Herring, *Djuna*.
35. Joanne Winning, 'Dreams of a Lost Modernist: A Reevaluation of Thelma Wood', *Modernist Cultures* 8, no. 2 (2013): 288–322 (315–16). See also Joanne Winning, 'Djuna Barnes, Thelma Wood, and the Making of the Lesbian Modernist Grotesque', in Pender and Setz, *Shattered Objects*, 95–112.
36. Sigmund Freud's analysis of the dream-work is undertaken most fully in *Die Traumdeutung* (1900). For an English translation, see *The Interpretation of Dreams*, trans. James Strachey, ed. James Strachey with Alan Tyson, rev. Angela Richards (Harmondsworth: Penguin, 1976).
37. Plumb corrects 'grandfather' to 'grandmother'. Plumb, *Nightwood: The Original Version*, 237.
38. Taylor, *Djuna Barnes and Affective Modernism*, 19.
39. Djuna Barnes, 'A Little Girl Tells a Story to a Lady', in *A Night among the Horses*, 233–47 (235, 236), repr. in *Modernism: An Anthology*, ed. Lawrence Rainey (Oxford: Blackwell, 2005), 938–42 (939). The story was first published as the first piece in *Contact Collection of Contemporary Writers* (Paris: Three Mountains Press, 1925), 1–10.
40. Quoted in Drake Stutesman, 'Whitehead, Djuna Barnes, and Freud's "Dora": Introduction to Two Treatments', *Framework: The Journal of Cinema and Media* 52, no. 2 (2011): 572–77 (574, ellipsis in Whitehead's original). See also Peter Whitehead, 'Cassation, Film Treatment', *Framework: The Journal of Cinema and Media* 52, no. 2 (2011): 584–89.
41. Barnes, 'The Robin's House', 117.
42. Herring, *Djuna*, 165. See Barnes to Emily Coleman, 7 April 1937, Djuna Barnes Papers.
43. Barnes to Emily Coleman, 5 January 1939, Djuna Barnes Papers.
44. Quoted by Plumb in *Nightwood: The Original Version*, ix. See Barnes to Coleman, 20 September 1935, Djuna Barnes Papers.
45. Plumb, in *Nightwood: The Original Version*, x. See Coleman to Barnes, 28 August 1932, Djuna Barnes Papers.

208 *The New Modernist Novel: Criticism and the Task of Reading*

46. Plumb, in *Nightwood: The Original Version*, 160, 194. See Barnes, *Nightwood*, 49.
47. Plumb, in *Nightwood: The Original Version*, 164, 184.
48. Barnes to Coleman, 5 January 1939, Djuna Barnes Papers; Barnes to Natalie Barney, 19 October 1937, quoted in Herring, *Djuna*, 214–15.
49. Spiro, *Anti-Nazi Modernism*, 155.
50. Spiro, *Anti-Nazi Modernism*, 157, 159.
51. Carlston, *Thinking Fascism*, 77, 85. See also Meryl Altman, 'Rereading *Nightwood*', in 'Djuna Barnes', special issue, *Review of Contemporary Fiction* 13, no. 3 (1993): 160–71.
52. Potter, '*Nightwood*'s Humans', 73. For discussion of the issues later raised by Spiro and Potter, see also Hanrahan, 'Djuna Barnes's *Nightwood*'.
53. Walter Benjamin, 'The Storyteller: Reflections on the Works of Nikolai Leskov' (1936), in *Illuminations*, trans. Harry Zorn, ed. and introd. Hannah Arendt (London: Pimlico, 1999), 83–107 (86, 89).
54. See, for example, Nikolai Leskov, *The Enchanted Wanderer*, trans. A. G. Paschkoff, introd. Maxim Gorky (1924; London: Soho Book Company, 1985).
55. Joseph Frank, 'Spatial Form in Modern Literature', in *The Widening Gyre: Crisis and Mastery in Modern Literature* (Bloomington: Indiana University Press, 1963), 3–62, repr. in Frank, *The Idea of Spatial Form* (New Brunswick, NJ: Rutgers University Press, 1991), 5–66. The essay was first published in *Sewanee Review* 53, nos. 2–4 (Spring, Summer and Autumn 1945): 221–40, 433–56, 643–53. I refer here to the slightly revised 1963 version of Frank's essay.
56. Frank, 'Spatial Form', 31–32.
57. Frank, 'Spatial Form', 35, 42, 38.
58. Frank, 'Spatial Form', 41.
59. Frank, 'Spatial Form', 42, 49.
60. For an argument that Joseph Frank's reading misses the critical qualities of *Nightwood*'s wit by aligning the novel with work by Joyce and Proust, see Milne, 'The Critique of Modernist Wit: Djuna Barnes's *Nightwood*'.
61. Frank, 'Spatial Form', 27, 34–35.
62. For this change, see Glavey, *Wallflower Avant-Garde*, 53. For Frank's later hesitation on *Nightwood*, see *The Idea of Spatial Form*, 109–10.
63. Paul de Man, *Blindness and Insight: Essays in the Rhetoric of Contemporary Criticism* (New York: Oxford University Press, 1971), ix.
64. For a reading that demonstrates the value of Joseph Frank's spatial form to reading *Nightwood* now, see Glavey, *Wallflower Avant-Garde*, chap. 3.
65. Paul de Man, 'Spacecritics', *Partisan Review* 31 (1964): 640–50 (643).
66. Miles L. Hanley, *Word Index to James Joyce's 'Ulysses'* (Madison: Wisconsin University Press, 1951). See also Wolfhard Steppe and Hans Walter Gabler, *A Handlist to Joyce's 'Ulysses': A Complete Alphabetical Index to the Critical Reading Text* (New York: Garland, 1985).
67. Louis F. Kannenstine, *The Art of Djuna Barnes: Duality and Damnation* (New York: New York University Press, 1977); on the word 'disqualification',

see Rachel Potter, 'Djuna Barnes's *Nightwood* and Disqualification', *Affirmations: Of the Modern* 1, no. 1 (2013): 178–95.

68. For discussion of this trope, see Steve Pinkerton, *Blasphemous Modernism: The 20th-Century Word Made Flesh* (Oxford: Oxford University Press, 2017), chap. 5.

69. Plumb, *Nightwood: The Original Version*, 226, following Barnes to Wolfgang Hildesheimer, 25 July 1959.

70. Howard Rye, 'The Southern Syncopated Orchestra', *Black Music Research Journal* 29, no. 2 (2009): 153–228 (194).

71. Glavey, *Wallflower Avant-Garde*, 74.

72. Trubowitz, *Civil Antisemitism, Modernism, and British Culture*, 92.

73. Scott Herring, *Queering the Underworld: Slumming, Literature, and the Undoing of Lesbian and Gay History* (Chicago: University of Chicago Press, 2007), 165.

74. Herring, *Queering the Underworld*, chap. 4.

75. Peter Adkins, *The Modernist Anthropocene: Nonhuman Life and Planetary Change in James Joyce, Virginia Woolf and Djuna Barnes* (Edinburgh: Edinburgh University Press, 2022), 103.

76. Carolyn Allen, '"Dressing the Unknowable in the Garments of the Known": The Style of Djuna Barnes's *Nightwood*', in *Women's Language and Style*, ed. Douglas Butturff and Edmund L. Epstein (Akron, OH: L&S Books, 1978), 106–18 (112). See also Carolyn Allen, *Following Djuna: Women Lovers and the Erotics of Loss* (Bloomington: Indiana University Press, 1996).

77. Tyrus Miller, *Late Modernism: Politics and the Arts between the World Wars* (Berkeley: University of California Press, 1999), 151.

78. This worked only on the second attempt. For an account of the exchange between Coleman and Eliot, see Miriam Fuchs, 'The Triadic Association of Emily Coleman, T. S. Eliot, and Djuna Barnes', *ANQ: A Quarterly Journal of Short Articles, Notes and Reviews* 12, no. 4 (1999): 28–39 (esp. 29–30). See also Emily Coleman to T. S. Eliot, quoted (abridged) in *Letters of T. S. Eliot*, vol. 7, *1934–1935*, ed. Valerie Eliot and John Haffenden (London: Faber and Faber, 2017), 812–14, with accompanying commentary, and vol. 8, *1936–1938*, ed. Valerie Eliot and John Haffenden (London: Faber and Faber, 2019), 45n–46n. See Emily Coleman, drafts of the two letters to T. S. Eliot, 25 October and 1 November 1935, series 1, box 2, folder 13, Emily Holmes Coleman Papers, Special Collections, University of Delaware Library, Newark.

79. Edwin Muir to T. S. Eliot, 28 September 1935, quoted (abridged) in *Letters of T. S. Eliot*, 7:813–814n1.

80. L. P. Hartley, 'The Literary Lounger', *The Sketch*, no. 177 (13 January 1937): 86, viii.

81. Muir, 'New Novels'; Dylan Thomas, 'Night Wood', *Light and Dark*, March 1937, 27–29; Alfred Kazin, 'An Experiment in the Novel; Djuna Barnes, in "Nightwood", Makes a Strange Excursion in the Technique of Fiction', *New York Times*, 7 March 1937, 6.

82. Frank, 'Spatial Form', 27, 49. See also 43–44: *Nightwood* is not 'only a collection of magnificent fragments'.

83. Hank O'Neal, *'Life is painful, nasty, and short – in my case it has only been painful and nasty': Djuna Barnes, 1978–1981; An Informal Memoir* (New York: Paragon House, 1990), 58–59; Herring, *Djuna*, 112. See also Melanie Micir, *Abandoned Lives: Impossible Projects and Archival Remains* (Princeton, NJ: Princeton University Press, 2019), 50–60.

84. Barnes to Coleman, 24 June 1938, Djuna Barnes Papers.

85. Ezra Pound, 'The Notes for "The Ivory Tower"', *The Little Review* 5, no. 5 (1918), 50–53 (51), continued from the previous (Henry James) issue of *The Little Review*.

86. For the novel's original title as *Anatomy of Night*, see *Letters of T. S. Eliot*, 8:195n–196n.

87. T. S. Eliot, preface (1937) to *Nightwood*, by Barnes, ix–xiv (x–xii).

88. Miriam Fuchs, 'Djuna Barnes and T. S. Eliot: Authority, Resistance, and Acquiescence', *Tulsa Studies in Women's Literature* 12, no. 2 (1993), 288–313 (291). For Eliot's preface eliding Matthew's gender and the novel's homoeroticism, see Ed Madden, *Tiresian Poetics: Modernism, Sexuality, Voice, 1888–2001* (Cranbury, NJ: Rosemont, 2008), 185–95.

89. Eliot, preface to *Nightwood*, x.

90. As relayed by Barnes to Coleman, 30 October 1938, Djuna Barnes Papers.

91. Coleman reports this in a letter to Barnes, 20 January 1936, Djuna Barnes Papers. However, Coleman wrote to Barnes on 26 January 1936, 'I don't think myself he half read the excerpts.' Quoted in Monika Lee (as Monika Faltejskova), *Djuna Barnes, T. S. Eliot and the Gender Dynamics of Modernism* (London: Routledge, 2010), 75.

92. Eliot, preface to *Nightwood*, xii. For 'whole pattern', see also xi.

93. Lee (Faltejskova), *Djuna Barnes, T. S. Eliot and the Gender Dynamics of Modernism*, 60–66; Plumb, in *Nightwood: The Original Version*, xii–xxiii.

94. Coleman to Barnes, 27 August 1935, Djuna Barnes Papers.

95. Plumb, in *Nightwood: The Original Version*, xvii; Coleman to Barnes, 5 November 1935, Djuna Barnes Papers.

96. Plumb, in *Nightwood: The Original Version*, xiv; Lee (Faltejskova), *Djuna Barnes, T. S. Eliot and the Gender Dynamics of Modernism*, 90.

97. Charles Baxter, 'A Self-Consuming Light: *Nightwood* and the Crisis of Modernism', *Journal of Modern Literature* 3 (1974): 1175–87 (1176) and Alan Williamson, 'The Divided Image: The Quest for Identity in the Works of Djuna Barnes', *Critique* 7, no. 1 (Spring 1964): 58–74 (66).

98. For this reaction and the full draft blurb, see Herring, *Djuna*, 276. For discussion, see Lee (Faltejskova), *Djuna Barnes, T. S. Eliot and the Gender Dynamics of Modernism* and Fuchs, 'Djuna Barnes and T. S. Eliot'. See also Lynda Curry, 'Tom, Take Mercy: Djuna Barnes's Drafts of *The Antiphon*', in Broe, *Silence and Power*, 286–98.

99. Herring, *Djuna*, 276–77. Dorothy Richardson's stance on genius as being more the province of women seems distant from Eliot's blurb. Dorothy Richardson, 'Genius and Talent', *Vanity Fair* 21, no. 1 (1923): 118–20, repr. in *The Gender of Modernism: A Critical Anthology*, ed. Bonnie Kime Scott (Bloomington: Indiana University Press, 1990), 407–11.

Notes 211

100. René Taupin, *Quatre essais indifférents pour une esthétique de l'inspiration* (Paris: Presses Universitaires de France, 1932), 161, as quoted in *Active Anthology*, ed. Ezra Pound (London: Faber and Faber, 1933), 14 (minor variations in Pound's text).

101. Étienne Bonnot de Condillac, *Essay on the Origin of Human Knowledge*, ed. and trans. Hans Aarsleff (Cambridge: Cambridge University Press, 2012), pt. 1, sec. 2, §104, p. 66.

102. *Oxford English Dictionary*, 3rd ed., s.v. 'genius', accessed 6 September 2022, https://www.oed.com/dictionary/genius_n?tab=meaning_and_use# 3071474.

103. Ezra Pound, *How to Read* (London: Harmsworth, 1931), 10. For the full schema, see *How to Read*, 21–24 and *ABC of Reading* (1934; New York: New Directions, 1987), 39–41.

104. Condillac, *Essay on the Origin of Human Knowledge*, pt. 1, sec. 2, §104, p. 66.

105. In her reply to Eliot, Barnes repeats the two sentences, contrasting them indignantly with the last sentence of his preface to *Nightwood*. See Barnes to T. S. Eliot, 9 January 1957, Djuna Barnes Papers. Her reply is quoted in Georgette Fleischer, 'Djuna Barnes and T. S. Eliot: The Politics and Poetics of *Nightwood*', *Studies in the Novel* 30, no. 3 (Fall 1998): 405–37 (408–9).

106. For a commentary on Barnes and Eliot on modernist language, see Peter Nicholls, afterword to Pender and Setz, *Shattered Objects*, 207–14.

107. 'Proclamation', *transition*, nos. 16–17 (1929), 13.

108. Muir, 'New Novels'. Both Muir and Clifton Fadiman are quoted referring to 'genius' in Lee (Faltejskova), *Djuna Barnes, T. S. Eliot and the Gender Dynamics of Modernism*, 6.

109. Muir to Eliot, 13 January 1956, Djuna Barnes Papers. For the correct date of Muir's letter, dated 1955, see Herring, *Djuna*, 273–76.

110. For discussion, see Fuchs, 'Triadic Association'.

111. Emily Holmes Coleman to T. S. Eliot, 26 October 1935, quoted in *Letters of T. S. Eliot*, 7:812n2. See Coleman, draft letters to T. S. Eliot, 25 October and 1 November 1935, Djuna Barnes Papers.

112. Coleman to Barnes, 27 August 1935, Djuna Barnes Papers.

113. *Letters of T. S. Eliot*, 7:812n2 and 8:46n and 45n4; Coleman, draft letters to Eliot, 25 October and 1 November 1935, Djuna Barnes Papers.

114. Eliot to Barnes, 23 July 1945, quoted in *Letters of T. S. Eliot*, 7:812n2.

115. Coleman to Eliot, 2 November 1935, quoted in *Letters of T. S. Eliot*, 8:46n.

116. Eliot, preface to *Nightwood*, x, xii. See also Coleman to Barnes, 20 January 1936, quoting Eliot on the superfluity of the last chapter, Djuna Barnes Papers.

117. *Oxford English Dictionary*, 3rd ed., s.v. 'genius', accessed 6 September 2022, https://www.oed.com/dictionary/genius_n?tab=meaning_and_use# 3071474.

118. Daniela Caselli points out that the (established) modernist canon opposes genius to talent, where, as she argues, the two need not be opposed. Caselli, *Improper Modernism*, 32–33.

212 *The New Modernist Novel: Criticism and the Task of Reading*

119. Eliot, preface to *Nightwood*, xiv.
120. For an overview of Barnes criticism to 2013, see Cathryn Setz, '"The Great Djuna": Two Decades of Barnes Studies, 1993–2013', 'Djuna Barnes', special issue, *Literature Compass* 11, no. 6 (2014): 367–87.

Chapter 4: *Adolphe 1920* in Modernism

1. Evi Heinz, 'John Rodker', ed. Anna Mukamal and Dominic Williams, Modernist Archives Publishing Project, accessed 18 December 2022, https://www.modernistarchives.com/person/john-rodker.
2. Andrew Crozier, notes to *Poems and Adolphe 1920*, by John Rodker (Manchester: Carcanet, 1996), 182–88 (182); Ian Patterson, 'The Translation of Soviet Literature: John Rodker and PresLit', in *Russia in Britain, 1880–1940: From Melodrama to Modernism*, ed. Rebecca Beasley and Philip Ross Bullock (Oxford: Oxford University Press, 2013), 188–208 (191). For details of Rodker's publications, including *Adolphe 1920*, see Ian Patterson, 'Cultural Critique and Canon Formation, 1910–1937: A Study in Modernism and Cultural Memory' (PhD thesis, University of Cambridge, 1996), chaps. 3 and 4, esp. 78–79.
3. Ford Madox Ford, 'Dedicatory Letter to Stella Ford', in *The Good Soldier*, ed. Martin Stannard (New York: Norton, 1995), 3–6 (5).
4. See Hugh Ford, *Published in Paris: American and British Writers, Printers and Publishers in Paris, 1920–1939*, foreword by Janet Flanner (London: Garnstone Press, 1975), 280. For a possible source of this statement, see Gerald W. Cloud, *John Rodker's Ovid Press: A Bibliographical History* (New Castle, DE: Oak Knoll Press, 2010), 17n25. For information and images relating to the Ovid Press, see Evi Heinz, 'Ovid Press', ed. Lise Jaillant and Nicola Wilson, Modernist Archives Publishing Project, accessed 18 December 2022, https://www.modernistarchives.com/business/ovid-press.
5. For details of the Ovid Press and Rodker's other publications at this time, including *To M. B. J.*, see Cloud, *John Rodker's Ovid Press*; for comment on Rodker's agency in selecting work to publish, see esp. p. 17.
6. For discussion, see Cloud, *John Rodker's Ovid Press*, 32–49; for further detail, see Eliot to John Rodker, 8 August 1921, in T. S. Eliot, *The Letters*, vol. 1 *1898–1922*, ed. Valerie Eliot (London: Faber and Faber, 1988), 463. See also Rodker to Wallace Stevens, 28 July 1920, cited in Lawrence Rainey, *Institutions of Modernism: Literary Elites and Public Culture* (New Haven, CT: Yale University Press, 1998), 46.
7. Cloud, *John Rodker's Ovid Press*, 42–44. On the failure of Rodker's initial plans to publish *Ulysses*, see also Rainey, *Institutions of Modernism*, 45–47.
8. For details on publication and manuscripts, see Crozier, notes to *Poems and Adolphe 1920*.
9. Pound to Margaret Anderson, 11 June 1917, in *Pound/The Little Review: The Letters of Ezra Pound to Margaret Anderson*, ed. Thomas L. Scott,

Melvin J. Friedman and Jackson R. Bryer (London: Faber and Faber, 1988), 63.

10. Crozier, introduction to *Poems and Adolphe 1920*, vii–xxiii (xvi).

11. On Rodker's publishing career, see Rémy Amouroux, '"A Serious Venture": John Rodker (1894–1955) and the Imago Publishing Company (1939–60)', *International Journal of Psychoanalysis* 92 (2011): 1437–54.

12. Crozier, introduction to *Poems and Adolphe 1920*, viii.

13. Cloud, *John Rodker's Ovid Press*, 37. See also Evi Heinz, 'Casanova Society', ed. Lise Jaillant and Nicola Wilson, Modernist Archives Publishing Project, accessed 18 December 2022, https://www.modernistarchives.com/business/casanova-society.

14. *Comprehensive Index to Little Magazines 1890–1970*, ed. Marion Sader, 8 vols. (Millwood, NY: Kraus-Thomson, 1976), 6:3830. On Rodker's translations, see Ian Patterson, 'Writing on Other Fronts: Translation and John Rodker', *Translation and Literature* 12, no. 1 (2003): 88–113.

15. Drew Milne, 'Modernist Poetry in the British Isles', in *The Cambridge Companion to Modernist Poetry*, ed. Alex Davis and Lee M. Jenkins (Cambridge: Cambridge University Press, 2007), 147–62 (157 and 153).

16. John Rodker, *The Future of Futurism*, Today and Tomorrow (London: Kegan Paul, Trench & Trubner, 1927), 8, 45.

17. David Trotter, *Cinema and Modernism* (Oxford: Blackwell, 2007), 152. See also Ezra Pound, 'Data', *The Exile*, no. 4 (Autumn 1928): 104–17 (114).

18. John Rodker, *Adolphe 1920*, in *Poems and Adolphe 1920*, 133–74 (133), ellipsis in the original. Further citations are given in the text, with original ellipses and punctuation.

19. Corrected typescript draft of *Adolphe 1920*, John Rodker Papers, Harry Ransom Centre, University of Texas at Austin.

20. John Rodker, 'Southern Syncopated Singers', in *Poems and Adolphe 1920*, 123–24.

21. Crozier, introduction to *Poems and Adolphe 1920*, xx.

22. Ezra Pound, 'Dr Williams' Position', *The Dial* 85, no. 5 (November 1928): 395–404 (403).

23. Edmond Jaloux, preface to *Montagnes russes*, by John Rodker, trans. Ludmila Savitzky (Paris: Librairie Stock, 1923), ix–xxviii (ix, xviii–xix), my translations.

24. See Patterson, 'Writing on Other Fronts', 106, 108.

25. See Patterson, 'Writing on Other Fronts', 108–10.

26. David Trotter, *Paranoid Modernism: Literary Experiment, Psychosis and the Professionalization of English Society* (Oxford: Oxford University Press, 2001), 211.

27. Benjamin Constant, 'Preface to the Second Edition or Essay on the Nature and Moral Effect of the Work', in *Adolphe*, ed. and trans. Margaret Mauldon (Oxford: Oxford University Press, 2001), 81–83 (83).

28. See Benjamin Constant, 'Préface de la troisième édition', in *Adolphe*, ed. Gustave Rudler (Manchester: Manchester University Press, 1961), xxi–xxii (xxii).

214   *The New Modernist Novel: Criticism and the Task of Reading*

29. On a decadent aesthetic where words 'tend to become things in themselves, opaque and material', see Peter Nicholls, *Modernisms: A Literary Guide*, 2nd ed. (Basingstoke: Palgrave Macmillan, 2009), 58.

30. See Rodker, *Poems and Adolphe 1920*, 23–33. For details on the composition and publication of the pieces collected as *Theatre Muet*, see Crozier, notes to *Poems and Adolphe 1920*, 184–85.

31. John Rodker, 'The Theatre', *The Egoist* 21, no. 1 (2 November 1914): 414–15. For discussion of Rodker's work with the theatre, including these short dramas, see Evi Heinz, 'John Rodker on Theatre: Rethinking the Modernist Stage from London's Jewish East End', *Open Library of Humanities* 6, no. 1 (2020): 3–27.

32. For the 'hesitation of the principle of non-contradiction' in Joyce's *Finnegans Wake*, see Stephen Heath, 'Ambiviolences: Notes for Reading Joyce', in *Post-structuralist Joyce: Essays from the French*, ed. Derek Attridge and Daniel Ferrer (Cambridge: Cambridge University Press, 1984), 31–68 (59). Originally published as 'Ambiviolences: notes pour la lecture de Joyce', *Tel quel* 50 (1972): 22–43.

33. Arthur Symons, *The Symbolist Movement in Literature*, with an introduction by Richard Ellmann (1899; New York: Dutton, 1958), 76.

34. John Rodker, 'God Bless the Bottle', *The Little Review* 6, no. 4 (1919): 31, repr. in Rodker, *Poems and Adolphe 1920*, 61.

35. For Woolf's response, see for example *The Diary of Virginia Woolf*, ed. Anne Olivier Bell and Andrew McNeillie (London: Hogarth Press, 1978), 2:188–89. For a brief history of the censorship of *Ulysses*, see Paul Vanderham, *James Joyce and Censorship: The Trials of 'Ulysses'* (New York: New York University Press, 1998), 1–4. For courtroom responses, see Joseph Brooker, *Joyce's Critics: Transitions in Reading and Culture* (Madison: University of Wisconsin Press, 2004), 19–22.

36. John Rodker, 'War Museum – Royal College of Surgeons', in *Poems and Adolphe 1920*, 125.

37. Laura Marcus, *The Tenth Muse: Writing about Cinema in the Modernist Period* (Oxford: Oxford University Press, 2007), 89–90.

38. Ian Patterson, 'John Rodker, Julius Ratner and Wyndham Lewis: The Split-Man Writes Back', in *Wyndham Lewis and the Cultures of Modernity*, ed. Andrzej Gasiorek, Alice Reeve-Tucker and Nathan Waddell (Farnham: Ashgate, 2011), 95–107.

39. Wyndham Lewis, *The Apes of God* (1930; London: Arco, 1955), 156–57. Punctuation and spacing follow this edition.

40. For Lewis's Ratner as an antisemitic portrait of Rodker and for discussion of the 'satirical attack' on Rodker and *Adolphe 1920*, see Patterson, 'John Rodker, Julius Ratner and Wyndham Lewis'.

41. Lewis, *The Apes of God*, 158. Punctuation and spacing follow this edition.

42. David Ayers, *Wyndham Lewis and Western Man* (New York: St Martin's Press, 1992), 156.

43. Patterson, 'John Rodker, Julius Ratner and Wyndham Lewis'.

44. *Pound/Lewis: The Letters of Ezra Pound and Wyndham Lewis*, ed. Timothy Materer (London: Faber and Faber, 1985), 13.

Notes   215

45. Harold Munro to John Rodker, 18 August 1920, cited in Cloud, *John Rodker's Ovid Press*, 34n40.
46. Richard Aldington, 'Flint and Rodker', *Poetry: A Magazine of Verse* 17, no. 1 (1920): 44–48 (47).
47. Aldington, 'Flint and Rodker', 47.
48. Max Nordau, *Degeneration*, translated from the second edition of the German work (London: Heinemann, 1898), 309.
49. For an account of how translating Lautréamont was important for Rodker's own writing, see Patterson, 'Writing on Other Fronts', 98–102, which includes comment on Aldington's review, 98–99.
50. Maxwell Bodenheim, 'In Defense of Rodker', *Poetry* 17, no. 3 (December 1920): 170–71.
51. On the complexity of Pound's relationship to Rodker, see Dominic Williams, 'Circulating Antisemitism: The "Men of 1914"', in *Modernist Group Dynamics: The Politics and Poetics of Friendship*, ed. Fabio A. Durão and Dominic Williams (Newcastle: Cambridge Scholars Press, 2008), 43–68.
52. Ezra Pound, 'The Exile', *The Exile*, no. 1 (Spring 1927): 88–92 (89); Pound, *How to Read* (London: D. Harmsworth, 1931), 24.
53. '*Adolphe 1920*. By John Rodker', *The Spectator*, 7 December 1929, 46.
54. Clere Parsons, review of *Adolphe 1920*, *The Criterion* 10, no. 39 (1931): 333–36 (335–36).
55. Parsons, review of *Adolphe 1920*, 334.
56. Wyndham Lewis, *The Diabolical Principle* (London: Chatto and Windus, 1931), 41–64.
57. See *transition*, no. 7 (October 1927). For discussion of Lewis's critique of *transition* and Lautréamont in relation to Rodker, see Patterson, 'Writing on Other Fronts', 102–3.
58. Richard Aldington to John Rodker, 6 August 1928, John Rodker Papers, Harry Ransom Centre, University of Texas at Austin.
59. T. S. Eliot, '*Ulysses*, Order and Myth', in *Selected Prose of T. S. Eliot*, ed. Frank Kermode (London: Faber and Faber, 1975), 175–78 (176). See also Richard Aldington, 'Mr. James Joyce's *Ulysses*', in *Literary Studies and Reviews* (London: Allen and Unwin, 1924), 192–207 (205); first published as 'The Influence of Mr. James Joyce', *The English Review*, April 1921, 333–41.
60. John Rodker, 'Preface for a New Edition of Lautréamont's *Lay of Maldoror*', *Lion and Crown* 1, no. 1 (1932): 34–38 (35).
61. Rodker, 'Joyce and His Dynamic', 143. For comment on this essay, see Laura Heffernan, 'The Secret, the Baffled, the True: John Rodker and Late Avant-Garde Reading', in *Joyce's Disciples Disciplined: A Re-exagmination of the 'Exagmination' of 'Work in Progress'*, ed. Tim Conley (Dublin: University College Dublin Press, 2010), 94–106.
62. For reflection on Rodker's omission from canons of modernist literature, see Heffernan, 'The Secret, the Baffled, the True', and Sean Pryor, 'Satyriast's Beatitudes: John Rodker's Hymns', *Texas Studies in Language and Literature* 55, no. 4 (Winter 2013): 473–92.
63. See Fredric Jameson, *Fables of Aggression: Wyndham Lewis, the Modernist as Fascist* (Berkeley: University of California Press, 1979), 4–6.

216 *The New Modernist Novel: Criticism and the Task of Reading*

64. Jeri Johnson, introduction to and composition and publication history of *Ulysses*, by James Joyce, ed. Jeri Johnson (1922; New York: Oxford University Press, 1993), xi–xiii, xli. For discussion of 'disgust' in responses to *Ulysses*, see Brooker, *Joyce's Critics*, 25–34.

65. Sianne Ngai, *Ugly Feelings* (Cambridge, MA: Harvard University Press, 2005), 332.

66. Ezra Pound, *Hugh Selwyn Mauberley* (London: Ovid Press, 1920), 26. For discussion see Hugh Witemeyer, 'Early Poetry 1908–1920', in *The Cambridge Companion to Ezra Pound*, ed. Ira B. Nadel (Cambridge: Cambridge University Press, 1999), 43–58 (55).

67. Émile Derlin Zinsou and Luc Zouménou, *Kojo Tovalou Houénou, précurseur 1887–1936: pannégrisme et modernité* (Paris: Maisonneuve et Larose, 2004), 45 and 187.

68. Prince Kodjo Tovalou Houénou, funeral notice of S. A. R. le Prince (Joseph) Tovalou Padonou Azanmodo Houénou, box 26, folder 2, Nancy Cunard Papers, Harry Ransom Centre, University of Texas at Austin. I am grateful to Ian Patterson, who told me of the existence of the Cunard invitation and showed me the alterations that Rodker had made in this page of the typescript draft.

69. Corrected typescript draft of *Adolphe 1920*, John Rodker Papers, Harry Ransom Centre, University of Texas at Austin.

70. Heinz, 'John Rodker'.

71. Lois Gordon, *Nancy Cunard: Heiress, Muse, Political Idealist* (New York: Columbia University Press, 2007), 102; see also Nancy Cunard, *These Were the Hours: Memories of My Hours Press, Réanville and Paris, 1928–1931* (Carbondale: Southern Illinois University Press, 1969), 142.

72. Howard Rye, 'The Southern Syncopated Orchestra', *Black Music Research Journal* 29, no. 2 (2009): 153–228 (163, 170, 180 and 186 for Lottie Gee; 196 for dates); Catherine Tackley (née Parsonage), *The Evolution of Jazz in Britain, 1880–1935* (Oxford: Routledge, 2005; repr., 2017), 148 on new lighting effects. Lottie Gee's return to the UK for 'untraced engagements' in October 2020 matches the orchestra's last set of Philharmonic Hall performances in London. See Howard Rye, 'Southern Syncopated Orchestra: The Roster', *Black Music Research Journal* 30, no. 1 (2010): 19–70 (33).

73. See Babacar M'Baye, 'Marcus Garvey and African Francophone Political Leaders of the Early Twentieth Century', *Journal of Pan-African Studies* 1, no. 5 (2006): 2–19.

74. Gordon, *Nancy Cunard*, 129.

75. See the incident described in Zinsou and Zouménou, *Kojo Tovalou Houénou*, 131–36.

76. *Ovid's Metamorphoses*, trans. Arthur Golding (1567), ed. John Frederick Nims (New York: Macmillan, 1965), 2, lines 1–458.

77. Lewis, *The Apes of God*, 144; Patterson, 'John Rodker, Julius Ratner and Wyndham Lewis'.

78. Rodker, *Future of Futurism*, 43.

79. Rodker, *Future of Futurism*, 90–91.

80. Jaloux, preface to *Montagnes russes*.

Notes 217

81. Patterson, 'Writing on Other Fronts', 104.
82. Rodker, *Future of Futurism*, 81–82.
83. Louis Aragon, *Paysan de Paris* (Paris: Gallimard, 1926), 29; Mina Loy, *Insel*, ed. Elizabeth Arnold, introd. Sarah Hayden (Brooklyn: Melville House, 2014), 33, 43, 45, 88, 95, 148.
84. Raymond Roussel, *Impressions of Africa* (1910), trans. Lindy Foord and Rayner Heppenstall (London: Calder, 1983), chap. 8 (122–39).
85. Jules Laforgue, 'Salomé', in *Moral Tales*, trans. William Jay Smith (New York: New Directions, 1985), 87–109 (95), quoted in Peter Nicholls, '"Arid clarity": Ezra Pound, Mina Loy, and Jules Laforgue', *Yearbook of English Studies* 32 (2002): 52–64 (61).
86. Jules Laforgue, 'Salomé', in *Moralités légendaires*, ed. Daniel Grojnowksi and Henri Scepi (Paris: Flammarion, 2000), 131–53 (141, ellipsis original).
87. Nicholls, '"Arid clarity"', 61.
88. Nicholls, '"Arid clarity"', 60–62.
89. Nicholls, '"Arid clarity"', 59.
90. John Rodker, 'Chanson on Petit Hypertrophique', *The Little Review* 7, no. 2 (1920): 16–17, repr. in Rodker, *Poems and Adolphe 1920*, 62–63; Jules Laforgue, 'La chanson du petit hypertrophique', in *Les complaintes; L'imitation de Notre-Dame la lune; Derniers vers* (Paris: Armand Colin, 1959), 5–6; Ezra Pound to Margaret Anderson, 21 June and 3 August 1917, in Scott, Friedman and Bryer, *Pound/The Little Review*, 77 and 99.
91. Vincent Sherry, 'Modernism under Review: Edmund Wilson's *Axel's Castle; A Study in the Imaginative Literature of 1870–1930*', *Modernist Cultures* 7, no. 2 (2012): 145–59.
92. John Rodker, 'Lettre de New-York', *La revue européenne*, no. 13 (1924): 70–72.
93. Rodker, 'Lettre de New-York', 70.
94. Tackley (née Parsonage), *Evolution of Jazz in Britain*, 144.
95. Howard Rye, 'The Southern Syncopated Orchestra', 157–62, 196; Howard Rye, 'Chronology of the Southern Syncopated Orchestra: 1919–1922', *Black Music Research Journal* 30, no. 1 (2010): 4–17.
96. Tackley (née Parsonage), *Evolution of Jazz in Britain*, 143.
97. As noted above. On dancing, see Rye, 'The Southern Syncopated Orchestra', 175–76.
98. The description of the band at time participates in *négrophilie*, as defined by Carole Sweeney: 'a modernist primitivism, brimming with the dynamic and vigorous energies and contradictions of all the various strands of modernisms' – which, as Merinda K. Simmons and James A. Crank explain, enabled formal, stylistic, and other kinds of experiment. As Urmila Seshagiri puts it, 'race *gives form* to experimental modernism', where race is an aesthetic category as well as a sociopolitical category. See Carole Sweeney, *From Fetish to Subject: Race, Modernism, and Primitivism, 1919–1935* (Westport, CT: Praeger, 2004), 4; cited and discussed in Merinda K. Simmons and James A. Crank, *Race and New Modernisms* (London: Bloomsbury Academic, 2019), 49; and Urmila Seshagiri, *Race and the Modernist Imagination* (Ithaca, NY: Cornell University Press, 2010), 9, 196, italics in original.

218 *The New Modernist Novel: Criticism and the Task of Reading*

99. Tackley (née Parsonage), *Evolution of Jazz in Britain*, 160.

100. Zora Neale Hurston, 'How It Feels to Be Colored Me' (1928), in *I Love Myself When I Am Laughing . . . and Then Again When I Am Looking Mean and Impressive*, ed. Alice Walker (New York: Feminist Press at the City University of New York, 1979), 152–56. Michael North discusses Hurston's passage in *The Dialect of Modernism: Race, Language, and Twentieth-Century Media* (New York: Oxford University Press, 1994), 179. Rodker's rhetoric similarly echoes the music critic Robert Goffin's in his essay on jazz in the 1934 *Negro Anthology* edited by Nancy Cunard. Goffin's references to the jungle are implicitly critiqued by another essay in the anthology, Ralph Matthews's, which offers an account of recent changes in Black American theatre performance. By contrast, Alain Locke praised Goffin's and [George] Antheil's 'serious analyses' of jazz to Cunard as 'path breaking'. See Robert Goffin, 'Hot Jazz', trans. Samuel Beckett, in *Negro Anthology*, ed. Nancy Cunard (London: Wishart and Co., 1934), 378–79; Ralph Matthews, 'The Negro Theatre – A Dodo Bird', in Cunard, *Negro Anthology*, 312–14; and Alain Locke, letter to Nancy Cunard, 14 April 1934, quoted in Jane Marcus, *Nancy Cunard: Perfect Stranger*, ed. Jean Mills (Clemson, SC: Clemson University Press, 2020), 244.

101. On literary primitivism and the 'remnant', see Ben Etherington, *Literary Primitivism* (Stanford, CA: Stanford University Press, 2017), chaps. 2, 3 and 4, esp. 37–43.

102. For commentary on Cunard's anthology, see Priyamvada Gopal, *Insurgent Empire: Anticolonial Resistance and British Dissent* (London: Verso, 2020), chap. 7, esp. 211–25.

103. On the complexity of such inclusions among modernists generally, see Simmons and Crank, *Race and New Modernisms*, chap. 1, esp. 40.

Chapter 5: *Insel* and Literary Value

1. Roger L. Conover, foreword to *Insel*, by Mina Loy, ed. Elizabeth Arnold (Santa Rosa, CA: Black Sparrow Press, 1991), 9–15 (15).

2. For detailed discussion, see Amy Morris, '"You should have disappeared years ago" – The Poetics of Cultural Disappearance in Mina Loy's Late Poems', *Critical Quarterly* 55, no. 2 (2013): 81–104.

3. For details see Carolyn Burke, *Becoming Modern: The Life of Mina Loy* (New York: Farrar, Straus and Giroux, 1996).

4. Roger L. Conover, 'Time-Table', in Mina Loy, *The Last Lunar Baedeker*, ed. Roger L. Conover (Manchester: Carcanet, 1985), lxiii–lxxix (lxxiv–lxxv).

5. Elizabeth Arnold, afterword to *Insel*, by Mina Loy, ed. Elizabeth Arnold, introd. Sarah Hayden (Brooklyn, NY: Melville House, 2014), 169–76 (171–74). See also Hayden's introduction, ix–xxxii (xiv). For Oelze's departure date, see Sarah Hayden, *Curious Disciplines: Mina Loy and Avant-Garde Artisthood* (Albuquerque: University of New Mexico Press, 2018), 196.

Notes **219**

6. Burke, *Becoming Modern*, ix and 381–84.
7. For details, see Conover, foreword to *Insel*, ed. Arnold, 9; Sandeep Parmar, *Reading Mina Loy's Autobiographies: Myth of the Modern Woman* (London: Bloomsbury, 2013), 151–52, 175; and Hayden, introduction to *Insel*, ix–xx, xxviii.
8. See Susan Rosenbaum, '"I'm not the Museum": Mina Loy, the Julien Levy Gallery, and Trans-Atlantic Surrealism', in *Mina Loy: Navigating the Avant-Garde*, ed. Suzanne W. Churchill, Linda A. Kinnahan, and Susan Rosenbaum, University of Georgia, accessed 17 September 2022, https://mina-loy.com/chapters/surreal-scene/4-loy-surrealism-the-levy-gallery/.
9. Burke, *Becoming Modern*, 400, 374; second draft, copy 1 of *Insel*, Mina Loy Papers, Yale Collection of American Literature, Beinecke Rare Book and Manuscript Library. See also Hayden, *Curious Disciplines*, 189n4; Hayden, introduction to *Insel*, xiv and xviii; Parmar, *Reading Mina Loy's Autobiographies*, 204n4; and Conover, foreword to *Insel*, ed. Arnold, 9.
10. Mina Loy, 'Visitation of Insel', in Loy, *Insel*, 155–67 (161).
11. See Burke, *Becoming Modern*, 380 and 462–63n; Hayden, *Curious Disciplines*, 131; and Hayden, introduction to *Insel*, xvi.
12. Loy, *Insel*, 42. Further citations are given in the text.
13. Hayden, *Curious Disciplines*, 130.
14. Tara Prescott similarly reads the cultural contexts of Loy's poetry in detail in her close readings. See, for example, *Poetic Salvage: Reading Mina Loy* (Lanham, MD: Lexington Books, 2017), 6–14 on the Cabaret du Néant.
15. See Loy's note: 'I read later that sugar was used for strengthening concrete' (*Insel*, 177n42).
16. Genêt [Janet Flanner], 'Stavisky', in *Paris Was Yesterday, 1925–1939*, ed. Irving Drutman (London: Angus and Robertson, 1973), 109–11, 114–16 and 154–55 (154).
17. Palmer White, *Elsa Schiaparelli: Empress of Paris Fashion*, foreword by Yves Saint-Laurent (London: Aurum, 1986), 154; Dilys Blum, *Shocking! The Art and Fashion of Elsa Schiaparelli* (Philadelphia: Philadelphia Museum of Art; London: Yale University Press, 2003), 102 and 124; Julien Levy, *Memoir of an Art Gallery* (New York: Putnam, 1977), 302. For reproductions of two advertisements for Shocking perfume, see Susan Rosenbaum, 'Surrealist Objects, Fashion, Design', in Churchill, Kinnahan, and Rosenbaum, *Mina Loy: Navigating the Avant-Garde*, accessed 17 September 2022, https://mina-loy.com/surrealist-objects-fashion-design/.
18. For comment on similarities between Loy's work and Schiaparelli's, see Susan E. Dunn, 'Mina Loy, Fashion and the Avant-Garde', in *Mina Loy: Woman and Poet*, ed. Maeera Schreiber and Keith Tuma (Orono, ME: National Poetry Foundation Press, 1998), 443–55 (452). On Loy's lampshades, see Susan Rosenbaum, 'Mina Loy's Lamp Shop', in Churchill, Kinnahan, and Rosenbaum, *Mina Loy: Navigating the Avant-Garde*, accessed 17 September 2022, https://mina-loy.com/chapters/surreal-scene/5-paris-era-exhibitions/; and Jessica Burstein, *Cold Modernism: Literature, Fashion, Art* (University Park: Pennsylvania State University Press, 2012), chap. 4.

220   *The New Modernist Novel: Criticism and the Task of Reading*

19. François Baudot, *Elsa Schiaparelli* (London: Thames and Hudson, 1997), 14.
20. Burke, *Becoming Modern*, 384–85 and 463n. On this point and for an image of *Erwartung*, see Rosenbaum, '"I'm not the Museum"'.
21. Renate Damsch-Wiehager, *Richard Oelze, Erwartung: Die ungewisse Gegenwart des Kommenden* (Frankfurt am Main: Fischer Taschenbuch Verlag, 1993), 6. See also Alfred Barr, '*Erwartung*', in *Richard Oelze 1900–1980: Gemälde und Zeichnungen*, ed. Wieland Schmied (Berlin: Akademie der Künste, 1988), 32–34, and the letter from Mathilde Visser to Werner Schmalenbach, 25 September 1982, quoted in Renate Damsch-Wiehager, *Richard Oelze: Ein alter Meister der Moderne* (Munich: Verlag C. J. Bucher, 1989), 227.
22. Wiehager, *Richard Oelze, Erwartung*, 6 and 8. See also Julien Levy, *Surrealism* (1936; New York: Da Capo, 1995), 177.
23. David Ayers also observes the difference and notes the relevance of the crowd to the painting, which was 'modelled on a photograph of a crowd waiting for the arrival of Charles Lindbergh's first transatlantic flight in 1927'. David Ayers, 'Mina Loy's *Insel* and Its Contexts', in *The Salt Companion to Mina Loy*, ed. Suzanne Hobson and Rachel Potter (London: Salt, 2010), 221–47 (230).
24. Barr, '*Erwartung*', 32. English original available in Württembergischer Kunstverein, Stuttgart, *Katalog 'Richard Oelze'* (Hanover: Kestner Gesellschaft, 1964).
25. Richard Oelze, 'Diktat für eine Fragebogen', in Schmied, *Richard Oelze 1900–1980: Gemälde und Zeichnungen*, 11, my translation.
26. Richard Oelze to Johannes Itten, 15 September 1948, in Wiehager, *Richard Oelze: Ein alter Meister der Moderne*, 230, my translation.
27. *Frieda* and *Frieda II* are reproduced in the 1933–1936 selection in *Richard Oelze: Einzelgänger des Surrealismus*, ed. Christine Hopfengart (Bremen: Kunstverein Bremen, 2000), 111 and 112. *Frieda* is also reproduced in Rosenbaum, '"I'm not the Museum"'. As Rosenbaum notes, this *Frieda* is a charcoal sketch of the destroyed original painting.
28. Wiehager, *Richard Oelze, Erwartung*, 51–53. See also Hopfengart, *Richard Oelze: Einzelgänger des Surrealismus*, 107.
29. For an investigation of Loy's interpretation of Freud and Christianity in *Anglo-Mongrels and the Rose*, see Keith Tuma, 'Mina Loy's *Anglo-Mongrels and the Rose*', in Schreiber and Tuma, *Mina Loy: Woman and Poet*, 181–202.
30. Wiehager, *Richard Oelze: Erwartung*, 8.
31. Hayden, *Curious Disciplines*, 195–96; for differences between Oelze and Insel, see 134, 138 and 140–41.
32. Burke, *Becoming Modern*, 405, 404, 464n.
33. Joseph Cornell, *The Magical Worlds of Joseph Cornell*, DVD-ROM, in Lynda Roscoe Hartigan et al., *Joseph Cornell: Shadowplay . . . Eterniday* (London: Thames and Hudson, 2003), in the section 'Early Objects and Boxes'.
34. Lynda Roscoe Hartigan, ed. *Joseph Cornell: Navigating the Imagination* (London: Yale University Press, 2007), 110–11.

Notes 221

35. Mina Loy, 'Phenomenon in American Art (Joseph Cornell)', in *Last Lunar Baedeker*, 300–302. At the end of the piece Loy uses sentences from *Insel* to gesture to Cornell's earlier work, including part of the sentence quoted from page 144 of *Insel*.
36. Hayden, *Curious Disciplines*, 201.
37. Helen Vendler, 'The Truth Teller', *New York Review of Books*, 19 September 1996, 57–60 (60).
38. For an account of metonymy as associated with the nineteenth-century realist novel and metaphor as associated with the modernist novel, see David Lodge, 'The Language of Modernist Fiction: Metonymy and Metaphor', in *Modernism: 1890–1930*, ed. Malcolm Bradbury and James McFarlane (Harmondsworth: Penguin, 1976), 481–96.
39. Denise Levertov, 'Notes of Discovery', in *Lunar Baedeker and Time-Tables: Selected Poems*, by Mina Loy, Jargon 23 (Highlands, NC: Jonathan Williams, 1958).
40. Hugh Kenner, 'To Be the Brancusi of Poetry', *New York Times*, 16 May 1982, 7, 30.
41. Ezra Pound, 'A List of Books', *The Little Review* 4, no. 11 (1918): 54–58 (58), repr. as 'Marianne Moore and Mina Loy', in Ezra Pound, *Selected Prose 1909–1965*, ed. and introd. William Cookson (London: Faber and Faber, 1973), 394–95. For comment, see Peter Nicholls, '"Arid clarity": Ezra Pound, Mina Loy, and Jules Laforgue', *Yearbook of English Studies* 32 (2002): 52–64.
42. William Carlos Williams, 'Mina Loy', in *Lunar Baedeker and Time-Tables*.
43. Pound, 'A List of Books'.
44. Alfred Kreymborg, ed., *Others: An Anthology of the New Verse (1917)* (New York: Alfred A. Knopf, 1917).
45. Ezra Pound, *How to Read* (London: Harmsworth, 1931), 25–26.
46. Virginia M. Kouidis, *Mina Loy: American Modernist Poet* (Baton Rouge: Louisiana State University Press, 1980), 87.
47. Peter Nicholls, 'Mina Loy and Lexicophilia', *Feminist Modernist Studies* 2, no. 3 (2019): 263–73 (266).
48. Rachel Potter, *Modernism and Democracy* (Oxford: Oxford University Press, 2007), 178.
49. Sean Pryor, *Poetry, Modernism, and an Imperfect World* (Cambridge: Cambridge University Press, 2017), 116–17.
50. Loy, 'Visitation of Insel', 159.
51. John Wilkinson, 'Stumbling, Balking, Tacking: Robert Creeley's *For Love* and Mina Loy's "Love Songs to Joannes"', in Hobson and Potter, *The Salt Companion to Mina Loy*, 146–65 (154).
52. Yvor Winters, 'Mina Loy', *Dial* 80, no. 6 (1926): 496–99 (496).
53. For an analysis of *Insel* as *Künstler(in)roman*, see Tyrus Miller, *Late Modernism: Politics and the Arts between the World Wars* (Berkeley: University of California Press, 1999), 207–22; for discussion of biography and autobiography in Loy's writing, including *Insel*, see Laura Scuriatti, *Mina Loy's Critical Modernism* (Gainesville: University Press of Florida, 2019), 176–91.

54. Marisa Januzzi, review of *Insel*, *Review of Contemporary Fiction* 12, no. 2 (1992), 202–4 (203).
55. For discussion, see Burke, *Becoming Modern*, 374–75, and Sandeep Parmar, 'Mina Loy's "Unfinishing" Self', in Hobson and Potter, *The Salt Companion to Mina Loy*, 71–98 (76–77 and 81).
56. Parmar, *Reading Mina Loy's Autobiographies*, 174–75.
57. Hayden discusses this plan and its failure to come to fruition in *Curious Disciplines*, 193–95.
58. For the situation of emigré artists in Paris, see Hayden, *Curious Displines*, 197–98.
59. See Hayden, *Curious Disciplines*, 131.
60. On graininess, see Beci Carver, *Granular Modernism* (Oxford: University Press, 2014), esp. 21–29.
61. Alberto Giacometti, 'Le rêve, le Sphinx et la mort de T.', *Labyrinthe* 22 (1946), 12–13. For an anecdote of the Sphinx, see Levy, *Memoir of an Art Gallery*, 143–44.
62. Diane Drouin, '"Like a Roll of Negative Film": montages optiques et fragmentation de soi dans *Insel* et "The Child and the Parent" de Mina Loy', *Études britanniques contemporaines* 56 (2019), para. 9, https://doi.org/10.4000/ebc.6190, my translation.
63. Levy, *Memoir of an Art Gallery*, 243–44.
64. Hayden, *Curious Disciplines*, 199–202.
65. David Trotter, *The Literature of Connection: Signal, Medium, Interface, 1850–1950* (Oxford: Oxford University Press, 2020), 127.
66. Susan Rosenbaum, 'Topsy-Turvy Aesthetics: Mina Loy, Jazz, Surrealism, and Race', in Churchill, Kinnahan, and Rosenbaum, *Mina Loy: Navigating the Avant-Garde*, accessed 17 September 2022, https://mina-loy.com/loy-surrealism-race/. Dalí describes the surrealist double image in 'L'âne pourri' ('The Rotten Donkey'), *Le Surréalisme au service de la révolution*, no. 1 (1930): 9–12, repr. in *Le Surréalisme au service de la révolution* (New York: Arno Press [1968]). For discussion of Dalí's double image, see Delia Ungureanu, *From Paris to Tlön: Surrealism as World Literature* (New York: Bloomsbury Academic, 2018), 52–53.
67. Rosenbaum, 'Topsy-Turvy Aesthetics'.
68. See *Frieda* and *Frieda II* in the 1933–36 selection in Hopfengart, *Richard Oelze: Einzelgänger des Surrealismus*, 111 and 112.
69. For Loy's feminism, see, for example, 'Feminist Manifesto', written 1914, in Mina Loy, *The Lost Lunar Baedeker*, ed. Roger L. Conover (Manchester: Carcanet, 1997), 153–56; Mina Loy, 'The Library of the Sphinx', in *Stories and Essays of Mina Loy*, ed. Sara Crangle (London: Dalkey Archive Press, 2011), 253–59.
70. On the politics of the artist's relationship to the art dealer in *Insel*, see Hayden, *Curious Disciplines*, 199–200.
71. Levy, *Memoir of an Art Gallery*, 283–95.
72. For Brancusi and Loy seeing the 'Thin Man' series together, which starred William Powell and Myrna Loy, see Burke, *Becoming Modern*, 380.

73. Phillip Herring, *Djuna: The Life and Work of Djuna Barnes* (New York: Viking, 1995), 179.
74. James Knowlson, *Damned to Fame: The Life of Samuel Beckett* (New York: Simon and Schuster, 1996), 100 and 253–54.
75. Robert McAlmon and Kay Boyle, *Being Geniuses Together, 1920–1930* (New York: Doubleday, 1968), 34.
76. Ernest Hemingway, *A Moveable Feast* (London: Vintage, 2000), 85–92 ('With Pascin at the Dôme').
77. Giacometti, 'Le rêve, le Sphinx et la mort de T.'
78. September 1932. See Raymond Federman and John Fletcher, *Samuel Beckett: His Works and His Critics* (Berkeley: University of California Press, 1970), 92–93.
79. Knowlson, *Damned to Fame*, 271.
80. On this period of study, see Burke, *Becoming Modern*, chap. 3.
81. Frank Kermode uses *Die Insel*'s image of dancer Loïe Fuller as the cover for his *The Romantic Image* (London: Routledge and Kegan Paul, 1957), noted on xi.
82. Otto Julius Bierbaum, Alfred Walter Henmel and Rudolf Alexander Schröder, 'Die Insel', *Die Insel* 1, no. 1 (1899): 1–4 (2), my translation.
83. F. T. Marinetti, 'The Founding and Manifesto of Futurism', in *Let's Murder the Moonshine: Selected Writings*, ed. R. W. Flint, trans. R. W. Flint and Arthur A. Coppotelli (Los Angeles: Sun & Moon Press, 1991), 47–52 (49).
84. Levy, *Memoir of an Art Gallery*, 71. The painting was stored in Loy's apartment (Burke, *Becoming Modern*, 377).
85. See, for example, Mina Loy, 'Auto-facial-Construction', in *Last Lunar Baedeker*, 283–84. For Insel as a 'soft machine', see also 'Visitation of Insel', 163.
86. Mina Loy, 'Nancy Cunard', in *Lost Lunar Baedeker*, 103.
87. For Man Ray's 1926 photograph of Cunard wearing African bracelets on her arms to each shoulder, see Man Ray, *Nancy Cunard* (1926), held at the Metropolitan Museum of Art, New York, accession number 1987.1100.131, accessed 17 September 2022, https://www.metmuseum.org/art/collection/search/265168
88. Surrealist Group in Paris, 'Murderous Humanitarianism', trans. Samuel Beckett, in *Negro Anthology*, ed. Nancy Cunard (London: Wishart and Co., 1934), 574–75, first published 1932. The Surrealist Group included two Martinique intellectuals and writers, Jules Monnerot and Pierre Yoyotte. See Natalya Lusty, 'Introduction: Surrealism's Critical Legacy', in *Surrealism*, ed. Natalya Lusty (Cambridge: Cambridge University Press, 2021), 1–28 (12). For the common history of Cunard's and the surrealists' interest in non-Western artefacts, see Carole Sweeney, *From Fetish to Subject: Race, Modernism, and Primitivism, 1919–1935* (Westport, CT: Praeger, 2004), 97–98.
89. On Loy's and Levy's role in shaping surrealism for the US, see Ungureanu, *From Paris to Tlön*, chap. 4; Wiehager, *Richard Oelze, Erwartung*, 6. See also Julien Levy, *Surrealism*, 177. For a contemporary version of surrealism closer to a Paris surrealism, see David Gascoyne, *A Short Survey of Surrealism* (1935), introd. Michael Remy, with a preface by Dawn Ades (London: Enitharmon Press, 2000).

90. For an account of Loy's links with Christian Science as a source of Insel's rays, see Ayers, 'Mina Loy's *Insel* and Its Contexts'.

91. Richard Oelze, *Phantastische Komposition*, 1935, in the Peggy Guggenheim Collection, Venice, 26.2 × 18.4 cm, accession number 76.2553 PG 104.

92. It is possible that Schulz first read Kafka's novel only after publishing his first collection *The Street of Crocodiles* in 1934. See Celina Wieniewska, 'Translator's Preface', in *Complete Fiction of Bruno Schulz: 'The Street of Crocodiles' and 'Sanatorium under the Sign of the Hourglass'* (New York: Walker and Company, 1989), ix–xiv.

93. Philippe Soupault, *Last Nights of Paris*, trans. William Carlos Williams (1929; Cambridge: Exact Change, 1992), 82. Originally published in French as *Les dernières nuits de Paris* (Paris: Calmann-Lévy, 1928).

94. Soupault, *Last Nights of Paris*, 156. Cf. the 'effulgence of phosphorus' around Robin in *Nightwood*: Djuna Barnes, *Nightwood* (London: Faber and Faber, 2015), 31.

95. For example, see Soupault, *Last Nights of Paris*, 46.

96. Philippe Soupault, 'Afterword: William Carlos Williams in Paris by Day and by Night', in *Last Nights of Paris*, 177–79 (179, 178).

97. Cited in the publisher's note to Soupault, *Last Nights of Paris*, v–ix (vii and ix).

98. André Breton, *Nadja*, rev. ed. ([Paris]: Gallimard, 1963), 99–100; André Breton, *Nadja* (1928), trans. Richard Howard, introd. Mark Polizzotti (London: Penguin, 1999), 100.

99. Breton, *Nadja*, 81.

100. Breton, *Nadja*, trans. Howard, 83.

101. Breton, *Nadja*, 134, 133; Breton, *Nadja*, trans. Howard, 142, 141.

102. Mark Polizzotti, introduction to *Nadja*, trans. Howard, ix–xxvii.

103. Alys Moody, 'Against Culinary Art: Mina Loy and the Modernist Starving Artist', in *Gastro-modernism: Food, Literature, Culture*, ed. Derek Gladwin (Clemson, SC: Clemson University Press, 2019), 83–98 (96–98).

104. Rosenbaum, 'Topsy-Turvy Aesthetics'.

105. Breton, *Nadja*, plates 39 and 40; Breton, *Nadja*, trans. Howard, plates 39 and 41

106. Will Atkin, 'Oceanic Metamorphoses: Easter Island, Paul Gauguin and "Magic Art" through the Eyes of the Surrealists', *Journal of Postcolonial Writing* 54, no. 5 (2018): 670–89 (674).

107. See the reproductions of artworks in the section 'Negro Sculpture and Ethnology' in Cunard, *Negro Anthology*, 655–733.

108. Breton, *Nadja*, trans. Howard, 122, 129.

109. Claire Howard, '*The Enchanters' Domain*: Oceania, the Northwest Coast, and New York', in *Surrealism beyond Borders*, ed. Stephanie D'Alessandro and Matthew Gale (New York: Metropolitan Museum of Art; New Haven, CT: Yale University Press, 2021), 180–83 (180).

110. André Breton, 'Crise de l'objet', in *Oeuvres complètes*, vol. 4, ed. Marguerite Bonnet (Paris: Gallimard, 2008), 681–88; Christina Rudosky, 'Surrealist Objects', in Lusty, *Surrealism*, 151–75.

111. Loy, 'Phenomenon in American Art', 302.

112. Atkin, 'Oceanic Metamorphoses', 688.
113. Maia Nuku, 'Power and Agency in Oceanic Art', in D'Alessandro and Gale, *Surrealism beyond Borders*, 184–85 (185).
114. Surrealist Group, 'Murderous Humanitarianism', 574.
115. André Breton, 'Qu'est-ce que le surréalisme?', in *Oeuvres complètes*, vol. 2 (1992), ed. Marguerite Bonnet (1992), 227–62. For commentary see Raymond Spiteri, 'Surrealism and the Demand of Politics', in Lusty, *Surrealism*, 63–77.
116. Peter Nicholls, *Modernisms: A Literary Guide*, 2nd ed. (Basingstoke: Palgrave Macmillan, 2009), 193–218; Michael Levenson, *Modernism* (New Haven, CT: Yale University Press, 2011), 158–63.
117. See, for example, the discussion of early twentieth-century French novels that might be called 'modernist' in Jean-Michel Rabaté, 'Modernism and the French Novel: A Genealogy (1888–1913)', in *A History of the Modernist Novel*, ed. G. Castle (Cambridge: Cambridge University Press, 2015), 86–109.
118. Carver, *Granular Modernism*, chap. 4.
119. Levin praises Marcel Proust as belonging to 'that class of novelists – eminently personified in Balzac – who still aspire towards wholeness' in 'Proust, Gide, and the Sexes', *PMLA* 65, no. 4 (1950): 648–52 (652), repr. in *Grounds for Comparison* (Cambridge, MA: Harvard University Press, 1972), 351–57 (354).
120. See Stephen Heath, 'The Folly of the Moon', in 'Remembering Frank Kermode', *Critical Quarterly* 54, no. 1 (2012): 1–15.
121. For Loy as a 'brilliant literary enigma', see Rachel Potter and Suzanne Hobson, introduction to *The Salt Companion to Mina Loy*, 1–11 (1). Reference is also made to *The Enigma of Isidore Ducasse* in Rosenbaum, '"I'm not the Museum"'. Roger L. Conover calls Loy an 'enigma' in his foreword to *Insel*, ed. Arnold, 10.

Epilogue: Vocabularies

1. Eric Hayot and Rebecca Walkowitz, introduction to *A New Vocabulary for Global Modernism*, ed. Hayot and Walkowitz (New York: Columbia University Press, 2016), 1–10.
2. Alys Moody and Stephen J. Ross, 'Global Modernism: An Introduction and Ten Theses', in *Global Modernists on Modernism: An Anthology*, ed. Moody and Ross (London: Bloomsbury Academic, 2019), 1–24 (7). For a critique of a diffusionist model of modernism, see Jahan Ramazani, 'Form', in Hayot and Walkowitz, *A New Vocabulary for Global Modernism*, 114–29, and Harsha Ram, 'The Scale of Global Modernisms: Imperial, National, Regional, Local', *PMLA* 131, no. 5 (2016): 1372–85; on circulation, see Susan Stanford Friedman, 'World Modernisms, World Literature, and Comparativity', in *The Oxford Handbook of Global Modernisms*, ed. Mark Wollaeger and Matthew Eatough (Oxford: Oxford University Press, 2012), 499–526.

3. In this paragraph's reflections I am indebted to the stimulus of Rabaté's lecture 'Joyce and Critical Theory', given at the Sydney Social Sciences and Humanities Advanced Research Centre, University of Sydney, December 2019. See his 'Joyce and Critical Theory', in *The New Joyce Studies*, ed. Catherine Flynn (Cambridge: Cambridge University Press, 2022), 252–67 (252). See also Jacques Derrida, *Ulysse gramophone: deux mots pour Joyce* (Paris: Galilée, 1987). Derrida's 1982 lecture was translated as 'Two Words for Joyce', in *Post-structuralist Joyce: Essays from the French*, ed. Derek Attridge and Daniel Ferrer (Cambridge: Cambridge University Press, 1984), 145–60.

4. On late modernism, see Rod Rosenquist, *Modernism, the Market, and the Institution of the New* (Cambridge: Cambridge University Press, 2009); Tyrus Miller, *Late Modernism: Politics and the Arts between the World Wars* (Berkeley: University of California Press, 1999); David Trotter, *Literature in the First Media Age: Britain between the Wars* (Cambridge, MA: Harvard University Press, 2013), 37.

5. Sue Thomas, 'Jean Rhys and Katherine Mansfield Writing the "Sixth Act"', in *Jean Rhys: Twenty-First Century Approaches*, ed. Erica L. Johnson and Patricia Moran (Edinburgh: Edinburgh University Press, 2020), 21–39.

6. Ford Madox Ford, preface to Jean Rhys, *The Left Bank and Other Stories* (1927; Freeport, NY: Books for Libraries Press, 1970), 7–27 (25).

7. Peter Kalliney, 'Jean Rhys: Left Bank Modernist as Postcolonial Intellectual', in Wollaeger and Eatough, *Oxford Handbook of Global Modernisms*, 413–33 (418).

8. Samuel Beckett, *How It Is* (New York: Grove, 1964), 7. Further citations of this edition are given in the text. Originally published in French as *Comment c'est* (Paris: Les Éditions de Minuit, 1961). Since I use the English-language text in these short comments, I have used the title *How It Is*.

9. I will use the term 'narrator' for the 'I' of this text. For Beckett's term 'narrator/narrated', see Hugh Kenner, *A Reader's Beckett* (London: Thames & Hudson, 1973), 94.

10. Arthur Rimbaud, 'Le bateau ivre', trans. Samuel Beckett, in Beckett, *Collected Poems 1930–1978* (London: Calder, 1984), 124–37 (126).

11. Dante Alighieri, *Divine Comedy*, trans. Mark Musa, vol. 1, *Inferno* (New York: Penguin, 1984), 7.125.

12. Daniela Caselli, *Beckett's Dantes: Intertextuality in the Fiction and Criticism* (Manchester: Manchester University Press, 2005), 3, 4.

13. James Knowlson, *Damned to Fame: The Life of Samuel Beckett* (New York: Simon & Schuster, 1996), 297–351.

14. Adam Piette, 'Torture, Text, Human Rights: Beckett's *Comment c'est/ How It Is* and the Algerian War', in *Around 1945: Literature, Citizenship, Rights*, ed. Allan Hepburn (Montreal and Kingston: McGill-Queen's University Press, 2016), 151–74 (151–52). See also Emilie Morin, *Beckett's Political Imagination* (Cambridge: Cambridge University Press, 2017), chap. 4; and the comments on 'violent years' in the general introduction to *The Letters of Samuel Beckett*, vol. 3, *1957–1965*, ed. George Craig, Martha Dow Fehsenfeld, Dan Gunn and Lois More Overbeck (Cambridge: Cambridge University Press, 2014), xii–xxiv (xiv–xvii).

Notes **227**

15. Piette, 'Torture, Text, Human Rights', 171.
16. Anthony Cordingley, 'The Afterlife of Empire in Beckett's *How It Is*', *Samuel Beckett Today/Aujourd'hui* 33 (2021): 88–105 (102).
17. Dominic Walker, 'Beckett's Safe Words: Normalising Torture in *How It Is*', in *Beckett Beyond the Normal*, ed. Seán Kennedy (Edinburgh: Edinburgh University Press, 2020), 117–32.
18. Walker, 'Beckett's Safe Words', 130.
19. Djuna Barnes, *Nightwood* (London: Faber and Faber, 2015), 134–35.
20. Mieke Bal, 'Over-Writing as Un-writing: Descriptions, World-Making, and Novelistic Time', in *The Novel*, ed. Franco Moretti (Princeton, NJ: Princeton University Press, 2006), 571–610 (593).
21. Dora Zhang, *Strange Likeness: Description and the Modernist Novel* (Chicago: University of Chicago Press, 2020), 27.
22. Beckett read Barnes's *Nightwood* in 1939 and knew Barnes at that time. See Knowlson, *Damned to Fame*, 295, and *Letters of Samuel Beckett*, vol. 1, *1929–1940*, ed. Martha Dow Fehsenfeld and Lois More Overbeck (Cambridge: Cambridge University Press, 2009), 668.
23. See Paul Sheehan, *Modernism and the Aesthetics of Violence* (Cambridge: Cambridge University Press, 2013).
24. Doug Battersby observes that 'late modernist prose', including Beckett's, 'often eludes understanding [. . .] and in ways that seem to implicate us in the most reprehensible sentiments', and that it does so by making use of 'modes of writing that give us intimate access to the inner lives of fictional characters'. *Troubling Late Modernism: Ethics, Feeling, and the Novel Form* (Oxford: Oxford University Press, 2022), 34.
25. Jean Rhys, 'Hunger', in *'Tigers Are Better-Looking', with a Selection from 'The Left Bank'* (London: Andre Deutsch, 1968), 181–84 (181, ellipsis original).
26. Rhys, 'Hunger', 182–84.
27. Jean Rhys, 'Till September Petronella', in *Tigers Are Better-Looking*, 11–39 (18, 27). Further citations are given in the text.
28. For the use of 'Gray' in the unpublished novel 'Triple Sec', an early version of *Voyage in the Dark* completed in 1924, and the connection with Oscar Wilde's Dorian Gray, see Thomas, 'Jean Rhys and Katherine Mansfield'. As Thomas notes, Rhys's lover between 1910 and 1912 was Lancelot Grey Hugh Smith (21).
29. Jean Rhys, *Voyage in the Dark* (1934; Harmondsworth: Penguin, 1969), 47, 45.
30. On the complexity of Rhys's white Creole protagonists' relation to race, see Mary Lou Emery, 'The Poetics of Labor in Jean Rhys's Global Modernism', *Philological Quarterly* 90, nos. 2–3 (2011): 167–97.
31. On the voices of migrant women in Rhys's *Voyage in the Dark*, see Mary Lou Emery, 'Caribbean Modernism: Plantation to Planetary', in Wollaeger and Eatough, *Oxford Handbook of Global Modernisms*, 48–78.

Index

Adkins, Peter, 100
Aldington, Richard, 12, 40, 122–23, 124–25
Algerian War, 178
Alleg, Henri, 178
Allen, Carolyn, 100–1
Altieri, Charles, 4 (188n14)
Anderson, Margaret, 109
Antheil, George, 218n100
Apollinaire, Guillaume, 16, 17
Aragon, Louis, 131, 161, 163, 169, 170
Arensberg, Walter and Louise, 139
Arnold, Elizabeth, 6, 138, 139
Ashbery, John, 56
Atkin, Will, 167–68
Attridge, Derek, 17, 18, 192n62, 207n28
Auden, W. H., 52, 199n67
Auerbach, Erich, 19, 23, 52
Ayers, David, 122, 220n23

Bachelard, Gaston, 167
Baker, Houston A., Jr, 50
Bal, Mieke, 86–88, 89, 92, 93, 180–81
Balzac, Honoré de, 109, 118–19
Barnes, Djuna, 1–21, 77–107, 172–76, 179–82
 The Antiphon, 104–7
 Ladies' Almanack, 7, 77, 101, 190n33
 'A Little Girl Tells a Story to a Lady' (*A Night among the Horses*), 91
 modernist studies and, 1–21, 31, 68, 74, 75, 78, 172–76

'The Robin's House' (*A Night among the Horses*), 87–88, 91
 see also Barnes, Djuna, *Nightwood*
Barnes, Djuna, *Nightwood*
 diffuseness of characters, 96, 99–101
 digression, 5, 79, 82, 86
 dream, 89–91, 180
 Eliot and Coleman on, 102–3, 104–7
 integration of figures, 97–101
 modernist studies and, 1–9, 13–15, 17–21, 67, 74–75, 84–85, 94–97, 107, 172–76
 passages and, 78, 101–2, 103–4, 106, 107, 182, 185
 performance, 4–6, 79, 80–85, 92–93
 Pound's limerick on, 77–78, 80, 104
 public readership, 6, 13, 56–57
 representation, of people and characters, 15, 18, 79–85, 86–89, 91–93, 99–100, 179–82
 'spatial form' (Frank), 94–97, 98, 101, 103
 storytelling, ethics of, 4–6, 78, 85–94, 101, 179–82
 tone, instability of, 4–6, 78, 79–80, 81, 83–89, 93, 94, 107
 wit, 77, 78–80, 81, 83–85, 88
 Wood, Thelma, 88–89, 90, 91–92, 93, 180–81
 see also unity
Barney, Natalie Clifford, 7, 91

Index   229

Barnhisel, Gregory, 11
Barr, Alfred, 141, 142, 161
Barry, Alyce, 207n32
Barthes, Roland, 'framework', 82;
   narration as exchange, 82
Battersby, Doug, 227n24
Baudelaire, Charles, 17, 109, 118–19,
   124, 130, 170
Baxter, Charles, 103
Beach, Sylvia, 195n7
Beardsley, Aubrey, 160
Bechet, Sidney, 135
Beckett, Samuel, 16, 65, 74, 159,
   172, 176–82
  academic construction of
    modernism and, 55, 56, 65,
    70, 74
  'Dante... Bruno. Vico.. Joyce',
    33–34
  style and modernism, 3, 20, 21
  see also Beckett, Samuel,
    Comment c'est / How It Is
Beckett, Samuel, *Comment c'est /*
   How It Is, 29, 176–82
  Barnes's *Nightwood* and, 179–82
  coherence, mockery of, 176–77,
    178, 182
  cultural history of the novel form,
    180–82
  literary reference, 177–78
  violence and, 178–80, 181
Benjamin, Walter, 'The Storyteller',
   93–94
Berrigan, Ted, 56
Best, Stephen, 27–28
Bierbaum, Otto Julius, 159
Blake, William, 130
Bluemel, Kristin, 4 (189n15)
Bodenheim, Maxwell, 123
Bois, Yve-Alain, 19
Booth, Wayne, 24, 66–68, 69–71
  on Barnes's *Nightwood*, 14, 67
  The Company We Keep, 67

criticism around 1960 and, 13,
   31–32, 57, 69–71, 72–73
  disunity of modernist fiction,
    66–67
  individual and community, 67
  The Rhetoric of Fiction, 66–68
borrowing, 44, 47, 71, 173
  Barnes's *Nightwood* and, 98,
    99–100
  Loy's *Insel* and, 143
  Rodker's *Adolphe 1920* and, 120,
    126–27, 130, 135, 136
Bourget, Paul, 72
Brancusi, Constantin, 159
Breton, André, 140, 159, 161, 162,
   169
  'Crisis of the Object', 167–68
  Nadja, 161–62, 163, 164–68, 181
  'What is Surrealism?', 168
Brooker, Joseph, 53, 61
Brooker, Peter, 75
Brooks, Cleanth, 11, 50, 52–53, 69
  (203n143)
Brown, Angus Connell, 26
Brown, Frederick, 170
Burke, Carolyn, 139, 141, 143–44,
   145
Butts, Mary, 56, 188n12
Buurma, Rachel Sagner, 39
Byron, Mark, 24

Calder, John, 178
Carlston, Erin, 93, 205–6n11
Carver, Beci, 153 (222n60),
   169
Casanova Press, 109
Caselli, Daniela, 3 (188n13),
   18 (192n62), 84, 177–78,
   211n118
Chambers, Ross, 85 (206n13)
Chekhov, Anton, 130
Cheyette, Bryan, 205n9
Childs, Donald J., 22–23

Chu, Patricia, 4 (189n16)
Cinema *see* film
circus, 17, 83, 111, 117, 128, 147–48
close reading *see* reading, close
clumsiness, 12, 77–78, 80, 84–85, 104, 150
coherence, 20, 58, 63, 64, 71–74, 75, 174
   Beckett's *How It Is* and, 177–78, 182
   consistency and, 64–65, 72, 73, 74
   'consonance' (Hough), 58, 72
   consonantia (Aquinas), 64, 72
   incoherence, 19, 59, 64
   Loy's *Insel* and, 153–54, 169
   'poetic synthesis' (Edel), 71
   Rhys's 'Till September Petronella' and, 183–85
   unity, 58, 64, 103–4
   see also consistency; correspondences; unity
Coleman, Emily Holmes, 91–92, 101, 102–104, 106
Collini, Stefan, 49
Collins, William, 'Ode to Evening', 24
Condillac, Étienne Bonnot de, 104–105
Connor, Steven, 67
Conover, Roger L., 6, 56
Conrad, Joseph, 46
consistency, 61, 64–65, 72, 73, 74, 170
   inconsistency, 61, 128
   see also correspondences; coherence
consonantia (Aquinas), 64, 72; *see also* coherence
Constant, Benjamin, *Adolphe*, 113–14, 118–19, 124, 127
Contact Collection of Contemporary Writers, 8, 20
Cook, Will Marion, 135
Cordingley, Anthony, 179

Cornell, Joseph, 140, 143–44, 147, 221n35
correspondences, 36–37, 62–64, 153, 174, 183–85
   mismatches, 128, 142–45, 153, 184
   see also consistency
Crane, R. S., 68–69
Crangle, Sara, 4 (189n15)
Crank, James A., 50, 83, 217n98
Crevel, René, 159
Crozier, Andrew, 6, 108, 109–10, 112–13, 125–26, 204n159
Cunard, Nancy, 128, 129, 136, 161, 167; *see also Negro Anthology*

Dada, 16, 20, 125, 161, 164, 169
Dalí, Salvador, 139, 140, 157
   The Persistence of Memory, 161
Dante Alighieri, 5, 72, 177–78
Davie, Donald, 198n46, 199n67
De Bolla, Peter, 29
decadence, 72, 132–33, 159–60, 174, 176
   gender and, 172
   passages and, 71–72, 104, 185
   see also Rodker, John, *Adolphe 1920*
De Chirico, Giorgio, 139
De Man, Paul, 96–97
Derrida, Jacques, 173
Dial, 7, 49, 123
Dickens, Charles, 35
Diepeveen, Leonard, 14–15, 190n32, 193n81
difficulty, 173
   as modernist aesthetic, 8, 14–15, 22–23, 33, 56
   resistance and, 15, 26
diffuseness, 19, 173; *see also* Barnes, Djuna, *Nightwood*
diffusionist model of modernism, 172, 225n2

digression, 174; *see also* Barnes, Djuna, *Nightwood*

disgust, 174; *see also* Rodker, John, *Adolphe 1920*

disintegration, 19, 169–70, 173; *see also* integration, reading as

disorder, 71, 72

distant reading *see* reading, distant

Dodge, Mabel, 139

Dorward, Nate, 199n67

Dostoevsky, Fyodor, 130

Dowson, Ernest, 183

dream, 16–17, 89–91, 180

Drouin, Diane, 154

Duchamp, Marcel, 139, 148

Dufy, Raoul, 140

Duncan, Robert, 56

Dürer, Albrecht, 160

During, Simon, 51

Edel, Leon, 14, 52, 54, 71

Eliot, George, 46

Eliot, T. S., 12, 41, 44, 57–60, 63, 102–7

  academic construction of modernism and, 2, 8, 10, 11, 48, 56, 94, 110

  Barnes's *The Antiphon*, draft blurb to, 104–7

  criticism and, 57–60, 63, 73, 74, 96

  The Love Song of J. Alfred Prufrock, 63

  modernist critic, 23, 24, 30, 39, 48, 51; *see also* essay titles

  modernist poet, 7, 23, 35, 46, 52, 84; *see also* poem titles

  New Criticism and, 11, 23, 30, 54

  Nightwood, editor of, 77, 91, 101, 102–3

  Nightwood, preface to, 6, 8, 102–3, 104, 106–7; Edel and, 14, 71

  Rodker's *Adolphe 1920* and, 108, 109, 110, 113, 130, 133

'Tradition and the Individual Talent', 41, 44, 63

'*Ulysses*, Order and Myth', 36, 125

The Waste Land, 48, 58–59, 63, 67, 85, 96, 174

Ellmann, Maud, 2 (188n7), 202n126

Ellmann, Richard, 53, 54

Éluard, Paul, 159

Emery, Mary Lou, 227n30

Empson, William, 22–23, 24, 30, 49, 59

Epstein, Jean, 120

Ernst, Max, 139, 140, 143–44

Etherington, Ben, 26, 218n101

evaluation, 18, 38, 40–41, 50–51, 124

Exile, The, 6, 7, 8, 108, 111

Faltejskova, Monika *see* Lee, Monika

feeling, 174; *see also* Rodker, John, *Adolphe 1920*

Felski, Rita, 22, 24, 27, 28

Ferrer, Daniel, 17, 18 (192n62)

Fiedler, Leslie, 14

Fielding, Henry, 79

film, 13, 16–17, 145, 159

  Rodker's *Adolphe 1920* and, 110–11, 120, 131

Filreis, Alan, 51

Fini, Leonor, 141

Firbank, Ronald, 71–72, 74

Flanner, Janet, 140, 205n5

Flaubert, Gustave, 56, 65, 70, 74, 94

  La tentation de St Antoine, 16, 17

  style, 46, 192n70

Flint, F. S., 122–23

Ford, Charles Henri, 56, 74

Ford, Ford Madox, 8, 43, 46, 114, 176, 182

  The English Novel, 194n4

  The Good Soldier, 108, 153, 181

232   *The New Modernist Novel: Criticism and the Task of Reading*

Ford, John, 107
Forster, E. M., *Aspects of the Novel*, 194n4
France, Anatole, 71
Frank, Joseph, on 'spatial form', 14, 71, 94–97, 98, 101, 103, 169
Freytag-Loringhoven, Baroness Elsa von, 101
Freud, Sigmund, 90, 141, 143
Friedman, Melvin J., 14
Friedman, Susan Stanford, 172 (225n2)
Frost, Laura, 19
Frost, Robert, 52
Frow, John, 18
Frye, Northrop, 18, 24
Fuchs, Miriam, 102 (210n88)
Fuller, Loïe, 223n81

Gascoyne, David, 223n89
Gaudier-Brzeska, Henri, 109
Gee, Lottie, 128
gender
  academic construction of modernism and, 4, 9, 10, 14, 50, 74, 172
  Barnes's *Nightwood* and, 82, 210n88
  Loy's *Insel* and, 158–59, 163, 166
Genet, Jean, 170
genius, and talent, 104–7
Gershwin, George, 134
Giacometti, Alberto, 139, 153–54, 159
Gide, André, 160, 199n67
Gilbert, Stuart
  James Joyce's 'Ulysses', 64, 65
  'Prolegomena to *Work in Progress*', 33–34
Giles, Paul, 39, 51, 196–97n31
Glavey, Brian, 14, 83, 99
global modernism, 1, 172

Goethe, Johann Wolfgang von, *Faust*, 16, 17, 60
Goffin, Robert, 218n100
Golding, Alan, 50
Golding, Arthur, *Ovid's Metamorphoses*, trans., 42–43
Gopal, Priyamvada, 218n102
Gorky, Arshile, 139, 159
Graff, Gerald, 66, 68–69
Graves, Robert, and Laura Riding, *A Survey of Modernist Poetry*, 22–23, 30, 35, 47, 48
Greenberg, Clement, 56
Gris, Juan, 139
Guillory, John, 28, 194n3

Hanley, Miles L., 97
Hardie, Melissa, 13 (191n46), 56–57
Hardy, Thomas, 46
harmony, 53, 64, 72, 73, 104, 144; disharmony, 66–67
Hartley, L. P., 101
Hartman, Geoffrey H., 28
Hayden, Sarah, 6, 138, 140, 143, 145
Hayot, Eric, 172, 187n5
Heath, Stephen, 56, 188n12, 192n70, 194n94, 214n32
Heffernan, Laura, 39
Heinz, Evi, 128
Hemingway, Ernest, 159
Henmel, Alfred Walter, 159
Herring, Phillip, 104
Herring, Scott, 100
Herrnstein Smith, Barbara, 18 (192n64)
Hildesheimer, Wolfgang, 84
Hilliard, Christopher, 45
Hobson, Suzanne, 225n121
Hofmannsthal, Hugo von, 160
Hoggart, Richard, 49
Homage, 83–84, 88, 170
Homer, *Odyssey*, 42, 65

Index 233

Hough, Graham, 44–45, 57–60
  criticism around 1960 and, 13,
    31–32, 57, 67, 70–71, 72–73
  An Essay on Criticism, 28, 58,
    203n139
  on modern criticism, 44–45, 57–59,
    63, 67, 69
  on modern poetry, 44–45, 57–60,
    63, 66, 67, 69
  'The Poet as Critic', 58
  *Reflections on a Literary
    Revolution*, 44–45, 57–60
Howard, Alexander, 56
Howard, Claire, 167
Howarth, Peter, 4 (188n14)
Hugo, Victor, 18
Hulme, T. E., 24, 58
Hurston, Zora Neale, 136
Huysmans, Joris-Karl, 118–19, 123,
    124, 125; *À rebours*, 118
Huyssen, Andreas, 51

'I Couldn't Hear Nobody Pray', 128,
    134, 135
inconsequence, 19, 173, 185; *see also*
    Rodker, John, *Adolphe 1920*
Insel, Die, 159–60
instability *see* Barnes, Djuna,
    Nightwood
integration, reading as, 97, 177;
    see also disintegration; Loy,
    Mina, *Insel*
integritas (Aquinas), 64; integrity, 65
Itten, Johannes, 142

Jacket and *Jacket2*, 204n159
Jaffe, Aaron, 10–11, 12, 190n34
Jaillant, Lise, 10
Jaloux, Edmond, 113, 125, 130–31
James, Henry, 46, 52, 56, 66–67, 69, 70
  The Aspern Papers, 66–67
  Barnes's *Nightwood* and, 94, 101
  Loy's *Insel* and, 153, 169

Jolas, Eugene, 'The Revolution of
    Language and James Joyce',
    32–34, 37; *see also transition*
Jouve, Pierre Jean, 113, 181
Joyce, James, 15–18, 32–35, 36–39,
    53, 60–66, 69–71, 182
  academic construction of
    modernism and, 10, 49, 52–53,
    60, 65–66, 69–71, 72–74, 110
  Barnes's *Nightwood* and, 16–18,
    84–85, 94–95, 97, 205n5
  critical labour and, 15–18, 30, 56,
    66–67, 69–71
  Finnegans Wake, 20, 32, 38–39,
    49, 64, 173; *see also Work in
    Progress*
  Kenner on, 53, 55, 61–66, 71,
    72–73, 74
  Levin on, 60–62, 71
  Loy's *Insel* and, 153, 154, 159,
    169
  *A Portrait of the Artist as a Young
    Man*, 62, 64, 153
  Rodker's *Adolphe 1920* and,
    108, 111, 112–13, 125, 130,
    133
  Wilson on, 30, 31, 36–39, 72
  Work in Progress, 12, 20, 31,
    32–35, 37, 49, 125, 173
  style and, 46, 198n53
  see also Joyce, James, *Ulysses*
Joyce, James, *Ulysses*
  academic construction of
    modernism and, 13, 48, 49, 52,
    53, 60, 95, 173
  criticism and, 16–18, 36–39,
    60–63, 64–65, 85, 97, 174
  Loy's *Insel* and, 153, 154
  publication of, 7, 20, 109
  Rodker's *Adolphe 1920* and,
    112–13, 119–20, 124, 125,
    126, 127–28
  style, 20, 182

Kafka, Franz, 72, 143, 150, 151, 162
Kalliney, Peter, 176
Kenner, Hugh, 49, 54–55, 56, 61–66,
  72–74
  academic construction of
    modernism and, 2, 13, 53, 65,
    72–74, 133, 169
  criticism around 1960 and, 13,
    31–32, 57, 69–71, 72–73
  Dublin's Joyce, 61–63, 64, 65, 66
  Flaubert, Joyce and Beckett,
    64–65
  The Invisible Poet: T. S. Eliot, 63
  Joyce's Voices, 66; 'Uncle Charles
    Principle', 5, 80
  Levin and, 61–63, 64, 65, 66
  The Poetry of Ezra Pound, 11–12,
    53, 54–55
  'To Be the Brancusi of Poetry', 56,
    147 (221n40)
Kermode, Frank, 72, 73, 74, 133,
  169
Kipling, Rudyard, 35
Koch, Kenneth, 56
Kouidis, Virginia, 148
Krauss, Rosalind, 19
Kreymborg, Alfred, 8
Kristian, Roald, 109

Laforgue, Jules, 17; *Salomé*, 132–33
Lassner, Phyllis, 4 (189n15)
late modernism, 3, 21, 174–75
Latham, Sean, 54
Latour, Bruno, 28
Laughlin, James, 11, 52, 60, 138,
  139, 170
Lautréamont, Comte de (Isidore
  Ducasse), 109, 123–25, 130,
  133
  *Chants de Maldoror / The Lay of
    Maldoror*, 109, 123, 124, 125
learnedness, 74, 75, 85, 171, 177–78;
  see also literary reference

Leavis, F. R., 22–24, 43–48, 54–55
  on fiction, 46–48
  The Great Tradition, 46, 52
  How to Teach Reading, 12, 31,
    40, 43–48, 54–55
  New Bearings in English Poetry,
    45, 52
  reception of modernism and,
    50–51, 52, 53, 199n67
Leavis, Q. D., *Fiction and the
  Reading Public*, 47–48, 52, 59
Lee, Monika, 103
Leftwich, Joseph, 8
Lennard, John, 205n6
lesbian, gay, bisexual, transgender
  and queer (LGBTQ+) writing,
  7, 14, 15, 57, 82, 100
  modernist studies and, 9, 35, 50,
    74, 210n88
Les continents, 129
Leskov, Nikolai, 93–94
Lessing, Gotthold Ephraim, 94
Levenson, Michael, 48, 52, 169
Levertov, Denise, 56, 147 (221n39)
Levin, Harry, 55–56, 60–62, 153, 169
  criticism around 1960 and, 13,
    31–32, 57, 69–71, 72–73
  The Gates of Horn, 55–56, 61
  James Joyce, 52, 60–62, 64
  Kenner and, 61–63, 64, 65, 66
  'A Personal Retrospect', 48–49
  on the study of the novel, 55–56
  'What Was Modernism?', 60,
    69–70
Levinson, Marjorie, 23–24
Levy, Julien, 139, 140, 141, 161
  Memoir of an Art Gallery, 154, 159
  Surrealism, 142, 144, 159
Lewis, Wyndham, 3, 21, 55, 58, 63,
  109, 199n67
  The Apes of God, 120–22
  The Diabolical Principle, 124–25
  Little Review and, 23, 48

on Rodker's *Adolphe 1920*, 12,
108, 120–22, 129, 130, 136
'taxi-cab driver test' (*Men without Art*), 47
Time and Western Man, 121
unpalatability of, 126
Lindon, Jérôme, 178
Linett, Maren Tova, 80
literary reference, 46, 84–85, 130,
174, 177–78
close reading and, 16–18, 24–25
literary value
Barnes's *Nightwood* and, 19–21,
68, 102–3, 106
close reading and, 21–29, 40–46,
73, 126
coherence, consistency and,
64–65, 71–73, 74, 169, 173,
177, 184
construction of, 18–19, 32, 52,
70–71, 74–76, 125–26, 175–76
critical labour and, 18–19, 67–69
gender, sexuality, culture and
ethnicity and, 9, 50, 74
Loy's *Insel* and, 19–20, 145–50,
169–70
new modernist studies and, 126,
175–76, 186
reception of decadence and,
123–25, 172
Rodker's *Adolphe 1920* and,
19–20, 112–13, 122–26
style and, 19–21, 71–72, 73, 169,
173
little magazines *see* periodicals
Little Review, The
Barnes, Rodker and Loy and, 7,
109, 118, 133
reading and, 23, 30, 40, 48
short pieces in, 20
Llona, Victor, 'I Dont Know What
to Call It But Its Mighty Unlike
Prose [*sic*]', 33–34

local momentum, 173; *see also* Loy,
Mina, *Insel*
Locke, Alain, 218n100
The New Negro, 20, 167
Lodge, David, 67–68, 69
Longus, 124
Loy, Mina, 1–4, 6–9, 17, 19–21,
104, 138–70, 172–76, 180–82
Anglo-Mongrels and the Rose, 8,
148
'The Child and the Parent',
151
'Crab-Angel', 17
'Islands in the Air', 140
'John Rodker's Frog', 190n33
The Last Lunar Baedeker, 6,
56
Lunar Baedeker, 147
Lunar Baedeker and Time-Tables,
6, 56
modernist studies and, 1–4, 6–9,
12, 17–21, 31, 68, 75, 110,
172–76
'Nancy Cunard', 161
'Phenomenon in American Art
(Joseph Cornell)', 144, 167
poems in *Others Anthology*, 8,
147–48
'Visitation of Insel', 138, 139,
140, 149–50, 166
see also Loy, Mina, *Insel*
Loy, Mina, *Insel*
avant-garde art and artists and,
104, 159–61, 165–66
Breton's *Nadja* and, 161–62, 163,
164–68
close reading and, 25, 138,
140–45
gender and, 158–59, 166
Last Nights of Paris and, 161–64,
165–66, 168
local momentum, 145–50, 156–57,
162, 167–68, 170

236 The New Modernist Novel: Criticism and the Task of Reading

Loy, Mina, *Insel (cont.)*
  modernist studies and, 1–4, 6–9,
    12, 17–21, 75–76, 107, 138,
    153–54, 168–70, 172–76
  novel form, 138, 144–57, 161–66,
    168–70, 179–82
  publication history, 138, 139–40,
    169–70
  reading as integration, 150–56,
    169, 170
  surrealism and, 131, 140–44, 153,
    155, 157–59, 161–69
Loy, Myrna, 222n72
Lustig, Alvan, 56–57
Luther, Martin, 84–85

MacKillop, Ian, 45
McAlmon, Robert, 159
Madden, Ed, 210n88
Maeterlinck, Maurice, 160
Magritte, René, 139
Mahoney, Dan, 84, 92
Mallarmé, Stéphane, 116, 130, 173,
    183
Mann, Heinrich, 160
Mao, Douglas, 4, 31
Marcus, Jane, 85
Marcus, Laura, 120
Marcus, Sharon, 27–28
Marinetti, F. T., 160–61
Martin, Wallace, 51
Mason, Ellsworth, 53
Matthews, Ralph, 218n100
Matthiessen, F. O., 52
Maupassant, Guy de, 130, 176
Melville, Herman, 154
Menand, Louis, 39
Messerli, Douglas, 188n8
Metcalf, Henriette, 88, 91, 92, 180
Middleton, Thomas, 107
Miller, J. Hillis, 97
Miller, Tyrus, 3, 21, 101
Milne, Drew, 28 (194n100), 85,
    110, 204n159

Milton, John, 39
Mirrlees, Hope, *Paris*, 189n25
Mitchell, Pamela, 179
Mondrian, Piet, 142
Monnerot, Jules, 223n88
mood *see* Rodker, John, *Adolphe
    1920*; Rhys, Jean, 'Hunger'
Moody, Alys, 166, 172 (225n2)
Moore, Marianne, 46, 74, 147,
    199n67
Moretti, Franco, 25–26
Morin, Emilie, 178
Morley, Frank, 77, 91
Morris, Amy, 138 (218n2)
Morrison, Blake, 199n67
Movement, the, 199n67
Muir, Edwin, 23, 101, 105, 205n5
  The Structure of the Novel, 194n4
Munro, Harold, 122–23
Murry, John Middleton, 60

Nabokov, Vladimir, *Lolita*, 67,
    203n139
Negro Anthology, 136, 161, 167,
    168, 218n100
New Criticism
  close reading and, 22–24, 50,
    55
  construction of modernism and,
    10–11, 50–51, 52–53, 70, 72
  critiques of, 54–56
  fiction and, 10, 13, 50, 52–53,
    55, 70
  productivity and, 69, 70
New Directions, 11, 49, 56, 60
  Loy's *Insel* and, 138, 139, 170
new modernist studies
  close reading and, 1–4, 171–72
  critiques of, 4
  periodicals and, 2, 21, 172–73
  poets as readers and, 56, 75,
    204n159
  related to mid-century modernist
    studies, 9, 31, 57, 74

Ngai, Sianne, 126
Nicholls, Peter, 72, 84, 132–34, 148, 169, 214n29
Nietzsche, Friedrich, 160
Nordau, Max, 123
Norris, Margot, 66
North, Joseph, 22–23, 24
North, Michael, 55, 201n92
Nuku, Maia, 168

O'Faolain, Sean, 340
Oelze, Richard
  Erwartung, 141–42, 161
  Frieda and *Frieda II*, 143, 158
  original for Insel, 139, 141–43, 145, 155, 158–59, 162
  Phantastische Komposition, 162
O'Hara, Frank, 56
Our Exagmination round His Factification for Incamination of Work in Progress, 31, 32–35, 37, 48
Ovid, *Metamorphoses*, 129–30; trans. Arthur Golding, 42–43
Ovid Press, 7, 109, 127

Parataxis, 204n159
Parmar, Sandeep 139, 151
Parsonage, Catherine *see* Tackley, Catherine
Parsons, Clere, 124
Pascin, Jules, 159
passages, style in, 19–20, 43, 46, 104, 154, 169, 173–74, 182
  Barnes's *Nightwood* and, 101–102, 104, 106, 107
  decadence and, 71–72, 185
  Rhys's stories and, 183, 185
  see also reading, selection of passages for; Pound, Ezra, *How to Read*

Patterson, Ian
  on *Adolphe 1920*, 108, 113, 125, 128
  on Lewis's response to Rodker, 120–21, 122, 124, 130
Patterson, Isobel, 104
Pender, Elizabeth, 14, 71, 197n35
performance, 16, 28, 85; *see also* Barnes, Djuna, *Nightwood*
periodicals, 2, 20, 21, 23, 31, 172–73
  Barnes, Rodker and Loy and, 6–8, 108–109, 159–60, 174–75
Petherbridge, Jenny, 88, 90, 181
Picasso, Pablo, 17, 60
Piette, Adam, 178–79
Plumb, Cheryl J., 82, 92, 103
point of view, 5, 52–53, 112, 174
Potter, Rachel, 80, 93, 148, 225n121
Pound, Ezra
  ABC of Reading, 40–43, 44–45, 46, 61, 105
  academic construction of modernism and, 2, 10–12, 50–51, 53, 56, 74, 110, 169
  Active Anthology, 41, 104–105, 106
  Barnes's *Nightwood* and, 12, 77–78, 80, 84, 104
  The Cantos, 20, 44, 55, 132–33, 85, 174
  decadence and, 72, 132–33
  'Dubliners and Mr James Joyce', 198n53
  Hough on, 44–45, 58
  Hugh Selwyn Mauberley, 127
  Kenner on, 11, 53, 54–55, 63, 72, 74
  on Loy's poetry, 8, 147–48
  modernist critic, 8, 23, 30, 46, 73, 94, 101, 169
  New Criticism and, 11, 55, 72
  Rodker and, 6, 7, 8, 108, 109, 127, 130, 132–33

Pound, Ezra *(cont.)*
    on Rodker's *Adolphe 1920*, 8,
        111, 112–13, 123–24
    see also Pound, Ezra, *How to Read*
Pound, Ezra, *How to Read*, 12, 31,
    40–48, 54–55, 61, 105
    Kenner on F. R. Leavis and, 54–55
    Leavis, F. R., on, 12, 31, 40,
        43–48, 54–55
    style in excerpts and, 42–43, 46,
        48, 73
Powell, William, 159
Prendergast, Christopher, 201n101
presentism, and historicism, 19–20,
    192n68
Prévost, Antoine-François, abbé, 124
Prins, Yopie, 21 (192n73)
productivity, 15–21, 58–71, 75
Proust, Marcel, 56, 61, 70, 169, 170
    À la recherche du temps perdu, 20
        (192n70), 94–95, 153
    Edmund Wilson on, 35–36, 37, 72
Prynne, J. H., 15, 24
Pryor, Sean, 148, 189n25, 192n68
puzzlement, 58, 83, 101, 173

Rabaté, Jean-Michel, 173, 225n117
Rabelais, François, 79, 205n5
Rainey, Lawrence, 3, 29
Ransom, John Crowe, 30, 56
Ray, Man, 140, 157, 170
reading, as a task, 28, 29, 30
reading, as unfinishable, 27–28, 29,
    78, 173
reading, close, 1–2, 3–4, 15, 21–29,
    54–55, 173–74, 186
    contexts and, 24–25, 138, 140–45,
        173–74
    interdependence of, with
        modernist literature, 22–24,
        30–32, 46
    meaning of, 21–22, 24–25, 27
    New Criticism and, 22–24, 50–51,
        55

new modernist studies and, 1–2,
    3–4, 19, 21, 24, 126, 175–76,
    186
see also Pound, Ezra, *How to
    Read*; Leavis, F. R., *How to
    Teach Reading*
reading, distant, 25–26
reading, professional vs lay, 28, 31
reading, selection of passages for, 27
    fiction and, 42–43, 46–48
    in this book, 78, 81, 115, 127,
        140, 150, 178
    quotation and, 45–46, 197n35
    see also passages
reading, strategies of, 10–12, 13, 32,
    65–66, 171–72
    canon and, 10, 12, 13, 32, 65–66,
        70
    modes of reading, 24, 26, 27,
        53–54, 57, 127, 175–76, 186
    new modernist studies and, 18–19,
        26–27, 175
    reputation and, 10–11
    resistance to, 15, 19–21, 80, 170,
        171–72
reading, surface, 27–28, 78
representation, of people and
    characters, 15, 18, 25, 29, 173,
        179–81, 185
    Loy's *Insel* and, 161, 165, 168
    Rodker's *Adolphe 1920* and, 125,
        134–36
    see also Barnes, Djuna,
        Nightwood
reputation, 10, 11
Revue européenne, La, 6, 7, 108,
    134
Rexroth, Kenneth, 56
Rhys, Jean
    Good Morning Midnight, 185
    new modernist studies and, 29,
        172, 176
    Stories of the Left Bank, 176,
        182; 'Hunger', 182–83, 185

Tigers Are Better-Looking,
176, 182; 'Till September
Petronella', 183–85
Voyage in the Dark, 176, 184,
227n28
Richards, I. A., 22–23, 24, 30, 45,
47, 51
Richardson, Dorothy, *Pilgrimage*,
20, 71
Riding, Laura, and Robert Graves,
A Survey of Modernist Poetry,
22–23, 30, 35, 47, 48
Rilke, Rainer Maria, 160
Rimbaud, Arthur, 35, 130, 170,
177
Rodker, John, 1–4, 6–9, 17–21,
108–37, 172–76, 182
'An Ape of Genius', 122
'Chanson on Petit
Hypertrophique', 133
The Future of Futurism, 110, 130,
131
Hymns, 109, 122–23
'Joyce and His Dynamic', 33–34,
37, 125
Loy, exchange with, 190n33
Memoirs of Other Fronts, 119
modernist studies and, 1–4, 6–9,
12, 17–21, 31, 68, 75, 109–10,
172–76
Montagnes russes, 108, 113, 124,
130
reception of, 120–26
'Southern Syncopated Singers',
112, 135
'The Theatre', 118
Theatre Muet, 118
'War Museum – Royal College of
Surgeons', 120
see also Rodker, John, *Adolphe
1920*
Rodker, John, *Adolphe 1920*
decadence and, 117, 118–19,
123–25, 127, 132–34, 182

disgust, 120, 121–23, 126; taste
and distaste, 122–26
inconsequence, 113–15, 117, 119
modernist studies and, 1–4, 6–9,
17–21, 75–76, 107, 108–11,
125–27, 133, 172–76
mood, 108, 117, 118, 127–29,
134; feeling, 108, 112, 115,
117, 129, 137
perspective, 111–12
Southern Syncopated Orchestra,
128, 135–37
temporality of reading, 112,
116–18, 121, 182
Wyndham Lewis on, 12, 108,
120–22, 129, 130, 136
Rogers, Gayle, 54
Rosenbaum, Susan, 157, 166
Rosenberg, Isaac, 8
Rosenquist, Rod, 10, 12
Ross, Stephen J., 172 (225n2)
Roussel, Raymond, 130, 131–32;
Impressions of Africa, 131–32
Rudosky, Christina, 167
Ruttmann, Walter, *Berlin: City
Symphony*, 111

Sage, Robert, 'Before *Ulysses* – and
After', 33–34
Saint-Amour, Paul K., 4 (189n17)
Salton-Cox, Glyn, 191n54
Sartre, Jean-Paul, 169, 170
Saunders, Max, 23
Savitzky, Ludmila, 108
Scalability, 25–27, 43
Schiaparelli, Elsa, 141
Schröder, Rudolf Alexander,
159
Schulz, Bruno, 162
Scott, Bonnie Kime, 14, 50
Scrutiny, 50, 52
Seshagiri, Urmila, 4 (189n15),
217n98
Setz, Cathryn, 14, 21, 71

240 *The New Modernist Novel: Criticism and the Task of Reading*

Shakespeare, William, 65; criticism of, 67
Sheehan, Paul, 181 (227n23)
Sherry, Vincent, 72, 133
Simmons, Merinda K., 50, 83, 217n98
Sinclair, May, 23
Slingsby, G. V. L. (pseudonym), 34–35, 195n17
Sohmers, Harriet, 57
Sontag, Susan, 57
Soupault, Philippe
    editor of Lautréamont's *Oeuvres*, 124
    Les dernières nuits de Paris, 161–62, 163–64, 165
Southern Syncopated Orchestra, 98, 128, 135, 137
'spatial form', 174; *see also* Barnes, Djuna, *Nightwood*; Frank, Joseph
Spicer, Jack, 56
Spiro, Mia, 93
Spivak, Gayatri Chakravorty, 26
Stavisky, Alexandre, 140
Stein, Gertrude, 20, 35, 74, 139, 168
    Three Lives, 38
Stendhal, 61
Sterne, Laurence, *Tristram Shandy*, 79
Stevens, Wallace, 74
storytelling, 5–6, 85–94, 174, 180–82, 184; *see also* Barnes, Djuna, *Nightwood*
strategies of reading *see* reading, strategies of
Strindberg, August, 160; *A Dream Play*, 16
surface reading *see* reading, surface
surrealism, 56, 101, 104, 124–25, 157–70
    global consciousness of, 166–68
    Loy's *Insel* and, 131, 140–44, 153, 155, 157–59, 161–69
    the novel and, 161–66, 168–70

Surrealist Group, 161, 168, 223n88
Sussman, Matthew, 19
Sweeney, Carole, 217n98

Tackley, Catherine, 135
Taupin, René, 104–105
Taylor, Julie, 90–91
Tchelitchew, Pavel, 139
temporality of reading, 173; *see also* Rodker, John, *Adolphe 1920*
Thomas Aquinas, Saint, 64, 73
Thomas, Sue, 176
tone, 63, 154–56, 174; *see also* Barnes, Djuna, *Nightwood*
Toulouse-Lautrec, Henri de, 139
Tourneur, Cyril, 107
Tovalou Quénum (Houénou), Joseph, 128
Tovalou Houénou, Kojo, 128–29, 136
transition, 7, 20, 21, 32, 33, 49
    Lautréamont translated in, 124
    'Revolution of the Word', 105
Trilling, Lionel, 39, 51
Trotter, David, 110–11, 113–14, 156, 191n45
Trubowitz, Lara, 99–100
Tuma, Keith, 199n67
Turner, Catherine, 10

Undine, 115
unity, 36, 53, 55, 58, 64, 66–67, 72
    decadent style and, 72
    disunity, 66–67, 96
    see also coherence

Vadda, Aarthi, 193n91
value *see* literary value
Veltman, Laura J., 84
Vendler, Helen, 145–46
Verlaine, Paul, 122, 160
Virgil, 5, 177

Index   **241**

Wadsworth, Edward, 109
Walker, Dominic, 178–79
Walkowitz, Rebecca, 172, 187n5
Warren, Diane, 85
Warren, Robert Penn, 50, 52–53
Wedekind, Frank, 160
West, Rebecca, 119; 'The Strange
    Case of James Joyce', 34
Whitehead, Peter, 91
Whiteman, Paul, 134
Wiehager, Renate, 141, 142, 143
Wilde, Oscar, 5, 7, 20, 71, 109, 124,
    176
    The Picture of Dorian Gray, 104,
        118, 181, 227n28
Wilkinson, John, 150
Williams, Jonathan, 6, *56*
Williams, Raymond, 49, 73, 75
Williams, William Carlos, 112, 139,
    147, 170
    Last Nights of Paris, 162–64
    'A Point for American Criticism',
        34
Williamson, Alan, 103–104
Wilson, Edmund
    'The Antrobuses and the
        Earwickers', 38–39

Axel's Castle, 12, 30, 31, 35–40,
    72, 133
decadent style and, 71–72
'A Dissenting Opinion on Kafka',
    72
'The Dream of H. C. Earwicker',
    38
the figure of 'the reader', 38–39, 48
'A Revival of Ronald Firbank', 71
'Thoughts on Being
    Bibliographed', 39, 48–49
Winning, Joanne, 89
Winters, Yvor, 12, 30, 150
wit, 119, 148–50, 163, 174, 177
    New Critical wit, 11, 54
    see also Barnes, Djuna,
        Nightwood
Wood, Thelma *see* Barnes, Djuna,
    Nightwood
Woolf, Virginia, 23, 46–47, 52

Yeats, W. B., 35, 52, 56, 110,
    199n67
Yellow Book, The, 177
Yoyotte, Pierre, 223n88

Zhang, Dora, 88, 181